Cognition
and Language:

Perspectives from New Zealand

edited by

Claire M. Fletcher-Flinn and Gus M. Haberman

AUSTRALIAN ACADEMIC PRESS
Brisbane

First published in 2006
Australian Academic Press
32 Jeays Street
Bowen Hills Qld 4006
Australia
www.australianacademicpress.com.au

National Library of Australia
Cataloguing-in-Publication data:

Cognition and Language: Perspectives from New Zealand.

ISBN 1 875378 72 3.

1. Cognitive psychology - New Zealand.
2. Psycholinguistics - New Zealand. 3. Cognitive learning -
New Zealand. 4. Cognitive science - New Zealand.
I. Fletcher-Flinn, Claire M. II. Haberman, Gus M.

153

Cover and text design by Roberta Blake of Australian Academic Press, Brisbane.

Contents

continued over

continued over

Part 4

Theoretical Insights and Future Challenges

List of Contributors

Gjurgjica Badzakova-Trajkov
Research Centre for Cognitive Neuroscience, and Department of Psychology, University of Auckland, Auckland, New Zealand

Dr Kylie J. Barnett
Research Centre for Cognitive Neuroscience, and Department of Psychology, University of Auckland, Auckland, New Zealand

Amy Bird
Department of Psychology, University of Otago, Dunedin, New Zealand

Dr Heather Buttle
School of Psychology, Massey University, Auckland, New Zealand

Professor James W. Chapman
Professor of Educational Psychology and Pro Vice-Chancellor, College of Education, Massey University, Palmerston North, New Zealand

Dr Zhe Chen
Department of Psychology, University of Canterbury, Christchurch, New Zealand

Dr Michael Colombo
Department of Psychology, University of Otago, Dunedin, New Zealand

Professor Michael Corballis
Professor of Psychology, School of Psychology, University of Auckland, Auckland, New Zealand

Dr Scott L. Fairhall
Research Centre for Cognitive Neuroscience, and Department of Psychology, University of Auckland, Auckland, New Zealand

Dr Claire M. Fletcher-Flinn
Department of Psychology, and Research Centre for Interventions in Teaching and Learning (RCITL), University of Auckland, Auckland, New Zealand

Dr Michelle Gulya
Department of Psychology, Rutgers University, New Jersey, United States of America

Dr Jen Hay
Department of Linguistics, University of Canterbury, Christchurch, New Zealand

Dione Healey
Department of Psychology, University of Canterbury, Christchurch, New Zealand

Dr Stephen R. Hill
School of Psychology, Massey University, Palmerston North, New Zealand

Dr Peter Jackson
formerly at the Psychology Unit, The Open Polytechnic of New Zealand, Hutt City, New Zealand

Dr Lucy Johnston
Social Perception Laboratory, University of Canterbury, Christchurch, New Zealand

Dr Todd C. Jones
School of Psychology, Victoria University of Wellington, Wellington, New Zealand

Dr Anthony Lambert
Research Centre for Cognitive Neuroscience, Department of Psychology, University of Auckland, Auckland, New Zealand

Dr Jason Low
School of Psychology, Victoria University of Wellington, Wellington, New Zealand

Lynden Miles
Social Perception Laboratory, University of Canterbury, Christchurch, New Zealand

Clare Morton
Research Centre for Cognitive Neuroscience, and Department of Psychology, University of Auckland, Auckland, New Zealand

Dr Ewald Neumann
Department of Psychology, University of Canterbury, Christchurch, New Zealand

Dr Rhiannon Newcombe
Department of Psychology, University of Otago, Dunedin, New Zealand

Dr John V. Podd
School of Psychology, Massey University, Palmerston North, New Zealand

Verena E. Pritchard
Department of Psychology, University of Canterbury, Christchurch, New Zealand

Professor Elaine Reese
Department of Psychology, University of Otago, Dunedin, New Zealand

Professor Carolyn Rovee-Collier

Department of Psychology, Rutgers University, Piscataway, New Jersey, United States of America

Dr Steve Stewart-Williams

Postdoctoral Research Fellow, Department of Psychology, Neuroscience, and Behaviour, McMaster University, Hamilton, Ontario, Canada

Formerly at School of Psychology, Massey University, Palmerston North, New Zealand

Dr G. Brian Thompson

School of Education, Victoria University of Wellington, Wellington, New Zealand

Professor William E. Tunmer

Distinguished Professor of Educational Psychology, College of Education, Massey University, Palmerston North, New Zealand

Dr Paul Warren

School of Linguistics and Applied Language Studies, Victoria University of Wellington, Wellington, New Zealand

Preface

Andrew J. Lock

This volume represents a 'coming of age' for cognitive psychology in New Zealand. Like other branches of psychological inquiry in New Zealand, the study of the means by which people act needs to be placed in context. Here, the geographic isolation of the country is one of the most important factors to consider as contributing to the current scene. Because of its isolation, New Zealand was the last significant land mass to be inhabited by people, first by Polynesian seafaring people — the Māori — and later by peoples from the far side of the world, particularly from colonially ambitious Victorian Britain. Reaching New Zealand has always been tied up with the technologies underwriting travel. A good trip from Britain 150 ago years could be completed in 3 months. A return trip could take 7 months. Fifty years ago, 6 weeks was the norm. Jet aircraft have brought this down to 24 hours since then, and the 'death of distance' as a result of Internet technology has made the virtual trip almost instantaneous. These historical constraints on the speed of two-way communication with the intellectual resources of western culture have been a major factor in the development of all aspects of New Zealand life.

It has led to particular individuals having enormous influence in all walks of professional life. One person might well be the only 'expert' in a country that stretches the equivalent distance between Oslo and Rome. The knowledge and skills they bring with them will be applied without recourse to developments elsewhere, and a distinct 'furrow' can ensue, creating a trajectory in the history of professional life unique to New Zealand's situation. This, as Michael Corballis points out in chapter 1 of this book, is certainly the case in cognitive psychology. The study of cognition has subsequently developed alongside the other branches of psychology, and this has had both positive and negative consequences.

On the downside, 'academic' psychology in New Zealand was originally an underdog to the 'applied' branches of the discipline, as one would expect in accord with the needs of a developing nation. To have an 'ivory tower' psychologist in an academic setting was a luxury. And that luxury was, for a long time, an individual with behaviourist leanings, unconcerned with the inner workings of the psyche. The furrow of behaviourism was ploughed long and deep in this country. But, once travel technology enabled the faster import of ideas, the legacy of behavioural work provided an important context for the development of cognitive work — the intellectual rigour of meticulous experimentation. This rigour is clearly reflected in the empirical chapters in this book, and is a major strength of the field here.

Another influence follows not only from developments in travel technology, but also from the fact that New Zealand is a country that people want to visit. This leads to a continuing international interchange of ideas and collaborations that stimulate and refresh the discipline. This is again clear in this book, with contributions from psychologists who have come to live here from many other countries, and local psychologists who are engaged in international research teams, across the whole gamut of cognitive study: perception, memory, language, cognitive development, social cognition, representations, intentionality. These are further signs that cognitive psychology is in good health in New Zealand universities. In addition, its continuing good health can be predicted from the fact that the non-empirical chapters in this book indicate the willingness of cognitive work to be both reflective and open to new perspectives.

A Conspectus of Cognitive Inquiry in New Zealand/Aotearoa: An Introduction

Claire M. Fletcher-Flinn and Gus M. Haberman

This volume marks the first comprehensive collection of reports from research projects in cognitive psychology in New Zealand. The existence of such a book is a reflection of the remarkable and ongoing growth in cognitive inquiry in this part of the world. Although most influential models and theories on cognition have originated in North America and Europe, the last two decades have seen an upsurge of cognitive research in the Australasian region.

The term 'cognitive' as used in the discourse of psychology is polysemic; according to Bindra's (1984) semantic analysis, it encompasses five distinct conceptual meanings. The first relates 'cognitive' to a central knowledge state (in contrast to peripheral events), and includes, for example, concepts of mental set and expectancy. The second relates cognition to reasoning and problem-solving, with 'cognitive' distinguished from rote learning. A third sense of 'cognitive' is pertinent to transformations assumed in an information-processing framework (encoding, storage, retrieval, schemata), as opposed to a traditional associative framework. Bindra (1984) also demarcated a fourth sense of 'cognitive' as mentalistic, as opposed to behaviouristic, and a fifth sense relating to self-control systems, as opposed to situationalist views.

It can be claimed on good grounds (cf. chapter 1, this volume) that New Zealand cognitive psychologists have contributed to the study of cognition under each of these interpretations. However, in the last 10 years more emphasis has been placed on models presented in an information-processing framework. For the cognitivist, 'information' can be translated to 'representations derived by a person from environmental stimulation or from processing that influences selections among alternative choices for belief or action' (Massaro & Cowan, 1993, p. 383). According to the same review, information processing 'refers to how the information is modified so that it eventually has its observed influence' (op.cit., p. 384). It is the study of sequentially ordered models of formally statable mental operations, related to representation formation and modification, that forms a pervasive theme through chapters of this book.

This introduction is intended to provide a bird's-eye view of the research scene in today's New Zealand. The sections that follow will suggest a context for summarising the cognitive research themes appearing in the 17 chapters of the book.

New Zealand Scholarship

In the last 20 years or so, research on cognition in New Zealand has shown signs of becoming theoretically significant, vigorous, and diversified. Developments can be understood when examined in the context of a renewal of New Zealand academia. As with every country, New Zealand is uniquely shaped by its geography, history, and the groups contributing to its societal fabric. New Zealanders have forged a society from the meshing of Pacific, European, and Asian cultures. Its unique position in the world has facilitated value systems favouring self-reliant, resourceful, creative action. As a modern nation of 4 million, New Zealand upholds pluralism. Aotearoa[1] is a multi-ethnic society with an emphasis on a particular brand of biculturalism, with Mâori culture providing an upfront and alternative view of education and tradition. For better or worse, the habit of thinking laterally and independently has established itself in the Kiwi psyche.[2] For a relatively small population, New Zealanders have been noted for enormous contributions to sciences and arts (physicist Ernest Rutherford, writers Katherine Mansfield and Witi Ihimaera, operatic soprano Kiri Te Kanawa, visual artist Shane Cotton are examples).

As a country located on the fringe of the Pacific rim, always quick to take advantage of cultural tools and opportunities, New Zealand has embraced the arrival of the Internet for business and personal use. At the time of writing, over 1 million households in New Zealand are connected. This reduces New Zealand's geographical isolation, prompts awareness of the latest research findings, and provides opportunity for a strong voice in further developments.

In 2006, New Zealand has approximately 32 government-supported tertiary institutions (eight full universities, as well as institutes of technology, polytechnics, Mâori colleges called 'wananga'). The number of recognised private tertiary providers is in the hundreds. New Zealand scholarship and New Zealand universities have a high international standing that can be appraised more than ever before, through the Internet site of each university (cf. Endnote 3). The global standing of New Zealand academia was reflected, among others, in the so-called *Academic Ranking of World Universities* report (Jiao Tong University).

Cognitive Science in New Zealand

Growth and development in cognitive work in New Zealand have been stimulated both by American, British, and Continental European scholars permanently settling in New Zealand, and by academics who graduated from local universities. Concurrent with basic research, further teams of New Zealand researchers reap results of applying cognitive models in fields of practical significance.

Psychology has been established at each of the eight full universities of New Zealand. Seven universities (University of Auckland, Auckland University of Technology, University of Waikato, Massey University, Victoria University of Wellington, University of Canterbury, and University of Otago) have well-supported psychology departments of international reputation.[3]

While this introduction emphasises psychologists working in the cognitive disciplines, other departments contributing to cognitive science in New Zealand — such as philosophy, theoretical linguistics, and computer science — have equally respectable, sometimes longer, histories of scholarly enquiry and advanced teaching. Most universities offer courses in branches of cognitive science at undergraduate, postgraduate, and doctoral levels. (For a precise analysis of the origins and historical threads of cognitive psychology in New Zealand, see chapter 1).

In view of the need to establish interdisciplinary centres of excellence, it comes as no surprise that several New Zealand universities already have such centres in the cognitive area. Others contemplate the creation of centres. Examples include the Research Centre for Cognitive Neuroscience at the University of Auckland, and the postgraduate program in Cognitive Science and Philosophy of Mind at the University of Canterbury. This brief overview demonstrates that cognitive science is not only 'alive and well' in New Zealand but rapidly becoming a moving force within several domains.

Aims of This Volume

Cognition and Language is intended to make accessible and integrate theoretically significant outcomes of cognitive science in New Zealand research centres. Our intention was to edit the first volume on the international publishing scene reflecting the depth, quality, and some of the thematic diversity of cognitive psychology in New Zealand centres. It reflects some of the perspectives and approaches that New Zealand scientists take to internationally well recognised cognitive topics. It also indicates more unique themes that are investigated reliant on the Australasian context.

Scope and Limitations

As printed, our book is a lean collection of high-quality chapters written by New Zealand cognitive psychologists and a small number of non-psychologists. There is no claim that this collection is representative of all the impressive studies being carried out in cognition in New Zealand. However, it does promote a more profound and more accurate insight into contemporary New Zealand cognitive psychology than pre-existing publications. In particular, it is meant to integrate studies in the technical field of perception, the interfaces between cognition and language (psycholinguistics, psychology of communication), and cognitive–developmental studies — three domains that become increasingly salient in New Zealand cognitive science.

Outline and Synopsis

The book is designed to consist of four major sections, each integrating a few chapters. The sections correspond to the broader disciplinary themes within cognitive research that the 29 authors address, viz. perception and cognition, including chapters on the neural substrate, language and communication, and cognitive development. The fourth section contains chapters on current and future theoretical challenges in cognitive inquiry. As obvious from the design, the editors intended to highlight some of the current and best examples of cognitive research and whet the readers' appetite for more.

We have identified four main areas within cognitive research, without trying to be overly comprehensive. Some readers may find the diversity of research targets daunting at first. However, the chapters complement one another (especially within sections), as well as existing publications in cognition; they consolidate research findings worldwide; and they offer some new data and insights. All share a common thread based on Bindra's five interpretations of a cognitive approach, especially the information-processing view. The editors believe there is much to be gained by a collection that cuts across the usual boundaries. Readers may share in the excitement generated by this diversity, and benefit from a cross-fertilisation of knowledge and methodology.

Special attention was directed to New Zealand efforts to use a cognitive approach to the study of language and communication, given both editors' interest in psycholinguistic research. This is justified not only by the centrality of linguistic interaction, discourse, and narrative as empirical phenomena, but as Carpenter, Miyake, and Just (1995, p. 91) have observed, 'language has been the venue in which several key questions about cognition have been asked'. They point to examples that should be familiar to most readers, for example, Lashley's work on the problem of serial order in behaviour, Chomsky's cognitive perspective gaining ascendancy over Skinner's behaviorist view in the context of a linguistic battlefield, and Fodor's modular arguments to explain language processing. With many cognitive scientists worldwide, the editors share the view that 'language has been considered a prototype of a complex, well-learned, multi-tiered ... activity that reflects the fundamental architecture of cognition' (Carpenter et al., 1995, p. 92).

Sections, Chapters, and Findings

A theoretical scene for all empirical and theoretical work in subsequent chapters is set by chapter 1, a painstaking but also entertaining analysis of historical trends of how cognition was introduced and approached in New Zealand, and how cognitive research gained momentum. This is followed by Parts 1, 2, 3, and 4.

Part 1

The largest section of the volume, consisting of seven chapters, encompasses perception and cognition. It starts with a fitting topic, an illustration of the complexity of visual perception phenomena. Repetition blindness is a curious perceptual deficit that weakens our belief that the human visual system provides a veridical visual image of the world. Chapter 2 provides a theoretical account of repetition blindness and its applications. The question posed in chapter 3 is whether learning is a more satisfactory explanation of orienting effects than notions of derived attention, or exogenous and endogenous processing factors. In this chapter, the theoretical implications of the attentional effects of central and peripheral cues on visual attention are critically examined.

In the next two chapters, the focus is turned to social aspects of visual perception. It has been assumed that attending to one dimension of a stimulus results in the processing of other dimensions of that stimulus regardless of their behavioural relevance. However, what about the processing of names and faces — are they special? The experiments reported in chapter 4 suggest that top-down processing has little control over the selection of personally relevant information once an object has received focal attention. The next chapter is an investigation of the perceived impact of posed and genuine smiles on the perceiver.

Data are presented in chapter 5 that demonstrate an implicit sensitivity to the meaningful differences between the two kinds of smiles, and findings are discussed in the context of person perception and deception detection. Part 1 concludes with two chapters placing considerable emphasis on issues of methodology and theory. Chapter 6 uses complementary EEG and fMRI technologies in a study that provides converging evidence on the involvement of the anterior cingulate and prefrontal cortices in attentional aspects of the Stroop task. It is suggested that it is an oversimplification to assign a particular cognitive construct to a particular neural substrate.

Two approaches to measuring intentional and unintentional memory — the retrieval intentionality criterion method and the process dissociation procedure — are reviewed in chapter 7 within the context of alternative theoretical models of human memory. Experiments directly comparing the procedures are reported with study manipulations (level of processing; and reading versus anagram solution) used as critical variables.

Part 2

The three chapters in Part 2 provide challenging data for conventional psycholinguistic theories. Most models of spoken word recognition and lexical access assume a stable input representation. Sound change represents a challenge to this position and evidence for the spreading merger of [ɪə] and [ɛə] diphthongs in New Zealand speech is discussed in chapter 8. Recent research is presented about the consequences of ongoing sound change for spoken word recognition.

In chapter 9, evidence regarding two conflicting views of the nature of the developmental sequence of the subsyllabic division between onset and rime in children's phonological segmentation ability is reviewed. Findings supporting the 'psychological processing account' are explained. The final chapter in this section is on reading acquisition. Knowledge Sources theory is unique in postulating two forms of phonological recoding, one implicit and the other explicit. An updated version of the theory is presented in chapter 10 with new data from experimental studies of normal children, and case studies of atypical children and precocious readers.

Part 3

This part integrates four chapters on cognitive development. Chapter 11 reviews extant and current research on the child as a notator. Data are presented that supports the Karmiloff-Smith model by demonstrating that exogenous information is only temporarily beneficial with no transfer effects, and both procedural and conceptual information must be re-described before children can exhibit cognitive flexibility. An important question is posed in chapter 12 — how do children develop a way of talking about past life events? Recent theories about the development of autobiographical memory are examined, including primary and multiple influence theories. An integrated approach to the development of autobiographical memory is advocated that relies on cognitive, linguistic, and social factors in the early steps of creating a life story.

Chapter 13 presents evidence for the development of serial order knowledge in children. The findings suggest that it is not until 7 years of age that children can reliably extract knowledge of ordinal position. This section concludes with chapter 14 on the assessment of selective attention abilities in ADHD, highly creative, and normal boys using a Stroop task. Although the boys with ADHD demonstrated more Stroop interference, the magnitude of the effect did not differ across the groups. It is suggested that boys with ADHD have greater difficulty processing irrelevant information, however, the specific inhibitory mechanism that resolves Stroop interference is intact.

Part 4

Finally, we hear from researchers addressing theoretical dilemmas and asking us to ponder the future. On the basis of evolutionary arguments, it is suggested that there is a basic category framework of human experience. Evidence for the universality, innateness, and evolutionary importance of the elements is scrutinised in chapter 15. In the next chapter, a new type of summary is presented of several twists in the dispute on 'Do machines think as we humans do, or do they simulate the process of thinking?', and Searle's Chinese Room proposal. We end this section by being asked to consider an embodied approach to cognitive science. This approach has forced the re-thinking of structural elements of cognitive architectures in computer science; it is suggested that theorising in psychology should be constrained by evolutionary and developmental considerations, environmental factors, and the dynamics of construction.

Endnotes

1   Aotearoa (Mâori for 'long white cloud') is a name for the country used by New Zealanders of Mâori as well as non-Mâori ancestry.

2   'Kiwi' is the Mâori term for an avian genus indigenous to New Zealand. People born in New Zealand, as well as residents, often refer to themselves as 'Kiwis'; the bird is a jocular symbol of the nation.

3   New Zealand universities:
http://www.auckland.ac.nz/
http://www.aut.ac.nz/
http://www.waikato.ac.nz/
http://www.massey.ac.nz/
http://www.vuw.ac.nz/
http://www.canterbury.ac.nz/
http://www.lincoln.ac.nz/
http://www.otago.ac.nz/
See also websites of
UNITEC New Zealand: http://www.unitec.ac.nz/
The Open Polytechnic of New Zealand: http://www.topnz.ac.nz/
Psychology:
http://www.psych.auckland.ac.nz/
http://www.aut.ac.nz/schools/psychology/
http://www.waikato.ac.nz/wfass/subjects/psychology/
http://psychology.massey.ac.nz/
http://www.vuw.ac.nz/psyc/
http://www.psyc.canterbury.ac.nz/
http://www.lincoln.ac.nz/section204.html
http://psy.otago.ac.nz/index.html
Linguistics:
http://www.arts.auckland.ac.nz/departments/index.cfm?S=D_DALSL (Department of
   Applied Language Studies and Linguistics)
http://www.waikato.ac.nz/wfass/subjects/linguistics/
http://www.waikato.ac.nz/wfass/subjects/linguistics/ (School of Language Studies)
http://www.vuw.ac.nz/lals/ (School of Linguistics and Applied Language Studies)
http://www.ling.canterbury.ac.nz/
http://www.otago.ac.nz/departments/humanities/h_d_lang_perform_arts.html (School of
   Language, Literature and Performing Arts)
Philosophy:
http://www.arts.auckland.ac.nz/phi/
http://www.waikato.ac.nz/wfass/subjects/phil-rels/philosophy/
http://hpp.massey.ac.nz/ (School of History, Philosophy and Politics)
http://www.vuw.ac.nz/phil/
http://www.phil.canterbury.ac.nz/
http://www.lincoln.ac.nz/section200.html
http://www.otago.ac.nz/philosophy/
Computer Science:
http://www.cs.auckland.ac.nz/
http://www.cs.waikato.ac.nz/
http://www-ist.massey.ac.nz/ResearchGroups/
http://www.mcs.vuw.ac.nz/comp/
http://www.cllc.vuw.ac.nz/ (Centre for Logic, Language and Computation)
http://www.cosc.canterbury.ac.nz/
http://www.lincoln.ac.nz/section185.html
http://www.cs.otago.ac.nz/

Acknowledgments

The editors wish to gratefully acknowledge the assistance of Victoria University of Wellington, as well as Massey University, in providing a modest start-up grant to Australian Academic Press for the creation of this book. We would like to thank Dr. David Crabbe, Dr. Paul Warren (Victoria University of Wellington) as well as Professor Ian M. Evans, Dr. John V. Podd, and Dr. Nikolaos Kazantzis (Massey University) for their efforts.

References

Bindra, D. (1984). Cognition: Its origin and future in psychology. In J. R. Royce & L. P. Mos (Eds.), *Annals of theoretical psychology* (Vol. 1, pp. 1–29). New York: Plenum Press.

Carpenter, P. A., Miyake, A., & Just, M. A. (1995). Language comprehension: Sentence and discourse processing. *Annual Review of Psychology, 46,* 91–120.

Massaro, D. W., & Cowan, N. (1993). Information processing models: Microscopes of the mind. *Annual Review of Psychology, 44,* 383–425.

History of Cognitive Psychology in New Zealand

Michael Corballis

Experimental psychology really began as a cognitive science, although it was not labelled as such. As we all know, or used to know, the first psychological laboratory was established by Wilhelm Wundt in Leipzig, Germany, in 1879. Wundt was essentially a Cartesian dualist. Just as we understand the physical world by looking outwards, he thought, so we might study the mind by looking inwards, through *introspection*. Although little of his legacy remains, Wundt had a prodigious output, and a wide influence. Among his disciples was the British psychologist, Edward B. Titchener, who transported Wundt's introspectionism to Cornell University in the United States, where it came to be known as *Titchenerism*. Psychologists of today who look into the psychological journals of the late 19th and early 20th centuries may be surprised to discover discussions of many of the topics that are fashionable today, such as memory, attention, language, and consciousness.

It was in this tradition that New Zealand psychology was born, largely through the efforts of one remarkable man. Thomas Alexander Hunter was born in London in 1876, but was brought up in Dunedin from the age of four. He gained his MA with first-class honours in mental and moral philosophy at the University of Otago in 1899, and then taught for a while at Waitaki Boys High School. A man of many parts, he also played rugby as a half-back for the University of Otago and for Otago province. In 1904 he was appointed lecturer in Mental Science and Political Economy at Victoria University College, and in 1906 completed MSc at Victoria. In 1907 he went to the United States to study with Titchener at Cornell, with whom he continued to correspond for many years. On his return he was appointed to a combined Chair in Philosophy and Economics, but in 1909 he dropped economics and took a new Chair in Mental and Moral Philosophy. He maintained his interest in rugby as player-coach of the Victoria College rugby team, and in 1949 was elected President of the Wellington Rugby Union. In 1939, he became the first academic in New

Zealand to be awarded a knighthood. He was awarded an honorary Litt.D. by the University of New Zealand in 1949, and died in 1953.

Hunter had correspondence with Wilhelm Wundt in Leipzig and the psychiatrist W. H. R. Rivers in Cambridge, but it was his association with Titchener that was most influential in his early career, leading him to create the first psychological laboratory in Australasia, and to establish a diploma in experimental psychology (Brown & Fuchs, 1969). Although several generations of students were introduced to experimental studies of reaction time, visual acuity, and hand–eye coordination, there appear to have been no original publications in basic experimental psychology arising from this laboratory, although Hunter himself wrote a number of articles with psychological themes in the 1920s (e.g., Hunter, 1924, 1927, 1928 — see Taylor, 2003 for more details). Two of his legacies to New Zealand psychology are the Hunter Memorial Prize for the top student in psychology at Victoria University of Wellington, and the premier Hunter Award for psychological research offered annually by the New Zealand Psychological Society. The Hunter Building at Victoria University is also named after him (although the present-day Department of Psychology is located in the Easterfield Building).

Hunter did not continue with basic psychological research, however, but devoted himself increasingly to broader and more practical social concerns. He was first President of the Wellington branch of Workers' Educational Institute and was chairman of the New Zealand Council for Educational Research from its inception in 1938 until 1947. He worked for university reform, and was chairman of Massey Agricultural College (now Massey University) from 1936 to 1938. In the 1930s he took a stand against the eugenics movement that swept the western world, including New Zealand, with horrific consequences in Nazi Germany. Later on, in the 1940s, he persuaded Peter Fraser, the Prime Minister and Minister of Education, to provide funds for a School of Social Science for the training of social workers.

Given Sir Thomas's increasingly public role and broadening interest in the social sciences, it is perhaps not surprising that when the first Chair of Psychology in New Zealand was established at Victoria University College in Wellington, Titchener's legacy was long forgotten, although Hunter himself was influential. Professor Ernest Beaglehole was appointed to that Chair in 1947. He was trained as an ethnopsychologist, perhaps closer to anthropology than to mainstream psychology, and was a protégé and admirer of Sir Thomas Hunter. He edited the *festschrift* to Sir Thomas — the first ever to a New Zealand academic (Beaglehole, 1946). Nevertheless, while paying tribute to Hunter's immense contribution to academic, political, and social life in New Zealand, Beaglehole (1966) remarked that 'he was never a great or profound scholar in the professional sense' (p. 124).

But this may not have been the only or even principal reason why Hunter's early vision of psychological science did not survive. Rather, it may have had to do with a profound sea-change within academic psychology itself. When he went to study with Titchener in 1907, the Wundtian era and Titchenerism itself were in fact drawing to a close, and by the middle of the century were largely forgotten. From late in the 19th century, in fact, there had been growing unease over the introspective method, some of it based on doubt as to whether all thought processes were accessible to introspection. In 1894 one of Wundt's former students, Oswald Kulpe, established what came to be known as the Wurzburg school, which began to challenge the introspective method. Their investigations led to the notion of *unanschlauliche Bewusstheit*, later translated as 'imageless thought' (Boring, 1929). In the United States, Titchener (1909) tried to argue against such notions, but a year later even he seemed to accept that some forms of habitual thought could be entirely unconscious (Titchener, 1910).

The Dark Ages

The more decisive onslaught came, however, not from arguments over imageless thought, but rather from a radical change in ideas as to what psychology should be about. A critical event was the publication, in 1913, of J. B. Watson's article 'Psychology as a behaviorist views it' in the influential *Psychological Review*. Psychology quickly ceased to be the study of the mind, and instead, especially in the United States, became the study of behaviour. Cartesian dualism effectively gave way to the Darwinian idea of a continuity between humans and other animals, and out the window went most of those concepts we like to think of as cognitive. Mentalistic terms such as attention, memory, and even consciousness were effectively banished from scientific analysis. The appropriate matter for study was not what humans and animals think, but rather what they do. Moreover, the laws governing behaviour were supposed to be the same for animals as for humans, so it did not really matter which animal you studied.

For cognitive psychologists this marked the beginning of the dark ages, where rats and pigeons seemed to take precedence over people. Behaviourism dominated, especially in the United States, until well into the 1960s, and was also the dominant approach, at least among experimental psychologists, in New Zealand when psychology began to break away from philosophy in the late 1940s and 1950s.

Other universities followed Victoria's lead and established departments of psychology over the next two decades. While none of the professorial appointments could be described as a radical behaviourist, behaviourism was still the dominant paradigm, although psychophysics retained a thread of continuity going back to the 19th century. Beaglehole's influence kept social and clinical psychology relatively distinct, although much of clinical psychology was later colonised by behaviourism through the so-called scientist–practitioner model. Nevertheless, as a student at Victoria University College in the late 1950s, I can recall that most of the experimental psychology I was taught had to do with the behaviour of rats in mazes, or in pressing bars to obtain food. The influential theorist of the time was the United States psychologist Clark L. Hull, whose 1952 book, *A Behavior System*, seemed the ultimate in theoretical sophistication.

One of the main theoretical issues that we discussed had to do with whether rats negotiated mazes by learning particular turning responses, or whether they learned which places to go to, as proposed by Edward Chase Tolman (1951). Tolman's idea of a 'cognitive map' was at least a wink toward cognitivism.

The behaviourist who was to become more influential, in New Zealand as in the United States, was the radical behaviourist B. F. Skinner. One of his innovations was to introduce pigeons in place of rats, and as if through the influence of some pied piper, the rats gradually disappeared from the laboratories of experimental psychology and in flew the birds. This change was not due to any belief that humans might be more closely related to birds than to other mammals, much as I find that idea appealing, but was simply a matter of convenience. Pigeons can peck keys more rapidly than rats can press bars, so that data can be accumulated more quickly. They are also less likely to draw blood. I still shudder when I think back to when I was a demonstrator for undergraduate laboratories at the University of Auckland in the early 1960s, when students were assigned rats and required to taken them through various conditioning routines. It was my job to transport rats from cage to Skinner box and back, and mediate when there was a stand-off between rat and student. Blood, usually human, was often shed in the call of duty, although I do remember trying to pick up a rat by the tail, and was left holding the end-piece of the tail while the rest of the animal escaped. In the more benign company of pigeons, behavioural psychology remains a persistent if dwindling influence in several departments of psychology in New Zealand, notably at the Universities of Auckland, Canterbury, and Otago, and at Waikato University.

It is of interest to speculate why behaviourism gained such a persistent hold in this country, since it was never such a strong influence in Europe, or even in mother England, as it was in the United States. Perhaps its anti-intellectualism was appealing to a small country without a strong intellectual or academic tradition, or perhaps our farming background caused us to recognise the practical usefulness of behavioural techniques in the control of animal (not to mention human) behaviour. Curiously, though, behaviourism had much less of an impact in neighbouring Australia. A fledgling discipline in a small country may perhaps owe more to one or two influential individuals than to any national trait. One wonders how it might have developed had Hunter had a more enduring influence on the discipline itself.

But in any case, behaviourism itself was riding for a fall.

The International Cognitive Revolution

According to the American author Howard Gardner (1985), the critical date for the 'cognitive revolution' was September 11, 1956, when the speakers at a conference held at the Massachusetts Institute of Technology included Noam Chomsky on syntactic structures, Herbert Simon (later to win the Nobel Prize in Economics!) and Alan Newell on the first complete proof of a theorem by a computing machine, and George A. Miller on the magical number 7. It was Chomsky who was to provide the most direct challenge to Skinnerian behaviourism.

In 1957 Skinner was at the height of his reputation. This was the year in which his book *Verbal Behavior* appeared. To many, language is the ultimate intellectual challenge, and *Verbal Behavior* was Skinner's attempt to reach the summit. Descartes (1647/1985) had argued that, because of its open-endedness and freedom from constraint, human language could not be reduced to mechanical principles, but must be governed by some nonmaterial influence operating through the pineal gland. Indeed, this was one of Descartes' principal arguments for mind–body dualism. For Skinner, the Cartesian challenge actually came from a remark made to him by the eminent British philosopher Alfred North Whitehead. Skinner had dined with Whitehead in 1934 and tried to explain to him the nature and power of behaviourism, whereupon Whitehead had uttered the sentence, 'No black scorpion is falling upon this table', and asked Skinner for a behaviourist explanation of why he might have said that. It took over 20 years for Skinner to reply. His explanation, in an appendix to *Verbal Behavior*, actually seems to owe more to Freudian psychology than to behaviourism, which is ironic given Skinner's antipathy to psychoanalysis. He suggested that the 'black scorpion' was to Whitehead a symbol of behaviourism, and Whitehead was unconsciously expressing the determination that it would not take over.

As fate would have it, *Verbal Behavior* was published in the same year as Chomsky's *Syntactic Structures*, which was essentially a demonstration that language could not be reduced to associationistic or Markovian principles. Two years later, in 1959, Chomsky published his famous review, or rather demolition, of *Verbal Behavior*. According to Chomsky, syntax depends on rules, of the sort that might be implemented on a digital computer, and not through learned associations. His arguments clearly won the day, and the new field of psycholinguistics was born. In the more general sense, cognitive psychology probably entered the mainstream of United States academic psychology with the publication in 1967 of Ulric Neisser's eloquent and influential book, *Cognitive Psychology*.

Outside of the United States, the behaviourist revolution was perhaps less dramatic. In British psychology, for example, the work of Frederic C. Bartlett in the 1930s was a clear forerunner of present-day cognitive psychology, emphasising an experimental, objective approach to memory and thinking, without resort to introspection (e.g., Bartlett, 1932). This led to a tradition of studying humans as communication systems, often in applied settings, such as airplane cockpits. The study of the limits of human performance assumed special importance during the Second World War. In many respects, Donald E. Broadbent's 1958 book *Perception and Communication*, which summarised and gave theoretical backing to much of the wartime work, was a precursor to Neisser's *Cognitive Psychology*, and gave British psychologists something of a jump start in the cognitive revolution. The British psychologists effectively defined what came to be termed the 'information-processing' approach to the human mind, later enthusiastically embraced by experimental psychologists in the United States. The rats and pigeons were replaced by humans. This was not a return to introspectionism, though, since the methods of study were objective rather than subjective. Human performance was measured in terms of accuracy or reaction time, leading to models, often based explicitly on computer systems, of how the mind works.

The McGill Connection

In New Zealand, it was perhaps Canada, not Britain, that was to have the most important influence in the slow rise of cognitive psychology. In 1949, Donald O. Hebb, a professor of psychology at McGill University in Montreal, published *Organization of Behavior*. This book was influential in reviving physiological psychology, and continues to have an important influence in modern neuroscience. It was also through Hebb's influence, along with that of the legendary neurosurgeon Wilder Penfield, that Dr Brenda Milner, a McGill PhD, became the first psychologist to be appointed in a neurological hospital — the Montreal Neurological Institute. Neuropsychology inevitably focuses interest on cognition, and on the understanding of deficits in language, perception, attention, and the like.

A New Zealander who studied at McGill in the heady 1950s was one T. H. (Harry) Scott. Scott had been interned as a conscientious objector in New Zealand during World War II, and after the war went to McGill for his PhD. There, he was influenced by Hebb's ideas, and in particular by Hebb's view that the brain needed constant stimulation in order to function properly. Scott was co-author of a famous paper on the destabilising effects of sensory deprivation on psychological function (Bexton, Heron, & Scott, 1954) — a study that was later to lead to the controversial use of sensory deprivation as a 'brainwashing' technique. There is perhaps an irony here, given Scott's earlier role as a conscientious objector to war. After completing his PhD, Scott returned to teach psychology in the philosophy department at the University of Auckland, and in 1960, at the age of 41, was tragically killed in a climbing accident near the summit of Mt Cook.

At McGill, Hubert ('Barney') Sampson, a Canadian who had served in the Canadian Navy during the war, had befriended Scott, who persuaded him to take up a post as lecturer in psychology at the University of Canterbury. In 1961, Sampson was appointed to head the newly created Department of Psychology at the University of Auckland. He had completed his PhD at McGill University in 1954, and before coming to Canterbury had worked for the Defence Research Board in Canada, where he developed an interest in human information processing. To several of us, he seemed to represent a new wave in psychology in New Zealand, and Auckland was the place to be. David Quartermain, a lecturer at Victoria University, shifted to a lecturing post at Auckland, and a number of students, including myself, transferred from other universities to join the first masters class in psychology at Auckland in 1961.

Barney Sampson taught us about physiological psychology, and a young British psychologist called William S. Anthony, appointed as a lecturer in that same year, introduced us to Broadbent's *Perception and Communication*. In these two respects, we may have been more in tune with what was to come in psychology than most graduate students throughout the world. But it still took a long time for cognitive psychology to take hold. Quartermain went to the United States, eventually to become Professor of Neurology at New York University, Anthony returned to Britain, and those of us in that masters class who went on to academic careers went to graduate schools overseas, as was the accepted practice in those days. Paul Spong went to University of California, Los Angeles (UCLA), Guy von Sturmer to the University of Melbourne, Denis Lander (as a post-doc) to Dalhousie University in Nova Scotia, Canada, while I went to McGill. Peter MacNeilage, who had been a student of Sampson's at Canterbury, had also gone to McGill as a PhD student, and since graduating has become internationally known for his work in speech science.

Perhaps this exodus delayed the development of cognitive psychology. When I returned from McGill in 1978 to take up a third Chair in Psychology at Auckland, I found that Sampson had rather paradoxically built up a strong emphasis on operant psychology, with the appointments of, among others, Ivan L. Beale and Michael C. Davison, who was to go on to become an international leader in the field. Nevertheless the appointment of R. John Irwin to the second Chair of Psychology at Auckland in 1963 had at least ensured a presence for human experimental psychology. Irwin's specialty was psychoacoustics rather than human cognition, although even he flirted for a time with operant psychology. There were other gradual shifts toward cognition. Beale and I blended operant and human experimental psychology in a series of studies of left–right discrimination in both pigeons and human children (Corballis & Beale, 1970), leading Beale himself to shift his interest from the operant behaviour of pigeons to the study of learning disabilities in children. Elsewhere, at Victoria University, Murray J. White had developed an interest in human information processing, and was author of a classic review paper on lateralisation in visual processing (White, 1969), and his namesake, K. Geoffrey White, gradually and successfully blended operant and cognitive psychology in studies of memory. Geoffrey White later took up a Chair at Otago University, now a mecca for studies of memory.

The Rise of Neuropsychology

Sampson's main contribution to cognitive psychology was the paced serial adding task (PSAT), which he had developed while employed by the Defence Research Board in Canada, prior to coming to New Zealand. A number of us, including Spong, MacNeilage, and myself, had completed masters theses under Sampson's supervision, working on different aspects of performance on this task; and Roger Ratcliff, who was trained in physics, developed a sophisticated mathematical model of PSAT performance. Ratcliff then went on to a distinguished career as an experimental and mathematical psychologist in the United States. Despite this activity, though, none of us was quite sure what the PSAT was supposed to measure, but it was another PhD student of Sampson's, Dorothy Gronwall, who found that it provided a sensitive index of information-processing deficits following closed head injury. Gronwall and Sampson (1974) established the PSAT internationally as a neuropsychological test and, in 1981, with the collaboration of a neurosurgeon, Philip Wrightson, Gronwall set up the Concussion Unit at Auckland Hospital. Her books with Wrightson and another Auckland graduate, Peter Waddell, are widely used as practical guidelines for recognition and management of the effects of concussion (Gronwall, Wrightson, & Waddell, 1990; Wrightson & Gronwall, 1999). Gronwall received the OBE for services to clinical neuropsychology in 1994, and died suddenly, at the age of 70, in 2001. She was New Zealand's first clinical neuropsychologist.

Gronwall also taught a now legendary masters paper in clinical neuropsychology in the Department of Psychology at Auckland, and Sampson ensured that physiological psychology retained a presence. Some continuity with Gronwall's work was ensured when Jennifer A. Ogden, under the supervision of myself and Gronwall, completed a PhD on hemispatial neglect, based on patients at Auckland Hospital. In 1986, after a postdoctoral year working at Massachusetts Institute of Technology with Suzanne Corkin, a former student of Brenda Milner's, Ogden was appointed Senior Lecturer in charge of the clinical psychology program at Auckland, which retains a strong emphasis in clinical neuropsychology.

Physiological psychology petered out at Auckland, but was installed with a flourish at the University of Otago in 1981 with the appointment of Graham V. Goddard as Professor of Psychology. Goddard was yet another graduate of McGill, having completed his PhD there in 1963. After graduating, he went on to academic appointments at the University of Waterloo and then Dalhousie University in Canada, and discovered that low-level electrical stimulation of the limbic system in rats eventually leads to epilepsy-like seizures, a phenomenon known as 'kindling'. This work laid the foundation for subsequent work on long-term potentiation (LTP), in which trains of electrical stimulation to the brain — and notably to the hippocampus — induces long-term changes in synaptic responsivity. This phenomenon is widely held to be the neural basis of memory. Echoing the earlier death of Harry Scott, Goddard was tragically killed in 1987 while trying to cross a flooded stream in Arthurs Pass National Park. His work on LTP was carried on by others, notably Wickliffe C. Abraham, who had been a post-doc with Goddard, and eventually became Professor and Head of the Department of Psychology at Otago. That department is a world-class centre for research into memory at all levels, including the neurophsyiological, the neuropsychological, the developmental, and (perforce) the cognitive.

In the meantime, a Research Centre for Cognitive Neuroscience had been established at Auckland, focusing at first on the psychological examination of brain-injured patients, but supplemented later by high-density electrophysiological analysis of brain activity in normal human volunteers. In 2004 facilities for functional and structural magnetic resonance imaging were established at the University of Auckland, so the Centre now has access to state-of-the-art imaging.

Whither Cognitive Psychology?

Cognitive psychology can take either of two paths. One is basically computational, based on the digital computer as a model for the mind. This approach was partly diverted into connectionist modelling from about the early 1980s, but still effectively relies on a computational approach to simulate mental function, or to provide appropriate metaphors for cognition. The alternative path has been through the study of brain function, whether through behavioural neuroscience, which involves direct neurophysiological recording or intervention in nonhuman species, or through cognitive neuroscience, involving brain imaging or neuropsychological testing of human subjects. These two paths need not be mutually exclusive, but on the whole cognitive psychology in New Zealand has taken the second path — through the brain rather than the machine.

One can only speculate as to why New Zealand cognitive psychology has taken this path, which is again not nearly so evident across the Tasman. Perhaps it was simply the colonising influence of McGill, where D. O. Hebb effectively introduced psychologists to the brain. The reader can best judge whether this tradition persists, or whether there are new influences afoot, by reading the remaining chapters of this volume.

References

Bartlett, F. C. (1932). *Remembering: A study in experimental and social psychology*. Cambridge, England: Cambridge University Press.

Beaglehole, E. (Ed.). (1946). *The university and the community: Essays in honour of Thomas Alexander Hunter*. Wellington, New Zealand: New Zealand University Press.

Beaglehole, E. (1966). Hunter, Thomas Alexander, KBE. In A. H. McLintock (Ed.), *An encyclopaedia of New Zealand*, (Vol. 2, pp. 123–124). Wellington, New Zealand: Government Printer.

Bexton, W. H., Heron, W., & Scott, T. H. (1954). Effects of decreased variation in the sensory environment. *Canadian Journal of Psychology*, 8, 70–76.

Boring, E. G. (1929). *A history of experimental psychology*. New York: Appleton-Century-Crofts.

Broadbent, D. E. (1958). *Perception and communication*. Oxford, England: Pergamon.

Brown, L. B., & Fuchs, A. H. (1969). *The letters between Sir Thomas Hunter and E. B. Titchener*. Wellington, New Zealand: Victoria University of Wellington School of Psychology Publication No. 23.

Chomsky, N. (1957). *Syntactic structures*. The Hague, the Netherlands: Mouton.

Chomsky, N. (1959). A review of B. F. Skinner's 'Verbal behavior'. *Language*, 35, 26–58.

Corballis, M. C., & Beale, I. L. (1970). *The psychology of left and right*. Hillsdale, NJ: Erlbaum.

Descartes, R. (1985). *The philosophical writings of Descartes* (J. Cottingham, R. Stoothoff, & D. Murdock, Ed. and Trans.). Cambridge, England: Cambridge University Press. (Original work published 1647)

Gardner, H. (1985). *The mind's new science: A history of the cognitive revolution*. New York: Basic Books.

Gronwall, D. M. A., & Sampson, H. (1974). *The psychological effects of concussion*. Wellington, New Zealand: Oxford University Press.

Gronwall, D. M. A., Wrightson, P., & Waddell, P. A. (1990). *Head injury: The facts: A guide for families and caregivers*. Oxford, England: Oxford University Press.

Hebb, D. O. (1949). *Organization of behavior*. New York: Wiley.

Hull, C. L. (1952). *A behavior system*. New Haven, CT: Yale University Press.

Hunter, T. A. (1924). Some reflections on social institutions. *Australasian Journal of Psychology and Philosophy, 2*, 51–57.

Hunter, T. A. (1927). Some concepts in relation to social science. *Australasian Journal of Psychology and Philosophy, 5*, 161–185.

Hunter, T. A. (1928). Psychological clinic for children, Victoria University College, Wellington. *Australasian Journal of Psychology and Philosophy, 2*, 51–57.

Neisser, U. (1967). *Cognitive psychology*. New York: Appleton-Century-Crofts.

Skinner, B. F. (1957). *Verbal behavior*. New York: Appleton-Century-Crofts.

Taylor, A. J. W. (2003). In praise of an all-round psychologist: Sir Thomas Hunter. *Bulletin of the New Zealand Psychological Society*, No. 101, 26–35.

Titchener, E. B. (1909). *Lectures on the experimental psychology of the thought process*. New York: Macmillan.

Titchener, E. B. (1910). *A textbook of psychology*. New York: Macmillan.

Tolman, E. C. (1951). *Collected papers in psychology*. Berkeley, CA: University of California Press.

Watson, J. B. (1913). Psychology as a behaviorist views it. *Psychological Review, 20*, 1–14.

White, M. J. (1969). Laterality differences in perception: A review. *Psychological Bulletin, 72*, 387–405.

Wrightson, P., & Gronwall, D. M. A. (1999). *Mild head injury: A guide to management*. New York: Oxford University Press.

Part 1

Perceiving and Cognising: Information Processing and Neural Substrate

Repetition Blindness: An Illustration of the Complexity of Visual Perceptual Phenomena

Heather Buttle

Consider the hypothetical case of a man, Alf, who exhibits a number of perceptual deficits. These deficits became evident in the following ways: Alf being a keen All Blacks rugby supporter watches their matches whenever he can. On one occasion, while intently following the left wing's break toward the try line, he failed to notice that a streaker had run across the pitch. On another occasion, Alf was carefully trying to match his chosen paint colour to one of the paint palettes in his local DIY store. At one point the assistant he had originally approached swapped places with a different assistant. On putting the paint palette down, Alf failed to notice the assistant had changed and resumed the conversation as if it were the original assistant. Furthermore, when watching television programs or films that contain rapid sequences he is unaware of a number of the items shown and if two items are repeated, he is frequently only aware of one. What neurological impairment is it that Alf has? Well, it is likely that Alf is actually neurologically typical; all of these deficits have been found in 'normal' individuals.

Literature on the study of attention has described a number of 'normal' perceptual phenomena that characterise these perceptual deficits. The All Blacks example is a case of *inattentional blindness* (Mack & Rock, 1998). Here the movement of the left wing and his location on the pitch were attended, but the streaker and his location was unattended. Inattentional blindness is a case of an event outside the focus of attention failing to be brought into conscious awareness. Similarly, the DIY incident is an example of *change blindness* (Rensink, O'Regan, & Clark, 1997), where changes to a non-attended region (the assistant) are not noticed. If the paint palette had changed this would have probably been noticed, as it was the attended region of interest. Alf's problem with failing to notice items that are rapidly presented refers to the *attentional blink* (Raymond, Shapiro, & Arnell, 1992), where the second of two to-be-reported targets is not consciously processed if presented within 200 to 500 ms of the first target. And finally, a further additive deficit, known as *repetition blindness* (Kanwisher, 1987), occurs when two identical items are presented within 200 ms of each other; this leads to awareness of only one of the repetitions.

This hypothetical case demonstrates that while people go about their daily lives relying on their highly functioning visual systems, they take it for granted that they have a veridical impression of the visual world that surrounds them. In fact, while the human visual system generally operates efficiently, as would be hoped from several thousand years of human evolution, there are 'failings' in perception that reveal invaluable clues as to how the visual system operates. One of these mysterious failings is the phenomenon of repetition blindness. What follows is a journey through this particular example of a visual perceptual phenomenon, from how it has been accounted for (including whether it is truly a perceptual deficit or a memory deficit), to what types of stimuli produce the effect, and through to applied uses (including measuring brand associations). Note, however, that the debate surrounding the nature of repetition blindness is still ongoing, and while this chapter attempts to sum up the state of play it is far from exhaustive. For instance the discussion has been kept to the visual domain and does not attempt to cover the literature on *repetition deafness* (e.g., Soto-Faraco, & Spence, 2001). But, first a basic account of repetition blindness will be explored.

Repetition Blindness

The term 'repetition blindness', herein referred to as RB, was first coined by Kanwisher (1987) to describe her participants' failure in reporting the presence of repeated words when presented in a rapid serial visual presentation (RSVP). Kanwisher tested serial lists of words, as well as sentences, that either did or did not contain a repeated word. For example, the sentence, 'It was work time so work had to get done' contains the repeated word 'work'. Each of these words would be presented one after another in the centre of a computer screen for between 117 to 250 milliseconds (see Figure 1). Both serial lists and sentences revealed that participants were significantly less likely to recall both occurrences of the repeated words than two critical items that were not identical. This is a surprising finding for two reasons: (a) typically the presence of a repeated item leads to facilitation in recognition, known as *repetition priming* (e.g., Hintzman & Block, 1971; Scarborough, Cortese, & Scarborough, 1977), (b) the RB effect persisted even when the omission of the repeated word rendered the sentence ungrammatical (e.g., the example above would be recalled, 'It was work time so had to get done').

So how can this finding be explained? Kanwisher (1987) proposed the *token individuation hypothesis* as an account of her results. The key to understanding this hypothesis lies in the distinction made between two forms of information: *types* and *tokens*. Type information is created from the identity of the item and token information is created from the visual episode of the item. As each new item from the RSVP task is recognised its type node is activated. In parallel with this

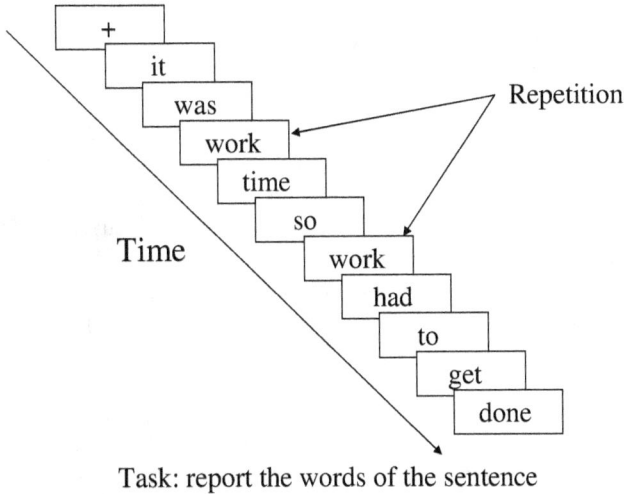

Figure 1
An example of a sentence presented in RSVP. Each word would have been presented for between 117–250 ms.

process, token nodes are activated to encode the current episode, allowing serial order information to be preserved. For instance, in learning the alphabet we need to be able to identify what type of letters were presented (e.g., 'S' and 'Y'), and what order they were presented in (e.g., 'S' then 'Y'). It is this latter process that involves 'token individuation'. In the case of RB, once a type node (the identity of the word 'work') has been token individuated (the episode registered) it is temporarily unavailable for subsequent token individuation (the second episode). Note that this is not to say that the second occurrence cannot be typed — its identity is activated a second time, but the token information is not. If there is no new token for the repeated item, the two identical items are not encoded as separate events, leaving the participants only aware of one occurrence.

This is a perceptual account of how RB occurs: there is an online failure in token, but not type, activation for the repeated item. While this provides a parsimonious account, consideration is needed of whether RB is truly a perceptual effect or if it can be explained in terms of memory limitations. Perhaps participants forget to report, or confuse, the repeated items? And if RB is a perceptual effect, are there any other accounts that can explain the effect?

Perception or Memory?

The account of repetition blindness presented so far views RB as an online perceptual phenomenon. However, a number of researchers have interpreted RB as a memory retrieval failure. In simple terms, were the repeated items lost from memory after being seen or were they never seen at all?

The use of traditional RB procedures, where participants report the items following the presentation, brings obvious comparisons to a memory phenomenon known as the *Ranschburg effect* (Ranschburg, 1902). In this case, short-term recall for repeated items presented in serial lists is impaired. This occurs even at very slow rates of presentation, where perceiving each item should not be a problem. However, the Ranschburg effect differs from the RB effect. Most notably, the Ranschburg effect is least prevalent when repeated items are positioned in close proximity to each other. In contrast, RB effects tend to be larger when the repeated items are close together. Moreover, RB is evident even in displays with a low demand on memory, where perhaps only two or three items are presented (e.g., Bavelier, 1994; Kanwisher, Yin, & Wojciulik, 1999; Neill, Neely, Hutchinson, Kahan, & VerWys, 2002).

Despite the apparent dissociation between the two effects, a number of researchers have accounted for RB effects in terms of memory retrieval failure. These accounts can be grouped into two forms of argument: memory interference/bias and memory-migration. The memory interference account suggests that as serial report tasks require items to be recalled in order of occurrence, the overt report of the first occurrence of the item interferes with the subsequent report of the second item. Furthermore, a response bias may make it unlikely that a second occurrence of an item is reported. Explicitly, Fagot and Pashler (1995) suggested that a guessing bias might lead participants to report a 'not yet reported' item when an item had not been seen. Naturally, this would lead to repeated trials being incorrect, while non-repeated trials may by chance be correct. They also suggested that a censorship bias might occur, where participants were reluctant to make the same report twice. Evidence for the response bias account comes from a number of sources where the repeated stimulus was specifically cued for report (Armstrong & Mewhort, 1995; Fagot & Pashler, 1995; Lewandowsky, Neely, VerWys, & Amos, 1997). For instance, Fagot and Pashler (1995) presented a sequence of six letters, one of which was coloured red and was either a repeated or non-repeated letter. After each presentation a cue appeared to indicate which of two tasks was to be performed first: (a) report the identity of the red item, and (b) report the whole letter series. The authors found that when participants reported the whole series, RB occurred. However, when asked to simply report the red letter, responses were equivalent in both repeated and non-repeated conditions. This could indicate that all the items were available for report, but in the whole report task participants refrained from reporting both the first and second identical items.

The *memory-migration account* is suggested by Whittlesea, Dorken, and Podrouzek (1995). They posited that during recall from short-term memory, one occurrence is tagged as recalled, but when the second occurrence is later recalled it is confused with the already tagged first occurrence. This would be less likely to occur for non-repeated items, as the inconsistency between the two items would tend to be noticed. Hence, the distinctiveness in memory of two non-repeated items facilitates reporting, compared to the repeated items.

Having considered the possibility that RB is actually a memory phenomenon, what evidence do we have to maintain that RB is perceptual in origin? The most straightforward case for discounting the memory account is the abundance of RB research that uses minimal memory load tasks (Hochhaus & Johnston, 1996; Johnston, Hochhaus, & Ruthruff, 2002; Luo & Caramazza, 1995; Kanwisher, Kim, & Wickens, 1996; Neill et al., 2002; Park & Kanwisher, 1994). These techniques have ranged from counting tasks (e.g., Anderson & Neill, 2002; Johnston et al., 2002; Park & Kanwisher, 1994), to two-item displays (e.g., Luo & Caramazza, 1995; Neill et al., 2002), to online detection tasks (Johnston et al., 2002). To elaborate, a counting task only requires the presence of certain specified items to be counted, as opposed to recalling the whole series. For instance, Park and Kanwisher (1994) observed RB effects when participants were asked to count whether one or two vowels occurred among a sequence of consonants. Here, it was less demanding on memory load to recall one or two items than it was to retrieve the entire sequence.

Similarly, when only two items are presented memory demands should also be low. This was evident in Neill et al.'s (2002) study where a target letter was displayed for 50 ms to the left or right then masked by a '£' sign and followed by a second 50 ms target letter and mask in the opposite location. Despite the reduced item presentation, RB was still observable. An even more convincing technique is the online task used by Johnston et al. (2002). Here the authors required participants to respond to the targets as they occurred on screen, via a keyboard press, thus bypassing the need to retrieve serial information. Again strong RB was observed.

Consistent with a perceptual encoding account is an ERP (event-related potential) study by Schedan, Kanwisher, and Kutas (1997). The ERPs indicated that RB modulated cortical responses with relatively early latencies. Early latencies would be expected with a perceptual account, while later latencies would have been expected with a memory account. An interesting addition to this evidence is an *apparent motion* account of RB. According to Chun and Cavanagh (1997), RB can be modulated by the perceived grouping of moving objects. In their study, when repeated items were presented in the same apparent motion stream a larger RB effect was found compared to when the repeated items were presented in different but simultaneously displayed streams. This links RB mechanisms to those involved in apparent motion, and affords us a perceptual account of RB with real-world implications. Consider the following: imagine you are driving along a highway when you suddenly see a motorcycle appear in your wing mirror, it then just as suddenly disappears, perhaps into your blind spot, and then reappears again in your wing mirror. Did you see two motorcycles or just one? In real environments objects are frequently out of view for small amounts of time, either from occlusion by other objects or from the rapid saccades the eyes make to other portions of the visual scene. In these rapid instances, it makes sense for the visual system to bind the events together as one occurrence.

Having set out a number of reasons why RB should not be discounted as a perceptual effect, it should be added that this is not to rule out a memory-based account entirely. Current research is still debating the memory versus perceptual account of RB and it is entirely possible that both memory and perceptual factors contribute to the RB effects observed. Perceptual factors certainly seem to contribute to RB effects. But, is the token-individuation account the only perceptual explanation?

The token individuation hypothesis makes the distinction between types (identity: what?) and tokens (temporal or spatial events: when or where?), where RB is a failure in creating two tokens even though both occurrences have been successfully typed[1]. A simpler perceptual explanation is the *type refractoriness* hypothesis (Luo & Caramazza, 1995). In this account, after a perceptual category has been activated a first time, there is difficulty in reactivating this category a second time. This corresponds to a temporary reduction in neurons after firing (Luo & Caramazza, 1996).

Again, as with the memory versus perception debate, numerous investigations have tried to tease apart these perceptual accounts. What emerges from this research are a variety of RB tasks that make the type refractory account unlikely. Kanwisher (1987) tried to rule out the type refractory account by simply requiring participants to report the last word of a rapid word sequence. Half the time the last word was a repeated item and half the time it was a non-repeated item. According to the type refractory account, RB arises through a difficulty in activating two types, whereas the token individuation account attributes the effect to a problem with distinguishing the events. The first account anticipates that the repeat condition would produce a decrement in performance, while the latter account does not (only one token needs to be created). On this task, participants actually demonstrated facilitation in recalling the repeated item, thus favouring the token individuation account. Further support for this view arises from studies demonstrating spatial RB (Kanwisher, 1991; Kanwisher, Driver, & Machado, 1995; Mozer, 1989). In Kanwisher, Driver, and Machado's (1995) RB task, the repeated items were actually presented simultaneously. After a fixation point, two letters would be presented to the left and right of fixation and then followed by visual masks. According to the type refractory account there should be no difficulty in recalling both items, while the token individuation account would anticipate a problem in creating two distinct tokens. Again, the token individuation account was favoured, as large RB effects were found in this spatial task.

One further study that dismisses the type refractory account investigated the issue of whether it is the first or second item that is 'blinded'. Neill et al. (2002) used a two-letter procedure, where one letter appeared to the left or right of fixation and was followed by a second letter to the opposite location. Experiments 1a, 1b, 2, 4 and 5 used a spatial cue and Experiments 3, 4, and 5 used a temporal cue. In the spatial cue task an arrow indicated which target was to be reported, and the phrases 'first letter?' or 'second letter?' indicated which target was to be reported in the temporal cue task. In all experiments, two repeated letters resulted in RB for both the first and second presented letters. Moreover, RB was greater for the second letter if participants expected temporal cues, while RB was greater for the first letter if participants expected spatial cues. RB occurring for the first item is incompatible with the type refractory account, as it is activation of the first category type that inhibits activation of the second item type. However, this research, as well as posing a problem for the type refractory account, also poses a problem for the token individuation account. Neill et al. (2002) point out that according to Kanwisher's (1987) theory of token individuation, RB is assumed to operate in a forward direction only, with only the second occurrence of the same target impaired. Impaired tokenisation of the first item could only occur if by chance the identification of the second target was completed sooner than the first. This means that the magnitude of RB on the second target should never be equal to or greater than RB on the first. So how do we reconcile these accounts with the data?

Neill et al. (2002) suggest that the token individuation hypothesis can be modified to accommodate these findings. They suggest that 'tokenisation' involves two separate processes: *instantiation* and *contextualisation*. Instantiation is the process whereby there is recognition that an instance of a conceptual category has occurred, and is determined by the first occurrence. For example, if 'when' is of primary import the first item is most relevant (temporal focus). Contextualisation is the process whereby an instance is assigned or attributed to a specific context, such as list position, and may be influenced by the second occurrence. For example, if 'where' is of primary import the second item is most relevant (spatial focus). This could occur for two reasons: (a) contextualisation is slow and sensitive to new information, or (b) contextualisation is fast, but can be undone by new information. Which of these two possibilities account for the pattern of RB for first versus second occurrences will surely be vigorously examined in future.

In summary, memory accounts, while they may contribute to RB effects, fail to resolve all the issues of RB. Furthermore, the type refractory hypothesis as a perceptual account seems to be an unlikely candidate. At present, the token-individuation account of RB is the 'best-fit' in terms of explaining the pattern of RB effects observed across a variety of paradigms. In future, it will be interesting to see whether 'contextualisation' is established as an inherent part of the tokenisation process.

Visual, Phonological, and Semantic RB

So far the discussion of RB has been limited to word or letter stimuli. However, there are dissociations between the repetition effects found for word and picture stimuli. Both words and pictures produce RB for exact repetitions. However, in assessing the type of information overlap necessary and/or sufficient to produce RB (e.g., visual, orthographic, phonological, or semantic), differences arise that have been attributed to different levels of processing for these two types of stimuli (Bavelier, 1994). Before discussing why these differences occur, the RB findings are reviewed for words and pictures.

Kanwisher (1987) demonstrated that RB was evident over changes in letter case, indicating that RB can occur at an abstract level rather than one that just encodes the visual form. This raises the question 'does the effect occur at a lexical (the word unit) or sub-lexical (e.g., letter clusters) level?' Kanwisher and Potter (1990) argued that the units involved in RB were not strictly lexical as a compound word and a noun component (e.g., 'My neighbour's *dogs* like *hotdogs* in the park') produced RB, even though the compound and noun were different words. This view has been strengthened by evidence from the illusory word paradigm (Harris & Morris, 2001; Morris & Harris, 1999), where in the sequence *lake brake ush* the report of *brush* indicated that the recognition of *ake* in *brake* is disrupted by its occurrence in *lake*, leaving the *br* available to be combined with *ush*. Furthermore, Harris and Morris (2000) demonstrated that the amount of RB increased as a function of the proportion of repeated letters.

Kanwisher and Potter (1990) suggested that RB could occur at either an orthographic level or a case-independent letter level, but this is dependent on which unit (words or single letters) is the processing focus. They found that both homographs (e.g., (she) rose and (the) rose) and homophones (e.g., (the) wound and (he) wound) produced equivalent amounts of RB, but RB for homophones was attenuated, though not eliminated, if they were not orthographically similar (e.g., 'The *pair* bought a *pear* and an apple in the market'). Therefore, while different pronunciations of orthographically similar words demonstrated equivalent RB, orthographically dissimilar words, albeit with the same pronunciation reduced RB. Moreover, letter level RB was successfully obtained when participants reported the letters of a word, where each letter of the word was presented sequentially (e.g., 'manager'). However, a single letter overlap between two words separated by another word did not produce RB for the repeated letter. Hence, the level at which RB occurs is determined in part by the visual unit that is task relevant.

While there is evidence that RB can occur at the letter or word level, are there other relationships between two items that might produce RB? Is there any evidence for phonological and semantic forms of RB? Bavelier and Potter (1992) focused on cases in which visually distinct stimuli shared the same phonology. Varying visual similarity by letter case (A/a) or symbol type (eight/8) did not eliminate RB effects, indicating that visual similarity was not a necessary condition for the RB effect. While both these cases could imply that shared phonology was the basis of the effect, the role of shared meaning was also possible. To distinguish these possibilities the authors used homophonic pairs (won/one) that shared phonology, but not meaning. These homophone pairs showed RB effects when presented in simple 3-item displays (low-memory demand), in sentences (where context was provided), and persisted even with irrelevant articulation, thus ruling out the possibility that the observed effect was due to phonological confusion in short term memory. Instead, they proposed the *early phonological hypothesis*, where the locus of the RB effect occurs at an early stage of phonological coding. Hence, in this case, RB reflects an inability to select for a second time a phonological representation that has recently been used for registration of information into short-term memory. Moreover, the authors proposed that RB is not dependent on the complete type identity for the item pairs, but on the attributes of the type that are selected for initial registration in short term memory. Again, the view is held that task relevancy is a key factor in predicting which attributes will produce RB effects.

Compelling evidence supporting this explanation comes from a study that combined words and pictures into 'rebus' sentences (Bavelier, 1994). In a rebus sentence a picture can take the place of the written word; for example, 'The duck quacked when the 🦆 was hungry'. Here the two occurrences of the homophone 'duck' are represented by a lexical and a pictorial form. This form of repetition allowed Bavelier to examine whether RB could occur with stimuli types other than words. Explicitly, Bavelier hypothesised that RB between visually different items should not be restricted to words, but should occur with any stimuli, as long as the task required the stimuli to be encoded along dimensions on which they were similar (i.e., in this case phonology). When the participants' task was to name the items presented (note they were encouraged to read the picture as part of the sentence) significant RB was found. However, when the participants' task was to both name the items and report whether they were in word or picture format the RB effect was diminished in size. In the former case the task biased participants towards phonological encoding, while the latter biased them towards visual encoding. With the visual encoding bias, visual dissimilarity is more likely to counteract the role of the similarity of the other codes. Therefore, RB between visually different items appears to arise because participants are biased toward the use of a similar code for registration in short-term memory.

Moreover, when Bavelier (1994) introduced a concurrent articulation task, homophonic RB was eliminated between pictures and words when similar phonology was all they shared. However, when the pictures and words also shared semantic and lexical representations, RB was evident, indicating that semantic and lexical information could also have a role in RB effects for pictures and words. From these studies Bavelier concluded:

> ... that there were three main properties for tokens: (1) the instantiation of the episodic token of an event is a dynamical process during which one or more codes that specify the object or event are registered in the token. The stability of the token is a function of the number and saliency of the codes registered into it. (2) A given code cannot efficiently be registered into more than one token in a short amount of time. (3) The codes that will be registered in STM are determined both by the perceptual properties of the stimulus and by the nature of the preferred encoding in STM. (Bavelier, 1994, pp. 224–225).

The nature of the similarity required for pictures to exhibit RB effects was further explored by Kanwisher et al. (1999). They argued that as RB is sensitive to the identity of two visual stimuli, it can be used to ask what kind of stimuli are treated as the same by the visual system. To address this question, the authors conducted a series of experiments that looked at effects of phonology, size, orientation, viewpoint, visual similarity, and semantics on RB effects for pictures. Neither varying the size and orientation of two repeated pictures nor varying the viewpoint by rotating the objects in depth (even when the views were selected to be as visually distinct a possible) eliminated RB. If pictures are invariant to these types of visual change, could it be that phonology, as witnessed with Bavelier's (1994) RB effects between words and pictures, could account for the observed RB? Kanwisher et al. (1999) tested phonological RB with pictures by selecting two pictures of different objects that shared the same name but were otherwise unrelated, such as a picture of a baseball bat and a picture of the animal bat. An interesting contrast was observed for RB between words and pictures: Kanwisher et al. (1999) failed to find any evidence for phonological RB with pictures, despite the occurrence with words previously described.

A further dissociation for RB effects between words and pictures was observed by Kanwisher et al. (1999). While phonological similarity was not sufficient to produce RB for pictures, semantic or conceptual similarity between items revealed significant RB for pictures. For instance, a picture of a 'helicopter' and a picture of an 'airplane' would produce RB. However, the same items used as words did not produce RB. This dissociation between words and pictures has been corroborated by a number of sources. Buttle, Ball, Zhang, and Raymond (2005) tested the semantic relationship between brand words and products where the association between the items was more exclusive. For example, 'Pepsi' and 'Coca-Cola' have an immediate connection with the category 'cola soft drink', whereas a similar shaped pair of items 'Pepsi' and 'Heinz beans' do not. These semantically related stimuli produced significant RB effects when presented as the brand object (the product with brand name visible) but failed to show RB when the brand words were presented alone. Similarly, other studies have failed to show semantic RB for words either with within-language or between-language synonym pairs (Altarriba & Soltano, 1996; Kanwisher & Potter, 1990). One exception to this is MacKay and Miller's (1994) finding that RSVP sentences containing two synonyms in different languages ('horses' and the Spanish equivalent 'caballos') did successfully produce semantic RB in bilingual speakers. However, to date this study seems to be an anomalous finding.

It is important to point out that just as RB for words could occur simply with orthographic overlap, RB for pictures could also occur based just on visual similarity. Kanwisher et al. (1999) showed that two unrelated items that looked similar (a pear and a guitar) produced RB, just as Arnell and Jolicouer's (1997) use of novel non-object stimuli (with no established phonology or semantic meaning) successfully produced RB.

In summary, visual similarity is sufficient to produce RB for both words and pictures. However, visual similarity is not necessary for RB to occur. Words exhibit RB effects for phonological similarity, but not semantic similarity and pictures exhibit RB effects for semantic similarity but not phonological similarity. So, how can we explain these differences for words and pictures?

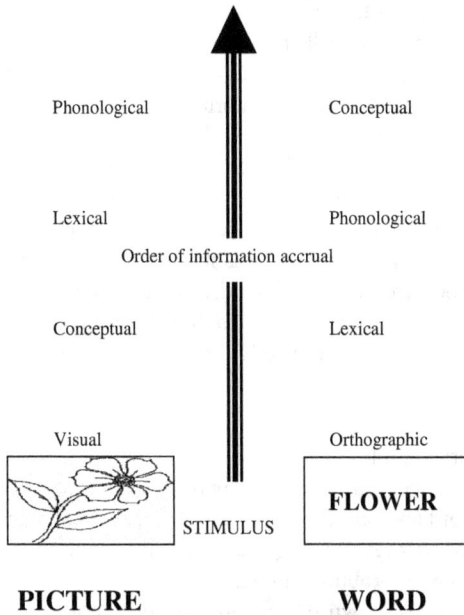

Figure 2
A sketch of the order of information accrual for words and pictures.

The order of information accrual for the two types of stimulus may provide an answer to why RB effects diverge (Bavelier, 1994). Figure 2 sketches the order of information accrual for words and pictures. There is considerable evidence that phonology is involved in the early stages of processing words, where phonological information about a written word is available almost immediately (Ferrand & Grainger, 1993; Lukatela & Turvey, 1991; Perfetti & Bell, 1991; Van Orden, 1987; Van Orden, Pennington, & Stone, 1990).[2] This explains why phonological similarity produces RB effects for words: there is successful activation of the same phonological codes (types) but separate tokens fail to be established. However, semantic information occurs at a much later stage of processing for words. Hence, the presentation time of the RSVP task does not permit semantic activation to occur and so there is no semantic RB. Contrary to words, pictures are believed to first activate their semantic or conceptual representations (Potter & Faulconer, 1975; Theios & Amrhein, 1989), with phonological codes activated at a later stage of processing. Therefore, with pictures we find the opposite effects: there is semantic RB but no phonological RB.

To recap on where this perceptual adventure has journeyed so far: The discussion of the original finding that two identical items presented close in succession produce a deficit in report accuracy, led to the exploration of the nature of RB by weighing the current evidence of a perceptual account against that of a memory based account. Moreover, it was suggested that Kanwisher's (1987) token individuation hypothesis still offers the most robust perceptual explanation of the data, with modifications to the theory providing the most parsimonious account (e.g., Neill et al., 2002). The information overlap that is sufficient to produce RB effects was then explored. Evidence for visual, phonological and semantic effects were discussed in relation to the order of information available in the early stages of processing for words and pictures. In summary, RB occurs where type information, accessed at an early stage of processing, is shared between two items. The type information is successfully accessed both times, but the tokens for each occurrence fail to be individuated. However, a further aim of this introduction to repetition blindness is to show how perceptual effects studied at the theoretical level in cognitive psychology can also inform applied matters.

Applied RB

The study of repetition blindness is an intriguing topic in its own right. However, its importance comes in the opportunity it presents in informing theories of visual word and object recognition. In the case of visual word recognition, Harris and Morris (2001) suggest that the illusory word paradigm could be used as a technique for probing sublexical representations. As previously discussed, this paradigm has shown that when the words 'china', 'cheat' and 'thr' are presented, the 'ch' from the second instance is unavailable to awareness, allowing the 'eat' and 'thr' to be recalled as 'threat'. With this paradigm, Harris and Morris (2001) have been able to establish that sequences of letters are marked for their position in words prior to word recognition, and that such words do not appear to be marked for phonology. For example, in the case of a participant reporting the word 'threat' the pronunciation of 'eat' is different to its pronunciation in the original word 'cheat'. The author suggests that the paradigm could be used to investigate theories of the units mediating visual word recognition.

Similarly, Kanwisher et al. (1999) view RB as an important method for developing theories of visual object recognition. They point out that RB can characterise the abstractness of the representations that are extracted within a few hundred milliseconds of picture presentation, providing evidence about the nature of short-term visual memory. In particular, they argue that any complete theory of object recognition must specify the nature of the perceptual representations that can be generated outside of awareness. In most demonstrations of perception without awareness one task is used to demonstrate that perception occurred and another task is used to demonstrate that awareness did not occur. Here RB has an advantage because it can demonstrate that an item was perceived but was not available for conscious report. For example, Arnell, Shapiro, and Sorensen (1999) demonstrated that there was reduced RB for the presentation of one's own name, a salient stimulus, compared to other nouns. This indicates that selective attention can modulate what items are available for conscious report in the RB paradigm.

A more applied approach to the RB paradigm has been taken by Buttle et al. (2005) who addressed the issue of semantic RB for words and pictures by using consumer products that were familiar through both brand name and product design. While this research further established that semantic association could produce RB effects for pictures but not words, it also offered a potential technique for assessing brand association. When the colas 'Pepsi' and 'Coca-Cola' were presented in an RSVP stream, an effect of semantic RB, comparable in size to trials were the critical items were identical (e.g., 'Pepsi' repeated), was observed. This occurred even though products that were of a similar shape but different category did not show RB effects. Moreover, Buttle (2002) suggested that the semantic RB effect for products observed in her change detection task was mediated by the familiarity of the items. For example, there was greater semantic RB for the famous shampoos 'Pantene' and 'Organics' than when an unfamiliar brand was introduced ('Pantene' and a generic store brand). These studies offer the potential for semantic RB to be used as a measure of brand association and familiarity, where a new market entrant could measure how successfully their product had been associated with its category over time (e.g., measures could be taken before and after advertising campaigns and so on).

On a similar theme, research has examined semantic RB as a measure for assessing whether companies have successfully associated their brand name and brand logo in consumers' mind sets (Buttle & Westoby, in press). For instance, some companies use a logo that has a direct phonological link with the brand name (e.g., the logo for the oil company 'Shell' is a picture of a clam shell), while others use a logo that has no obvious meaning until the association between name and logo is learnt (e.g., the logo for 'Nike' is its swoosh-type tick mark). The data indicate that regardless of how abstract a brand's logo is it will produce semantic RB. Further testing of semantic RB may lead to a technique for testing a number of brand issues that relate to visual cognition. Moreover, it is my suggestion that researchers in other fields may find other opportunities for exploiting this phenomenon for applied purposes.

To conclude, RB is just one of a number of visual perceptual phenomena that have and are still being investigated with controversial discussions still ongoing. However, while a definitive explanation is yet to be agreed upon, such phenomena, despite their complexity, are already being utilised to address both issues of basic visual cognition and more applied issues. All research should be more than just an intellectual exercise, it should have a view to contributing to or even improving everyday life. Perceptual phenomena are important for this very reason: they inform on how our visual system operates, while also allowing development and improvement of ways to impart visual information with greater efficiency.

Endnotes

1   This is a narrower use of type/token distinctions than observed in other fields, such as psycholinguistics (e.g., Lacher & Riegel, 1970).

2   It is beyond the discussion of this chapter, but worth noting that there remains controversy over how many processing routes are involved in naming, especially naming of words versus non-words (Coltheart, Rastle, Perry, Langdon, & Zeigler, 2001; Reynolds & Besner, 2002) and similarly between whether non-words can or can not produce RB (Campbell, Fugelsang, & Hernberg, 2002; Coltheart & Langdon, 2003; Harris & Morris, 2004).

References

Altarriba, J., & Soltano, E. G. (1996). Repetition blindness and bilingual memory: Token individuation for translation equivalents. *Memory & Cognition, 24,* 700–711.

Anderson, C. J., & Neill, W. T. (2002). Two Bs or not two Bs? A signal detection theory analysis of repetition blindness in a counting task. *Perception & Psychophysics, 64,* 732–740.

Armstrong, I. T., & Mewhort, D. J. K. (1995). Repetition deficit in RSVP displays: Encoding failure or retrieval failure? *Journal of Experimental Psychology: Human Perception and Performance, 21,* 1044–1052.

Arnell, K. M., & Jolicoeur, P. (1997). Repetition blindness for pseudo-object pictures. *Journal of Experimental Psychology: Human Perception and Performance, 23,* 999–1013.

Arnell, K. M., Shapiro, K. L., & Sorensen, R. E. (1999). Reduced repetition blindness for one's own name. *Visual Cognition, 6,* 609–635.

Bavelier, D. (1994). Repetition blindness between visually different items: The case of pictures and words. *Cognition, 51,* 199–236.

Bavelier, D., & Potter, M. C. (1992). Visual and phonological codes in repetition blindness. *Journal of Experimental Psychology: Human Perception and Performance, 18,* 134–147.

Buttle. H. (2002). *Visual fame effects: The processing benefits of highly learnt images.* Unpublished doctoral dissertation, University of Wales, Bangor.

Buttle, H., Ball, C. K., Zhang, J., & Raymond, J. E. (2005). Semantic association of brand images at the implicit level: Evidence of repetition blindness. *Applied Cognitive Psychology, 19,* 1199–1210.

Buttle, H., & Westoby, N. (in press). Brand logo and name association: It's all in the name. *Applied Cognitive Psychology.* Retrieved July 14, 2006, from www3.interscience.wiley.com/cgi-bin/fulltext/112664986/PDFSTART

Campbell, J. I. D., Fuselgang, J. A., & Hernberg, V. D. (2002). Effects of target distinctiveness and lexicality on repetition blindness. *Journal of Experimental Psychology: Human Perception and Performance, 28,* 948–962.

Chun, M. M., & Cavanagh, P. (1997). Seeing two as one-linking apparent motion and repetition blindness. *Psychological Science, 8,* 74–78.

Coltheart, V., & Langdon, R. (2003). Repetition blindness for words yet repetition advantage for nonwords. *Journal of Experimental Psychology: Learning, Memory, and Cognition, 29,* 171–185.

Coltheart, M., Rastle, K., Perry, C., Langdon, R., & Ziegler, J. (2001). DRC: A dual route cascaded model of visual word recognition and reading aloud. *Psychological Review, 108,* 204–256.

Fagot, C., & Pashler, H. (1995). Repetition blindness: Perception or memory failure? *Journal of Experimental Psychology: Human Perception and Performance, 21,* 275–292.

Ferrand, L., & Grainger, J. (1993). The time course of orthographic and phonological code activation in the early phases of visual word recognition. *Bulletin of the Psychonomic Society, 31,* 119–122.

Harris, C. L., & Morris, A. L. (2000). Orthographic Repetition blindness. *Quarterly Journal of Experimental Psychology: Human Experimental psychology, 53A,* 1039–1060.

Harris, C. L., & Morris, A. L. (2001). Illusory words created by repetition blindness. *Psychonomic Bulletin & Review, 8,* 118–126.

Harris, C. L., & Morris, A. L. (2004). Repetition blindness occurs in nonwords. *Journal of Experimental Psychology: Human Perception and Performance, 30*, 305–318.

Hintzman, D. L., & Block, R. A. (1971). Repetition and memory: Evidence for a multiple-trace hypothesis. *Journal of Experimental Psychology, 88*, 297–306.

Hochhaus, L., & Johnston, J. C. (1996). Perceptual repetition blindness effects. *Journal of Experimental Psychology: Human Perception and Performance, 22*, 355–366.

Johnston, J. C., Hochhaus, L., & Ruthruff, E. (2002). Repetition blindness has a perceptual locus: Evidence from online processing of targets in RSVP streams. *Journal of Experimental Psychology: Human Perception and Performance, 28*, 477–389.

Kanwisher, N. (1987). Repetition blindness: Type recognition without token individuation. *Cognition, 27*, 117–143.

Kanwisher, N. (1991). Repetition blindness and illusory conjunctions: Errors in binding visual types with visual tokens. *Journal of Experimental Psychology: Human Perception and Performance, 17*, 404–421.

Kanwisher, N., Driver, J., & Machado, L. (1995). Spatial repetition blindness is modulated by selective attention to colour and shape. *Cognitive Psychology, 29*, 303–337.

Kanwisher, N., Kim, J., & Wickens, T. (1996). Signal detection analyses of repetition blindness. *Journal of Experimental Psychology: Human Perception and Performance, 22*, 1249–1260.

Kanwisher, N., & Potter, M. C. (1990). Repetition blindness: Levels of processing. *Journal of Experimental Psychology: Human Perception and Performance, 16*, 30–47.

Kanwisher, N., Yin, C., & Wojciulik, E. (1999). Repetition blindness for pictures: Evidence for the rapid computation of abstract visual descriptions. In V. Coltheart (Ed.), *Fleeting memories: Cognition of brief visual stimuli* (pp. 119–150). London: The MIT Press.

Lacher, M. R., & Riegel, K. F. (1970). Word recognition thresholds as a function of instructions, type of word relations, and associative frequency. *Journal of General Psychology, 83*, 23–33.

Lewandowsky, S., Neely, J. H., VerWys, C. A., & Amos, A. (1997, November). *Repetition blindness under serial versus paired encoding*. Poster presented at the 38th annual meeting of the Psychonomic Society, Philadelphia.

Lukatela, G., & Turvey, M. T. (1991). Phonological access of the lexicon: Evidence from associative priming with pseudohomophones. *Journal of Experimental Psychology: Human Perception and Performance, 17*, 951–966.

Luo, C. R., & Caramazza, A. (1995). Repetition blindness under minimum memory load: Effects of spatial and temporal proximity and the encoding effectiveness of the first item. *Perception and Psychophysics, 57*, 1053–1064.

Luo, C. R., & Caramazza, A. (1996). Temporal and spatial repetition blindness: Effects of presentation mode and repetition lag on the perception of repeated items. Journal of Experimental Psychology: Human Perception and Performance, 22, 95–113.

Mack, A., & Rock, I. (1998). *Inattentional blindness*. London: The MIT Press.

Mackay, D. G., & Miller, M. D. (1994). Semantic blindness: Repeated concepts are difficult to encode and recall under time pressure. *Psychological Science, 5*, 52–55.

Morris, A. L., & Harris, C. L. (1999). A sublexical locus for repetition blindness: Evidence from illusory words. *Journal of Experimental Psychology: Human Perception and Performance, 25*, 1060–1075.

Mozer, M. C. (1989). Types and tokens in visual letter perception. *Journal of Experimental Psychology: Human Perception and Performance, 15*, 287–303.

Neill, W. T., Neely, J. H., Hutchison, K. A., Kahan, T. A., & VerWys, C. A. (2002). Repetition blindness, forward and backward. *Journal of Experimental Psychology: Human Perception and Performance, 28*, 137–149.

Park, J., & Kanwisher, N. (1994). Determinants of repetition blindness. *Journal of Experimental Psychology: Human Perception and Performance, 20*, 500–519.

Perfetti, C. A., & Bell, L. (1991). Phonemic activation during the first 40 ms of word identification: Evidence from backward masking and priming. *Journal of Memory & Language, 30,* 473–485.

Potter, M. C., & Faulconer, B. A. (1975). Time to understand pictures and words. *Nature, 253,* 437–438.

Ranschburg, P. (1902). Über Hemmung gleichzeitiger Reizwirkungen. *Zeitschrift für Psychologie, 30,* 39–86.

Raymond, J. E., Shapiro, K. L., & Arnell, K. M. (1992). Temporary suppression of visual processing in an RSVP task: An attentional blink? *Journal of Experimental Psychology: Human Perception and Performance, 18,* 849–860.

Rensink, R. A., O'Regan, J. K., & Clark J. J. (1997). To see or not to see: The need for attention to perceive changes in scenes. *Psychological Science, 8, 368–373.*

Reynolds, M., & Besner, D. (2002). Neighbourhood density effects in reading aloud: New insights from simulations with the DRC model. *Canadian Journal of Experimental Psychology, 56,* 310–318.

Scarborough, D. L., Cortese, C., & Scarborough, H. S. (1977). Frequency and repetition effects in lexical memory. *Journal of Experimental Psychology: General, 114,* 50–77.

Schendan, H. E., Kanwisher, N., & Kutas, M. (1997). Early brain potentials link repetition blindness, priming, and novelty detection. *Neuroreport, 8,* 1943–1948.

Soto-Faraco, S., & Spence, C. (2001). Spatial modulation of repetition blindness and repetition deafness. *The Quarterly Journal of Experimental Psychology, 54A,* 1181–1202.

Theios, J., & Amrhein, P. C. (1989). Theoretical analysis of the cognitive processing of lexical and pictorial stimuli: reading, naming, and visual and conceptual comparisons. *Psychological Review, 96,* 5–24.

Van Orden, G. C. (1987). A rows is a rose: Spelling sound and reading. *Memory & Cognition, 15,* 181–198.

Van Orden, G. C., Pennington, B., & Stone, G. (1990). Word identification in reading and the promise of subsymbolic psycholinguistics. *Psychological Review, 97,* 488–522.

Whittlesea, B. W. A., Dorken, M. D., & Podrouzek, K. W. (1995). Repeated events in rapid lists: Part 1. Encoding and representation. *Journal of Experimental Psychology: Learning, Memory, and Cognition, 21,* 1670–1688.

Effects of Derived Peripheral Cues on Visual Attention

Anthony Lambert

In his celebrated text of 1890 William James distinguished between several 'varieties' of attention. According to James, attention could be 'passive, reflex, non-voluntary, effortless' or 'active and voluntary' (James, 1890/1983, p. 394). This distinction between reflexive and voluntary attention is endorsed by a substantial body of modern research on attention (see Wright & Ward, 1998, for review). However, William James also drew a further distinction between 'immediate' and 'derived' attention. This distinction has received much less consideration in modern work on attention. According to James (1890/1983), attention can be 'immediate, when the topic or stimulus is interesting in itself, without relation to anything else; derived when it owes its interest to association with some other immediately interesting thing' (p. 393). In a series of recent papers we have reexamined the Jamesian notion of derived attention (Lambert & Duddy, 2002; Lambert, Naikar, McLachlan, & Aitken, 1999; Lambert, Norris, Naikar, & Aitken, 2000; Lambert & Roser, 2002) using a variant of the spatial cueing technique commonly employed in studies of spatial attention (see Wright & Ward, 1998, for review). In the experiments reported by Lambert and Duddy (2002) participants made a simple detection response to a target object (a small white square) that could appear on the left or right of a visual display. Targets were accompanied or preceded by bilateral letter cues (X or T), which predicted its likely location. For example, in Experiments 1, 3A, 4 and 5 (Lambert & Duddy, 2002) participants were informed that the target would probably appear on the same side as one of letter cues (e.g., 'X') and on the opposite side to the other letter cue (e.g., 'T'). The spatial arrangement of the letter cues (i.e., $X_{left} + T_{right}$ or $T_{left} + X_{right}$) varied randomly from trial to trial. Response latencies were compared between valid trials, where the target appeared at the location predicted by the cue letters, and invalid trials where it did not. This technique can be viewed as assessing Jamesian derived attention, since there is a predictive association between cue letters and the object of interest — the target. In order to assess the speed with which participants were able to make use of the predictive information carried by the cues, the delay between onset of the letters and onset of the target was varied from 0 ms (i.e., cue letters and target appeared simultaneously) to 500 ms. A surprising feature of our results was the speed with which participants were able to make effective use of the predictive information carried by the cue. For example, in Experiments 3A, 4 and 5 (Lambert & Duddy, 2002) response latencies were faster on valid than invalid trials, even when there was no delay between onset of peripheral cue letters and onset of the target. This suggests very rapid interaction between the attentional system and perceptual processing of the cue letters. Since cue and target appeared simultaneously, this must have involved interaction between parallel processing of cue and target information, in the period between target onset and response execution, which was approximately 400 ms.

The nature of this rapid interaction between spatial attention and processing of peripheral cue information is of considerable interest theoretically. It suggests that shifting attention in response to peripheral stimuli is far more sophisticated than is implied by current notions of 'reflexive orienting' in response to peripheral onsets or luminance changes (e.g., see Folk & Gibson, 2001). Our findings show that participants can orient very rapidly indeed, not merely in response to peripheral onsets per se, but in response to the *nature* of the peripheral object. However, the results reported in our earlier studies leave an important question unanswered, concerning characteristics of the rapid attention shift elicited by derived peripheral cues. In all of the experiments reported by Lambert et al. (1999), Lambert and Duddy (2002) and Lambert and Roser (2002) we measured simple response time (RT): participants pressed a key as quickly as possible in response to the onset of a luminance target (a small white square). A limitation of this design is that while it furnished valuable information concerning response latency, it provided no information concerning response accuracy. This is because in the simple RT paradigm participants press a single key in response to target onset — there are no 'correct' or 'incorrect' responses. The absence of response accuracy information makes it possible to interpret the results in at least two ways. First, the improvement in RT observed on valid trials could reflect a real improvement in perceptual efficiency. That is, information was encoded more rapidly from the target location, without compromising perceptual accuracy. Alternatively, the effect could reflect a shift in response criterion, with no improvement in perceptual efficiency. That is, participants may simply be more willing to release a response on the basis of perceptual evidence accumulating at the valid location.

The aim of the experiment reported here was to test between these alternative hypotheses. The design was similar to the peripheral cue conditions described in Lambert and Duddy (2002). In this case, however, participants judged whether an oblong shape presented on the left or right of a display screen was tall or short. As before, participants were presented with bilateral letter cues (V, O), and were informed that the target shapes would usually appear on the same side as one of the letters. Three different stimulus onset asynchronies (SOAs) between cue and target onset were used: 0 ms, 100 ms and 600 ms. Participants were instructed to perform the discrimination task as rapidly as possible, without making too many errors. Two dependent measures were assessed: response time and perceptual sensitivity (d'). If the effects of peripheral letter cues reported in our earlier studies do indeed reflect a real improvement in perceptual sensitivity then performance should be better on valid than on valid trials, with respect to both RT and d'.

Method

Participant
Fifty-one adult University of Auckland students participated in the experiment.

Apparatus
The experiment was run in a computer laboratory equipped with 24 IBM-compatible Pentium III PCs. The software for display presentation and timing was written in Turbo Pascal v.7.0. The experiment was performed under normal levels of room illumination. Viewing distance was approximately 60 cms.

Display and Stimuli
All stimuli were presented in white against a black background. The fixation display comprised a central cross subtending approximately $0.4° \times 0.4°$. The target stimuli were white filled oblong shapes subtending $0.9°$ in width. Target height was either $2.1°$ (tall targets) or $1.7°$ (short targets). In the horizontal dimension, the inner edge of each target was approximately $6.5°$ from the central cross. In the vertical dimension, target stimuli were presented centrally. The letters 'V' and 'O' served as cue stimuli. Each cue letter subtended $0.9° \times 0.9°$. The inner edge of each letter was presented $6.5°$ from the horizontal centre of the screen. The lower edge of each cue letter was presented $1.2°$ from the vertical centre of the screen.

Procedure
Participants were informed that their task was to discriminate between tall and short oblong shapes that would be presented on the left or right of visual display. They were instructed to press the '/' key on the keyboard in response to a long oblong and the 'z' key in response to a short oblong. They were instructed to make this response as rapidly and as accurately as possible. Participants in the 'V' group were instructed that the target shapes would usually ($p = .8$, i.e., on 4 out of 5 occasions) appear on the same side as the V and opposite to the O. This was reversed for participants in the 'O' group, for whom the target usually appeared on the same side as the O. Participants were instructed to fixate the central cross throughout the experiment, and the importance of maintaining central fixation was emphasised. The central cross disappeared for 100 ms one second before the cues were presented; that is, the central cross blinked at the beginning of every trial. This was to draw participants' attention to the fixation cross, and to

remind them to fixate centrally on every trial. The two cue letters were then presented for 100 ms. Participants were instructed to use the letter cues in order to prepare for a target shape on the side indicated by the cue. Subjects were instructed to pay attention covertly when doing this: that is, to pay attention to one side of the screen without moving their eyes from the central fixation cross. An oblong target was then presented 6.5° to the left or right of fixation for 100ms. The delay between cue onset and target onset (stimulus onset asynchrony; SOA) was varied. There were three SOAs: 0 ms, 100 ms and 600 ms. After an interval that varied randomly from 500 ms to 1000 ms the central cross blinked to signal the beginning of the next trial.

Participants were requested to avoid making anticipatory responses, and were informed that pressing a response key before the target appeared would result in the message 'Warning! Anticipation Error' being presented for 1 s at the bottom of the screen.

At the beginning of the testing session, participants were presented with 16 practice trials to familiarise them with the task. Subjects then performed 5 blocks of 60 trials.

Design

There were 29 participants in Group O and 22 participants in Group V. Each experimental session comprised 300 trials. There were 240 valid trials and 60 invalid trials. There were 100 trials at each of the three SOAs. There were equal numbers of trials with a tall and short oblong target, and with a target in the left and right visual field. Trial type varied pseudorandomly with respect to target size, target location, SOA and cue validity.

Results

Response Time

Response time results from the experiment are shown in Figure 1. Mean response times were calculated for each condition and were then entered into a four factor mixed analysis of variance. There was one between-groups factor, letter group (Group O vs. Group V), and there were three repeated measures factors, size (tall vs. short targets), SOA (0 ms, 100 ms, 600 ms) and validity (valid vs. invalid). The main effect of size was significant, $F(1, 49) = 4.08$, $p < .05$: participants responded more quickly to tall than to short oblongs (701 ms vs. 716 ms). The main effect of SOA was also significant, $F(2, 98) = 17.42$, $p < .001$: response latencies decreased with increasing SOA (SOA 0 ms mean RT = 734 ms; SOA 100 ms mean RT = 705 ms; SOA 600 ms mean RT = 685 ms). This is most plausibly interpreted as a warning signal effect. Onset of the cue letters acts as a general warning signal that the target is about to be presented, in addition to providing spatial information concerning probable target location (Lambert & Duddy, 2002; Niemi & Naataanen, 1981). Most importantly, for our purposes, the main effect of validity was significant, $F(1, 49) = 11.16$, $p < .005$: overall, response latencies were quicker on valid than on invalid trials (682 ms vs. 734 ms). However, validity also entered

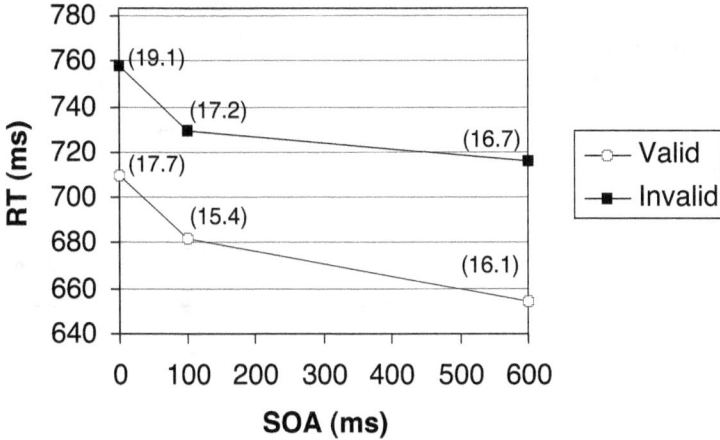

Figure 1

Mean response time results.

Note: The numbers in parentheses represent the error rate (%) in each condition.

into, two higher order interactions. The interactions between validity, SOA and size, $F(2, 98) = 4.44$, $p < .025$, and between validity, SOA, size and letter group, $F(2, 98) = 8.24$, $p < .001$, were both significant. Means for the latter interaction are shown in Appendix A. As this appendix shows, the interaction arises from a complex pattern of variation in the size of validity effects as a function of SOA, target size, and letter group. For participants in Group O, validity effects tended to increase with SOA for large targets, but decrease with SOA for small targets. For participants in Group V, validity effects showed much less variation as a function of SOA. The factors responsible for this very complex interaction are not entirely clear. However, in relation to the hypothesis addressed by the experiment, the important point to note is that in all conditions response latencies were quicker on valid than on invalid trials.

Perceptual Sensitivity

A measure of perceptual sensitivity (d') derived from signal detection theory was calculated for valid and invalid conditions, at each of the three SOAs. However, at each of the three SOAs there were some participants who made no errors in either the valid or invalid condition; this made calculation of d' problematic for these conditions. Although methods are available for estimating d' in such cases (see McMillan & Creelman, 1991), it was decided that these were not appropriate here. This is because when using the techniques described by MacMillan and Creelman (1991), d' estimates are related to the number of trials sampled, and the number of trials sampled was four times greater for valid than invalid trials. Hence, in this case use of estimated d' values would confound our

Table 1

Perceptual Sensitivity for Valid and Invalid Trials in Each SOA Condition

	Valid d' (SD)	Invalid d' (SD)	t (df)	p
SOA 0 ms (N = 26)	2.06 (.47)	1.77 (.54)	2.42 (25)	< .025
SOA 100 ms (N = 34)	2.00 (.48)	1.73 (.46)	2.44 (33)	< .025
SOA 600 ms (N = 29)	2.03 (.53)	1.66 (.55)	2.69 (28)	< .025

comparison of valid and invalid conditions. In light of this, comparisons of perceptual sensitivity within each SOA condition were based on data from participants who made at least one error in both the valid and invalid conditions. The number of participants (out of 51) who satisfied this criterion in the three SOA conditions (0 ms, 100 ms, 600 ms) were 26, 34 and 29 respectively. Mean d' values for these participants are displayed in Table 1. Three repeated measures t tests compared d' in the valid and invalid conditions, at each SOA. As Table 1 shows, d' was significantly higher on valid than on invalid trials at each of the three SOAs ($p < .025$ in all three cases).

Discussion

Results from this single experiment provide important clarification concerning the findings reported by Lambert and Duddy (2002). It appears that the shortening of response latency that occurs on valid trials following spatial correspondence cues does not simply reflect a response criterion shift, whereby participants are more willing to release a key-press in response to perceptual evidence from the valid location. Rather, it appears that spatial correspondence cues produce a real improvement in perceptual efficiency at the location indicated by spatial correspondence cues. Furthermore, this attentional shift appears to occur with extreme rapidity: perceptual sensitivity is better at valid than invalid locations even with zero delay between cue onset and target onset. Indeed, as Table 1 illustrates, the magnitude of the sensitivity effect is comparable across all three SOAs (0 ms, 100 ms, 600 ms).

The speed with which attention was shifted in response to the letter cues employed in this experiment is indeed surprising. Even with no delay between onset of the cues and onset of the target, participants responded more rapidly and with superior perceptual sensitivity to the oblong shapes presented at the valid location. Theoretically, this may be taken as implying the following scenario. At stimulus onset, participants begin to process both the target (oblong shape) and the cue letters simultaneously. Encoding of the latter leads to a shift of visual attention towards the location indicated by the cues. This occurs with sufficient rapidity that perceptual processing of the target is facilitated, even though cue processing and target processing began together. However, one presumes that target processing would normally be well underway before sufficient information had been extracted from the cue letters to determine whether attention should be oriented leftwards or rightwards. To achieve this, it would have been necessary to discriminate whether the two letters, each of which was presented 6.5° from fixation comprised either $V_{left} + O_{right}$ or $O_{left} + V_{right}$. Clearly, this scenario implies extremely rapid interaction between encoding of the parafoveal cue letters and mechanisms that control covert orienting of attention. On the other hand, it is worth noting that, on average, participants took 660 ms to 760 ms to produce a correct response. The relationship between this overall response latency and the time-course of subprocesses, such as encoding, decision and response execution remains unclear. Nevertheless, the results may be taken as implying that the time-course of encoding and decision processes was long enough to enable attentional facilitation of target processing at the valid location.

However, an alternative interpretation is also feasible. It is possible that the processes involved here do *not* occur as a cascaded sequence such as that just described, that is, cue letter encoding + early target encoding — followed by attention shift — followed by facilitation of late target encoding at the valid location. An alternative interpretation is that participants encode cues and targets together, as compound stimulus events. For participants in the 'O' group the pairing of O with a tall or short oblong shape (on the left or right of the display) is much more likely as a perceptual event than the pairing of V with an oblong shape. Obviously, the converse state of affairs would obtain for participants in the V group. It may be that within this context, participants develop an attentional set which enables them to respond more rapidly and efficiently to the distinction between tall and short oblongs when these are paired with a particular cue letter. One way in which this might occur is as follows. For participants in the V group, both tall and short oblongs are frequently presented with the letter 'V' situated directly above them, but only infrequently presented with the letter 'O'. After practice, a form of perceptual learning may occur in which participants tune in to complex configural features of the compound stimulus 'oblong + V', which makes performance on these (valid) trials faster and more accurate than 'oblong + O' (invalid) trials. The converse would of course need to occur for participants in the O group: that is, better performance on valid trials, due to perceptual learning of configural features that emerge from repeated pairing of the oblong shape with O.

Which interpretation is likely to be correct: rapid attention shifting or perceptual learning of complex configural features? The influence of SOA on validity, or rather the lack of an effect of SOA on validity provides quite strong grounds for preferring the former interpretation, surprising as that may seem to some readers. As Table 1 and Figure 1 illustrate, the validity effect undergoes no detectable change as SOA increases from 0 ms to 600 ms. If the validity effect is driven by perceptual learning of configural features that emerge from repeated pairing of the oblong shapes with either O or V then one might expect the effect to diminish or disappear in the SOA 600 ms condition, since on these trials the letter cue disappeared from the display fully half a second before onset of the oblong target stimulus.

Regardless of which interpretation is preferred, it is clear that the results demonstrate an exquisite sensitivity of the human perceptual–attentional system to statistical relationships between elements of the visual world, represented in this experiment by the association between peripheral cue letters and target oblong shapes.

Acknowledgments

I would like to acknowledge the support of Auckland University Research Committee for the work reported in this chapter. I am very grateful to Michael Hautus for valuable comments on an earlier draft of this chapter.

References

Folk, C. L., & Gibson, B. S. (Eds.). (2001). *Attraction, distraction and action: Multiple perspectives on attentional capture*. (In Advances in psychology series, Vol. 133.) Amsterdam, the Netherlands: Elsevier.

James, W. (1983). *Principles of psychology*. Cambridge, MA: Harvard University Press. (Original work published 1890)

Lambert, A., & Duddy, M. (2002). Visual orienting with central and peripheral precues: Deconfounding the contributions of cue eccentricity, cue discrimination and spatial correspondence. *Visual Cognition*, 9, 303–336.

Lambert, A., Naikar, N., McLachlan, K., & Aitken, V. (1999). A new component of visual orienting: Implicit effects of peripheral information and sub-threshold cues on covert attention. *Journal of Experimental Psychology: Human Perception and Performance*, 25, 321–340.

Lambert, A., Norris, A. Naikar, N., & Aitken, V. (2000). Effects of informative peripheral cues on eye movements: Revisiting William James' 'derived attention'. *Visual Cognition*, 7, 545–570.

Lambert, A., & Roser, M. (2002). Effects of bilateral colour cues on visual orienting: Revisiting William James' 'Derived attention'. *New Zealand Journal of Psychology*, 30, 16–22.

Macmillan, N., & Creelman, C. D. (1991). *Detection theory: A user's guide*. Cambridge: Cambridge University Press.

Niemi, P., & Naataanen, R. (1981). Foreperiod and simple reaction time. *Psychological Bulletin*, 89, 133–162.

Wright, R., & Ward, L. (1998). The control of visual attention. In R. D. Wright (Ed.), *Visual attention* (pp. 132–186). New York: Oxford University Press.

Appendix A

		SOA 0 ms		SOA 100 ms		SOA 600 ms	
		Tall	Short	Tall	Short	Tall	Short
Group O	Valid RT (ms)	691	809	733	709	701	656
	Invalid RT (ms)	804	812	805	758	740	766
	Invalid–Valid	113	3	72	48	38	110
Group V	Valid RT (ms)	647	693	638	647	630	629
	Invalid RT (ms)	663	753	680	674	674	684
	Invalid–Valid	16	60	41	27	44	56

Visual Attention and the Selection of Non-Target Objects

Zhe Chen and Murray Simmonds

Until recently, it had been assumed that when an object is attended, all of its features are processed regardless of whether they are task relevant or irrelevant (Duncan, 1984; Kahneman & Treisman, 1984). Perhaps the most famous example is the Stroop interference effect (Stroop, 1935). When observers are asked to identify the colour of a word which is itself a colour name (e.g., the word RED written in blue colour), they are almost invariably slower and/or make more mistakes when the colour of the word is incongruent with its meaning rather than when the two are congruent (see MacLeod, 1991, for a review). Furthermore, the magnitude of the effect is positively correlated with the amount of attention participants pay to the stimulus (Chen, 2003a; Kahneman & Henik, 1981).

Additional support for the close relationship between attention and encoding comes from recent research on object-based attentional selection. It has been shown that observers are faster and/or more accurate when they respond to features that belong to a single object rather than to two different objects (Baylis & Driver, 1993; Duncan, 1984). Faster reaction times have also been reported when participants are required to switch attention within one object rather than between two different objects (Chen, 1998; Egly, Driver, & Rafal, 1994; Moore, Yantis, & Vaughan, 1998). Moreover, interference from irrelevant objects is larger when the target and distractors share the same features than when they do not (Harms & Bundesen, 1983; Kramer & Jacobson, 1991). These findings support the view that task irrelevant features are processed along with the relevant feature when they pertain to the same object.

However, despite the above empirical findings, this view has been recently challenged by Remington and Folk (2001). They demonstrated that attention per se does not guarantee involuntary processing of all aspects of an object. They suggested that it is important to distinguish between an attended object which is a target and one which is a distractor. They noted that evidence supporting the attention-encoding assumption is based largely on the results of those experiments in which the attended object is itself a target object (Baylis & Driver, 1993; Duncan, 1984; Stroop, 1935). In other words, it is unclear whether the processing of an irrelevant object feature is primarily caused by the allocation of attention to the object or by the status of that object as being a target. To be consistent with Remington and Folk's usage, in the rest of this chapter we will use the words *attention* and *attend* to refer to the act of paying attention and the words *selection* and *select* to refer to the processing or encoding of a stimulus.

To determine whether attention and selection could be dissociated, Remington and Folk (2001) employed a spatial cuing paradigm in which the participants' attention was directed to a location that was subsequently occupied by either a target or a distractor. The task was to respond to one of two features of the target (e.g., colour or orientation) on the basis of a response cue at the beginning of each trial. The results show that whether the task irrelevant feature of the attended object was processed or not depended on the status of that object. When it was a target, the irrelevant feature was processed along with the relevant feature. However, when it was a distractor, only the relevant feature was encoded. These results led Remington and Folk to the conclusion that selection involves more than the allocation of attention, and that task demands play a key role in determining the level of processing of an attended non-target object.

Factors That Influence the Selection of an Attended Non-Target Object

Remington and Folk's (2001) research underscores the importance of identifying factors that influence selective attention. However, an important feature in their study is the cuing of the participants' attention to the location of an object rather than to a non-spatial object feature such as colour or shape. In light of the many differences regarding the role of location versus the role of colour or shape in selective attention (see Lamy & Tsal, 2001, for a review) and the many differences between object-based and location-based attentional selection (see Cave & Bichot, 1999, for a review), it is possible that the specific design characteristics in Remington and Folk's study have given rise to their reported results.

To investigate whether the processing of a non-target object differs as a function of attention to its spatial location as opposed to an object features, Chen (2005) conducted a series of experiments in which the participants were shown two stimuli in quick succession: a prime followed by a probe. The prime varied in two features (e.g., colour and orientation), and the task was to respond to a specific feature of the probe on the basis of a response cue that was presented at the beginning of each trial. Thus, on every trial there was a relevant feature and an irrelevant feature. Of particular interest was whether the participants' reaction times to the probe would be influenced by the compatibility of the relevant and irrelevant features of the prime. The results show that whether the participants processed the irrelevant feature of the prime depended on the specific feature that the participants paid attention to. When the task was to respond to an object feature such as colour, shape, or orientation, reaction times to the probe were faster when the relevant and irrelevant features of the prime indicated the same response key relative to when they indicated different response keys. This suggests that the irrelevant feature of the prime was processed. However, when one of the two response features of the stimulus was location, a processing asymmetry was observed. Whereas the participants processed the location of the prime when attention was cued to an object feature such as the shape of the prime, similar processing was not found when attention was cued to the location of the prime. These results suggest that in addition to the status of an attended object (Remington & Folk, 2001) the effect of attention on selection depends on the nature of the specific feature dimension that receives attention. Whereas attending to a target object entails the processing of all its feature dimensions, the effect of attention on the processing of a non-target is more complex than was previously understood.

The involuntary encoding of location when an object feature is attended has also been reported in previous experiments where the attended object is a target instead of a distractor (see Lamy & Tsal, 2001, for a review). Several experiments have shown that the selection of an object by colour or shape is accompanied by the selection of its location, even in conditions where location is task-irrelevant (Kim & Cave, 1995; Tsal & Lavie, 1993). For example, Kim and Cave (1995) asked their participants to detect a small black dot that could occasionally appear at a location previously occupied by a target or by a distractor that did not share any of the target's features. The participants' reaction times were faster in the former case than in the latter one. This suggests that location plays a special role in selective attention, and that location encoding is involuntary when attention has selected a specific dimension of an object.

In addition to the processing asymmetry reported above, whether or not an irrelevant feature of an attended non-target object is selected also appears to depend on an observer's overall reaction time for a given task (Chen, 2003b, 2005). One consistent finding across several experiments is that evidence for the selection of the irrelevant feature occurs only on those trials where the relevant features of the prime and probe are different, but not when they are the same. Because the participants' reaction times are substantially slower on the *different* trials than on the *same* trials, Chen proposed that the efficiency with which a target is processed, which is directly associated with the participants' overall reaction times in a given task, is a critical factor in the selection of the task irrelevant feature. To verify this hypothesis empirically, she conducted an experiment employing two groups of participants who were required to respond to the probe's shape or orientation on the basis of a response cue (Chen, 2005, Experiment 5). The only difference between the two groups was the spatial separation between the prime and probe. Consistent with prior research (Hughes & Zimba, 1985; Zimba & Hughes, 1987), the participants in the *near* group were significantly faster than their counterparts in the *far* group. More importantly, only the *far* group showed evidence of processing the irrelevant prime dimension. A similar compatibility effect was not found with the *near* group.

The finding that the degree of processing of an attended non-target object depends on the processing efficiency of the target is not only in agreement with the data regarding the differential reaction times between the *same* and *different* trials, but is also consistent with a commonly held assumption about perception. It is believed that perception is a limited resource process which proceeds from relevant to irrelevant information (Lavie & Tsal, 1994) and that it self-terminates when the target representation emerges (Treisman & Gelade, 1980). If we accept the above assumption, it is not difficult to see why processing time available for a stimulus might be an important factor in determining the degree of encoding of its irrelevant feature. At one extreme, participants may not process the irrelevant feature. This will happen when the processing of the target is so efficient that its representation becomes available before the process of selecting the task irrelevant feature is completed. At the other extreme, the irrelevant feature may be fully identified. This is likely to occur when target processing is inefficient so that target representation does not emerge until after the irrelevant feature is identified.

Experiments

Although the experiments reviewed above have identified a number of factors that influence the relationship between attention and selection, many questions remain unanswered. One such question is whether personally and/or socially important stimuli such as one's own name or a human face are more likely to capture attention than impersonal or less significant stimuli such as other people's names or geometric shapes. If that is the case, we might expect to find the stimuli in the former category more likely to be selected even when they are the task-irrelevant feature in a location task.

Highly personal information, such as one's own name, appears to be particularly powerful at capturing an individual's attention. Using a dichotic listening procedure that required the participants to repeat aloud passages that were presented to one ear while ignoring passages that were delivered to the other ear, Moray (1959) found that whereas the participants would fail to notice a list of words that had been presented up to 35 times to their unattended ear, they were much more likely to notice their own name when it was presented to the unattended ear. More recently, Mack and Rock (1998) reported that inattentional blindness, an inability to detect suprathreshold stimuli that were presented unexpectedly, was substantially reduced when the unexpected stimulus was the participant's own name or a smiling face rather than when it was other people's name or a sad face. These findings provide evidence that one's own name may have a lower recognition threshold, and may capture attention even when it is task irrelevant.

In two experiments we explored the processing of an attended non-target stimulus when that stimulus was either one's own name (Experiment 1) or a cartoon smiling face (Experiment 2). Of particular interest was whether or not the processing asymmetry between location and an object feature would disappear when the irrelevant object feature was personally and/or socially important.

Intraprime Compatibility

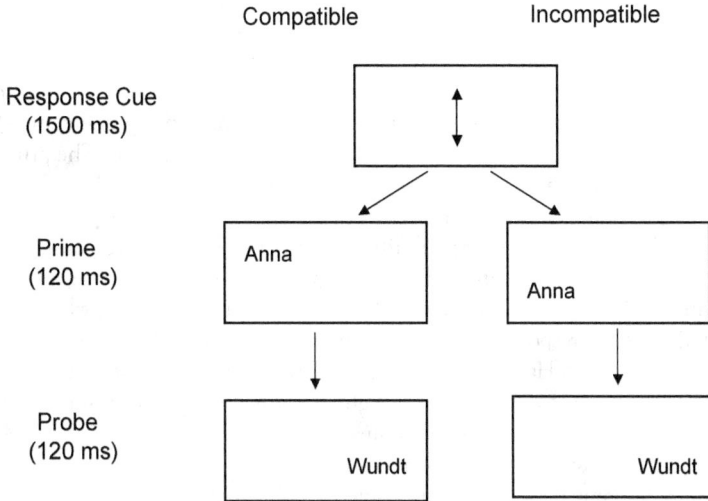

Compatible	Incompatible

Response Cue
(1500 ms)

Prime
(120 ms)

Anna

Anna

Probe
(120 ms)

Wundt

Wundt

Figure 1

Examples of stimulus displays in Experiment 1.

Note: The task was to respond to the probe's location (up or down) or name (one's own name or the name Piaget) as specified in advance by the response cue. The participant was to press one key if the response was his/her own name or 'up', and a different key if the response was Piaget or 'down'. The two trials illustrated here are examples of location-relevant trials. *Compatible* and *incompatible* conditions are defined with respect to the mapping of responses between the relevant and irrelevant features of the prime. Trials are termed compatible when they are mapped onto the same key (e.g., the participant's own name at an 'up' location). Trials are incompatible when they are mapped onto different keys (e.g., the participant's own name at a 'down' location).

Experiment 1: The Selection of One's Own Name

In Experiment 1, the participants were shown a series of trials, each consisting of a response cue, a prime, and a probe (see Figure 1). The response cue was presented at the center of the screen for 1500 ms, and it consisted of either the word NAME or a vertical two-headed arrow ($\updownarrow$). Upon its offset, the prime, which was either the participant's personal name or the name Piaget, appeared for 120 ms at one of four locations at the ends of a $10.51° \times 3.43°$ imaginary rectangle. The probe also consisted of a name, and was displayed for 120 ms. However, the name and its location depended on the specific response cue that pertained to a given trial. On name-relevant trials, it was either the participant's personal name or Piaget, either of which appeared $5.26°$ to the left or right from the center of the screen along the horizontal meridian. On location-relevant trials, it was always the name Wundt and appeared at one of the same four locations as those used for the prime. All stimuli were white against a neutral grey background, and the prime and probe were both written in 48-point Geneva font. To avoid the possible effects of masking, the prime and probe occurred on different sides of the screen on any given trial.

The task was to respond to the probe's identity (the participant's own personal forename or Piaget) when the cue was NAME or to its location (up or down) when the cue was an arrow. Participants pressed one key if the response was their own name or up, and a different key if it was Piaget or down. Eighteen people took part in the study.

The experiment employed a within-participants design, with task (name or location), prime-probe similarity (same vs. different), and intraprime compatibility (compatible vs. incompatible) as the principal manipulations. The prime-probe similarity refers to the inter-object relationship between the relevant features of the prime and probe. There were as many *same* trials as there were *different* ones. The intraprime compatibility refers to the intra object response compatibility between the relevant and irrelevant features within the prime, and the two features of the prime were equally likely to be compatible (i.e., when they indicated the same response key) or incompatible (i.e., when they indicated different response keys). Half the trials were name relevant, and the other half were location relevant. In total, there were eight experimental conditions: location-same-compatible, location-same-incompatible, location-different-compatible, location-different-incompatible, name-same-compatible, name-same-incompatible, name-different-compatible, and name-different-incompatible.

To illustrate the various conditions, imagine that a participant named Anna was presented a trial that commenced with an arrow, followed by her own name Anna at the upper left location of the screen, and then the word Wundt appeared at the lower right location. As indicated by the arrow, the relevant feature on this particular trial was location, so the correct response should be down. The prime-probe similarity was different, because the prime was located up the screen and the probe was down the screen. The intraprime compatibility would be compatible, because the two prime features, that is, Anna and up, shared the same response key. This trial is an example of the location-different-compatible condition.

Table 1A shows the results of Experiment 1. In agreement with prior research (Kornblum, 1973; Meyer & Schvaneveldt, 1971), the participants showed a positive priming effect of similarity. They were faster when the relevant features of the prime and probe were the same compared to when they were different. There was also a three-way interaction between task, similarity and compatibility. Consistent with previous experiments (Chen, 2003b, 2005), there was a processing asymmetry between the name and location trials. When attention was directed to the location of the prime on location relevant trials, the participants showed no evidence of processing the name. By contrast, when attention was directed to the name of the prime on name relevant trials, the location of the prime was involuntarily selected on those trials when the relevant features of the prime and probe were different. Based on these results, one might be tempted to conclude that the processing of one's name is not fundamentally different from the processing of other stimuli such as letters or geometric shapes. However, before that conclusion can be drawn, we need to separate those trials where the irrelevant prime feature was the participant's

Table 1A

Mean Reaction Times and Error Rates for Experiment 1

			Intraprime compatibility		
		Location-relevant		Name-relevant	
Prime-probe similarity	C	I		C	I
			Reaction times (ms)		
Same	666	684		655	635
Different	749	748		720	743
			Error rates (%)		
Same	3.30	3.72		3.12	1.56
Different	4.32	5.51		3.83	5.42

Note: C, compatible; I, incompatible.

name from those trials where it was Piaget. Because there was no reason to expect Piaget to have a particularly low recognition threshold, it is possible that our null result was caused by combining these two types of trials together.

To determine whether this might indeed be the case, we analysed the two types of name trials separately (see Table 1B). Our results suggest that the processing of one's own name is very different from the processing of the word Piaget. When the prime was the participant's own name, the name was processed even when the task was location. This was evidenced by faster reaction time when the two features of the prime indicated the same response than when they indicated different responses. In contrast, when the prime was Piaget, the participants showed a reversal of the compatibility effect. In other words, they were slower when the two prime features were compatible than when they were incompatible. No speed accuracy tradeoff was observed.

The most important finding of Experiment 1 is that the participants processed their own names even when they were part of a non-target object in a location task. Previous experiments using letters as the critical stimuli have shown that similar processing does not occur when attention is paid to the location of the letters (Chen, 2005; Remington & Folk, 2001). Our results suggest that although

Table 1B

Mean Reaction Times and Error Rates for the Location Task in Experiment 1

			Intraprime compatibility		
		One's own name		Piaget	
Prime-probe similarity	C	I		C	I
			Reaction times (ms)		
Same	666	699		669	671
Different	727	799		773	704
			Error rates (%)		
Same	3.80	3.34		2.83	4.03
Different	2.96	7.97		5.72	3.02

Note: The irrelevant prime dimension was participant's own name or 'Piaget'.
    C, compatible; I, incompatible.

the dissociation between attention and selection applies to common stimuli, it does not necessarily generalise to a special group of stimuli that possess high attention capturing capacity. These stimuli include one's own name, and possibly also include danger signals such as 'look out' or 'fire' (Treisman, 1960). The fact that in the present experiment one's own name was processed on location-relevant trials provides converging evidence that its perception may be fundamentally different from that of other stimuli, a finding which is consistent with prior studies that have used different paradigms (Mack & Rock, 1998; Moray, 1959).

The special status of one's own name is also supported by the absence of a similarity by compatibility interaction in our participants' reaction time data. In all other previous studies using the same paradigm, if the irrelevant prime dimension was selected, it appeared only on those trials where the relevant dimensions of the prime and probe were different (Chen, 2003b, 2005). With one's own name, however, evidence of its processing was observed regardless of the inter object relationship between the prime and probe. A plausible interpretation of this finding is that because one's own name had a low recognition threshold in long-term memory due to its significance in our daily lives (Treisman, 1960), it captured attention as soon as it was presented. Consequently, its selection did not appear to depend on the efficiency with which the probe was processed, at least in the present paradigm.

One aspect of the data that we did not predict was the reversal of the compatibility effect on those trials where the irrelevant prime feature was Piaget. Similar effects have not been reported in the research literature to date, and we are puzzled by it. Further experiments are required to explore this issue.

Experiment 2: The Selection of a Smiling Face

In Experiment 2, we examine the degree of processing of stimuli that are socially important but which are not as personally significant to an individual as one's own name. The stimuli we chose were schematic cartoon faces.

There is considerable evidence that faces are interpersonally meaningful stimuli whose processing differs from that of other common objects. For example, single-cell recordings have found face-selective neurons in the superior temporal sulcus of macaques (Desimone, 1991; Gross, Roche-Maranda, & Bender, 1972). Furthermore, patients who suffer from prosopagnosia, a severe inability to recognise familiar faces by sight, can be relatively intact in recognising common objects (De Renzi, 1986; Farah, Levinson, & Klein, 1995). Researchers using fMRI on normal people have also reported a 'face area' in the fusiform gyrus that becomes more active when observers view photographs of faces compared to those of other objects such as houses, scrambled faces, hands or animals (Kanwisher, McDermott, & Chun, 1997; Kanwisher, Stanley, & Harris, 1999). Moreover, Mack and Rock (1998) reported that, as with one's own name, participants' inattentional blindness reduced when a schematic happy face rather than a sad or a scrambled face was presented unexpectedly. In light of these findings, a schematic face appeared to be a good candidate for our purposes.

Table 2A

Mean Reaction Times and Error Rates for Experiment 2

| | | Intraprime compatibility | | | |
| | | Location relevant | | Face relevant | |
Prime-probe similarity	C	I		C	I
			Reaction times (ms)		
Same	686	687		758	723
Different	723	715		733	787
			Error rates (%)		
Same	3.83	4.46		5.13	2.43
Different	4.93	4.33		2.82	4.76

Note: C, compatible; I, incompatible.

As in Experiment 1, each trial consisted of three displays. The response cue was a double headed arrow as that in Experiment 1 or a face like symbol ($\ddot{\cup}$) which subtended 0.96° × 1.43° in length and width. The prime was either a happy face or a sad face that subtended 2.39°. The probe was the same as the prime on face relevant trials, but it was an outline circle without any internal facial features on location relevant trials. The participants' task was to respond to the probe's location (up or down) or facial expression (happy or sad). They pressed one key for 'up' or 'a happy face', and another key for 'down' or 'a sad face'. Seventeen participants completed Experiment 2. All other aspects of the experiment were identical to those of Experiment 1.

The data appear in Table 2A. As was expected, the participants' reaction times showed a positive priming effect. In addition, they were faster in the location task than in the face task. Because of the three-way interaction, we again examined the data for the two tasks separately. In the location task, the participants showed no evidence that they processed the irrelevant prime feature. Their reaction times to the probe did not differ as a function of the response compatibility between the relevant and irrelevant features of the prime. However, in the face task, there was a significant response compatibility effect when the relevant dimensions of the prime and probe were different, but a reversed compatibility effect when these dimensions were the same. There was no evidence of a speed accuracy tradeoff.

To examine whether a happy face was processed differently from a sad face, we analysed the two types of trials individually (see Table 2B). No significant effects regarding the processing of the irrelevant prime feature were found with either type of stimuli. Thus, there was no evidence to suggest that the participants processed the two types of trials differently.

Unlike Mack and Rock (1998), who reported reduced inattentional blindness when a happy face rather than a sad face was shown unexpectedly, we did not observe any processing differences between these two types of stimuli. Our finding that a happy face was processed differently from one's own name suggests that the deciding factor in the selection of an attended non-target object is

Table 2B

Mean Reaction Times and Error Rates for the Location Task in Experiment 2

| | Intraprime compatibility | | | |
| | Happy | | Sad | |
Prime-probe similarity	C	I	C	I
	Reaction times (ms)			
Same	683	693	692	681
Different	713	720	736	713
	Error rates (%)			
Same	3.36	3.73	4.35	5.20
Different	4.29	5.04	5.44	3.66

Note: The irrelevant prime dimension was a happy face or a sad face.
   C, compatible; I, incompatible.

likely to be the extent of personal significance a stimulus holds for an individual. It is possible that if we had used photographs of the participants' own faces rather than schematic cartoon faces, our results might have been different.

Perhaps it is not surprising that one's own name was processed differently from abstract cartoon faces. The two types of stimuli differ in several important ways. First, whereas one's own name is personally important, a cartoon face is less personal, and definitely less important. Second, compared to cartoon faces, one's own name is presumably recognised at a more specific level of categorisation (e.g., Anna, John). Finally, there is empirical evidence that the two types of stimuli differ in their ability to capture attention (Mack & Rock, 1998; Nothdurft, 1993). Whereas Mack and Rock (1998) found a pop-out effect when their participants searched for his or her own name among words as distractors, Nothdurft (1993) reported inefficient search when his participants searched for a happy face among sad faces. Our results provided further evidence that the perception of one's own name and that of faces may be very different.

Is it possible that the processing asymmetry revealed in Experiment 2 was caused by the slower reaction times in the location task than in the face task rather than by a difference in the way in which attention was directed between the two types of features? Although this interpretation is possible, it is not very likely. The fact that a similar asymmetry existed in previous experiments (Chen, 2005) where there were no significant differences between the location and shape tasks, argues against such an account. Further evidence comes from the studies of Remington and Folk (2001), who used a very different paradigm from ours. Yet no selection of the irrelevant feature of a non-target object was found when attention was directed to the object's location.

Admittedly, the finding that the participants showed a reversal of the compatibility effect in the face task when the relevant dimensions of the prime and probe were the same was puzzling. The fact that a similar effect was found in Experiment 1, even though it occurred in the location task, raises the possibility that this may relate in some way to the specific types of stimuli used in our experiments. We do not yet have a satisfactory explanation for this observation.

The Level of Processing of an Attended Non-Target Object

So far, all the experiments we have reported or reviewed had one characteristic in common: the specific features that constituted the irrelevant prime feature were the same as the features that were required to be reported for the probe within an experiment. This raises the question as to whether the processing of the irrelevant feature of an attended non-target object only occurs when it is physically identical to the reporting feature of the target object. Although this question was not addressed in the experiments reported here, it has been investigated in two recent studies (Chen, 2003b, 2005). These experiments employed the same general paradigm as those that we have described here. The participants' task was to report the identity (T or V) or the orientation (30° left or right tilt) of the probe as indicated by the response cue. A unique characteristic of these experiments is that neither the relevant nor irrelevant feature of the prime were physically identical to the features that were required to be reported for the probe. Specifically, whereas the probe was an uppercase 'T' or 'V' with a 30° orientation, the corresponding prime was a lowercase 't' or 'v' with a 60° orientation. The results show that the participants demonstrated both a positive priming effect and a response compatibility effect. As in other experiments, the compatibility effect occurred only on those trials where the relevant features of the prime and probe were different. Furthermore, the compatibility effect was comparable regardless of whether the probe was informative or uninformative. These findings suggest that the processing of the irrelevant prime feature did not require identical stimulus features between the prime and probe.

Conclusion

The evidence presented in this chapter suggests that the relationship between visual attention and selection is more complex than was previously assumed to be the case. Taken together, the research indicates that selection is object-based when the attended stimulus has been selected as a target. However, when the attended stimulus is a distractor, selection depends on such factors as the direction of attention, the processing efficiency of the target, and the personal significance of the attended stimulus. Although experimental task demands can guide the extraction of features in some circumstances, selection is largely involuntary when attention has been directed towards an object feature of a non-target object or when personally significant information such as one's own name is the critical stimulus.

References

Baylis, G. C., & Driver, J. (1993). Visual attention and objects: Evidence for hierarchical coding of location. *Journal of Experimental Psychology: Human Perception & Performance, 19,* 451–470.

Cave, K. R., & Bichot, N. P. (1999). Visuospatial attention: Beyond a spotlight model. *Psychonomic Bulletin & Review, 6,* 204–223.

Chen, Z. (1998). Switching attention within and between objects: The role of subjective organization. *Canadian Journal of Experimental Psychology, 52*, 7–16.

Chen, Z. (2003a). Attentional focus, processing load, and Stroop interference. *Perception & Psychophysics, 65*, 888–900.

Chen, Z. (2003b). *Attention and selection: The level of processing of an attended non-target object.* Paper presented at the 4th International Conference on Cognitive Science, Sydney, New South Wales, Australia.

Chen, Z. (2005). Selective attention and the perception of an attended non-target object. *Journal of Experimental Psychology: Human Perception and Performance, 31*, 1493–1509.

De Renzi, E. (1986). Current issues in prosopagnosia. In H. D. Ellis, M. A. Jeeves, F. Newcombe, & A. Young (Eds.), *Aspects of face processing* (pp. 243–252). Dordrecht, the Netherlands: Martinus Nijhoff.

Desimone, R. (1991). Face-selective cells in the temporal cortex of monkeys. Special issue: Face perception. *Journal of Cognitive Neuroscience, 3*, 1–8.

Duncan, J. (1984). Selective attention and the organization of visual information. *Journal of Experimental Psychology: General, 113*, 501–517.

Egly, R., Driver, J., & Rafal, R. D. (1994). Shifting visual attention between objects and locations: Evidence from normal and parietal lesion participants. *Journal of Experimental Psychology: General, 123*, 501–517.

Farah, M., Levinson, K. L., & Klein, K. L. (1995). Face perception and within-category discrimination in prosopagnosia. *Neuropsychologia, 33*, 661–674.

Gross, C. G., Roche-Maranda, C. E., & Bender, D. B. (1972). Visual properties of neurons in inferotemporal cortex of the macaque. *Journal of Neurophysiology, 35*, 96–111.

Harms, L., & Bundesen, C. (1983). Color segregation and selective attention in a nonsearch task. *Perception & Psychophysics, 33*, 11–19.

Hughes, H. C., & Zimba, L. D. (1985). Spatial maps of directed visual attention. *Journal of Experimental Psychology: Human Perception and Performance, 11*, 409–430.

Kahneman, D., & Henik, A. (1981). Perceptual organization and attention. In M. Kubovy & J. R. Pomerantz (Eds.), *Perceptual organization* (pp. 181–211). Hillsdale, NJ: Laurence Erlbaum.

Kahneman, D., & Treisman, A. (1984). Changing views of attention and automaticity. In R. Parasuraman & D. R. Davies (Eds.), *Varieties of attention* (pp. 29–61). Orlando, FL: Academic Press.

Kanwisher, N., McDermott, J., & Chun, M. M. (1997). The fusiform face area: A module in human extrastriate cortex specialized for face perception. *Journal of Neuroscience, 17*, 4302–4311.

Kanwisher, N., Stanley, D., & Harris, A. (1999). The fusiform gyrus is selective for faces not animals. *Neuroreport, 10*, 183–187.

Kim, M-S., & Cave, K. R. (1995). Spatial attention in visual search for features and feature conjunctions. *Psychological Science, 6*, 376–380.

Kornblum, S. (1973). Sequential effects in choice reaction time: A tutorial review. In S. Kornblum (Ed.), *Attention and performance IV* (pp. 107–132). Hillsdale, NJ: Lawrence Erlbaum.

Kramer, A. F., & Jacobson, A. (1991). Perceptual organization and focused attention: The role of objects and proximity in visual processing. *Perception & Psychophysics, 50*, 267–284.

Lamy, D., & Tsal, Y. (2001). On the status of location in visual attention. *European Journal of Cognitive Psychology, 13*, 305–342.

Lavie, N., & Tsal, Y. (1994). Perceptual load as a major determinant of the locus of selection in visual attention. *Perception & Psychophysics, 56*, 183–197.

Mack, A., & Rock, I. (1998). *Inattentional blindness*. Cambridge, Massachusetts: MIT Press.

MacLeod, C. M. (1991). Half a century of research on the Stroop effect: An integrative review. *Psychological Bulletin, 109*, 163–203.

Meyer, D. E., & Schvaneveldt, R. W. (1971). Facilitation in recognizing pairs of words: Evidence of a dependence between retrieval operations. *Journal of Experimental Psychology: General, 90*, 227–234.

Moore, C. M., Yantis, S., & Vaughan, G. (1998). Object-based visual selection: Evidence from perceptual completion. *Psychological Science, 9*, 104–110.

Moray, N. (1959). Attention and dichotic listening: Affective cues and the influence of instructions. *Quarterly Journal of Experimental Psychology, 11*, 56–60.

Nothdurft, H-C. (1993). Faces and facial expressions do not pop out. *Perception, 22*, 1287–1298.

Remington, R. W., & Folk, C. L. (2001). A dissociation between attention and selection. *Psychological Science, 12*, 511–515.

Stroop, J. R. (1935). Studies of interference in serial verbal reactions. *Journal of Experimental Psychology, 18*, 643–662.

Treisman, A. M. (1960). Contextual cues in selective listening. *Quarterly Journal of Experimental Psychology, 12*, 242–248.

Treisman, A. M., & Gelade, G. (1980). A feature-integration theory of attention. *Cognitive Psychology, 12*, 97–136.

Tsal, Y., & Lavie, N. (1993). Location dominance in attending to color and shape. *Journal of Experimental Psychology: Human Perception and Performance, 19*, 131–139.

Zimba, L. D., & Hughes, H. C. (1987). Distractor-target interactions during directed visual attention. *Spatial Vision, 2*, 117–149.

Not All Smiles Are Created Equal: Perceiver Sensitivity to the Differences Between Posed and Genuine Smiles

Lynden Miles and Lucy Johnston

The face plays a central and undeniable role in everyday social interaction. Attending to only the face, we can easily discriminate males from females, strangers from acquaintances, and the young from the old (Zebrowitz, 1997). In addition, by virtue of a complex musculature and rich innervation, faces have a capacity for multifaceted and intricate movement (Ekman, 2003). These dynamic properties of the face have particular function when considered in the context of interpersonal communication. Specifically, the exhibition and perception of facial expressions can be an essential component to ensuring smooth social transaction (Lazarus, 1991). Indeed, such communication is a cornerstone of social interaction and employed extensively by both humans and other higher-order animals (Plutchik, 2003).

Within the context of facial expressions, expressions of emotion have a special prominence in that they serve as a reliable source of information pertinent to predicting an individual's emotional state, and therefore their likely future behaviour (Keltner & Haidt, 1999). While all facial expressions convey socially relevant information, expressions of emotion have specific biological and psychological significance in that they are thought to be indicators of an underlying affective experience (Ekman, 2003). Knowledge of another person's psychological state is helpful for guiding interaction with that person. At the most basic level, it is well advised to interact quite differently with a smiling, happy person compared to a frowning, angry individual. A smile informs the perceiver that the sender is happy and therefore likely to be amenable to subsequent interaction, whereas a frown, in contrast, suggests the sender is unlikely to be happy and consequently relatively less approachable or perhaps even potentially harmful. It follows, therefore, that the ability to accurately perceive facial expressions of emotion is a significant modulator of social interaction. It is important for the social perceiver to be sensitive to the information conveyed in facial expressions of emotion in order to both facilitate desirable and advanta-geous interaction, and to avoid potentially deleterious social transactions.

However, such social utility of facial expressions may be compromised if a particular expression of emotion is exhibited without experiencing the corre-sponding emotional state. While the perceiver is generally well served by being able to recognise facial expressions of emotion in others, it is not always advan-tageous to the sender to reveal such information in a consistently open and honest manner (Frank, 1988). If the goals of the respective parties in a social interaction conflict, informing others of intended behaviour may be counter-productive to the attainment of those goals. For instance, if one is angered suf-ficiently to want to harm another, signaling intention may actually thwart the achievement of this goal. Upon recognising an expression of anger, the perceiver is granted an opportunity to anticipate the potential harm and react accordingly (perhaps by fleeing, preemptively attacking, or attempting some form of non-violent conflict resolution).

Consequently, in the context of social exchange, there is often incentive for senders to produce disingenuous facial expressions. Veracious expressions can serve as signals of intended action to perceivers that may not always be desirable or advantageous to the expresser. Simultaneously, there is incentive for per-ceivers to be sensitive to such attempts at deception. In turn, there is further incentive to deceive in more subtle ways and, of course, to detect more subtle attempts at deception. Commonly termed a cognitive 'arms race', several theo-rists (e.g., Cosmides, 1989; Cosmides & Tooby, 1992; Trivers, 1985) have sug-gested that during our evolutionary history this interplay between dishonesty and detection of dishonesty has played a fundamental role in the development of human intelligence. In a more contemporary sense, it remains important for individuals to have the ability to regulate and simulate expressions of emotion, or risk exploitation, and concurrently to be sensitive to dishonest expressions of emotion, or risk incorrectly inferring emotional state.

In this chapter we will apply the framework outlined above to the case of our most common facial expression of emotion: the smile. First, we will review lit-erature pertinent to difference between spontaneous, veridical facial expressions of positive affect, the genuine smile, and the intentional counterpart to this expression, the posed smile. Research in this area has suggested that there are categorical psychological distinctions between posed and genuine smiles that are evident physiognomically (Frank, 2002). Second, we will review the available literature regarding the ability of perceivers to detect the differences between posed and genuine smiles. Finally, we will present data from our own laboratory that demonstrate sensitivity to the meaningful differences between posed and genuine smiles, consistent with the ontological origins of the respective expres-sions. The results of this research will be discussed in terms of person perception and consideration given to the methodological implications of using simulated expressions of emotion in social psychological research.

Posed and Genuine Smiles

French neurologist and anatomist Duchenne de Boulogne (1862/1990) first noted the distinction between genuine smiles of enjoyment and posed smiles. Duchenne observed that genuine smiles involved concomitant bilateral contraction of the *zygomatic major* muscle (which pulls the corners of the mouth obliquely upward toward the cheekbones) and the *orbicularis oculi* muscle (which pulls the skin surrounding the eye toward the eyeball). By comparison, intentional or posed smiles consisted of *zygomatic major* contraction only, and did not involve *orbicularis oculi* contraction. Importantly, contraction of the *orbicularis oculi* results in folds or creases in the skin, sometimes termed 'crow's feet', at the outer corners of the eye. Duchenne concluded that this particular feature, the wrinkling at the corners of the eyes, was a perceivable marker of a spontaneous smile of enjoyment, a genuine smile.

Since these early observations, many areas of research have confirmed that there are distinctions between posed and genuine facial expressions of enjoyment (for a review see Frank, 2002). At the neuro-anatomical level, it has been shown that there are two relatively distinct neural pathways associated with the display of facial expressions that differentially support voluntary and involuntary facial movements (for a review see Rinn, 1984). Neurologically, voluntary facial movements originate from areas in the motor cortex, predominantly in the left hemisphere, and are innervated via the pyramidal motor system. By comparison, spontaneous facial movements employ phylogenetically older neural pathways originating in the subcortical areas within the brain, specifically, according to Damasio (1994), the anterior cingulate region, limbic cortices and basal ganglia, which innervate the facial muscles via the extrapyramidal motor system (Gazzaniga, Ivry, & Mangun, 2002). Clinical evidence for the distinction of these neural pathways can be seen in stroke patients. Patients who have experienced damage to the motor cortex show asymmetrical voluntary facial movements, but symmetrical involuntary expressions. In contrast, stroke patients with damage to the anterior cingulate region exhibit asymmetry contralateral to the damaged hemisphere during spontaneous facial expressions, but no such asymmetry when wilfully contracting their facial muscles (Damasio, 1994). Such is the reliability of the neurological distinction between voluntary and involuntary facial movements that prior to the use of soft-tissue imaging, facial movements were used as a diagnostic criteria for brain injury (DeMyer, 1980).

The neurological distinction between volitional and spontaneous facial expressions, supports Duchenne's (1862/1990) original observations regarding posed and genuine smiles. Damasio (1994) suggests that while the *zygomatic major* can be contracted either wilfully or involuntarily (i.e., is innervated by both the pyramidal and extrapyramidal motor systems), *orbicularis oculi* is not under volitional control. In support of this claim Ekman, Roper, and Hager (1980) demonstrated that while most people can deliberately contract the medial aspect of *orbicularis oculi*, only around 20% of the population are able to voluntarily contract the lateral portion of this muscle. Importantly, as noted by

Duchenne, and later confirmed by Ekman, Friesen, and O'Sullivan (1988), it is only the lateral parts of the eye sphincter that are involved when spontaneously expressing positive affect. Thus, it appears there is a sound neurological basis for distinguishing between posed and genuine facial expressions.

Studies of neurological function have provided evidence that the distinction between posed and genuine smiles has a direct relationship to an underlying psychological state, that is, the relative presence or absence of positive emotion. Ekman, Davidson, and Friesen (1990) measured central nervous system (CNS) activity using electroencephalography (EEG), facial movements and self-reports of emotional experience of participants viewing film clips designed to induce positive or negative affect. Smiles involving *orbicularis oculi* activity, genuine smiles, were shown to occur more frequently than smiles not involving *orbicularis oculi* activity, posed smiles, when viewing positive films and were correlated with reports of positive subjective experience. Furthermore, genuine smiles were accompanied by a pattern of CNS activity systematically different from that of posed smiles. The particular pattern of CNS activity associated with genuine smiles, but not posed smiles, closely resembled that of a more general approach-related emotional response (Davidson, Ekman, Saron, Senulis, & Friesen, 1990). Fox and Davidson (1988) found similar patterns of brain activity in 10-month-old infants who showed genuine smiles in response to the approach of their mother, but not strangers. It appears that, consistent with the functionally separable neural pathways, posed and genuine smiles are associated with different patterns of underlying neurological activity relative to specific environmental events (e.g., mother vs. stranger approach).

On the basis that there is evidence in support of a neuro-cognitive disparity between posed and genuine smiles, it follows that this same distinction should be apparent in more ecological contexts than the laboratory studies reviewed above. If Duchenne's (1862/1990) original observations are valid, we should be able to observe a greater incidence of genuine smiles when individuals are known to be experiencing positive emotional experiences, and in turn, an absence of genuine smiles when there is no such affective state. To this extent, further support for the emotion-specific difference between posed and genuine smiles can be found in clinical settings. As would be expected, clinically depressed individuals, in line with their negative affective experience, exhibit fewer genuine smiles than those not depressed (Katsikitis & Pilowsky, 1991), but show increases in the incidence of genuine smiling in line with reductions in the symptoms of their depression (Steiner, 1986). Also in the clinical domain, Bonanno and Keltner (1997) studied the course of the bereavement process of adults who had experienced the death of a romantic partner. They conducted a videotaped interview 6-months post-loss, and subsequently coded participant's facial expressions. It was found that the incidence of genuine smiles in this interview was negatively correlated with the grief experienced 25 months after the death of the partner. The participants in this study who had exhibited more positive emotion, as evidenced by a greater frequency of genuine smiles, also showed greater success in coping with, and recovery from the death of their conjugal partner.

While these studies of facial expressions are generally correlational in nature, the findings are consistent with Duchenne's (1862/1990) original observations in that occurrence of spontaneous genuine smiles, but not voluntary, posed smiles appears to be linked to the experience of positive emotion. In addition, the findings from the neurological studies of facial expression provide sound evidence for an anatomical and functional distinction between posed and genuine smiles, also in line with Duchenne's initial interpretation. Taken together, this body of research provides a strong basis for concluding that smiles that include the contraction of *orbicularis oculi*, marked by the characteristic 'crow's feet' or wrinkling at the outer corners of the eyes, are spontaneous, genuine facial expressions indicative of a positive emotional experience. Alternatively, smiles that do not involve recruitment of *orbicularis oculi*, are intentional, voluntary facial expressions for which there is no substantive underlying positive emotional state (as evidenced by an absence of markers of a spontaneous genuine smile). With this in mind, in social contexts it is important for perceivers not to conflate posed and genuine smiles into a general, amorphous form of positive facial expression or else they risk misperceiving happiness, and potentially the behavioural intentions of the smiler. Although the motives for the posed smile may vary widely from a simple greeting to a deliberate attempt to deceive (Ekman, 2003), it remains a volitional communicative mechanism intended to influence the perceiver in a specific manner. In line with the 'cognitive arms-race' logic outlined above, it is advantageous to the perceiver to be sensitive to such attempted forms of interpersonal manipulation. In the next section of this chapter we will examine the sensitivity of the social perceiver to the distinction between posed and genuine smiles.

Perceiver Sensitivity

Only a decade after Duchenne's (1862/1990) original observations, Darwin (1872/1998) began to explore the social significance of the distinction between posed and genuine smiles. Using a set of photographs given to him by Duchenne, Darwin observed that while the differences between the posed and genuine smiles were slight, almost everyone he showed the pictures to could readily determine which was a real expression of emotion and which was posed. Although Darwin never conducted any rigorous scientific examination of this effect, evidence consistent with his findings was reported over a century later. Frank, Ekman, and Friesen (1993) reported that participants could reliably distinguish between posed and genuine smiles when viewing short video clips of these expressions. Furthermore, participants also rated targets who exhibited a genuine smile more positively across a range of behavioural dimensions compared to targets exhibiting a posed smile. Together, these findings suggest that perceivers can exhibit sensitivity to the meaningful differences between posed and genuine smiles.

Subsequent to the work of Frank et al. (1993) several studies have examined factors relevant to the perception of posed and genuine smiles. Williams, Senior, David, Loughland, and Gordon (2001) investigated the patterns of eye-fixations of participants viewing photographs of 'neutral', 'sad' and 'happy' faces. These authors reported that compared to neutral and sad facial expressions, perceivers made proportionately more and longer eye fixations to the outer corners of the eye when viewing happy faces. Given that this is the location on the face where indications of genuine smiling are likely to occur, it appears that when a smile is detected generically (most probably by the presence of *zygomatic major* contraction), attention is shifted specifically to the area around the eyes where the characteristic 'crow's feet' marker is shown. No parallel 'eye checking' strategy was found for either neutral or sad facial expressions. The patterns of ocular dynamics revealed in this study when viewing 'happy' faces were consistent with a perceptual approach that would function as a means to help establish the veracity of smiles.

Further, Surakka and Hietanen (1998) reported research that employed facial electromyography (EMG) to investigate participant's facial activity when viewing genuine smiles, posed smiles, and neutral facial expressions. The results revealed that facial reactions to genuine smiles differed from those to neutral faces, while no difference was found between posed smiles and neutral faces. Specifically, muscular contraction around the periocular region (including *orbicularis oculi* contraction) when viewing genuine smiles was more intense than when viewing neutral expressions, but this was not observed when comparing posed smiles to neutral expressions. Again, the result from this study suggests that the social perceiver is sensitive to the veracity of a smile.

Scherer and Ceschi (2000) provided additional support for the notion that perceivers are sensitive to the distinctions between posed and genuine smiles using evidence from a more naturalistic setting, a major international airport. Airline passengers whose luggage had failed to arrive were identified and surreptitiously videotaped as they reported their loss to the appropriate airline staff. After dealing with each passenger, the staff member, who was blind to the purposes of the study, was asked to rate that passenger's mood. The videotapes of each passenger were also coded for the frequency of posed and genuine smiles. The authors reported a positive relationship between the incidence of genuine smiles exhibited by passengers with lost luggage and ratings of their mood made by the airline agents who were blind to the purposes of the study. Importantly, the frequency of posed smiles exhibited was not related to the passenger's mood. In effect, this finding supports Frank et al.'s (1993) results from laboratory studies in that the airline agents displayed sensitivity to the difference between posed and genuine smiles. Passengers perceived to be in better moods exhibited more genuine smiles, whereas the display of posed smiles was not related to perceived emotional state.

It appears therefore that perceivers can, and do, exhibit sensitivity to the meaningful distinctions between posed and genuine smiles. Anecdotal and experimental evidence suggests that perceivers are able to accurately determine the veracity of a smile (e.g., Darwin, 1872/1998; Frank et al., 1993). Additionally, such ability has been shown to be supported by specific patterns of ocular dynamics when viewing smiles (Williams et al., 2001) as well as different behavioural responses to posed and genuine smiles (Scherer & Ceschi, 2000; Surakka & Hietanen, 1998). However, a number of methodological limitations do hinder the generalisation of the results of these studies. The practice of obtaining explicit ratings of personality traits and constructs (e.g., see Frank et al., 1993; Scherer & Ceschi, 2000) as a proxy measure for impression formation is, arguably, not suitable for application to this domain (Baron & Bordeau, 1987). Ordinarily, the social perceiver does not make such considered, deliberate judgments of others along preordained, segmented dimensions or categories, but instead spontaneously detects relevant opportunities for interaction with others (Baron & Miscovich, 1993; Gibson, 1979; McArthur & Baron, 1983). Hence, requiring participants to make ratings of personality qualities of smiling individuals does not approximate well to the reference situation of an actual social interaction.

A second and perhaps more serious methodological concern regards the nature of the target facial expressions. In their study of perceivers' reactions to emotional faces, Surakka and Hietanen (1998) operationalised genuine smiles by guiding actors to produce facial expressions consistent with the definition of this expression (i.e., *zygomatic major* and *orbicularis oculi* contraction). We see this as potentially problematic in that a 'posed genuine' smile, aside from the oxymoron, may not resemble the naturalistic occurrence of this expression. Given that there is strong evidence to suggest separate neural pathways are associated with the exhibition of spontaneous and deliberate facial movements (Damasio, 1994; Gazzaniga et al., 2002; Rinn, 1984), it is unlikely that even a very accomplished actor could perfectly recreate a spontaneous genuine smile on demand. Furthermore, Surakka and Hietanen provide no indication as to the on-line emotional state experienced by the actor when the stimuli expression was produced. Consequently, there is no means to verify the genuine smiles employed in this study were actually indicative of any underlying affective state. This presents a problem in that it is unclear whether participants viewing these expressions were actually responding to the intended genuine smile, or some other artefact of simulating this expression. We suggest, therefore, that it is vital to the validity of any research examining differences when perceiving posed or genuine facial expressions, to operationalise stimuli material according to complete and functional definitions of the expression. Specifically, genuine smiles should operationalised as spontaneous expressions of positive emotional experience.

The Present Research

We sought to address the methodological issues discussed above and in doing so replicate and extend the current literature regarding the sensitivity of perceivers to the meaningful differences between posed and genuine smiles. An initial challenge was to generate ecologically valid facial displays that conformed to both morphological and emotional criteria for posed and genuine smiles respectively.

In short, genuine smiles should be accompanied by a positive emotional experience and show evidence of both *zygomatic major* and *orbicularis oculi* contraction, while posed smiles should occur in the absence of any particular emotional state and show evidence of *zygomatic major* contraction only.

Facial Display Generation

Initially we recruited volunteers ($n = 19$) who were aware that our procedure involved videotaping their facial expressions, but not the particular purpose: the generation of posed and genuine smiles. Participants were invited to our laboratory individually and seated at a table across from a computer monitor. All instructions and materials were delivered via the computer monitor, on top of which was mounted a digital video camera. The procedure consisted of five phases: (a) neutral expression, (b) posed smile, (c) positive mood induction, (d) genuine smile sound stimuli and (e) genuine smile image stimuli. In the first phase participants were asked to relax their face and look into the camera with a neutral facial expression. In the second phase, participants were asked to look into the camera and smile as if they were having a photograph taken in various everyday circumstances (e.g., for their passport, their CV, a family portrait). The third phase was intended to induce positive mood in the participants in order to provide an affective state relevant to genuine smiling, and consisted of participants listening to approximately 4 minutes of classical music previously shown to have such an effect (Halberstadt & Niedenthal, 1997). During the fourth phase, participants listened to 11 short sound clips (each approximately 10 seconds long) of positively valenced sounds sourced from the International 'Affective Digitized Sounds' (IADS) database (Bradley & Lang, 1999b). In the final phase participants viewed 21 positively valenced static images sourced from the International Affective Picture System (IAPS) database (Lang, Bradley, & Cuthbert, 2001). Participants reported their mood at the end of each phase using analogue mood scales. Finally, each participant's video was subsequently coded for the evidence of *zygomatic major* and/or *orbicularis oculi* contraction using the Facial Action Coding System (FACS; Ekman, Friesen, & Hager, 2002), an anatomically based classification system for codifying all visually discernable facial movements. In total genuine smiles were obtained from 9 participants while posed smiles and neutral expressions were obtained from all 13 participants.

Our preliminary studies using this pool of facial expressions provided confirmation that perceivers could accurately judge whether a smiling individual was happy or not; that is, whether their smile was posed or genuine (Miles, 2005). Participants in these studies were simply asked to identify whether a target individual was happy or not happy. The results indicated that perceivers were indeed sensitive to the differences between posed and genuine smiles with respect to the presence or absence of an underlying positive emotional state. Sensitivity was similar regardless of whether judgments were made from static photographs or dynamic video clips, or whether participants were judging the emotion shown or the emotion felt by the target. Response bias varied as a function of the judgment type (i.e., judging the emotion shown versus the emotion felt) and whether the target expression involved the exposure of the teeth. Specifically, open mouth smiles were more likely to be considered to reflect happiness than closed mouth smiles regardless of the veracity of the expression, as were judgments of the emotion shown compared with those of the emotion felt. Nevertheless, judgments of the emotion felt by targets exhibiting closed mouth smiles (i.e., with no teeth exposed) were typically not accompanied by any significant bias, but did indicate sensitivity to the differences between posed and genuine smiles. When taken together, the results from these studies suggested that, consistent with a functional account of social perception, perceivers can exhibit sensitivity to the information contained within facial expressions that specifies a positive emotional experience.

However, we suggest that the requirement to explicitly judge emotional state may not generalise well to actual social interactions where perceivers are not ordinarily in the practice of employing such overt decision making strategies regarding the detection of the emotional state of conspecifics (Baron & Miscovich, 1993; McArthur & Baron, 1983). By drawing attention specifically to emotional state, participants may have been led to scrutinise the target facial displays in ways they may not during real-time social intercourse. To address this issue we have conducted a series of studies investigating the implicit impact of posed and genuine smiles on the social perceiver. In the next section of this chapter we outline an experiment representative of both the methods employed and the results obtained from this program of research that further elucidates the functional role of the perceiver in accurately detecting expressed positive emotion.

Affective Priming and Expression Veracity

In order to further our investigations into the sensitivity of perceivers to the differences between posed and genuine smiles without requiring participants to judge facial expressions directly we employed an affective priming procedure adapted from Sternberg, Wiking, and Dahl (1998). These authors reported that exposure to a happy face induced an automatic and involuntary response whereby words congruent with the expression (i.e., semantically positive words) were processed more rapidly than were words incongruent with the expression. This result indicated a priming effect characterised by facilitation of the identification of concepts related to the prime. Exposure to 'happy' faces spontaneously facilitated identification of 'happy' words. However, in terms of the target facial expressions used, Sternberg et al. did not explicitly differentiate between posed and genuine smiles, instead simply using 'happy expressions' (p. 761). While we acknowledge that the purpose of this study was not to examine differences between reactions to posed and genuine smiles, we agree with Frank (2002), in that it is an error to categorise all smiles together as expressions of positive affect.

To this end, in the present study we partially replicated Sternberg et al. (1998) with the addition of ecologically valid posed and genuine smiles as primes. We were concerned with the effect of exposure to posed and genuine smiles on the subsequent identification of positive words. Assessing automatic behavioural responses to socially relevant events, in this case exposure to posed and genuine smiles, provides a means to index sensitivity to these events in a meaningful and socially relevant manner without requiring explicit judgments or decisions from participants. Genuine smiles, as expressions of positive affect, were predicted to increase the efficiency with which conceptually similar information was apprehended, while posed smiles, as expressions unrelated to positive affect, were not predicted to show this effect. Thus, consistent with the previous research reported above, we hypothesised that genuine smiles would facilitate the identification of positive words to a greater extent than would posed smiles.

Method

In this study we replicated the priming procedure employed by Sternberg et al. (1998). Two target individuals drawn from the pool of expressions generated for this research (see above for details) were selected and a neutral expression, a posed smile and a genuine smile from each was employed. A control shape was also constructed by inverting the eyes and mouth of each target individual's neutral expressions. Thirty target words (15 positive, 15 negative) were selected from the Affective Norms for English Words (ANEW) database (Bradley & Lang, 1999a), and 17 female volunteers served as participants.

The experiment was administered using a custom-written software package (Walton, 2003) whereby participants were required to indicate with a key press whether a word presented on the screen was positive or negative. Order of face and word presentation was completely randomised. Each trial began with a fixation-cross presented in the centre of the screen and was replaced with a target expression (the duration between the onset of the fixation cross and that of the stimuli face was varied randomly between 1 and 3 seconds to avoid participants making anticipatory responses). The face, which served as the affective prime remained on the screen for 100 ms, and was immediately replaced by the target word. Participants were instructed to ignore the face and concentrate on responding to the word categorisation task as quickly and accurately as possible. Accuracy and response latency were recorded for each trial.

Due to the sensitivity of reaction time data to outliers and skewness (Bargh & Chartrand, 2000), the data set was cleaned and transformed prior to analysis. Errors (i.e., identifying a positive word as negative and vice versa) were omitted without replacement, and the remaining data was $\log_{10}$ transformed to meet the assumption of normality. In addition, after transformation any remaining data points outside the range of 3 standard deviations above or below the mean response time were removed for each participant as recommended by Uleman, Hon, Roman, and Moskowitz (1996). In total 7.5% of the data (6% errors and 1.5% outliers) was removed during data cleaning.

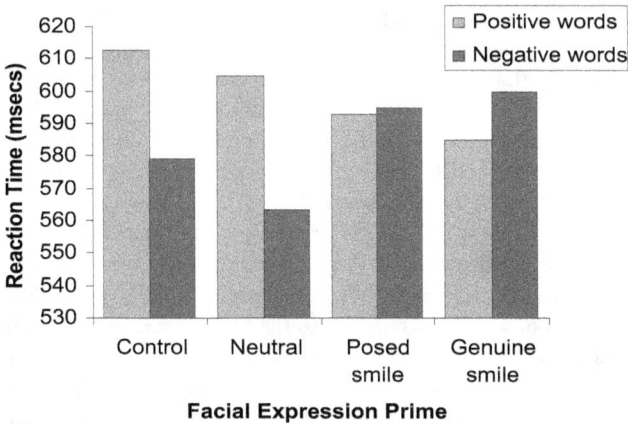

Figure 1
Reaction time to identify target words as a function of facial expression prime.

Results and Discussion

Median (log) reaction times were calculated by condition for each participant and compared using a 4 (facial expression: control/neutral/posed/genuine) × 2 (word valence: positive/negative) repeated measures analysis of variance. This revealed a significant interaction between facial expression prime and word type, F (3, 42) = 5.46, p < .01, as displayed in Figure 1. Post-hoc testing (Tukey a) indicated that a genuine smile prime facilitated identification of positive words compared to a neutral expression prime, but no such difference was observed between the posed smile and neutral expression primes. Brief exposure to a genuine smile impacted on the perceiver in a manner that facilitated subsequent access to positive words. By comparison, exposure to a posed smile did not appear to influence the perceiver in this manner, or at least no differently from exposure to a non-emotional, neutral expression.

We interpret these results as further evidence in support of the proposition that perceivers are sensitive to the meaningful difference between posed and genuine smiles. Semantically positive concepts were more readily identified when preceded by a facial expression specifying positive affect, compared to an expression, the posed smile, which, while physiognomically similar to a genuine smile, was in fact ontologically distinct. Furthermore, exposure to a posed smile did not influence subsequent behaviour (i.e., word identification) any differently from exposure to a relatively 'emotion*less*' target, the neutral facial expression.

The present data builds on the previous studies in this area (e.g., Frank et al., 1993; Scherer & Ceschi, 2000; Surakka & Hietanen, 1998), and thereby furthers our understanding of the perception of facial expressions of happiness. We have demonstrated that perceivers do evidence sensitivity to the distinction between posed and genuine smiles without instruction to pay attention to emotional state or expression veracity, when such sensitivity was indexed by a behavioural priming task. It is unlikely that participants in the current study were able to intentionally adjust their responses as a function of the facial expression prime, thereby suggesting that the perception of the facial expression prime influenced their behaviour in a relatively automatic manner.

Considering these findings within the wider context of person perception research, it appears as though perceivers are not only sensitive to the differences between posed and genuine smiles, but that upon detection of one of these expressions, ensuing behaviour is influenced in a manner consistent with the expression perceived. Specifically, detection of the markers of positive mood (i.e., a genuine smile) resulted in enhanced sensitivity to subsequent positive information. In terms of social interaction, such sensitivity equips the social perceiver to be better positioned to engage in likely subsequent interaction, that is, behaviour that accompanies positive moods. Alternatively, in the case of posed smiles, where there is no underlying positive affect, perceivers did not show any enhanced sensitivity to the positive information that followed, again in line with a functional account of this perceptual attunement. Ongoing research in our laboratories is aimed at addressing more fully the behavioural implications of perceptual sensitivity to the difference between posed and genuine smiles. In particular, we are focusing on enhancing the ecological validity of this research by utilising experimental methods that provide participants opportunities to interact with individuals exhibiting posed and genuine smiles rather than to passively view representations of these expressions. Presenting opportunities for interaction allows participants to behave in ways that more closely resemble how they would in everyday social interaction, thereby enhancing the mundane realism of the experimental setting, and in turn the generalisability of the research to the real world. Having a high degree of external validity is crucial when we attempt the laboratory study of psychological phenomena, such as the sensitivity to posed and genuine smiles, which exist in the relationship between the individual perceiver and their environment.

Conclusions

There is robust evidence to distinguish posed from genuine smiles in terms of both the exhibition and recognition of these facial expressions. Genuine smiles, that is, those that include contraction of *orbicularis oculi* in concert with *zygomatic major*, are argued to be spontaneous expressions indicative of underlying positive affective states. These expressions have been associated with neural pathways, patterns of brain activity and perceptual responses functionally distinct from that of posed smiles, which, in terms of physiognomy, do not involve recruitment of *orbicularis oculi*. We contend that the difference between posed and genuine smiles has particular significance in the context of social interaction, where facial expressions have a substantial communicative function. There is incentive in any social exchange to simultaneously regulate one's own emotional expression, and be sensitive to attempts by others to do the same. Smiles provide an example of such mechanisms at work in that we can effectively simulate this expression to the extent that morphologically, posed smiles only differ subtly from genuine smiles, but this difference can be detected in a socially relevant manner. Research from our laboratories has provided novel empirical support for the sensitivity of perceivers to the distinction between posed and genuine smiles, using ecologically valid stimuli. We have shown that detection of a genuine smile influences the perceiver in a manner that readies him or her for likely subsequent interaction. These results provide an important step toward a more integrated understanding of the role of posed and genuine smiles in social interaction, by examining perceivers' implicit sensitivity to these facial expressions in a manner that more closely approximates the on-line processes that occur in social contexts. Finally, we contend that it is critical that all research concerned with the exhibition and perception of emotion in social settings takes account of the meaningful differences between posed and genuine facial expressions.

References

Bargh, J. A., & Chartrand, T. L. (2000). The mind in the middle: A practical guide to priming and automaticity research. In H. T. Reis & C. M. Judd (Eds.), *Handbook of research methods in social and personality psychology* (pp. 253–285). Cambridge, UK: Cambridge University Press.

Baron, R. M., & Boudreau, L. A. (1987). An ecological perspective on integrating personality and social psychology. *Journal of Personality and Social Psychology, 53*, 1222–1228.

Baron, R. M., & Misovich, S. J. (1993). Dispositional knowing from an ecological perspective. *Personality & Social Psychology Bulletin, 19*, 541–552.

Bradley, M. M., & Lang, P. J. (1999a). *Affective norms for English words (ANEW)*. Gainesville, FL: The NIMH Center for the Study of Emotion and Attention, University of Florida.

Bradley, M. M., & Lang, P. J. (1999b). *International affective digitised sounds (IADS): Stimuli, instruction manual and affective ratings*. Gainesville, FL: The Center for Research in Psychophysiology, University of Florida.

Bonanno, G. A., & Keltner, D. (1997). Facial expressions of emotion and the course of conjugal bereavement. *Journal of Abnormal Psychology, 106*, 126–137.

Cosmides, L. (1989). The logic of social exchange: Has natural selection shaped how humans reason? Studies with the Wason selection task. *Cognition, 31*, 187–276.

Cosmides, L., & Tooby, J. (1992). Cognitive adaptations for social exchange. In J. H. Barkow, L. Cosmides, & J. Tooby (Eds.), *The adapted mind: Evolutionary psychology and the generation of culture* (pp. 163–228). New York: Oxford University Press.

Damasio, A. R. (1994). *Descartes' error: Emotion, reason and the human brain*. London: Picador.

Darwin, C. (1998). *The expression of emotion in man and animals* (3rd ed.). New York: Oxford. (Original work published 1872)

Davdison, R. J., Ekman, P., Saron, C. D., Senulis, J. A., & Friesen, W. V. (1990). Approach-withdrawal and cerebral asymmetry: Emotional expression and brain physiology I. *Journal of Personality and Social Psychology, 58*, 330–341.

DeMyer, W. (1980). *Technique of neurological examination*. New York: McGraw-Hill.

Duchenne, B. (1990). *The mechanisms of human facial expression or an electro-physiological analysis of the expression of emotions* (A. Cuthbertson, Trans.). New York: Cambridge University Press. (Original work published 1862)

Ekman, P. (2003). *Emotions revealed: Recognizing faces and feelings to improve communication and emotional life*. New York: Times Books/Henry Holt.

Ekman, P., Davidson, R. J., & Friesen, W. V. (1990). The Duchenne smile: Emotional expression and brain physiology II. *Journal of Personality and Social Psychology, 58*, 342–353.

Ekman, P., Friesen, W. V., & Hager, J. C. (2002). *Facial Action Coding System* [CD-Rom]. Salt Lake City, UT: Nexus.

Ekman, P., Friesen, W. V., & O'Sullivan, M. (1988). Smiles when lying. *Journal of Personality and Social Psychology, 54,* 414–420.

Ekman, P., Roper, G., & Hager, J. (1980). Deliberate facial movement. *Child Development, 51,* 886–891.

Fox, N. A., & Davidson, R. J. (1988). Patterns of brain electrical activity during facial signs of emotion in 10-month-old infants. *Developmental Psychology, 24,* 230–236.

Frank, M. G. (2002). Smiles, lies and emotion. In M. H. Abel (Ed.), *An empirical reflection on the smile* (pp. 15–43). Lewiston, NY: Edwin Mellen Press.

Frank, M. G., Ekman, P., & Friesen, W. V. (1993). Behavioral markers and recognizability of the smile of enjoyment. *Journal of Personality and Social Psychology, 64,* 83–93.

Frank, R., H. (1988). *Passions within reason: The strategic role of emotions.* New York: W. W. Norton.

Gazzaniga, M. S., Ivry, R. B., & Mangun, G. R. (2002). *Cognitive neuroscience: The biology of the mind* (2nd ed.). New York: W. W. Norton.

Gibson, J. J. (1979). *The ecological approach to visual perception.* Boston: Houghton Mifflin.

Halberstadt, J. B., & Niedenthal, P. M. (1997). Emotional state and the use of stimulus dimensions in judgement. *Journal of Personality and Social Psychology, 72,* 1017–1033.

Katsikitis, M., & Pilowsky, I. (1991). A controlled quantitative study of facial expression in Parkinson's disease and depression. *Journal of Nervous and Mental Disease, 179,* 683–688.

Keltner, D., & Haidt, J. (1999). Social functions of emotions at four levels of analysis. *Cognition & Emotion, 13,* 505–521.

Lang, P. J., Bradley, M. M., & Cuthbert, B. N. (2001). *International affective picture system (IAPS): Instruction manual and affective ratings.* Gainesville, FL: The Center for Research in Psychophysiology, University of Florida.

Lazarus, R. S. (1991). *Emotion and adaptation.* New York: Oxford University Press.

McArthur, L. Z., & Baron, R. M. (1983). Toward an ecological theory of social perception. *Psychological Review, 90,* 215–238.

Miles, L. (2005). *Smiles, affordances and social interaction.* Unpublished PhD dissertation, University of Canterbury.

Plutchik, R. (2003). *Emotions and life: Perspectives from psychology, biology, and evolution.* Washington, DC: APA.

Rinn, W. E. (1984). The neuropsychology of facial expression: A review of the neurological and psychological mechanisms for producing facial expressions. *Psychological Bulletin, 95,* 52–77.

Scherer. K. R., & Ceschi, G. (2000). Criteria for emotion recognition from verbal and nonverbal expression: Studying baggage loss in the airport. *Personality and Social Psychology Bulletin, 26,* 327–339.

Steiner, F. (1986). Differentiating smiles. In E. Branniger-Huber & F. Steiner (Eds.), *FACS in psychotherapy research* (pp. 13–28). Zürich: Universität Zürich.

Sternberg, G., Wiking, S., & Dahl, M. (1998). Judging words at face value: Interference in a word processing task reveals automatic processing of affective facial expressions. *Cognition & Emotion, 12,* 755–782.

Surakka, V., & Hietanen, J. K. (1998). Facial and emotional reactions to Duchenne and non-Duchenne smiles. *International Journal of Psychophysiology, 29,* 23–33.

Trivers, R. L. (1985). *Social evolution.* Menlo Park, CA: Benjamin Cummings.

Uleman, J. S., Hon, A., Roman, R. J., & Moskowitz, G. B. (1996). Online evidence for spontaneous trait inferences at encoding. *Personality & Social Psychology Bulletin, 22,* 377–394.

Walton, P. R. (2003). The Lexical Decision Computer Task (Version 1.7.21) [Computer software]. Christchurch, New Zealand: Dexterware.

Williams, L. M., Senior, C., David, A. S., Loughland, C. M., & Gordon, E. (2001). In search of the 'Duchenne smile': Evidence from eye movements. *Journal of Psychophysiology, 15,* 122–127.

Zebrowitz, L. A. (1997). *Reading faces: Window to the soul?* Boulder, CO: Westview Press.

Involvement of Anterior Cingulate and Prefrontal Cortices in the Stroop Colour–Word Task: EEG and fMRI Studies

Kylie J. Barnett, Scott L. Fairhall,
Gjurgjica Badzakova-Trajkov, Clare Morton,
and Ian J. Kirk

The Stroop colour naming task was introduced some 60 years ago (Stroop, 1935) and has become 'a paradigmatic measure of selective attention' (Carter, Mintun, & Cohen, 1995). In what might be described as the classic Stroop task, subjects are asked to name the colour in which the word is printed. Response times to the relevant task dimension are longer in incongruent conditions (e.g., the word BLUE printed in red ink), relative to a control condition (e.g., JUMP printed in red; or XXXX printed in red). It has also been repeatedly found that employing a congruent condition (e.g., BLUE printed in blue) results in what is known as Stroop task facilitation. That is, response times are shorter in this condition relative to that in the control condition.

It is generally agreed that the behavioural results from the Stroop task are due to a conflict between stimuli or responses that results in a competition for the allocation of attention to aspects of the stimuli, and/or in the selection and monitoring of responses. The majority of studies also implicate the anterior cingulate cortex (ACC) in at least some aspects of the task. However, in spite of, or perhaps because of, the recent plethora of imaging experiments investigating Stroop task performance, the neural correlates underlying different aspects of the Stroop effect remain an area of contention. As will be outlined below, the relative contributions of the ACC and the dorsolateral prefrontal cortex (DLFPC) is a particular source of much current debate.

The neural correlates of control in the Stroop task are of more than academic interest, due to the utility of the Stroop task as a diagnostic tool in disorders such as schizophrenia, mania, obsessive-compulsive disorder, attention-deficit hyperactivity disorder (ADHD; McGrath, Scheldt, Welham, & Clair, 1997; Carter, Mintun, Nichols, & Cohen, 1997; Carter & Barch, 2000), and in patients with memory disturbances (Hanninen et al., 1997; Fisher, Freed, & Corkin, 1990). Disturbances in ACC functioning in particular have been observed in a variety of these patient groups (Carter & Barch, 2000) and it is important therefore to clarify its relative role in tasks such as the Stroop.

In the following brief review, recent work employing either functional imaging (positron emission tomography (PET) and functional magnetic resonance imaging (fMRI)) or scalp recorded event-related potentials (ERPs) will be described. In the process, different recent perspectives regarding the specific contributions of ACC and DLPFC will be outlined. Subsequently, recent investigations carried out in our laboratory into the neural substrates of the Stroop effect will be outlined. Our experiments have employed both fMRI and ERPs. It is well known that fMRI has excellent spatial resolution, but poor temporal resolution, whereas in contrast ERPs have excellent temporal, but relatively poor spatial resolution. We argue here that a combination of techniques of this sort will be required to address not only the issue of the neural substrates of the Stroop effect currently under discussion, but many similar questions in cognitive neuroscience in general.

fMRI and PET Imaging and the Neural Substrates of Control in the Stroop Task

In a recent review MacLeod and MacDonald (2000) note that a large number of recent PET (e.g., Pardo, Pardo, Janer, & Raichle, 1990; Bench et al., 1993; George et al., 1994; Carter et al., 1995) and fMRI (e.g., Bush et al., 1998; Carter et al., 2000) studies have been performed where cerebral activity in the incongruent condition is compared to that in a variety of control conditions. In the overwhelming majority of these experiments, maximal differential activation between incongruent and control conditions has been observed in the ACC (see also the meta-analysis of Bush, Luu, & Posner, 2000).

However, a number of other regions have been observed to be differentially activated also. Most consistently activated among these appear to be regions of the prefrontal cortex and, in particular, the DLPFC (e.g., MacDonald, Cohen, Stenger, & Carter, 2000; Milham, Banich, Claus, & Cohen, 2003). Nevertheless, MacLeod and MacDonald (2000) conclude that given the consistent observation that ACC is most activated in the incongruent condition, this structure seems certain to be involved in mediating processes underlying Stroop task interference resolution. However, as will be discussed in some detail below, it is still a matter of some debate as to whether the ACC is involved in the application of attentional control per se, or in the detection of some informational conflict, or in the monitoring of some aspect of performance.

Perhaps the most influential general view of ACC functioning in tasks such as the Stroop task is that outlined by Posner and Dehaene (1994). On this view, the ACC performs an 'executive' role in the control of attention. In this view, the ACC is involved in the top-down implementation of selection and processing of stimuli that need to be acted upon, playing an executive role in the control of attention.

In contrast, Carter and colleagues proposed that the ACC is principally acts as an 'error detector', or at least a detector of conditions in which errors are likely to occur (Carter et al., 1998), a 'performance monitor' (Carter et al., 1998; MacDonald et al., 2000), or, in its most recent guise, a 'conflict monitor' (van Veen & Carter, 2002). According to this general view, ACC activity will most likely be observed in conditions of information conflict. The ACC detects these conditions and signals the need for a high degree of attentional control. Carter and colleagues maintain that the top-down attentional control itself may be mediated by other structures such as the DLPFC (e.g. MacDonald et al., 2000).

A similar perspective to that of Carter and colleagues is held by the Milham/Banich/Cohan group (see e.g., Banich et al., 2000; Milham et al., 2001; Milham, Banich, Claus, & Cohen, 2003). They also propose that the DLPFC, rather than the ACC, plays the predominant role in implementing top-down attentional control. The ACC, they argue, is involved primarily in response related processes such as conflict monitoring (discussed above), error detection (see also Gehring & Knight, 2000; Gehring, Goss, & Coles, 1993), or response facilitation or inhibition (see also Paus, 2001; Paus, Petrides, Evans, & Meyer, 2003). Another similar, but more extreme, position is taken by Zysset, Muller, Lohmann, and von Cramon (2001), who suggest that the ACC is not specifically involved in input processes at all in the Stroop task. They suggest that ACC is involved instead in motor output preparation processes.

The suggestions that ACC is principally involved in response-related processes is, as has been pointed out by MacLeod and MacDonald (2000), difficult to reconcile with the observation that in the Stroop congruent condition increased ACC activation has been observed relative to a control (e.g., Bench et al., 1993: Carter et al., 1995). They argue that in the congruent case, any conflict must arise in deciding which dimension to attend to (colour or word). As the two sources of information are in accord in the congruent condition, response conflict is unlikely.

As will be detailed below, we attempted to determine the extent to which response-related processes contribute to activations observed in the Stroop task by employing a covert Stroop paradigm in both ERP and fMRI experiments, in which no motor response is required (either manual or verbal). This is compared to an overt paradigm in which a motor response is made (a key press).

ERP and the Stroop Task

Relative to the number of studies employing PET and fMRI, those employing event-related potentials (ERPs) are surprisingly rare. This is perhaps surprising, given that ERPs provide temporal resolution in the millisecond range and potentially allow investigation of the temporal dynamics of neural activity underlying the Stroop effect.

The earliest studies to take advantage of the ERP technique to investigate the Stroop task were those of Duncan-Johnson (Duncan-Johnson & Kopell, 1981). She identified a P300 (a positive going wave with a latency of about 300 msec) elicited in various Stroop test conditions. However, whereas the subjects' reaction time varied with the congruence of the word and the colour in which it was printed in the usual way, the latency of the concomitantly evoked P300 wave remained constant. It was suggested therefore, in agreement with some of the proposals discussed above, that the behavioural Stroop effect is largely due to competition at the level of the response.

Subsequent studies using ERPs to investigate the Stroop task have found significant differences in the amplitude of the waveform evoked in the congruent relative to the incongruent condition for instance (Aine & Harter, 1984; Schack, Chen, Mescha, & Witte, 1999; West & Alain, 1999; Rebai et al., 1997; Liotti et al., 2000). Duncan-Johnson and Kopell (1981) on the other hand found no systematic relationship between the amplitude of the P300 and the eliciting stimulus. This somewhat constrains their interpretation. In addition, most of the subsequent studies do not interpret the Stroop-related waveform as a P300. Although comparison between studies is complicated by the number of different referencing systems in use (i.e. potentials at each electrode are recorded with reference to another (reference) electrode), the majority of studies have found that a frontal, or fronto-central negative-going wave is systematically related to manipulations in Stroop task conditions (Aine & Harter, 1984; Schack, Chen, Mescha, & Witte, 1999; West & Alain, 1999; Rebai, Bernard, & Lannou, 1997; Liotti, Woldorff, Perez, & Mayberg, 2000). This is consistent at least with an assumed frontal site of generation. It is possible that the 'P300' observed by Duncan-Johnson and Kopell was a passive reflection of a frontal negative-going wave.

Most of the studies mentioned above employed relatively few electrodes, which makes estimations of the neural sources of the elicited potentials difficult. One recent exception is the study of Liotti et al. (2000). These authors employed a relatively dense electrode array (64 electrodes) and found a significant amplitude difference between the evoked potentials elicited by congruent and incongruent Stroop stimuli. This difference was maximal in the 350 to 450 ms latency window. Further, these authors employed equivalent dipole source modeling (Scherg & Picton, 1984) to estimate the neural source of the differences in evoked potential, and found that the estimated sources were in the ACC. Thus, the data of Liotti et al. support the position that the ACC is relatively more activated during, and thus relatively more involved in mediating, the conflict in the incongruent Stroop condition (relative to the congruent condition).

The Current Experiments

The experiments described below were designed to resolve, if possible, some of the discrepancies in the preceding overview of the literature. In general, it seems that the two major experimental techniques employed (EEG vs. fMRI or PET) may themselves be responsible for some of these discrepancies. This is not surprising, given that the two procedures measure rather different aspects of neurodynamic processes. EEG has relatively good temporal resolution, but relatively poor spatial resolution, and the reverse is true of fMRI or PET. However, the spatial resolution of EEG can be considerably improved by the use of high-density EEG (we used 128 channels), combined with neural source estimation (e.g., LORETA, see Methods). We employed both EEG and fMRI to determine the extent to which similar conclusions can be reached regarding the contribution of different neural regions to different aspects of the Stroop task.

A second issue is the extent to which response-related processes contribute to conclusions regarding the contribution of various anatomical regions in the Stoop task. Hence, we performed an initial EEG study to determine if the activation patterns in a covert Stroop task (one in which no motor response is required) are similar to those obtained in the more commonly employed response task. A covert task is of considerable benefit in fMRI, as movement artifacts due to a verbal or manual response can be eliminated. Finally, most (though certainly not all; see e.g., Carter et al., 1995) work on the Stroop task concentrates on the difference in neural activity (or behaviour) in the incongruent condition relative to that in the congruent condition. Here we illustrate in our fMRI studies that also considering congruent-control and incongruent-control contrasts gives a broader picture of the networks involved in various aspects of the Stroop task.

Methods

EEG

Subjects

Participants were nine males (six right-handed) and six females (five right-handed). They were all post-graduate students of the University of Auckland, had an average age of 24 years, had no history of neurological disorder, and all had normal or corrected normal vision.

Stimuli and Procedure

The display consisted of a series of characters of three types corresponding to the control, congruent and incongruent Stroop conditions. In the control Stroop condition, coloured non-word X-strings (e.g., XXX) were presented, printed in red blue, green or yellow. String lengths of 3, 4, 5, or 6 were randomly presented to match the string lengths of the congruent and incongruent conditions below. In the congruent Stroop condition, letters spelling the words RED BLUE GREEN or YELLOW were presented. The colour of the word-strings matched the word meaning (i.e., the print colour of RED was red, and so on).

In the incongruent condition, the stimuli were the same except the print colour never matched word meaning (e.g., RED would be printed in blue). Each letter subtended two degrees of visual angle, vertically and horizontally. The conditions were presented randomly.

Subjects performed the task in two response conditions. The overt task required the subjects to make a manual key-press corresponding to the four possible ink-colour targets (RED BLUE GREEN or YELLOW). In the covert condition, no response was required, and the participant was asked to name the ink colour silently to themselves.

EEG Apparatus and ERP Averaging

EEG was recorded using 128 channel Ag/AgCl nets (Electrical Geodesics, Inc.). Signals were recorded continuously (250 Hz sampling rate; 0.1–39.2 Hz analogue band pass) with Electrical Geodesics Inc. amplifiers (200 MV input impedance) and acquisition software running on a Power Macintosh 9600/200 computer with a National Instruments PCI-1200 12 bit analogue to digital conversion card. Electrode impedances ranged from 10 to 40 k, which is an acceptable range for the high impedance amplifiers of the system. EEG was initially acquired using a common vertex (Cz) reference and re-referenced in off-line analyses to the average reference (Bertrand, Perrin, & Pernier, 1985). Use of the average reference recovers Cz as an active electrode, resulting in 129 channels of data. Eye artefact was removed from individual trial epochs using procedures from Jervis, Nichols, Allen, Hudson, and Johnson (1985).

Data Analysis

Time windows for analysis were determined by the following procedure. First, the global field power (GFP) of the ERPs for the three Stroop conditions were calculated and visually examined. GFP is computed as the mean potential deviation of all electrodes in the recording array. From this potential distribution a reference-independent measure of GFP is computed as the mean of all potential differences within the field (Skrandies, 1995). GFP thus reflects the spatial standard deviation across all electrodes at a particular time. Potential fields at a particular time with high peaks and troughs and steep gradients are associated with high field power values. Time frames were selected from the GFP for further investigation. For instance, the topography of the difference between the ERPs elicited in incongruent minus congruent Stroop stimuli can be examined.

Although the details will not be reported here, in general, the degree to which (and the topographic location) of significantly larger ERPs to one stimulus type relative to another were calculated with PCA-derived Bonferroni corrected t tests at each electrode using the method of Hopf and Mangun (2000). Comparison of scalp distributions were tested by analysis of variance (ANOVA) of normalised data, employing using Greenhouse–Geisser corrected degrees of freedom as employed by McCarthy and Wood (1985; see also Hamm, Johnson, & Kirk, 2002). Source localisations were performed using low-resolution electromagnetic tomography (LORETA; Pascual-Marqui, Michel, & Lehmann 1994). This method is preferred over single dipole modelling because it is unlikely that ERPs in the Stroop reflect activation differences arising from a single brain area.

fMRI

Subjects

Participants were five right-handed males and one left-handed male (average age = 26 years). They were all postgraduate students of the University of Auckland with no history of neurological disorder, and all had uncorrected normal vision. All had participated in the EEG experiments.

Stimuli

The stimuli were generated on a computer and projected to a screen visible via a prism from the scanning bed. The display consisted of a series of characters of three types — the three Stroop conditions, and a baseline condition. In the baseline condition a crosshair ('+') was displayed at the centre of the screen. The crosshair subtended two degrees of visual angle vertically and horizontally. The physical characteristics of the stimuli for the control, congruent and incongruent conditions were the same as for the EEG experiments.

fMRI Scanning Apparatus and Procedure

Functional imaging was performed on a 3 Tesla GE LX Horizon MR scanning system. A block design was employed. Each activation epoch consisted of a 30-second baseline followed by a 30-second experimental block of either control, congruent, or incongruent stimuli. In each experimental block, stimuli were randomly presented for 3 seconds, every 3 seconds. Each of the baseline-experimental block cycles was presented twice.

Gradient echo EPI images were aquired during testing, using the following parameters: repetition time (TR) = 3000 msec.; TE = 40 msec.; Flip = 40; 1 NEX, 22 slices (whole brain coverage), slice thickness = 4 mm, with 1 mm gap; acquisition matrix = 128×128; field of view = 240 mm; pixel size = 1.875 $\times$ 1.875 mm^2. Imaging time per subject was 6 minutes, and resulted in 120 images. The subjects' task in each experimental block was to covertly name the ink colour of the stimuli.

Data Analysis

Statistical parametric mapping (SPM99; Wellcome Department of Imaging Neuroscience, 2000) was used to realign data, normalise, smooth, and analyse task-related differences in fMRI activation. Head movement correction was performed, and realigned images were spatially normalised to correct for subject differences in brain size and shape. The normalised images were then spatially soothed with a Gaussian filter (FWHM = 4 mm). Condition effects were estimated according to the general linear model at each voxel in brain space ($p < .001$; uncorrected).

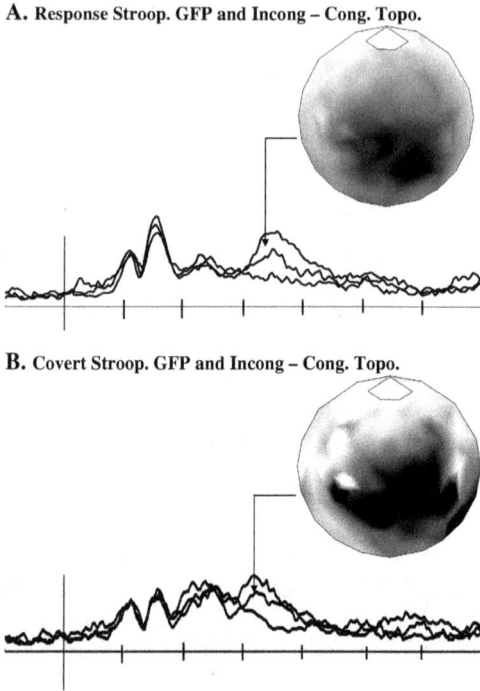

A. Response Stroop. GFP and Incong – Cong. Topo.

B. Covert Stroop. GFP and Incong – Cong. Topo.

Figure 1

The Global Field Power (GFP) is shown for the incongruent, congruent and control conditions for the Stroop task requiring a manual response (A), and the covert version (B). Extent of Y axes = 1 µV, tick marks on X axis = 100 msec. The significant differences between ERPs are seen in the 300 to 400 msec time window in both response and covert tasks. In this time window, maximum GFP is observed in the incongruent condition, and minimum GFP in the control condition. The congruent condition evokes an intermediate GFP. The scalp topography of the incongruent minus congruent difference wave is also shown. Average reference, white is negative potential, black is positive. Note similarities between the topographies of the response and covert tasks.

Results

EEG

In both the overt and the covert conditions, GFP showed the expected significant differences in ERP between the control, congruent and incongruent conditions of the Stroop task. These differences also occurred in the expected time window of 300 to 400 ms. (see Figure 1). The incongruent versus congruent difference waveforms for the overt and covert conditions exhibited scalp distributions that were not significantly different, suggesting that they result from a similar configuration of brain generators.

Loreta source localisation was performed for a number of difference-wave comparisons. The result of localising the incongruent versus congruent difference waveform for the covert condition is shown in Figure 2. Of particular

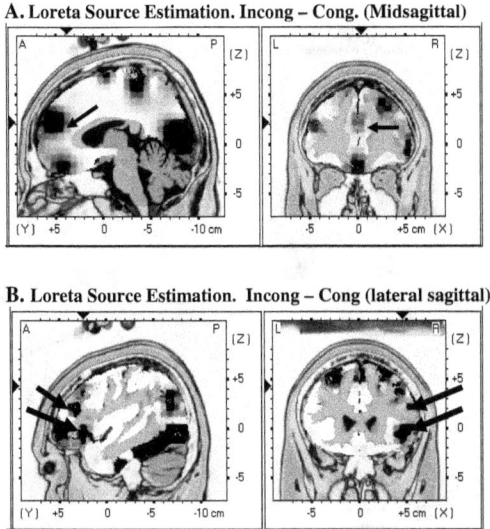

A. Loreta Source Estimation. Incong – Cong. (Midsagittal)

B. Loreta Source Estimation. Incong – Cong (lateral sagittal)

Figure 2
Results of Loreta source estimation for the incongruent minus congruent difference wave in the covert version of the Stroop task. A. Midsagittal and equivalent coronal view. Arrow points to ACC. B. Lateral sagittal and equivalent coronal view. Top arrows point to dorsolateral frontal cortex, bottom arrows point to ventolateral frontal cortex.

interest here is that a network of neural sources that include the ACC (and an area dorsal and anterior to it), the DLPFC, and the ventral lateral prefrontal cortex is activated in this task. It should be noted too that a similar pattern was observed with the incongruent versus congruent difference waveform in the overt condition, and in the congruent-control and the incongruent-control subtractions in both overt and covert versions of the task (data not shown).

fMRI

Significant activations in the congruent versus control, incongruent versus control, and incogruent versus congruent comparisons are shown in Figure 3. In both the congruent versus control and incongruent versus control comparisons (Figures 3A and 3B), an area of the cingulate gyrus is activated, although in the incongruent versus control contrast, activation is more caudal and dorsal than in the congruent versus control contrast, in which activation is in the ACC. Both these comparisons show significant activations in fronto-lateral areas also, particularly in the left hemisphere.

The most obvious difference in the incongruent versus congruent comparison is the absence of any activation in the cingulate. Instead, significant activations in frontal cortex are confined to the dorsal and ventrolateral frontal cortex. In contrast to the left frontal activations in the comparisons involving

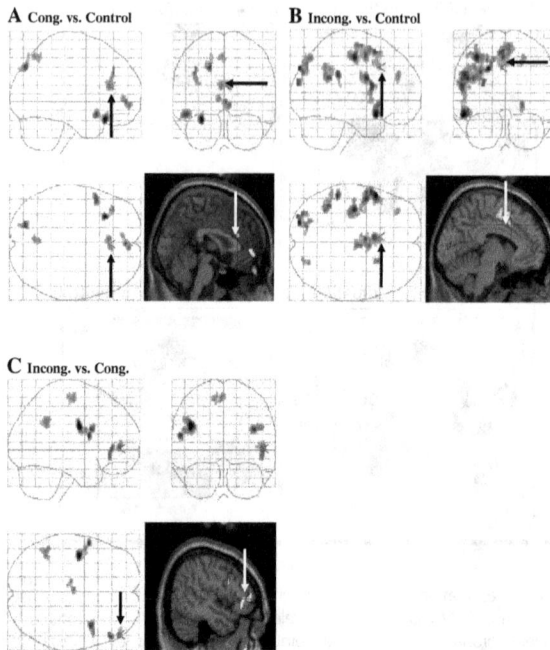

Figure 3
Significant (p <.001; uncorrected; voxel threshold = 40) activations for the congruent vs. control (A), incongruent vs. control (B), and incongruent vs. congruent (C) contrasts. Arrows in A and B point to cingulate gyrus, and in C to the dorsolateral and ventrolateral frontal cortex.

the control condition, however, activations in the incongruent versus congruent comparison are right lateralised.

Discussion

The initial goal of the EEG experiments reported here was to determine if the covert version of the Stroop task leads to similar differences in ERPs as those that have been repeatedly shown in various overt response paradigms. Comparison of GFPs in the timeframe in which task differences have previously been observed, comparison of the topography of differences in ERPs evoked in various Stroop conditions, and the use of low-resolution source estimates, suggest that similar neural processes are indeed involved in the overt and covert versions of the task. That the Stroop task can be performed covertly has considerable practical value, as activations can be measured in fMRI without confounds from motor processes or movement artifacts produced by overt responding. As noted above, it is also possible to determine the extent to which motor preparation processes are involved in generating activations observed during the task (see, for instance, Zysset et al., 2001). That being said, it should be noted that the absence of a required overt motor response does not necessarily preclude the preparation for one.

The fMRI studies reported here show the following general pattern. Cingulate and left lateral frontal activation is seen when either the congruent or the incongruent condition is compared to the control condition. When the incongruent condition is compared to the congruent condition, however, right frontal activation is observed, and cingulated activation is absent.

As can be seen in Figures 3A and 3B, somewhat different regions of the cingulate are activated in the two control contrasts in the current experiment. It is possible that these two task contrasts activate different regions of the cingulate. This might be expected, as the incongruent task involves conflicting information streams, while the congruent contrast does not. Certainly different regions of the cingulate have previously been shown to be activated in different tasks (e.g., Paus, 2001; Badgaiyan & Posner, 1998). However, when either of the control contrasts was exclusively masked with the other, a procedure that reveals activations in one contrast that are significantly greater than the other, all cingulate activation disappears. Hence, presumably widespread cingulate activation can be considered as equivalent in the two control contrasts. Consistent with this position, in the incongruent versus congruent contrast, cingulate activation also disappears, again suggesting the congruent and incongruent tasks are equivalent in terms of cingulate activation.

As both the control contrasts produce cingulate activation, it might be suggested that the equivalent additional cognitive process is being mediated by the cingulate in both the congruent and incongruent condition relative to the baseline. The baseline condition in the fMRI experiment is composed of coloured 'X's, and in terms of the task, represents a single source of information — the colour of the 'X's. Both the congruent and incongruent conditions have two sources of information, the colour of the printing and the colour represented by the word spelling. In only one condition (incongruent) is this information in conflict. Thus activation of the cingulate in the two contrasts with the control likely reflects the existence of two sources of information, rather than the presence or absence of conflict. Thus, it is likely that the cingulate is involved in top-down attentional allocation processes, and is involved here in the allocation of attention to one source of information rather than the other. Of course, given that left lateral areas are also equivalently activated in the two control contrasts, it is likely that these areas also contribute to the attentional allocation process (see below). Nevertheless, the involvement of the cingulate (including ACC) in control contrast activations reported here is in general agreement with the suggested role of the ACC in the 'executive' control of attention outlined by Posner and Dehaene (1994), rather than in error detection or some motor preparation process. That being said, lateral frontal cortices appear to be involved in this process also, although not exclusively, as has been suggested by the Carter or Banich groups (see Introduction).

In the incongruent versus congruent contrast, cingulate activation disappears entirely, suggesting that no additional activation of this region occurs in the incongruent condition. In this contrast, significantly more activation of the right dorsolateral and ventrolateral frontal regions is observed. It might be suggested therefore, that these right lateral frontal regions are more likely involved in conflict monitoring or error detection, rather than the ACC as has been suggested by the Carter or Banich groups (see Introduction).

These issues are complicated further, however, by the ERP source localisation data (see Figure 2). These data indicate that in the incongruent minus congruent condition, neural activations occur in the region of the ACC (in agreement with previous ERP studies), and also in the dorsal and ventral lateral frontal cortex. Further, although most marked when the sources of the incongruent minus congruent difference ERP are estimated, qualitatively similar distributions are seen in all contrasts.

That rather different conclusions regarding the neural substrates of a cognitive task might be reached from ERP data is not unexpected as EEG and fMRI measure quite different aspects of neural activity. For instance, an ERP component might reflect the entrainment (or resetting) of ongoing neural activity. This may result in a change of pattern of activity, rather than the increase in activity (synaptic drive or cell discharge) that is required for significant differences in an fMRI contrast.

On the combined evidence presented here then, it is perhaps reasonable to suggest that a network of regions that include the cingulate, the dorsolateral, and the ventrolatral frontal cortices, may contribute to all aspects of processing in the Stroop task. This suggestion is not inconsistent with those of Owen et al. (e.g., Rushworth & Owen, 1998), who propose that the ventrolateral frontal cortex is involved in conditional response selection and/or attentional switching, and the dorsolateral frontal cortex is involved in active manipulation or monitoring of information. These are similar to the 'executive' function usually assigned to the ACC, and all these regions may be necessary for coordinated executive processing to occur. However, it is likely that differential relative activation in different nodes of the network occurs in different subprocesses of the Stroop task, and indeed other attentional tasks as well. It is these changes that are amenable to study with fMRI. Nevertheless, it may be premature, and possibly an error as a general strategy, to attempt to assign a particular cognitive process to a particular anatomical neural substrate. Depending on the relative activity within particular nodes of a network, and the dynamics of coordinated activity between nodes, a neural system as a whole may contribute to different aspects of a cognitive task, and may indeed contribute to many different cognitive tasks. As a final suggestion, it is likely that a combination of experimental techniques, as employed here, will be necessary to elucidate the complexities of neural integration that underpin even the simplest of cognitive tasks.

References

Aine, C. J., & Harter, M. R. (1984). Event-related potentials to Stroop stimuli: Color and word processing. *Annals of the New York Academy of Science, 425,* 152–153.

Banich, M. T., Milham, M. P., Atchley, R. A., Cohen, N. J., Webb, A., Wszalek, T., et al. (2000). Prefrontal regions play a predominant role in imposing an attentional 'set': Evidence from fMRI. *Cognitive and Brain Research, 10,* 1–9.

Badgaiyan, R. D., & Posner, M. I. (1998). Mapping the cingulate cortex in response selection and monitoring. *Neuroimage, 7,* 255–260.

Bench, C., Frith, C. D., Grasby, P. M., Friston, K. J., Paulesu, E., Frackowiak, R. S. J., et al. (1993). Investigations of the functional anatomy of attention using the Stroop test. *Neuropsychologia, 31,* 907–922.

Bertrand, O., Perrin, F., & Pernier, J. (1985). A theoretical justification of the average reference in topographic evoked potential studies. *Electroencephalography and Clinical Neurophysiology, 62,* 462–464.

Bush, G., Whalen, P., Rosen, B., Jenike, M., McInerney, S., & Rauch, S. (1998). The counting Stroop: An interference task specialized for functional neuroimaging- validation study with fMRI. *Human Brain Mapping, 6,* 270–282.

Bush, G., Luu, P., & Posner, M. I. (2000). Cognitive and emotional influences in anterior cingulate cortex. *Trends in Cognitive Science, 4,* 215–222.

Carter, C. S., Mintun, M., & Cohen, J. D. (1995). Interference and facilitation effects during selective attention: An $H_2^{15}O$ PET study of Stroop task performance. *Neuroimage, 2,* 264–272.

Carter, C. S., Mintun, M., Nichols, T., & Cohen, J. D. (1997). Anterior cingulate gyrus dysfunction and selective attention deficits in schizophrenia: $H_2^{15}O$ PET study during single-trial Stroop performance. *American Journal of Psychiatry, 154,* 1670–1675.

Carter, C. S., Braver, T. S., Barch, D. M., Botvinick, M. M., Noll, D., & Cohen, J. D. (1998). Anterior cingulate cortex, error detection, and online monitoring of performance. *Science, 280,* 747–749.

Carter, C. S., & Barch, D. M. (2000). Attention, memory and language disturbances in schizophrenia: Characteristics and implications. In C. Andrade (Ed.), *Advances in psychiatry* (Vol. 3, pp. 45–72). London: Oxford University Press.

Carter, C. S., MacDonald, A. M., Botvinick, M. M., Ross, L. L., Stenger, V. A., Noll, D., et al. (2000). Parsing executive processes: Strategic vs, evaluative functions of the anterior cingulate cortex. *Proceedings of the National Academy of Science (U.S.A.), 97,* 1944–1948.

Duncan-Johnson, C. C., & Kopell, B. S. (1981). The Stroop effect: Brain potentials localize the source of interference. *Science, 214,* 938–940.

Fisher, L. M., Freed, D. M., & Corkin, S. (1990). Stroop color-word test performance in patients with Alzheimer's disease. *Journal of Clinical and Experimental Neuropsychology, 12,* 745–748.

Gehring, W. J., Goss, B., & Coles, M. (1993). A neural system for error detection and compensation. *Psychological Science, 4,* 385–390.

Gehring, W. J., & Knight, R. T. (2000). Prefrontal-cingulate interactions in action monitoring *Nature/Neuroscience, 3,* 516–520.

George, M. S., Ketter, T. A., Parekh, P. I., Rosinsky, N., Ring, H., Casey, B., et al. (1994). Regional brain activity when selecting response despite interference: An $H_2^{15}O$ PET study of the Stroop and emotional Stroop. *Human Brain Mapping, 1,* 194–209.

Hanninen, T., Hallikainen, M., Koivisto, K., Partanen, K., Laakso, M. P., Riekkinen, P. J., Sr., et al. (1997). Decline of frontal lobe functions in subjects with age-associated memory impairment. *Neurology, 149,* 148–153.

Hamm, J. P., Johnson, B. W., & Kirk, I. J. (2002). Comparison of the N300 and N400 ERPs to picture stimuli in congruent and incongruent contexts. *Clinical Neurophysiology, 113,* 1339–1350.

Hopf, J. M., & Mangun, G. R. (2000). Shifting visual attention in space: An electrophysiological analysis using high spatial resolution mapping. *Clinical Neurophysiology, 111,* 241–257.

Jervis, B. W., Nichols, M. J., Allen, E. M., Hudson, N. R., & Johnson, T. E. (1985). The assessment of two methods for removing eye movement artefact from the EEG. *Electroencephalography and Clinical Neurophysiology, 61,* 444–452.

Liotti, M., Woldorff, M. G., Perez, R., & Mayberg, H. S. (2000). An ERP study of the temporal course of the Stroop color-word interference effect. *Neuropsychologia, 38,* 701–711.

McCarthy, G., & Wood, C. C. (1985). Scalp distributions of event-related potentials: an ambiguity associated with analysis of variance models. *Electroencephalography and Clinical Neurophysiology, 62,* 203–208.

MacDonald, A. W., Cohen, J. D., Stenger, V. A., & Carter, C. S. (2000). Dissociating the role of the dorsolateral prefrontal cortex and anterior d cortex in cognitive control. *Science, 288,* 1835–1838.

MacLeod, C. M., & MacDonald, P. A. (2000). Interdimensional interference in the Stroop effect: Uncovering the cognitive and neural anatomy of attention. *Trends in Cognitive Science, 4,* 383–391.

McGrath, J., Scheldt, S., Welham, J., & Clair, A. (1997). Performance on tests sensitive to impaired executive ability in schizophrenia, mania and well controls. *Schizophrenia Research, 26,* 127–137.

Milham, M. P., Banich, M. T., Webb, A., Barad, V., Cohen, N. J., Wszalek, T., et al. (2001). The relative involvement of anterior cingulate and prefrontal cortex in attentional control depends on the nature of the conflict. *Cognitive and Brain Research, 12,* 467–473.

Milham, M. P., Banich, M. T., Claus, E. D., & Cohen, N. J. (2003). Practice-related effects demonstrate complementary roles of anterior d and prefrontal cortices in attentional control. *Neuroimage, 18,* 483–493.

Pascual-Marqui, R. D., Michel, C. M., & Lehmann, D. (1994). Low resolution electromagnetic tomography: a new method for localizing electrical activity in the brain. *International Journal of Psychophysiology, 18,* 49–65.

Pardo, J. V., Pardo, P. J., Janer, K. W., & Raichle, M. E. (1990). The anterior cingulate cortex mediates processing selection in the Stroop attentional conflict paradigm. *Proceedings of the National Academy of Science (U.S.A.), 87,* 256–259.

Paus, T. (2001). Primate anterior cingulate cortex, where motor control, drive and cognition interface. *Nature/Neuroscience, 2,* 417–424.

Paus, T., Petrides, M., Evans, C., & Meyer, E. (2003). Role of the human anterior cingulate cortex in the control of oculomotor, manual, and speech responses: A positron emission tomography study. *Journal of Neurophysiology, 70,* 453–469.

Posner, M. I., & Dehaene, S. (1994). Attentional networks. *Trends in Neuroscience, 17,* 75–79.

Rebai, M., Bernard, C., & Lannou, J. (1997). The Stroop test evokes a negative brain potential, the N400. *International Journal of Neuroscience, 91,* 85–94.

Rushworth, F. S., & Owen, A. M. (1998). The functional organization of the lateral frontal cortex: Conjecture or conjuncture in the electrophysiological literature. *Trends in Cognitive Sciences, 2,* 46–53.

Schack, B., Chen, C. A. N., Mescha, S., & Witte, H. (1999). Instantaneous EEG coherence analysis during the Stroop task. *Clinical Neurophysiology, 110,* 1410–1426.

Scherg, M., & Picton, T. W. (1984). Separation and identification of event-related potential components by brain-electrical source analysis (BESA). *Electroencephalography and Clinical Neurophysiology, 42,* 24–37.

Stroop, J. R. (1935). Studies of interference in serial verbal reactions. *Journal of Experimental Psychology, 18,* 643–662.

Skrandies, W. (1995). Visual information processing: Topography of brain electrical activity. *Biological Psychology, 40,* 1–15.

Van Veen, V., & Carter, C. S. (2002). The anterior cingulate as a conflict monitor: fMRI and ERP studies. *Physiology and Behavior, 77,* 477–482.

Wellcome Department of Imaging Neuroscience. (2000). Statistical Parametric Mapping 99 [Computer software]. Retrieved June 25, 2000, from http://www.fil.ion.ucl.ac.uk/spm

West, R., & Alain, C. (1999). Event-related neural activity associated with the Stroop task. *Cognitive and Brain Research, 8,* 157–164.

Zysset, S., Muller, K., Lohmann, G., & von Cramon, D. Y. (2001). Color-word matching Stroop task: Separating interference and response conflict. *Neuroimage, 13,* 29–36.

Intentional and Unintentional Memory Processes: A Tutorial on Measurements From the Retrieval Intentionality Criterion and Process Dissociation Procedures

Todd C. Jones

Considerable effort has been put into measuring intentional and unintentional memory processes in the past couple of decades. The retrieval intentionality criterion method (Schacter, Bowers, & Booker, 1989) and the process dissociation procedure (Jacoby, 1991; Jacoby, Toth, & Yonelinas, 1993) are two major approaches that have been developed to obtain accurate measures of intentional and unintentional processes. These two methods were directly compared with word stem retrieval cues. Below, the basic background information is summarised, two new experiments are described, and the merits and weaknesses of the different approaches are discussed.

Historical Background

Traditional tests of memory such as free recall, cued recall, and recognition are considered to measure intentional memory processes, though unintentional memory processes are likely to provide a basis of responding with stronger retrieval cues, as in recognition memory. Typically, these tests reflect the predominant use of conceptual memory processes, though conditions can be created that emphasise perceptual processes (Rajaram, 1993; Roediger, Weldon, & Challis, 1989). The instructions for these tests refer participants back to an earlier study episode, and participants are explicitly directed to retrieve items from the study episode. Thus, these tests are generally referred to as explicit or direct memory tests (e.g., Graf & Schacter, 1985; Richardson-Klavehn & Bjork, 1988).

Implicit or indirect memory tests, in contrast, measure unintentional memory processes (Graf & Schacter, 1985; for a tutorial review, see Roediger, Guynn, & Jones, 1994; for more full reviews, see Richardson-Klavehn & Bjork, 1988; Roediger & McDermott, 1993; Schacter, 1987). Intentional retrieval of items from an earlier study episode (i.e., consciously thinking back to the study episode) is not required to perform an implicit memory test and, in fact, the use of intentional memory on implicit tests is unwanted. Implicit tests can be separated into perceptual or conceptual tests (Roediger et al., 1989), but the focus here will be on perceptual implicit memory tests (e.g., word stem completion, word fragment completion, picture fragment identification, perceptual identification). On perceptual implicit tests, a benefit of a prior study presentation is established by comparing the accuracy or reaction time (RT) for briefly presented or perceptually degraded stimuli corresponding to studied items to that for stimuli corresponding to new items (a baseline condition). A higher accuracy rate for studied items (or faster RT in some experiments) relative to new items demonstrates *priming* or a *priming effect*. Perceptual implicit tests are sensitive to perceptual manipulations from study to test (e.g., higher priming for match compared to non-match conditions) but not conceptual manipulations (Roediger & McDermott, 1993).

The point to be highlighted here is that the retrieval mode or intention to retrieve study items differs for explicit and implicit tests: performance on explicit tests, particularly recall tasks, is thought to tap retrieval from an intentional (voluntary) memory process, whereas performance on implicit tests is thought to tap retrieval from an unintentional (involuntary) memory process.[1] The difference in retrieval mode is important in that amnesics can perform poorly relative to normal individuals on an explicit memory test but can produce intact priming scores for perceptual, as well as conceptual, implicit memory tests (e.g., Graf, Shimamura, & Squire, 1985).

There has been a concern that normal participants may think back to the study episode to aid performance on an implicit test (referred to as explicit contamination; Schacter et al., 1989). Some researchers have suggested that this worry has been overwrought (e.g., see Tulving's comment in Roediger & McDermott's, 1993, review), but the retrieval intentionality criterion method (Schacter et al., 1989) and process dissociation procedure (Jacoby et al., 1993) have aimed to address this potential problem.

Retrieval Intentionality Criterion (RIC)

The retrieval intentionality criterion (RIC) is meant to guard against an intentional retrieval strategy on an implicit test. The idea is to hold all conditions constant across implicit and explicit test conditions, including the retrieval cues, and to vary only the test instructions. If different patterns of data are obtained for the implicit and explicit test (i.e., a dissociation is obtained), then one gains assurance that explicit contamination was not a problem. Similar patterns of data for the two test conditions leave open the possibility that the measure on the implicit test may be contaminated. However, similar patterns on one variable for the two tests could be interpreted as a true similarity if a simultaneous dissociation is obtained with a second variable (e.g., Challis & Sidhu, 1993).

Process Dissociation Procedure (ProcessDP)

One possibility is that most, if not all memory tasks utilise intentional and unintentional processes (Jacoby, 1991). The process dissociation procedure (ProcessDP) attempts to measure the separate influences of intentional and unintentional memory. In the ProcessDP, after an initial study phase, there are two test conditions. For one test, called an inclusion test, participants try to recollect information from a prior study episode to complete a test retrieval cue (cued recall). If unable to recollect an item from the study phase to match the retrieval cue, participants are to guess with the first word that comes to mind. Performance on an inclusion tests is represented by the equation,

$$\text{Inclusion} = IM + (UM_E + UM_B)(1 - IM),$$

where IM is intentional memory, UM_E is unintentional memory from within the experiment, and UM_B is the unintentional memory baseline (based on pre-experiment experience; Toth, Reingold, & Jacoby, 1994).

For the second condition, called exclusion, participants try to recollect information from the prior study episode. If a participant recollects an appropriate word from the study episode, *then that word is not to be used as a response.* Instead, an alternative response (e.g., a new word) should be given. Thus, intentional memory is used to exclude studied words as responses. If a participant is unable to recollect a target word from the study phase, then he/she should guess with the first word that comes to mind. Exclusion performance is represented by the equation,

$$\text{Exclusion} = (UM_E + UM_B)(1 - IM).$$

Performance in an exclusion condition demonstrates the influence of unintentional memory when intentional memory fails (observed as an exclusion error). Unintentional memory could be strong but not be relied upon in the face of successful retrieval from IM. In this case, although unintentional memory would contribute information, the influence of that information would be relatively small. A simple way to think about the situation is to imagine that intentional memory has a veto power over unintentional memory.

To obtain a measure of intentional memory, one subtracts the exclusion score from the inclusion score. (If the inclusion and exclusion baselines are similar, the baseline term drops out of the equation.) To obtain a measure of unintentional memory from the experiment (UM_E), the scores for intentional memory and UM_B are substituted into one of the equations (i.e., divide the exclusion score by $1 - IM$, then subtract UM_B). If one is interested in a comparison of the measure of unintentional memory from an implicit test and the ProcessDP, as in the present case, then one is interested in the impact of the study episode itself. In this case, one needs to factor out the baseline completion rate (e.g., Roediger & McDermott, 1993; also see Toth et al., 1994). This approach was taken in the experiments reported below.

One important aspect of the ProcessDP is that it offers flexibility for measuring intentional memory because the experimenter can vary the exclusion criterion. Exclusion could be based on an item's occurrence (easy exclusion) or an item's list membership (difficult exclusion) in an earlier study phase. If the criterion is for list membership, then the experimenter can make the study lists relatively easy or difficult to differentiate. Alternatively, one could require the exclusion of a items studied in a particular condition (e.g., words generated from anagrams) where different study conditions (reading and generating) were intermixed in a single study list (e.g., Jones, 2006). The upshot is that one can measure intentional memory for a variety of situations.

A downside is some that intentionally retrieved but uninformative aspects of the study experience (i.e., with respect to the exclusion criterion; called noncriterial recollection, Yonelinas & Jacoby, 1996; or nondiagnostic memory, Mulligan & Hirshman, 1997) may shift into the measure of unintentional memory. For example, the results from ProcessDP studies on recognition memory have shown that a stricter exclusion criterion (e.g., exclusion based on list membership instead of occurrence) reduces estimates of recollection (intentional memory), as one would expect, but inflates estimates of familiarity (unintentional memory; e.g., Mulligan & Hirshman, 1997; Yonelinas & Jacoby, 1996; see also Gruppuso, Lindsay, & Kelley, 1997). The change in the estimate of the unintentional memory component in these recognition results has been criticised by some researchers (Humphreys, Dennis, Chalmers, & Finnigan, 2000; Mulligan & Hirshman, 1997) with the idea that the procedure should measure the whole contributions of each process.

An Alternative, Functional Viewpoint and Use of the Process Dissociation Procedure

In a functional viewpoint (Gruppuso et al., 1997), information that might contribute to intentional memory in one circumstance (e.g., easy conditions) might contribute to an unintentional memory measure in another circumstance (e.g., difficult conditions). This approach turns away from a dual-process approach that assumes unintentional memory and intentional memory processes are independent or an acceptance that the ProcessDP provides process pure estimates. Instead, the approach is based on the idea that 'some stored features can be retrieved independently of others' (Gruppuso et al., 1997, p. 265). From the functional viewpoint, it is important to think of measuring the *influences* of intentional memory and unintentional memory instead of measuring full *contributions*. The strengths of this approach are that violations of the process dissociation procedure appear to be circumvented and that measures are considered as influences that vary depending on the particular circumstances. A downside of this approach is that measures of intentional memory and unintentional memory may not be considered as whole contributions.

Direct Comparisons

Two experiments compared the measures of intentional memory and unintentional memory for word stimuli from the RIC method and two versions of the ProcessDP in full. In one ProcessDP, the exclusion criterion was relatively easy (occurrence of a word in an earlier study phase; e.g., Toth et al., 1994); in the other ProcessDP, the exclusion criterion was relatively difficult (occurrence of a word in a particular list in an earlier study phase; e.g., Jacoby et al., 1993). The present experiments represent the first full comparisons of these two versions of the ProcessDP with word stem retrieval cues.

During encoding, the level-of-processing (LOP; e.g., Craik & Tulving, 1975) was manipulated (shallow vs. deep) in Experiment 1, while reading versus solving anagrams was manipulated in Experiment 2. In both experiments, the perceptual overlap from the study words to the test cues (word stems) was the same for both study conditions. Thus, both experiments were designed to produce a typical single dissociation observed for explicit and perceptual implicit memory tests (Roediger & McDermott, 1993). An effect of study condition was expected on the explicit test, word stem cued recall, but little or no effect was expected on the implicit test, word stem completion.

Based on previous reseach (e.g., McBride & Dosher, 1999; Toth et al., 1994; see also Richardson-Klavehn & Gardiner, 1996, 1998) estimates of intentional memory for the easy ProcessDP group were expected to show a LOP effect consistent with that for the explicit test group. There was an expectation that similar results from the two procedures would extend to the read-anagram study manipulation. Also, in most ProcessDP experiments where a LOP study manipulation and word stem test cues have been used, a reverse LOP effect, even if slight, has been obtained on unintentional memory (Stern et al., 2003). Thus, this same pattern was expected in the current study. Whether this pattern would extend to the read-anagram manipulation was unclear. In some cases (e.g., McBride & Dosher, 1999; see also Richardson-Klavehn & Gardiner, 1996, 1998) estimates for unintentional memory have been fairly low (after correcting for baseline; for exceptions, see Stern, McNaught-Davis, & Barker, 2003; Toth et al., 1994). Thus, there was some expectation that, for both experiments, the estimates for unintentional memory from the easy ProcessDP would be lower than those for the implicit memory group.

The more stringent criterion for exclusion in the difficult ProcessDP group was expected to produce relatively low estimates of intentional memory (e.g., memory for list membership) but to boost the estimates of unintentional memory relative to the easy process dissociation condition. Such an increase in the unintentional memory measure could occur for two reasons. A greater influence of unintentional memory could be revealed because conflicting information provided by intentional memory would be relatively weak, thus allowing more of the contribution to become influential. Alternatively, uninformative recollection in the strict condition could be shifted into the measure of unintentional memory (noncriterial recollection). For example, a participant might remember (with an intentional process) that a word occurred in the study phase without remembering in which study list the word occurred. In this case, some influence of the intentional process could be absorbed into the unintentional memory estimate (Gruppuso et al., 1997; Yonelinas & Jacoby, 1996; also see Reingold & Toth, 1996).

Method

In each experiment, four groups of 20 United States Air Force recruits (80 recruits in total), participated at Lackland Air Force Base in San Antonio, Texas. Ten sets of 10 critical words (median frequency = 8.5, minimum = 0; maximum = 333; number of word with frequency higher than 100 = 4; word length: 5–8 letters; Francis & Kučera, 1982) were used in the study. Eighty words were presented in the study phase of both experiments. For the level-of-process-ing manipulation, the shallow task was counting consonants in a study word, while the deep task was rating the pleasantness of a study word. For the read-generate manipulation, participants simply read the study words on the computer screen or mentally rearranged the fourth and fifth letters of a letter string to produce the target word. All participants went through two study lists of 40 items where the type of trial was randomised within a list. On each study list, there were 20 items presented in each trial type. The words were presented one at a time, visually, for 4 s (per word). Six buffer words were used in each study list to eliminate primacy and recency effects. The only differences in these two study lists were their timing (one came before the other) and the actual items in lists. A 1-minute distracter task (writing down the names of United States Presidents) followed the second study list. The computer program for the experiment was created with Micro Experimental Laboratory Software (MEL; Schneider, 1988).

All groups received two tests where a word stem cue was given on each trial. The tests were self-paced with a time limit of 15 s per trial. Half of the items from each study list served as targets on each test. Two sets of 10 non-studied words were used as targets on the two tests (one for each test). For all partici-pants, the critical items were those for the first study list and the non-studied lists. The three-letter word stems for the targets, while unique within the exper-iment, could all be completed to form more than one word. Each set of critical stimuli appeared as an item in each type of trial (e.g., shallow vs. deep LOP or read vs. anagram) and in each study list (first or second) or as non-studied list equally often.

An explicit test group and an implicit test group each received two tests (both explicit or both implicit). The guidelines of the RIC procedure were followed such that the only difference for these two groups was in the test instructions. The explicit test group was told to use word stems presented on the test as retrieval cues for studied words. Word stems corresponding to new words were not to be completed. For the implicit test group, participants were instructed to write down the first word that came to mind to complete each word stem. In the second experiment participants also were told that some completions might be the same words as some words experienced earlier in the experiment (e.g., Tulving, Schacter, & Stark, 1982; for a comment on this procedure see Richardson-Klavehn & Gardiner, 1996) but that intentionally attempting to use words presented earlier would 'ruin their word completion score'. However, if participants realised that the first word to come to mind was a word that occurred earlier, then they were instructed 'to still write down that word'.

Following the two study lists, both ProcessDP groups received an inclusion test. The groups were told to try to complete the word stems with words that had been presented earlier. If a participant could not think of a study word, he was to guess with the first word that came to mind. Up to this point, the ProcessDP groups were treated identically. For the second test, both groups received exclusion instructions, but the criterion for exclusion was different for the two groups. One group (easy ProcessDP) was given a relatively easy exclusion criterion (occurrence in the study phase), and the other group (difficult ProcessDP) was given a relatively difficult exclusion criterion (list membership in the study phase). The easy ProcessDP group was told to try to remember words from the study phase that completed the word stems. If an appropriate word was remembered, then it was not to be written down. Instead, the word stem was to be completed with a new word. If an appropriate word from the study phase could not be remembered, the first word that came to mind was to be given as a response. The difficult ProcessDP group was told to try to remember words from the first study to complete the words stems. However, if a word was remembered as having occurred in the first list then that word was not to be given as an answer; a new word should be given as an answer in its place. If a participant could not remember a word from the study phase or was unsure of a study word's list membership, he was to write down the first word that came to mind. Inclusion and exclusion examples were given for both ProcessDP groups.

All four groups were compared for their performance on the first list of study words and on the non-studied words. For the two process dissociation groups, the inclusion and exclusion scores were used to estimate the influence of unintentional and intentional memory.

Results From the Retrieval Intentionality Criterion Method

The results for the RIC method are shown in Table 1. First, for the implicit test, the completion rates for the study conditions were higher than those for non-studied conditions, indicative of significant priming, Experiment 1: $F(1, 38) = 27.19$, $MSE = 0.02$; Experiment 2: $F(1, 38) = 28.41$, $MSE = 0.01$. Planned comparisons for each experiment showed that completion rates for the study conditions (combined) were significantly higher than that for the nonstudied baseline, Experiment 1: $F(1, 19) = 71.01$, $MSE = 0.02$; Experiment 2: $F(1, 19) = 58.02$, $MSE = 0.02$, but not different from each other (both $Fs < 0.12$). Second, processing words at a deep level produced a higher cued recall rate than processing words at a the shallow level, and solving anagrams produced higher cued recall rate than reading words as expected. Thus, the study manipulations

Table 1

Mean Cued Recall and Completion Rates for the RIC Procedure in Experiments 1 and 2

		Explicit			Implicit		
Exp.	Condition	Test 1	Test 2	Mean	Test 1	Test 2	Mean
1	Shallow	.29 (.25)	.25 (.21)	.27 (.23)	.35 (.25)	.38 (.25)	.37 (.25)
1	Deep	.53 (.49)	.53 (.49)	.53 (.49)	.38 (.28)	.39 (.26)	.38 (.27)
1	Non-studied	.04	.04	.04	.10	.13	.11
2	Read	.32 (.24)	.26 (.21)	.29 (.23)	.33 (.20)	.35 (.21)	.34 (.21)
2	Anagram	.46 (.38)	.42 (.37)	.44 (.38)	.31 (.18)	.37 (.23)	.34 (.21)
2	Non-studied	.08	.05	.06	.13	.14	.13

Note: Corrected means, where the non-studied base rate has been subtracted, appear in parentheses.

produced a robust effect on the explicit test, but little, if any, effect on the implicit test. These findings were supported by a study condition × test condition interaction effect from the corrected scores, Experiment 1: $F(1, 38) = 12.88$, $MSE = 0.04$; Experiment 2: $F(1, 38) = 9.27$, $MSE = 0.01$.

These results are consistent with previous findings (Craik, Moscovitch, & McDowd, 1994; Richardson-Klavehn & Gardiner, 1996, 1998; Roediger, Weldon, Stadler, & Riegler, 1992; for reviews, see Brown & Mitchell, 1994; Challis & Brodbeck, 1992; Roediger & McDermott, 1993). The small effects that sometimes occur on perceptual implicit tests have been thought to be due to intentional memory contamination on the implicit test (e.g., Challis & Brodbeck, 1992; Toth et al., 1994), a difference in lexical processing between study conditions (Richardson-Klavehn & Gardiner, 1998), or a difference in conceptual influences between study conditions (Toth & Reingold, 1996). The present experiments, however, showed only an extremely slight advantage for the deep over the shallow level of processing in Experiment 1 and no advantage for the anagram over the read condition in Experiment 2. While implicit tests may sometimes suffer from explicit contamination (e.g., Toth et al., 1994), on the whole, the level of explicit contamination has not warranted the amount of worry that some researchers have expressed. Also, potential cases of explicit contamination might be accounted for with other explanations (Richardson-Klavehn & Gardiner, 1996).

Some researchers have criticised the approach of obtaining dissociations with different tasks or for comparing performance on tasks with different baseline completion rates (e.g., Toth & Reingold, 1996; Reingold & Toth, 1996). Reingold and Toth point out that by using forced cued recall, where a response is forced on every trial, one can alleviate the concern about a response bias. However, a shift from a cued recall to a forced cued recall test may change what is actually being measured on the explicit test (Reingold & Toth, 1996). For example, forced cued recall may tap unintentional memory more than cued recall. Another criticism of the RIC approach is that tasks are assumed, or at least implied, to provide pure, separate measures of different underlying

Table 2

Mean Completion Rates for the ProcessDP Groups in Experiments 1 and 2

		Easy exclusion ProcessDP		Difficult exclusion processDP	
Exp.	Condition	Inclusion	Exclusion	Inclusion	Exclusion
1	Shallow	.34	.20	.35	.41
1	Deep	.53	.08	.53	.37
1	Non-studied	.14	.13	.12	.17
2	Read	.38	.16	.43	.34
2	Anagram	.47	.13	.48	.37
2	Non-studied	.16	.19	.18	.20

processes, and the relationship of the underlying processes often is unspecified (e.g., Jacoby, 1991; Toth & Reingold, 1996). This point is fair. Researchers should communicate their thoughts on what processes are being compared, the mapping of tasks to the processes (e.g., whether tasks tap different processes purely), and the assumed relationship of the processes. Nevertheless, the RIC procedure is a useful tool for showing dissociations between intentional and unintentional memory and for guarding against explicit contamination on the implicit test (also see Richardson-Klavehn, Lee, Joubran, & Bjork, 1994b).

Results From the Two Versions of the Process Dissociation Procedure

The data for the inclusion and exclusion conditions are shown in Table 2. To meet an assumption that memory retrieval is treated similarly under inclusion and exclusion conditions, it is important that the completion rates for nonstudied items are similar across inclusion and exclusion conditions. This was the case. A 2 (test: inclusion, exclusion) × 2 (test group: easy exclusion, difficult exclusion) ANOVA on the completion rates for new words produced no significant effects for either experiment (Experiment 1, all $Fs < 1.69$; Experiment 2, all $Fs < 0.79$).

Within each experiment the inclusion conditions for the two groups was quite similar. In Experiment 1, processing words at a deep level during encoding produced a higher cued recall rate than did processing words a shallow level. In Experiment 2, solving anagrams produced a small cued recall advantage over reading words. However, the pattern of results for the exclusion conditions was different, particularly for Experiment 1. The exclusion data for the easy ProcessDP group showed a reverse LOP effect, with the deep condition leading to a lower exclusion error rate than the shallow condition. This finding is consistent with the idea that better recollection for words studied under a deep LOP compared to a shallow LOP will likely lead to fewer exclusion errors. There was only a small, reverse LOP trend for the exclusion condition of the difficult ProcessDP. Finally, words studied under a shallow LOP were given as completions at a rate above baseline, but words studied under a deep LOP were given as completions at a rate below baseline. These results are generally similar to those obtained by McBride and Dosher (1999) and Toth et al. (1994; also see Richardson-Klavehn and Gardiner, 1996, 1998). In contrast, for the exclusion condition in the difficult ProcessDP, the shallow and deep LOP conditions yielded error rates well above baseline.

For Experiment 2, the differences between the exclusion error rates for the read and anagram conditions were slight. For exclusion in the easy ProcessDP, the error rate was slightly lower for the anagram condition than the read condition, but for exclusion in the difficult ProcessDP, the error rate was slightly higher for the anagram condition than the read condition. In terms of overall magnitude, the exclusion error rates were quite different for the two groups. For the easy ProcessDP, the error rates were a bit below the non-studied baseline. For the difficult ProcessDP, the error rates were well above non-studied baseline.

The estimates of intentional and unintentional memory were calculated for each individual and the means are shown in Table 3. As expected, exclusion based on list membership (difficult ProcessDP) produced much lower intentional memory estimates than that based on simple occurrence (easy ProcessDP). The study manipulations produced clear effects on intentional memory in the easy ProcessDP groups, Experiment 1: $F(1, 19) = 32.35$, MSE $= 0.03$, and Experiment 2: $F(1, 19) = 4.44$, MSE $= 0.03$. For the difficult ProcessDP group of Experiment 1, a LOP effect occurred on intentional memory, $F(1, 19) = 10.48$, MSE $= 0.05$, but this effect is probably a small overestimate because the negative estimate in the shallow condition should be considered as a zero. For the difficult ProcessDP in Experiment 2, there was no memorial benefit of generating a word from an anagram over reading a word, that is, a generation effect; $F(1, 19) < 0.06$.

The measures of unintentional memory contrasted sharply from those for intentional memory. (To correct for intentional memory estimates of less than zero, any negative intentional memory estimate was included in the overall intentional memory mean but was set to zero for the calculation of unintentional memory at the individual level.) First, the difficult ProcessDP produced much higher estimates of unintentional memory compared to the easy ProcessDP. For the easy ProcessDP, the deep LOP and the anagram solution conditions yielded lower estimates of unintentional memory than the shallow LOP and reading conditions, respectively. The effect was significant for Experiment 1, $F(1, 19) = 10.81$, MSE $= 0.01$, but not Experiment 2, $F(1, 19) = 0.97$, MSE $= 0.02$. In Experiment 1, this result was evident when the unintentional memory measure was calculated from the group means, and the trend was still apparent, though not as strong when participants with exclusion scores of zero were dropped (though see below about other changes from dropping zero exclusion scores). For the difficult ProcessDP, the deep LOP and the anagram solution conditions yielded slightly higher estimates of unintentional memory than the shallow LOP and reading conditions, respectively. Neither of these differences was significant (both Experiment 1 and 2 Fs < 0.71).

Table 3

Mean Estimates of Intentional and Unintentional Memory for the ProcessDP Groups in Experiments 1 and 2

		Easy exclusion ProcessDP		Difficult exclusion processDP	
Exp.	Condition	Intentional	Unintentional	Intentional	Unintentional
1	Shallow	.14	.09	−.06	.28
1	Deep	.45	−.04	.16	.31
2	Read	.22	.05	.09	.19
2	Anagram	.34	.01	.11	.23

Note: The mean base rate for each group has been subtracted out of the estimates for both intentional and unintentional retrieval components. Estimates of unintentional memory were calculated with negative intentional memory estimates set to zero.

Dissociations where the pattern reverses from intentional to unintentional memory have been described as *paradoxical* because, based on what is known from implicit memory findings and theory, there is no reason to predict a reversal. The reversal of the LOP effect in Experiment 1 for the easy ProcessDP is largely consistent with results from previous studies (e.g., Stern et al., 2003; McBride & Dosher, 1999; Toth et al., 1994; see also Richardson-Klavehn & Gardiner, 1996, 1998). In fact, across these studies and the present one (but excluding the ones by Richardson-Klavehn and Gardiner), this reversal, even if slight, has been obtained in 18 of 23 opportunities. Thus, this trend, which is opposite to that for perceptual implicit memory tests (e.g., Brown & Mitchell, 1994; Challis & Brodbeck, 1992), appears to be reliable. Although the read-anagram manipulation did not produce a strong paradoxical dissociation pattern, the effect on intentional memory was not as great as that for the LOP manipulation. A paradoxical pattern could likely be obtained by using a more potent generation condition (e.g., perhaps using conceptual cues with a word stem cue instead of anagram solution).

Paradoxical dissociations may occur because of an underlying dependent relationship of intentional and unintentional memory (Curran & Hintzman, 1995, 1997). A dependent relationship might also be induced from the editing of potential errors (a) when a target completion pops to mind involuntarily but with conscious awareness of its prior occurrence (called involuntary conscious memory; e.g., Richardson-Klavehn et al., 1994a) or (b) when possible completions are generated, then checked for their prior occurrence (a generate-recognise strategy; Bodner, Masson, & Caldwell, 2000; Jacoby, 1998). All of these possibilities represent violations of the independence assumption of the ProcessDP (for discussions, see Bodner et al., 2000; Curran & Hintzman, 1995, 1997; Dodson & Johnson, 1996; Hirshman, 1998; Humphreys, Dennis, Chalmers, & Finnigan, 2000; Mulligan & Hirshman, 1997; Richardson-Klavehn & Gardiner, 1995, 1996, 1998; Richardson-Klavehn et al., 1994a; Russo, Cullis, & Parkin, 1998; though see Jacoby, 1998; Jacoby, Begg, & Toth, 1997; Jacoby & Shrout, 1997; Toth, Reingold, & Jacoby, 1995).

Jacoby (1998) recommends boundary conditions for the use of the ProcessDP, and one boundary condition is to keep exclusion scores from being low (e.g., zero or below baseline). If the exclusion score equals zero, then the measure of unintentional memory must be zero, and one risks underestimating the contribution of unintentional memory. The easy ProcessDP in the present experiments produced exclusion scores that were on the low side. Why were these scores low? One possibility is that there was simply not much unintentional memory for the words, meaning that exclusion errors could not be observed. The implicit test showed robust priming, thus this possibility can be ruled out. Another possibility is that participants may have withheld responses to avoid making exclusion errors. If conservative responding were the case, then the completions for non-studied targets should be lower for the exclusion than the inclusion conditions. However, the non-studied completion rates were very similar. Thus, the withholding of responses is not supported, either.

Another possibility is that the low exclusion scores reflect the successful use of intentional memory to avoid exclusion errors. This possibility gains support by considering the intentional memory scores when participants with exclusion errors are dropped (e.g., Curran & Hintzman, 1995). Dropping the data for participants with exclusion scores of zero dramatically lowered the measures of intentional memory. In Experiment 1, the shallow condition dropped from .14 to −.10, and the deep condition dropped from .49 to .29. In Experiment 2, the read condition dropped from .22 to .16, and the anagram condition dropped from .34 to .25. Thus, the participants with high estimates of intentional memory were more likely to give an exclusion score of zero, indicating that the zero exclusion scores were based on successful recollection. Sometimes researchers have dropped zero exclusion scores with a focus on unintentional memory measures. However, as shown here and described elsewhere (Curran & Hintzman, 1995), dropping zero scores can have big implications for the measure of intentional memory. The recommendation here is that if a researcher is to report unintentional memory scores after dropping zero exclusion scores, then the corresponding intentional memory scores should be reported, too (see also Curran & Hintzman, 1995).

The drop in intentional memory when zero exclusion scores were eliminated, unfortunately, is consistent with the possibility that the relationship of intentional and unintentional memory is not independent. If one holds that the ProcessDP should measure full contributions instead of influences, then the results of the present experiments indicate that such a boundary condition may limit the viability of the ProcessDP to when intentional memory is relatively weak (see also Curran & Hintzman, 1995, 1997).

If the ProcessDP is viable only when intentional memory is relatively weak, then there is an additional concern regarding the pattern of unintentional memory measures. Hirshman (1998) points out that the ProcessDP equations, by their nature, will tend to produce invariance in the unintentional memory measure. Thus, dissociations where an effect is obtained on intentional memory

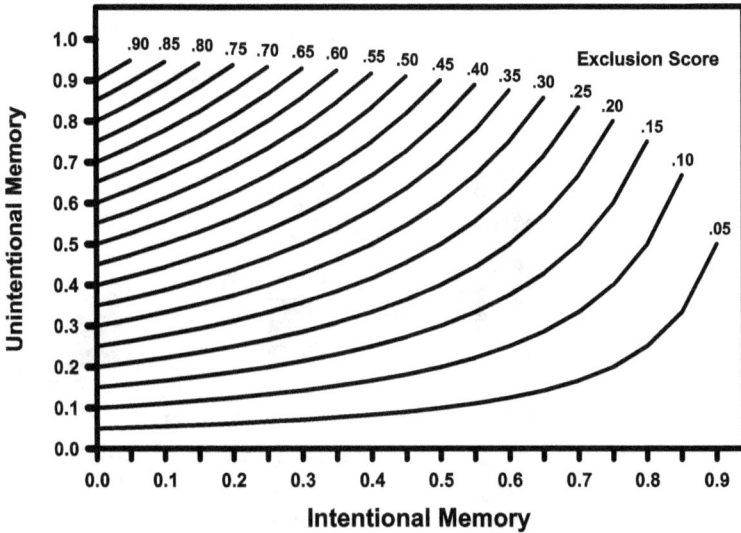

Figure 1
Unintentional memory score as a function of intentional memory score and level of exclusion performance.

but not on unintentional memory should be interpreted with caution. Figure 5 plots the measure of unintentional memory against intentional memory for given levels of exclusion performance. (The unintentional memory measure has not been corrected for a non-studied baseline.) The figure demonstrates Hirshman's point, but the problem of a tendency toward invariance is greatest for lower levels of exclusion, lower levels of intentional memory, and lower levels of unintentional memory. For example, for an exclusion error rate of .05, an increase in inclusion performance (e.g., from .10 to .50) would produce a large change of .45 in intentional memory, but almost no change in unintentional memory.

The problem stemming from low levels of exclusion errors fits with Jacoby's (1998) concern over boundary conditions. However, the problem still occurs for exclusion error rates that are off the floor. At exclusion error rates of .20 to .30, intentional memory could change from .00 to .20 with little effect on unintentional memory. Of course, if one expects an experimental condition to boost intentional memory relative to another condition, then one might well expect an increase in the inclusion score and a decrease in the exclusion score. An increase in the inclusion scores and a decrease in the exclusion score can promote a pattern of invariance in the unintentional memory estimate. The bottom line is that, due to the nature of the ProcessDP equations, it may be difficult to observe changes in unintentional memory (Hirshman, 1998; Stern et al., 2003), leading some researchers (e.g., Hirshman, 1998) to conclude that the

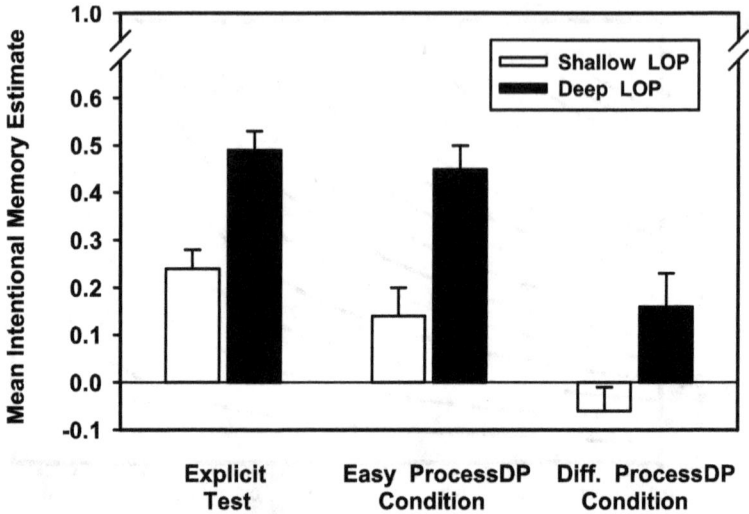

Figure 2

Mean intentional memory measure as a function of test procedure and level of processing.

Note: Error bars show the standard error of the mean within a condition.
Diff. = difficult.

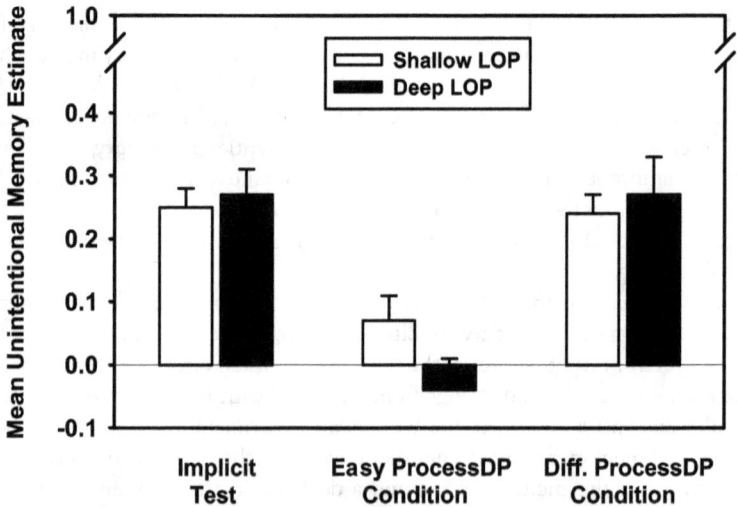

Figure 3

Mean unintentional memory measure as a function of test procedure and level of processing.

Note: Mean baseline completion rates for each test condition have been subtracted from the corresponding estimates.
Error bars show the standard error of the mean within a condition.
Diff. = difficult.

ProcessDP is useful for determining measures of intentional memory but not unintentional memory.

Despite concerns for a non-independent relationship of intentional and unintentional memory on completion tasks, it is important to note that the pattern of a 'paradoxical' dissociation has been found in recognition memory (Gruppuso et al., 1997), for which, involuntary conscious memory and a generate–recognise strategy can be ruled out. If intentional memory is much stronger for one condition than another, then it also seems reasonable that the influence of unintentional memory may be smaller for a strong memory condition over a weak memory condition. This interpretation follows a functional perspective of memory of Gruppuso and colleagues (1997). From this perspective, one would conclude that, overall, unintentional memory did not provide much *influence* in the easy ProcessDP when intentional memory was also meant to be used and that there was a greater *influence* of unintentional memory in the shallow than in the deep LOP condition.

Comparisons of the Procedures

Figures 2 to 5 show comparisons of the measures from the three different procedures. Figures 2 and 4 show that the measures of intentional memory are similar for the explicit test and easy ProcessDP procedure (where the exclusion criterion was based on occurrence). The only difference was that, overall, the measures from the explicit test are slightly higher than those obtained with the easy ProcessDP.

As expected, intentional memory measures from the difficult ProcessDP are much lower than those for the other two procedures. Figures 3 and 5 show that the measures of unintentional memory are similar for the implicit test and difficult ProcessDP procedure (where the exclusion criterion was based on list membership). Relative to these two procedures, the unintentional memory measure for the easy ProcessDP clearly underestimates unintentional memory, if considered as a full contribution.

For the difficult ProcessDP, although recollection was low, participants were sometimes able to retrieve list membership for the deep LOP, anagram solution, and read conditions. Items whose list membership could be retrieved with an intentional process would also be remembered (intentionally) as occurring in the easy ProcessDP. However, many of the items that were retrieved with an intentional process as occurring in the easy ProcessDP would have been remembered without their list membership. Thus, much of what constituted criterial recollection (memory for occurrence) in the easy ProcessDP constituted noncriterial recollection (memory for occurrence without list membership information) in the difficult ProcessDP.

The difference between intentional memory measures (easy minus difficult) represents a measure of intentionally remembering a word's occurrence while failing to retrieve list membership information (i.e., noncriterial recollection under the difficult ProcessDP; see Table 4). The intentional memory measures

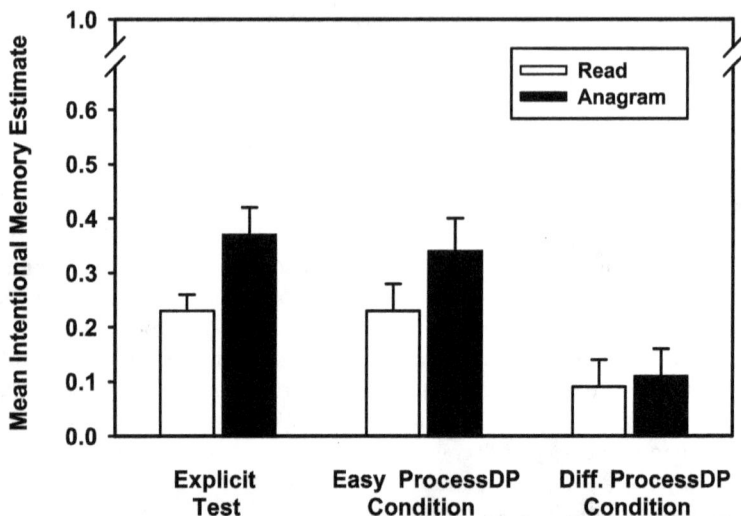

Figure 4

Mean intentional memory measure as a function of test procedure and study condition.

Note: Error bars show the standard error of the mean within a condition.
Diff. = difficult.

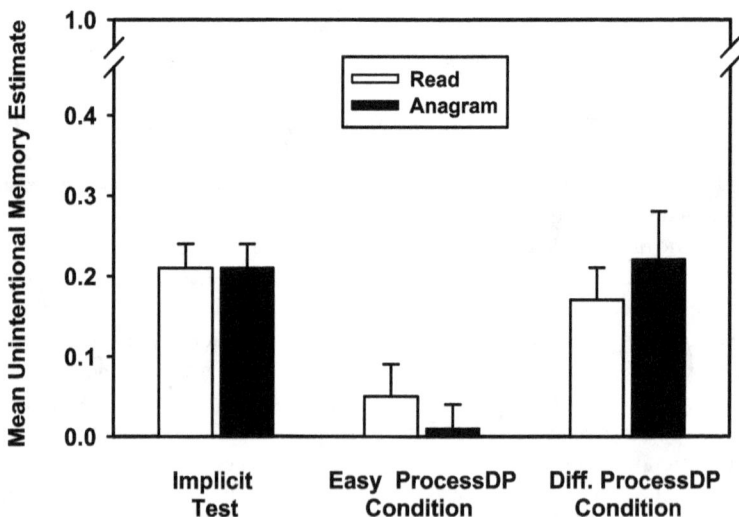

Figure 5

Mean unintentional memory measure as a function of test procedure and study condition.

Note: Mean baseline completion rates for each test condition have been subtracted from the corresponding estimates.
Error bars show the standard error of the mean within a condition.
Diff. = difficult.

Table 4

Mean Difference Between Intentional Memory Measures and Unintentional Memory Measures
for the ProcessDP Groups in Experiments 1 and 2

		Easy–difficult ProcessDP	
Exp.	Condition	Intentional	Unintentional
1	Shallow	.20 (.14)	−.19
1	Deep	.29	−.35 (.31)
2	Read	.13	−.14
2	Anagram	.23	−.22

Note: The numbers in parentheses are based on calculations with negative group means set to zero.

for occurrence without list information show clear effects of the study manipulations. Also, a portion of the intentional memory in the easy ProcessDP appears to shift to the measure of unintentional memory in the difficult ProcessDP. This shift can be seen readily by comparing difference scores (easy minus difficult ProcessDP) for intentional and unintentional memory (see Table 4). The difference scores for intentional and unintentional memory are similar but opposite in sign (direction), suggesting that all of the intentional memory of occurrence without list membership (intentional memory under the easy exclusion ProcessDP) shifted to the measure of unintentional memory under the difficult exclusion ProcessDP. One caveat for this comparison is that the values in unintentional memory are mathematically constrained such that similar values, though opposite in sign, are likely (cf., Hirshman, 1998).

Both the RIC method and the ProcessDP are valuable for stem completion tasks. Interestingly, both methods can suffer from unwanted participant strategies. Intentional retrieval of words on an implicit test can be a problem, and occurrences of involuntary conscious memory and a generate–recognise strategy in the ProcessDP can be a problem. Thus, for word completion tests, understanding the effects of a (potential) generation stage in different test conditions (e.g., Bodner et al., 2000; Weldon & Colston, 1995), and separating retrieval volition from awareness (e.g., Richardson-Klavehn & Gardiner, 1995) continue to be important. One unanswered question concerns the extent of violations in the ProcessDP. For example, if a generate–recognise strategy is employed only after an initial direct retrieval attempt after intentional memory fails (Rabinowitz, Mandler, & Barsalou, 1979), then the violation from the strategy might be quite minor. In a similar way, measurement problems introduced by involuntary conscious memory might be minor, too.

The instructions that attempt to set the retrieval mode for participants are different for the RIC method and the ProcessDP. On traditional explicit tests, the assumption has been that the measures or patterns obtained on these tests are not compromised by unintentional memory processes. By comparison, the absence of using an intentional retrieval process is what defines an implicit test. For the ProcessDP both intentional and unintentional processes are encouraged as retrieval modes, though the intentional retrieval process is given more weight (provided the criterial information required for exclusion is retrieved). The difference in retrieval modes that is set by the RIC for implicit and explicit tests (where the test cues are identical) produces the dissociations on implicit and explicit tests. Thus, perhaps similar measurements of unintentional retrieval should not be expected from implicit tests and a ProcessDP, particularly a ProcessDP where intentional retrieval is relatively easy.

The ProcessDP provides another means to obtain measures of intentional and unintentional processes. On the good side, the approach has spurred a considerable amount of interest, whether critical or not. The measures of intentional memory for the easy ProcessDP conditions roughly matched those for the explicit test groups in the present experiments. The procedure also appears to be a useful tool for identifying intentional memory deficits (Jacoby, Jennings, & Hay, 1996), and has been applied in a variety of situations (e.g., the Stroop paradigm; Lindsay & Jacoby, 1994). Another potential advantage of separating intentional and unintentional processes occurs when a given manipulation (e.g., reading vs. generating words at study) influences intentional and unintentional processes oppositely (Jacoby, 1983; Jacoby et al., 1993). The concern is that one may underestimate or fail to detect a significant effect on intentional memory in an explicit test because of an offsetting effect from an unintentional process. This concern may apply more to recognition than cued recall tasks because the recognition decision is likely to be based more heavily on familiarity.

What currently seems to be of some concern is whether the measures of unintentional memory from the ProcessDP, regardless of the exclusion criterion, accurately reflect the contribution of unintentional memory in the same way that an implicit test does. As shown in the present experiments, different exclusion criteria are likely to produce different measures of unintentional memory. Sometimes similar measures of unintentional memory will be found, but sometimes dissimilar measures will be obtained.

Also, there are concerns about violations of the independence assumption due to the use of a generate–recognise strategy or the occurrence of involuntary conscious memory.

The ProcessDP's strength seems to lie in measuring intentional memory and revealing susceptibility to memory errors in the exclusion condition (e.g., Jacoby, 1999; Jacoby, Jones, & Dolan, 1998) An alternative, functional approach (e.g., Gruppuso et al., 1997), though differing from the original rationale for the ProcessDP, clearly shifts the focus from contributions to influences. This shift makes use of the potential flexibility of the procedure but also emphasises the influences, instead of (full) contributions, of intentional and unintentional memory. The functional viewpoint opens the interpretation of paradoxical dissociation results to one where some conditions may be less influenced by unintentional memory than others when intentional memory is recruited. Such a viewpoint would appear to extend to findings with traditional implicit and explicit tests under the RIC and seems worth serious consideration.

Endnote

1 Different terms have been used for intentional and unintentional memory or retrieval processes. Graf and Schacter (1985) used the terms explicit memory and implicit memory. Since that study, the following combinations of terms have been used for tests using incomplete retrieval cues: conscious and unconscious or automatic (Jacoby et al., 1993; Toth et al., 1994), recollection and automatic (Jacoby et al., 1993), voluntary and involuntary (Richardson-Klavehn & Gardiner, 1995), or intentional and incidental (Richardson-Klavehn & Gardiner, 1996). In this chapter, for the sake of using consistent terminology throughout that (a) highlights the importance of retrieval intentionality and (b) keeps the spirit of the different terminologies, the terms intentional and unintentional memory (or retrieval processes) are used.

Acknowledgments

I thank Brennan Underwood, Janet Hereford, and the United States Air Force for their cooperation and assistance on data collection.

References

Bodner, G. E., Masson, M. E. J., & Caldwell, J. I. (2000). Evidence for a generate–recognize model of episodic influences on word-stem completion. *Journal of Experimental Psychology: Learning, Memory, & Cognition, 26,* 267–293.

Brown, A. S., & Mitchell, D. B. (1994). A reevaluation of semantic versus nonsemantic processing in implicit memory. *Memory & Cognition, 22,* 533–541.

Challis, B. H., & Brodbeck, D. R. (1992). Level of processing affects priming in word fragment completion. *Journal of Experimental Psychology: Learning, Memory, and Cognition, 18,* 595–607.

Challis, B. H., & Sidhu, R. (1993). Dissociative effect of massed repetition on implicit and explicit measures of memory. *Journal of Experimental Psychology: Learning, Memory, and Cognition, 19,* 115–127.

Craik, F. I. M., Moscovitch, M., & McDowd, J. M. (1994). Contributions of surface and conceptual information to performance on implicit and explicit memory tasks. *Journal of Experimental Psychology: Learning, Memory, and Cognition, 13,* 474–479.

Craik, F. I. M., & Tulving, E. (1975). Depth of processing and the retention of words in episodic memory. *Journal of Experimental Psychology: General, 104,* 268–294.

Curran, T., & Hintzman, D. L. (1995). Violations of the independence assumptions in process dissociation. *Journal of Experimental Psychology: Learning, Memory, and Cognition, 21,* 531–547.

Curran, T., & Hintzman, D. L. (1997). Consequences and causes of correlations in process dissociation. *Journal of Experimental Psychology: Learning, Memory, and Cognition, 23,* 496–504.

Dodson, C. S., & Johnson, M. K. (1996). Some problems with the process-dissociation approach to memory. *Journal of Experimental Psychology: General, 125,* 181–194.

Francis, W. N., & Kučera, H. (1982). *Frequency analysis of English usage: Lexicon and grammar.* Boston: Houghton Mifflin.

Graf, P., & Schacter, D. L. (1985). Implicit and explicit memory for new associations in normal and amnesic participants. *Journal of Experimental Psychology: Learning, Memory, and Cognition, 11,* 501–518.

Graf, P., Shimamura, A. P., & Squire, L. R. (1985). Priming across modalities and priming across category levels: Extending the domain of preserved function in amnesia. *Journal of Experimental Psychology: Learning, Memory, & Cognition, 11,* 386–396.

Gruppuso, V., Lindsay, D. S., & Kelley, C. M. (1997). The process-dissociation procedure and similarity: Defining and estimating recollection and familiarity in recognition memory. *Journal of Experimental Psychology: Learning, Memory, and Cognition, 23,* 259–278.

Hirshman, E. (1998). On the logic of testing the independence assumption in the process-dissociation procedure. *Memory & Cognition, 26,* 857–859.

Humphreys, M. S., Dennis, S., Chalmers, K. A., & Finnigan, S. (2000). Dual processes in recognition: Does a focus on measurement operations provide a sufficient foundation? *Psychonomic Bulletin & Review, 7,* 593–603.

Jacoby, L. L. (1983). Remembering the data: Analyzing interactive processes in reading. *Journal of Verbal Learning and Verbal Behavior, 22,* 485–508.

Jacoby, L. L. (1991). A process dissociation framework: Separating automatic from intentional uses of memory. *Journal of Memory and Language, 30,* 513–541.

Jacoby, L. L. (1998). Invariance in automatic influences of memory: Toward a user's guide for the process-dissociation procedure. *Journal of Experimental Psychology: Learning, Memory, and Cognition, 24,* 3–26.

Jacoby, L. L. (1999). Ironic effects of repetition: Measuring age-related differences in memory. *Journal of Experimental Psychology: Learning, Memory, and Cognition, 25,* 3–22.

Jacoby, L. L., Begg, I. M., & Toth, J. P. (1997). In defense of functional independence: Violations of assumptions underlying the process-dissociation procedure. *Journal of Experimental Psychology: Learning, Memory, and Cognition, 23,* 484–495.

Jacoby, L. L., Jennings, J. M., & Hay, J. F. (1996). Dissociating automatic and controlled processes: Implications for diagnosis and rehabilitation of memory deficits. In D. J. Hermann, C. L. McEvoy, C. Hertzog, P. Hertel, & M. K. Johnson (Eds.), *Basic and applied memory research: Theory in context* (Vol 1., pp. 161–193). Mahwah, NJ: Erlbaum.

Jacoby, L. L., & Hollingshead, A. (1990). Toward a generate/recognize model of performance on direct and indirect tests of memory. *Journal of Memory and Language, 29,* 433–454.

Jacoby, L. L., Jones, T. C., & Dolan, P. O. (1998). Two effects of repetition: Support for a dual-process model of know judgments and exclusion errors. *Psychonomic Bulletin & Review, 5,* 705–709.

Jacoby, L. L., & Shrout, P. E. (1997). Toward a psychometric analysis of violations of the independence assumption in process dissociation. *Journal of Experimental Psychology: Learning, Memory, and Cognition, 23,* 505–510.

Jacoby, L. L., Toth, J. P., & Yonelinas, A. P. (1993). Separating conscious and unconscious influences of memory: Measuring recollection. *Journal of Experimental Psychology: General, 122,* 139–154.

Jones, T. C. (2006). Editing (out) generated words on an exclusion recognition memory test. *Memory, 14,* 712–729.

Lindsay, D. S., & Jacoby, L. L. (1994). Stroop process dissociations: The relationship between facilitation and interference. *Journal of Experimental Psychology: Human Perception and Performance, 20,* 219–234.

Mandler, G. (1980). Recognizing: The judgment of previous occurrence. *Psychological Review, 87,* 252–271.

McBride, D. M., & Dosher, B. A. (1999). Forgetting rates are comparable in conscious and automatic memory: A process-dissociation study. *Journal of Experimental Psychology: Learning, Memory, and Cognition, 25,* 583–607.

Mulligan, N. W., & Hirshman, E. (1997). Measuring the bases of recognition memory: An investigation of the process-dissociation framework. *Journal of Experimental Psychology: Learning, Memory, and Cognition, 23,* 280–304.

Rabinowitz, J., Mandler, G., & Barsalou, L. W. (1979). Generation-recognition as an auxiliary retrieval strategy. *Journal of Verbal Learning and Verbal Behavior, 18,* 57–72.

Rajaram, S. (1993). Remembering and knowing: Two means of access to the personal past. *Memory & Cognition, 21*, 82–102.

Reingold, E. M., & Toth, J. P. (1996). Process dissociations versus task dissociations. A controversy in progress. In G. Underwood (Ed.), *Implicit cognition* (pp. 159–202). New York: Oxford University Press.

Richardson-Klavehn, A., & Bjork, R. A. (1988). Measures of memory. *Annual Review of Psychology, 39*, 475–543.

Richardson-Klavehn, A., & Gardiner, J. M. (1995). Retrieval volition and memorial awareness in stem completion: An empirical analysis. *Psychological Research, 57*, 166–178.

Richardson-Klavehn, A., & Gardiner, J. M. (1996). Cross-modality priming in stem completion reflects conscious memory, but not voluntary memory. *Psychonomic Bulletin & Review, 3*, 238–244.

Richardson-Klavehn, A., & Gardiner, J. M. (1998). Depth-of-processing effects on priming in stem completion: Tests of the voluntary-contamination, conceptual-processing, and lexical-processing hypotheses. *Journal of Experimental Psychology: Learning, Memory, and Cognition, 24*, 593–609.

Richardson-Klavehn, A., & Gardiner, J. M., & Java, R. (1994a). Involuntary conscious memory and the method of opposition. *Memory, 2*, 1–29.

Richardson-Klavehn, A., Lee, M. G., Joubran, R., & Bjork, R. A. (1994b). Intention and awareness in perceptual identification priming. *Memory & Cognition, 22*, 293–312.

Roediger, H. L., & McDermott, K. (1993). Implicit memory in normal human participants. In H. Spinnler & F. Boller (Eds.), *Handbook of neuropsychology* (Vol. 8, pp. 63–151). Amsterdam: Elsevier.

Roediger, H. L., III, Guynn, M. J., & Jones, T. C. (1994). Implicit memory: A tutorial review. In G. d'Ydewalle, P. Eelen, & P. Bertelson (Eds.), *Current advances in psychological science: An international perspective* (pp. 67–94). Hove, UK: Erlbaum.

Roediger, H. L., III, Weldon, M. S., & Challis, B. (1989). Explaining dissociations between implicit and explicit measures of retention: A processing account. In H. L. Roediger, III, & F. I. M. Craik (Eds.), *Varieties of memory and consciousness: Essays in honour of Endel Tulving* (pp. 3–41). Hillsdale, NJ: LEA.

Roediger, H. L., Weldon, M. S., Stadler, M. A., & Riegler, G. H. (1992). Direct comparison of word stems and word fragments in implicit and explicit retention tests. *Journal of Experimental Psychology: Learning, Memory, and Cognition, 18*, 1251–1269.

Russo, R., Cullis, A. M., & Parkin, A. J. (1998). Consequences of violating the assumption of independence in the process dissociation procedure: A word fragment completion study. *Memory & Cognition, 26*, 617–632.

Schacter, D. L. (1987). Implicit memory: History and current status. *Journal of Experimental Psychology: Learning, Memory, and Cognition, 13*, 501–518.

Schacter, D. L., Bowers, J., & Booker, J. (1989). Intention, awareness and implicit memory: The retrieval intentionality criterion. In S. Lewandowsky, J. C. Dunn, & K. Kirsner (Eds.), *Implicit memory: Theoretical issues* (pp. 47–65). Hillsdale, NJ: Erlbaum.

Schneider, W. (1988). Micro experimental laboratory [Computer program, Version 1.0]. Pittsburgh, PA: Psychology Software Tools.

Stern, L. D., McNaught-Davis, A. K., & Barker, T. R. (2003). Process dissociation using a guided procedure. *Memory & Cognition, 23*, 641–655.

Toth, J. P., Reingold, E. M. (1996). Beyond perception: Conceptual contributions to unconscious influences of memory. In G. Underwood (Ed.), *Implicit cognition* (pp. 41–84). New York: Oxford University Press.

Toth, J. P., Reingold, E. M., & Jacoby, L. L. (1994). Toward a redefinition of implicit memory: Process dissociations following elaborative processing and self-generation. *Journal of Experimental Psychology: Learning, Memory, and Cognition, 20*, 290–303.

Toth, J. P., Reingold, E. M., & Jacoby, L. L. (1995). A response to Graf and Komatsu's (1994) critique of the process-dissociation procedure: When is caution necessary? *European Journal of Cognitive Psychology, 7*, 113–130.

Tulving, E., Schacter, D. L., & Stark, H. A. (1982). Priming effects in word fragment completion are independent of recognition memory. *Journal of Experimental Psychology: Learning, Memory, and Cognition, 8*, 336–342.

Weldon, M. S., & Colston, H. L. (1995). Dissociating the generation stage in implicit and explicit memory tests: Incidental production can differ from strategic access. *Psychonomic Bulletin & Review, 2*, 381–386.

Yonelinas, A. P., & Jacoby, L. L. (1996). Noncriterial recollection: Familiarity as automatic, irrelevant recollection. *Consciousness & Cognition: An International Journal, 5*, 131–141.

Part 2

Cognition, Language, and Communication

Using Sound Change to Explore the Mental Lexicon

Paul Warren and Jen Hay

Variation and Change

Ask two speakers to produce the same sentence and you will undoubtedly find a number of differences in the ways in which they say that sentence. Ask a single speaker to say the same sentence on more than one occasion and the same will be true. Such variation arises for a number of reasons. Allophonic variation in the pronunciation of individual sounds frequently seems random, but may be constrained by linguistic factors such as the position of a sound in a word or phrase (e.g., unaspirated variants of /p/ occur after initial /s/ as in *spot*, but aspirated versions occur in initial position as in *pot*). Connected speech processes, which are abundant in fluent speech, often involve the influence of one sound on its neighbours, resulting in a wide range of different pronunciations for the 'same' word. But such processes can also be quite variable in operation, since they may depend on aspects of speech style, which is in turn linked to the level of formality of the speech situation, as well as to interlocutor effects and other audience factors (Bell, 1984). Speakers are also influenced by environmental and paralinguistic factors (background noise, the expression of different emotions, and so on).

Inter-speaker differences are perhaps a more obvious source of variation. Some differences have physiological origins in differences in vocal tract size and shape. Others, such as the dialect and accent of a speaker, can depend on a number of factors, which include the region of origin of the speaker, their socioeconomic background and level of education, their age and sex, and their group membership.

As an indication of the extent of variation found within a reasonably homogenous speech community, consider the data in Table 1 from the ViC corpus of conversational American English (Johnson, 2004). Each of the listed variants was found at least once in the corpus. The extent of naturally occurring variation is underlined in Johnson's statistical analysis comparing recorded tokens of words in an extensive corpus of conversational speech with their canonical forms. For

Table 1

Variants of *until* Reported by Johnson (2004) From the ViC Corpus of American English Conversational Speech

Variant	# of deviating segments (compared with citation form, including deleted segments)	# of deleted segments (compared with citation form)
[ʌntɪl]	0	0
[ʌntəl] [ɛntɪl]	1	0
[ɛntəl] [ɪntɪw]	2	0
[n̩tɪl]	2	1
[əntʌ]	3	1
[n̩tl̩]	4	2
[tl̩]	4	3
[tə]	4	3

Note: Adapted from 'Massive reduction in conversational American English' by K. Johnson, 2004, in K. Yoneyama and K. Maekawa (Eds.), *Spontaneous Speech: Data and Analysis. Proceedings of the 1st Session of the 10th International Symposium*, p. 41. Copyright 2004 by author. Adapted with permission.

instance, 60% of words deviated from their citation form — that is, the pronunciation that might be listed for the word in a dictionary (i.e., [ʌntɪl] for the example in Table 1) — on at least one speech sound, and 28% on two or more. Such 'massive' reduction is frequently encountered in normal conversational speech.

While much variation exists even within an essentially stable system, variation can also be associated with change. The relationship between language variation and language change is complex. Variation within a linguistic category (e.g., different realisations of essentially the 'same' sound, such as differing degrees of aspiration of a /t/ in English) may not have major consequences in terms of language change, but variation that crosses category boundaries may impact on the linguistic system, resulting for instance in the merger of two formerly significantly different sounds. Mergers can take different forms — the collapse of a distinction may result in a single sound taking on a range of realisations previously covered by the two different sounds. Alternatively, a merger may entail the loss of the realisations previously associated with one of the sounds. Or the merger may result in a completely new set of realisations, perhaps intermediate between the earlier forms.

The mechanisms of change are also varied. Some changes may affect a complete linguistic category at the same rate, so that all words containing a certain speech sound seem to undergo simultaneous change. Other changes proceed by diffusion through the lexicon, with some words affected ahead of others. In this case the words initially affected may be the most frequently used words containing the sound in question, or if the sound change is triggered by a particular phonetic context (for instance, by a particular type of consonant before a vowel that is undergoing change), then the words affected may be the very words that contain such a context.

The particular form of variation that is of primary interest in our research program concerns the merger-in-progress in New Zealand English (NZE) of the front-centering diphthongs /iə/ and /eə/, which we will call NEAR and SQUARE, using Wells's (1982) lexical sets. As this is a change that is currently incomplete in NZE, it raises some interesting questions for aspects of spoken word recognition, as we will see below.

First, some brief comments on the progress of the NEAR–SQUARE merger. Gordon and Maclagan (2001) provide data from a 5-yearly survey among 14- to 15-year-old students in Christchurch. The dataset consists of recordings of words containing NEAR and SQUARE vowels, read in sentence contexts and word lists.[1] The results show quite clearly that the diphthongs, both still widely present in the initial 1983 survey, are almost completely merged on NEAR by 1998. Also, while there is considerable variation in the earliest samples, with some speakers showing no clear pattern of merger towards either NEAR or SQUARE, the more recent samples show more complete changes towards NEAR. In an apparent-time comparison of two age groups recorded in 1994 (Maclagan & Gordon, 1996) this more complete merger towards NEAR is confirmed for younger speakers (20–30 years old) but is not as evident for older speakers (45–60 years old). The NEAR-SQUARE merger is described as part of the chain-shift raising of the short front vowels of NZE (/pæt/ to /pet/, /pet/ to /pɪt/, and so forth), with the first element of the SQUARE diphthong raised towards that of the NEAR diphthong (Maclagan & Gordon, 1996, pp. 144–145).[2] Gordon and Maclagan (2001, p. 232) conclude that the change is most likely a 'merger of approximation' rather than a 'merger of expansion' (Labov, 1994, p. 321); that is, the two sounds are collapsing on a single form, in this case the higher or closer NEAR pronunciation, rather than continuing to use the whole range of pronunciations previously available to both NEAR and SQUARE. As a consequence, the more open SQUARE diphthong is heard mainly from the older speakers in the Christchurch survey.

A further claim about this sound change is that it has progressed through NZE by a process of lexical diffusion, that is, it has affected some words before others, and has then spread through the inventory of relevant words (Maclagan & Gordon, 1996, pp. 131–133). One potential pathway for this diffusion is revealed in a reanalysis of Holmes and Bell's (1992) auditory study of the NEAR-SQUARE merger. Warren (2006) looked at the preceding phonetic contexts in the materials investigated by Holmes and Bell, that is, the consonants that occurred before the NEAR or SQUARE vowels, to see whether they provide a phonetic conditioning factor that contributes to the likelihood of the merger (see Figure 1). This reanalysis found that SQUARE-raising, which increased over apparent time (so that mid-age speakers in that sample had higher forms than old speakers, and young speakers had even higher forms), was present for all phonetic contexts for the youngest speakers, but for the mid-age speakers was found only after coronal consonants. This pattern suggests that the change may

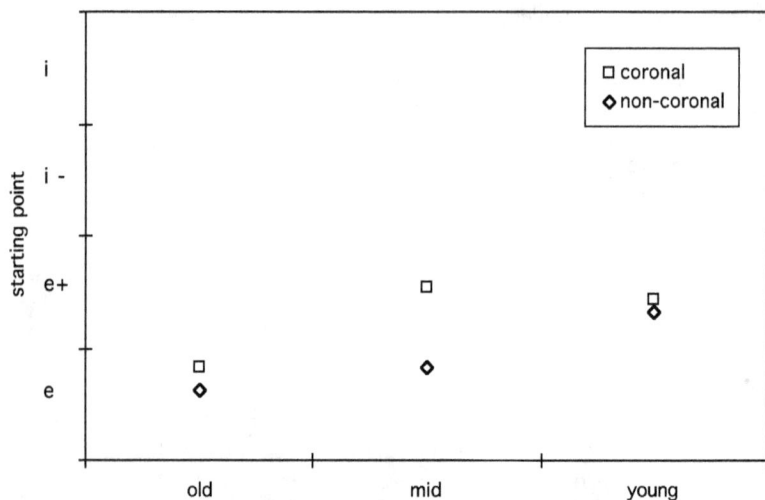

Figure 1
Median starting points for SQUARE diphthongs, by age group and place of articulation of preceding consonant.

Note: From the analysis in Warren (2006) of auditory data from Holmes and Bell (1992).

initially have been conditioned by the nature of the preceding consonant — the higher vowel position would be a natural consequence of coarticulation with a preceding coronal consonant, since the tongue is already in a high front position for such consonants. Subsequently the raising of SQUARE spread to other contexts. This pattern of diffusion is compatible with Ohala's (1992) comments that some sound changes are due to failure on the part of listeners to compensate for coarticulation. That is, speakers of NZE started to 'forget' that there was a conditioning factor responsible for the higher SQUARE vowel after coronals, and regarded these post-coronal forms as having NEAR vowels. At a subsequent stage, the NEAR vowel spread to other words formerly pronounced with SQUARE vowels.

As a change such as the NEAR-SQUARE merger proceeds, so different aspects of variation come to the fore. Initially the main type of variation might well be within-category variation, which increases as SQUARE forms take on higher (closer) articulations. Since the merger is asymmetric (moving towards NEAR) and a merger of approximation (consolidating on a single form rather than both vowels spreading their range of variation to include the total range of the two), variation at this stage may be greater for SQUARE than for NEAR. Subsequently, the boundary between the two categories becomes obscured as NEAR vowels increasingly get used for the SQUARE forms, and variation crosses the category boundary. While the change progresses through the speech community, there will be some speakers for whom the merger is complete, and who will primarily use NEAR forms for both NEAR and SQUARE words. Other (in this case older) speakers will still maintain a distinction between NEAR and SQUARE words. Clearly the nature of any variation will therefore be speaker dependent, while across the community as a whole there will be more variation in the realisation of SQUARE forms than of NEAR forms. An interesting question is whether listeners are able to utilise their knowledge of speaker differences in order to help interpret the variation that they hear (Strand, 1999; Johnson, Strand, & D'Imperio, 1999).

Word Recognition and Variation

Variation in the speech signal is not always problematic for word recognition, and may in some instances facilitate the processes involved. For instance, variation which results from the position of a sound in a word (e.g., the aspiration of an English voiceless stop when word initial, as in *pot*, but not when after /s/, as in *spot*) may be highly informative for the process of segmenting the continuous speech stream into words or other recognition units. However, there are many other occasions where variation is less predictable and therefore less useful for recognition. Yet despite the obvious extent of variation, listeners rarely complain of being unable to understand what is being said. Presumably, therefore, our comprehension system, including the processes involved in spoken word recognition, is well adapted to such variation, producing stability in perception despite the variability in pronunciation.

Historically, models of perception and recognition have sought islands of reliability in the speech signal, robust clues to the identity of speech sounds and/or the words that contain them. However, it has been claimed that most current models of spoken word recognition will ultimately fail in their attempts to deal with the issue of variation because they are constrained by at least one of two basic assumptions about the process of mapping from speech input to mental lexicon (Johnson, 2004). The first of these, the segmental assumption, supposes that stored lexical forms consist of speech segments (much like the alphabetic symbols in written words), and that an important goal of perception is to analyse the speech input into a similar segmental representation. This is problematic if the input is highly variable, with segments missing or different from those expected in a stored citation form. The second assumption is that there is a single lexical entry for each word, and so a further goal of input analysis is to remove or compensate for variation in order to arrive at a form that is well matched to this entry. These assumptions are similar to what Grosjean (1985) earlier referred to as the over-reliance of most models of spoken word recognition on the 'written dictionary' word as the assumed form of mental representations.

Not all current models of word recognition fall foul of both the *segmental* and the *single-entry* assumptions. Some depart explicitly from the assumption of a segment-based representation by allowing incomplete specifications of the segments that make up a word, thus permitting incomplete or ambiguous input information to continue to map on to the intended underlying form; or they may permit more detailed lexical representations, with subsegmental information therefore included also in the input analysis. For instance, Lahiri (Lahiri, 1999; Lahiri & Marslen-Wilson, 1991; Lahiri & Reetz, 2003) suggests that while there is only a single underlying representation for each word in the mental lexicon, these representations may be made up of overlapping arrays of subsegmental phonetic features (such as specifications for voicing, nasality, coronality, and so on) rather than consisting of sequences of quasi-discrete speech segments. Importantly, these featural representations make up a featurally underspecified lexicon (FUL). The nature of the underspecification is language-specific, and for English would include underspecification of coronal place of articulation. The lexical representations thus abstract away from the specific realisation of coronal place. This reflects the finding that coronal consonants frequently assimilate to neighbouring segments, as in *swee[p] boy* for *sweet boy*, while non-coronals are less likely to assimilate (so we tend not to find *ba[p] breaking* for *back breaking* or *clu[d] dances* for *club dances*). With a lexical representation for *sweet* that is underspecified for [coronal], the negative specification of this feature that arises from hearing the final stretch of speech in *swee[p]* does not clash with the lexical representation of *sweet* (in terms of the FUL model this is a 'no mismatch' situation), and thus *sweet* is still activated.

Gaskell and Marslen-Wilson (1996) develop such ideas further, and focus on the processes involved in retrieving the underlying lexical representation. Their research indicates that *sweet* is in fact accessed more successfully in a *swee[p] boy* context than in a *swee[k] boy* context. Consequently these authors argue for a model of recognition which includes phonological inferencing, in this case using information from the immediately following phonetic context (the [b]) to unravel the connected speech processes and thus to infer the underlying identity of the final consonant. While this provides sensitivity to the cause of assimilation, it has been pointed out that there may frequently be difficulty in determining what kinds of variation in production have led to the surface form encountered, making it problematic for the appropriate unravelling of these effects (Pitt & Johnson, 2003). Both FUL and phonological inferencing retain a single-entry approach and attempt to deal with variation resulting from assimilation by assuming that the acoustic featural structure of the input representation need not coincide completely with that of the lexical representation.

Other word recognition models which do not assume segmental analysis of the input include Klatt's Lexical Access from Spectra (LAFS; Klatt, 1979) and later versions of the Cohort model and allied approaches (Marslen-Wilson & Warren, 1994; Hawkins & Warren, 1994), which attempt to account for some of the subsegmental variation found in natural speech. While these models propose units smaller than the segment, they continue to posit single lexical representations for each word, and assume that recognition will proceed via some kind of measure of goodness-of-fit between input and representation. In practice, though, it turns out that the matching process can be just as sensitive to irrelevant detail as it is to the important phonetic distinctions between words (Klatt, 1989). In addition, single-entry models generally find it difficult to deal with the many segment and syllable deletions found in natural spontaneous speech, since such deletions reduce the extent of left-to-right match between the input and lexical representations.

Let us turn now to coping with variation by abandoning the single-entry assumption. Perhaps the most obvious modification in this direction is the addition of entries to the lexicon in order to permit greater recognition of regional variants in pronunciation. Thus the lexicon might be expanded to include both [baθ] and [bæθ] for *bath*, or [plʌg] and [plʊg] for plug, and so on. Different entires may also reflect free variation (e.g., the pronunciation of *economics* with different initial vowels). Some connected speech processes could also be accounted for with variants listed in the lexicon, such as [wen] for *went*. Here, though, experience in the domain of automatic speech recognition (ASR) suggests that the net gain may be rather small, because confusability within the lexicon can increase, with new variants being confused with other existing words, such as *went/when* for [wen], or [swip] analysed as either *sweep* or a possible assimilated form of *sweet* (for a review from the ASR perspective see Strik & Cucchiarini, 1999). Since assimilated forms often contain residual phonetic information that might help identify the underlying form (Pitt & Johnson, 2003), it might prove fruitful to add more detailed representations of words to the lexicon, capturing subsegmental distinctions such as those found in the formant transitions at the ends of vowels before assimilated (*sweet[p] boy*) and non-assimilated (*sweep paths*) segments (for evidence that listeners are sensitive to such detail in the course of word recognition see Marslen-Wilson & Warren, 1994).

Johnson (1997) has developed a model of word recognition which abandons both the assumption of segmental analysis/representation and the assumption of single-entries for lexical items. In Johnson's X-MOD model, a spectral representation of the input is calculated, much as in Klatt's (1979) LAFS model. But rather than being matched against a single stored representation, the input is compared with an exemplar 'map' based on previous encounters with relevant tokens. Weightings for exemplars are adjusted on the basis of experience and learning, and new exemplars can be added to the map as they are encountered. Such flexibility allows the model to be sensitive to variation encountered in the input.

Hawkins (e.g., 2003) takes this idea of an exemplar-based recognition system even further, and emphasises in her Polysp model the polysystemic nature of speech understanding. Individuals' prior experiences of language will influence how they use sensory information in order to arrive at speech comprehension. We would argue that in the set of prior experiences we should include implicit knowledge of how variation is socially distributed (see also Hay, Warren, & Drager, in press).

The NEAR-SQUARE Merger and Issues for Spoken Word Recognition

> Regional accents are wonderfully enriching contributions to the English language — but an accent becomes degenerate when the spoken word cannot differentiate between totally different meanings. Too often we hear of people crossing on the Cook Strait 'fairy' and flying 'Ear' New Zealand. (L. Bravery, letter to the editor, *Listener*, June 9, 2001)

Such comments are not unusual, and reflect a natural concern that speakers have when confronted with changes in the pronunciation of their language. If a change results in the loss of an earlier distinction, a common worry is that this will affect communicative ability in the language. Yet it is not clear that comprehension need be impaired by merger, since the language comprehension system is already equipped to cope with ambiguity. That is, there are many words in the English language (and not just in New Zealand English) that are already ambiguous, such as *bank*, or *write/right*. Existing research (e.g., Swinney, 1979) has demonstrated that when we encounter an ambiguous word, all meanings are initially accessed regardless of whether the word is actually ambiguous in the given context. A suitably constraining context will then quickly force the selection of the appropriate meaning, usually before we are even aware of ambiguity.

Now, given the progress of the NEAR-SQUARE merger outlined earlier, although all NZE speakers are currently still likely to hear both vowels, many younger speakers may produce only NEAR in both NEAR and SQUARE words. What is of interest is how this state of affairs may affect the ability to accurately recognise words containing these vowels. If the merger were complete across all speakers, then words like *cheer* and *chair* would be ambiguous, just like *bank* or *write/right*, and would presumably therefore be recognised in similar manner. However, since the NEAR-SQUARE merger is not complete in NZE, we might expect the processing of words like *cheer* and *chair* to differ somewhat from that of true homophones. This clearly relates to issues to do with variation and word recognition (as discussed above), because listeners have to be able to interpret the input that they are hearing in the context of what they 'know' about the scope and nature of variation in pronunciation. This is true just as much of variation resulting from change-in-progress as it is of variation determined by phonetic, phonological or social contexts.

The goals of our research program are to explore the consequences for spoken word recognition of variation resulting from change-in-progress. Ultimately this includes issues to do with how NZE speakers utilise information about speaker group membership in order to assess whether the spoken forms they hear reflect merged or unmerged systems (and our research program includes studies that explicitly manipulate clues to speaker identity).

Experimental Data

In this section we summarise some of our recent research results relating to the issue of how speech perception and word recognition are affected by the variation brought about by the change-in-progress described above. We hope that as our program develops we will be able to shed more light on the question of how listeners 'cope with' variation, and the role played in such a process by their experience of relevant variation in their environment. This experience includes variation in the listeners' own productions of the NEAR and SQUARE diphthongs, as well as in those spoken by other speakers. Importantly, we hypothesise, listeners will show sensitivity to the patterning of variation in the speech communities to which they are exposed.

The specific data reported here come from an initial series of speech production and perception tasks in Christchurch and Wellington. In each centre, we collected data using a number of paradigms. Here we refer to acoustic analyses of word-list reading data (Christchurch and Wellington), to the outcomes of binary forced-choice identification tasks between NEAR and SQUARE words (Christchurch and Wellington), and to the results of a timed lexical decision task exploring the issue of differential access to NEAR and SQUARE words on exposure to NEAR or SQUARE tokens (Wellington only). The data in each centre have been obtained from the same participant groups. Thus in Christchurch we have data on the differentiation in both production and perception of NEAR and SQUARE from one group of Christchurch participants, and in Wellington we have comparable data along with lexical access response time data, all from a single group of Wellington participants.

The first group of questions we pose with regard to the two data sets are whether there are any observable differences between and/or within the two communities in the degree to which NEAR and SQUARE words are distinguished (a) in production and (b) in the identification task, and (c) whether performance differences in these two tasks are interrelated. Finally, we ask of the Wellington group (d) whether performance data in the lexical access task reflect the observed asymmetry in the progression of the NEAR-SQUARE merger.

Production

Our interest in this section is the extent to which young NZE speakers distinguish NEAR and SQUARE tokens in a situation — reading minimal pairs — which favours distinctions being made. We are also interested in possible differences between Wellington and Christchurch speakers in this regard. Sixteen young participants (18–30 years old) from each centre were asked to read pairs of NEAR and SQUARE words. In each case they first read a list of words in which the NEAR form always preceded the SQUARE form (so *beer–bare*, *cheer–chair*, and so on), and then read the same word pairs with random ordering within pairs (so that the NEAR word did not always precede the SQUARE word). The first list would appear to be the optimal situation for obtaining clear distinctions.

Participants in the two centres had slightly different lists, and so the data reported below are based on the nine word pairs that were common to both lists (words beginning in /b, d, f, h, p, r, ʃ, sp/ and the pair *ear–air*. The Wellington data had these nine pairs plus *chair–cheer*, *stare–steer* and *tear–tier*, while the complete set of data from Christchurch had the nine pairs plus *mare–mere*). Note also that the analysis here uses data only from the female speakers in each group (12 in Christchurch, 13 in Wellington. The complete dataset also includes four males from Christchurch and three from Wellington). This is because the average acoustic values for the two regional groups would be differentially affected by the presence of differing proportions of male speakers in the total samples.

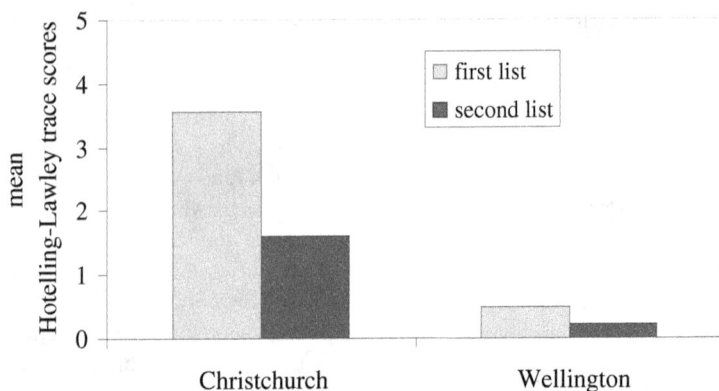

Figure 2

Mean Hotelling-Lawley trace scores, showing level of discrimination in production between NEAR and SQUARE vowels.

Our measure of the separation of the NEAR and SQUARE diphthongs is based on an acoustic analysis of the first two formants (F1 and F2) of the vowels at a point near the start of the diphthong.[3] For each speaker we obtained a statistical measure of the separation of NEAR and SQUARE articulations across the set of word pairs, using Bark values derived from the Hertz frequency measurements. (The Bark scale is a closer approximation than the Hertz scale to the perception of vowel formant information.) Compared with a simple distance metric such as the Euclidean distance between average /iə/ and /eə/ formant locations, the multivariate statistical measure we used, Hotelling-Lawley's trace, has the advantage that it takes into account the distribution of the formant locations over the different NEAR and SQUARE vowels for each speaker.

If our subjects find it difficult to produce differences between the two diphthongs, then we might expect the first reading of the word lists, with the fixed NEAR-SQUARE ordering of each word pair, to provide the clearest distinction. This is indeed what our data show, as seen in Figure 2. They also show a tendency for greater separation of the vowels for Christchurch speakers than for the Wellington group. These two findings are confirmed in analysis of variance (ANOVA) of the Hotelling-Lawley trace data, with Repetition (first vs. second reading, as described above) and City (Christchurch vs. Wellington) as factors. The effect of Repetition was significant, $F(1, 23) = 6.31$, $p < .02$, while that of City approached significance $F(1, 23) = 3.88$, $p = .06$. In addition, the interaction between these two factors approached significance, $F(1, 23) = 3.69$, $p < .07$. Wellington speakers show relatively small levels of distinction in either set of readings, while the Christchurch speakers are not only better able overall to distinguish the two diphthongs, but they also show a greater effect of the strict ordering of the first set. The relative success of the Christchurch speakers in distinguishing these vowels must however be kept in perspective — the first author,

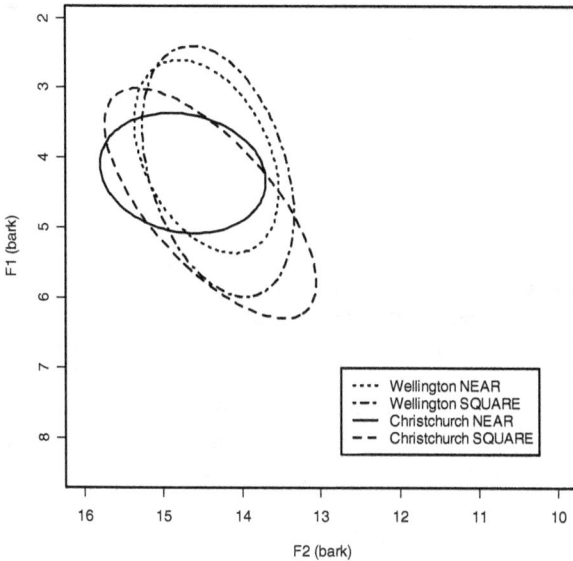

Figure 3

Ellipse plots in F1–F2 space of NEAR and SQUARE vowels produced by Wellington and Christchurch speakers reading the minimal pair lists.

a native speaker of a variety (Southern British English) that maintains a distinction between NEAR and SQUARE vowels, achieved a Hotelling-Lawley trace score of 18.4 for the same minimal pair list.

An indication of the greater separation for Christchurch than for Wellington speakers is given by the ellipse plots of the first two formants (in Bark) in Figure 3. This figure uses the conventional orientation of F1 on the vertical and F2 on the horizontal, each reversed, so that the position of a point on the chart is symbolic of the highest point of the tongue in a mouth facing towards the left (corresponding to the orientation of the standard vowel chart used in phonetics). The ellipses in the figure are based on 216 (Christchurch) or 234 (Wellington) F1 and F2 values for each diphthong. Each ellipse is centered on the mean for the relevant dataset and includes 95% of the data. The orientation of the ellipse reflects the distribution of the data in F1–F2 space.

The figure shows considerable overlap in the distributions of these acoustic values for NEAR and SQUARE diphthongs for both speaker sets, but with Christchurch speakers maintaining a greater distinction between the diphthongs, primarily by keeping more open articulations (higher F1 values) for SQUARE. For both speaker sets, note that the distribution for SQUARE is greater than that for NEAR, showing the variability in the pronunciation of the SQUARE diphthong.

It is not immediately clear why the Christchurch speakers produce a greater distinction between NEAR and SQUARE diphthongs. None of the factors previously

Table 2
Correct Identification Scores (%) for NEAR and SQUARE Diphthongs

	Christchurch	Wellington
NEAR	97.5	88.0
SQUARE	90.4	84.2

linked to the progress of the merger — speaker age, speaker sex, and phonetic context — seem to be likely. The speakers in the two groups have similar age ranges. When we prepared the data for analysis we removed data from the small number of male speakers in the experiment. We also ensured that both the analysed datasets had tokens with the same sets of consonants preceding the diphthongs. Remaining factors include the possibility that the merger is more advanced for the Wellington speakers, but there may also be a link to the same subject groups' performances in a perceptual identification task, to which we now turn.

Perceptual Identification

To get a measure of the ability of native speakers to distinguish between the NEAR and SQUARE diphthongs, we asked the same subjects to take part in binary forced-choice identification tasks. Individual recordings of the NEAR and SQUARE minimal pair words, recorded by female native speakers from the relevant region (i.e., a Wellington-based speaker and a Christchurch-based speaker, each of whom distinguishes the diphthongs in her speech), were played to subjects over closed-ear headphones, and the subjects were asked to identify the stimulus as one of two words (the correct word and its minimal-pair partner). Each token was presented twice during the course of the experiment. For the two presentations, the left–right display order of the words between which the subject had to choose was reversed. Order of presentation of items was pseudo-randomised, with care taken to ensure that presentations of the items from any one minimal pair were well separated in the test lists.

To allow close comparison between the Christchurch and Wellington data, and with the production data presented above, the results discussed here again relate only to the female participants from each city and include only the nine pairs of words used in both the Christchurch and Wellington production studies, so that the participants and word pairs are the same as those in the production task. The results for this subset of data are shown in Table 2. The results for the complete datasets do not differ greatly from those presented here.

Note first that overall scores were very high, showing that despite the ongoing merger of these vowels in NZE, including in their own speech, the participants were able to distinguish the two in this perceptual task. The proportions of correct scores for each participant for each diphthong type were subjected to an arcsin transform and entered into ANOVA with Diphthong (NEAR or SQUARE) and City (Wellington or Christchurch) as independent variables. The differences

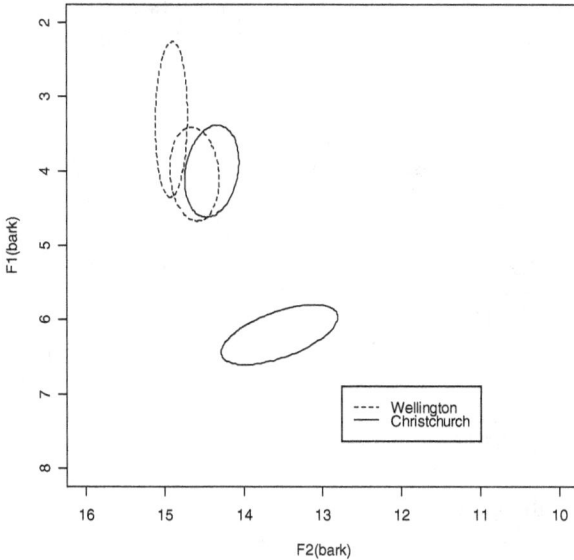

Figure 4
Ellipse plots in F1–F2 space of near and square vowels used in the Wellington and Christchurch identification task.

Note: NEAR vowels are in the upper ellipse in each case.

in identification rates for the two diphthongs and in the two cities are significant, Diphthong: $F(1, 23) = 5.51$, $p < .05$, and City: $F(1, 23) = 5.32$, $p < .05$; there was no interaction between these factors.

The most obvious explanation for the better correct response rate in the Christchurch data is that there are differences between the two recordings used. The speaker for the Christchurch data was older than the speaker used in Wellington, and in fact made clearer distinctions between the two diphthongs, as shown in Figure 4. It is interesting that the Wellington speaker's SQUARE vowels are in approximately the same area of the figure as the Christchurch speaker's NEAR vowels, and that the Wellington speaker has much closer NEAR vowels, though these are still within the range of the groups of speakers in Figure 3. Note that despite the smaller distinction in the vowels for the Wellington speaker, subjects still achieved a high level of correct identifications for this speaker.

Some data that suggest that the Christchurch/Wellington difference is not simply due to differences in the recordings comes from a further study with forty 14- and 15-year-olds from two Christchurch schools, schools which have contributed to the long-term study of the merger being carried out by Gordon and Maclagan. These 40 participants completed the exact same-identification task, with the same speaker, as the participants who provided the Christchurch data reported above. The correct scores for these school students were more similar to the Wellington scores than to those of the other Christchurch participants, at 90.75% for NEAR tokens and 86.6% for SQUARE tokens. Since these scores are for the same speaker as the other Christchurch data, the difference in this case cannot be attributed to speaker differences. Two further points are relevant here. One is that the NEAR/SQUARE difference in identification, though small, is highly robust, showing up in three listener groups for two different speakers. The other is that these younger Christchurch participants perform worse than the older ones in the identification task, but not by much. It seems that the ability to hear the difference between NEAR and SQUARE is going away, but it is disappearing at a much slower rate than the merger in production is occurring (as evidenced in the data presented by Gordon & Maclagan, 2001).

Possible interpretations for the finding of higher correct scores for NEAR words than for SQUARE words involve speaker effects, lexical effects and non-lexical bias. A possible speaker effect is that the speakers who provided the recordings used in the identification task are producing close variants of the SQUARE vowel. Yet as comparison of Figures 3 and 4 shows, this is not a likely explanation for the Christchurch speaker, though it may be a factor for the Wellington speaker.

A lexical interpretation is that the overall result arises because some of the SQUARE stimuli have close articulations, leading to NEAR responses for these items. We might therefore predict a significant correlation between the closeness of the SQUARE token and the rate of NEAR-for-SQUARE errors for individual items. No such significant correlation was found in Wellington or Christchurch.

An interpretation in terms of non-lexical bias might reflect the overall experience of the participants. Because the merger in NZE is towards a close first element for both diphthongs, this form is more frequent in the participants' environment. As a consequence, a 'fast phonological pre-processor' (Pierrehumbert, 2001) may be biased towards the closer diphthong, so that SQUARE tokens may occasionally be heard as NEAR.

Identification and Production

The two sets of data presented above, obtained from the same informants, allow us to investigate the relationship between the production and perception of the NEAR-SQUARE contrast. Of particular interest is the possibility that listeners may interpret acoustic phonetic information in a manner that shows an influence of their own production system. The (relatively small but statistically significant) difference reported above between the group of Wellington participants and the group of Christchurch participants in the extent to which they seem able to identify NEAR and SQUARE tokens is tantalising, since it appears to mirror the differences in the production data of these two groups (see the significant main effect of City in both the production and perception studies), and may reflect a difference in the extent of the merger in the two centres. However, if there is some kind of causal relationship involved here, it is not clear whether it is an influence of the participants' production system on their perception, or an influence of perception on production. This latter possibility arises because the production task was the final task carried out by participants in the experimental sessions, and may therefore have been influenced by prior exposure to the materials used in the identification task, which as we have seen were more distinct for the Christchurch stimuli.

A more detailed indication of a relationship between production and perception comes from an analysis that considers differences among individual participants. This analysis looks at correlations between the Hotelling-Lawley trace scores (indicating the extent of NEAR-SQUARE separation in production) and correct identification scores (for perception). For the two participant groups as a whole there is a significant correlation of overall Hotelling-Lawley scores (i.e., including both first and second recordings of each item) and overall correct identification scores (taking NEAR and SQUARE together), with $r = .427$, $p < .05$. Interestingly, when the overall correlation of Hotelling-Lawley and identification scores is examined separately for Wellington and Christchurch participants, only the latter show a significant relationship between production and perception ($r = .587$, $p < .05$). The absence of this effect for the Wellington group reflects the relatively small degree to which they distinguish NEAR and SQUARE in their productions — they would appear to be more solidly merged than the Christchurch group, though still able to identify NEAR and SQUARE words in the perceptual task at a high level of accuracy. This pattern of data across the two groups seems to suggest that listeners' sensitivity to differences between phonemic sets remains even after their production data fails to show consistent differentiation.

Lexical Access

Our final set of data relate to lexical access in a community undergoing sound change. Specifically, we consider speakers — our young Wellington participants — who are themselves no longer consistently able to produce a difference between the diphthongs, yet are able to identify the differences with a high level of reliability in the speech of others. The data come from an auditory lexical decision task with within-list priming (for more details, see Rae & Warren, 2002a, 2002b).

Test probes in the experiment were words associated in meaning to 12 pairs of NEAR and SQUARE words, which served as primes for these test probes. For instance *shout* or *sit* were probes following *cheer* and *chair* as primes. Probes were obtained from published association norms.[4] In addition, the same probes followed an unrelated control prime. All prime and probe words, filler items and non-words were recorded by the same speaker as used in the identification task for these participants. Our measure of the lexical activation of the primes is their facilitation of semantically related probes. This facilitation time (FT) is defined as the difference between the lexical decision response time (RT) to a probe word presented immediately after a test prime (e.g., *shout* after either *cheer* or *chair*) and the RT to the same test probe after a control prime (e.g., *shout* after *bee*).

If a variety reliably distinguishes NEAR and SQUARE, we would predict that each member of a NEAR–SQUARE pair would produce strongest facilitation for the

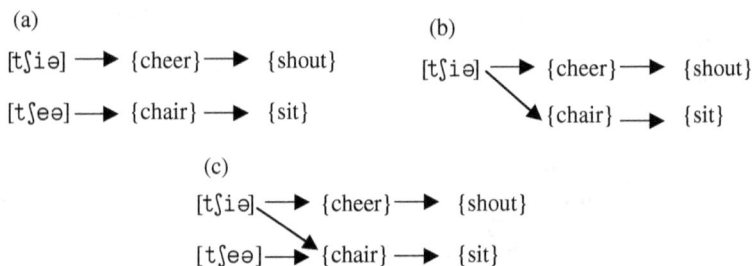

(a)

[tʃiə] ⟶ {cheer} ⟶ {shout}

[tʃeə] ⟶ {chair} ⟶ {sit}

(b)

[tʃiə] ⟶ {cheer} ⟶ {shout}
    ↘ {chair} ⟶ {sit}

(c)

[tʃiə] ⟶ {cheer} ⟶ {shout}

[tʃeə] ⟶ {chair} ⟶ {sit}

Figure 5

Hypothetical mappings from phonetic input onto lexical form for different states of merger of NEAR and SQUARE (see text for details).

appropriate semantically related word, as in panel (a) of Figure 5. Alternatively, given the pattern of the NEAR–SQUARE merger pointed out above, we might predict that younger speakers treat words like the *cheer–chair* pair as homophones merged on NEAR and access both words equally, as in panel (b), which assumes merger on NEAR. However, the presence of non-merged forms among older speakers means that this might not always result in successful recognition — recall that the identification task showed that our young subjects are able to categorise the SQUARE tokens appropriately. Because of this asymmetry in the merger, we predict that when listeners hear a NEAR form they retrieve both NEAR and SQUARE words, but that when they hear a SQUARE form they access only the SQUARE word, as illustrated in panel (c).

The statistical analysis of average FTs for each subject in each test condition (see Figure 6) confirmed that appropriate probes (e.g., *shout* after *cheer* or *sit* after *chair*) received greater priming than inappropriate probes (*sit* after *cheer* or *shout* after *chair*, $F(1, 15) = 5.85$, $p < .03$. In addition, there was a significant interaction of prime and probe type, $F(1, 15) = 4.90$, $p < .05$. In planned comparisons, SQUARE primes facilitated appropriate probes more than inappropriate probes ([tʃeə]–{sit} > [tʃeə]–{shout}), $F(1, 30) = 6.10$, $p < .02$, while there was no difference in the facilitation of different probes by NEAR primes ([tʃiə]–{shout} ≈ [tʃiə]–{sit}), $F(1, 30) = 0.23$.

These results show strong support for the predicted asymmetry in recognising words containing the NEAR and SQUARE vowels, consistent with the main trends shown in the production studies reviewed above, and supporting the hypothetical position displayed in panel (c) of Figure 5. In other words, on hearing items with a NEAR vowel, our young Wellington subjects access both NEAR and SQUARE words, just as the different meanings of *bank* are both automatically accessed on hearing the homophone. Hearing the SQUARE form leads to access of the SQUARE word (and not the NEAR word), reflecting the fact that the phonetic [eə] form is still heard in the subjects' environment.

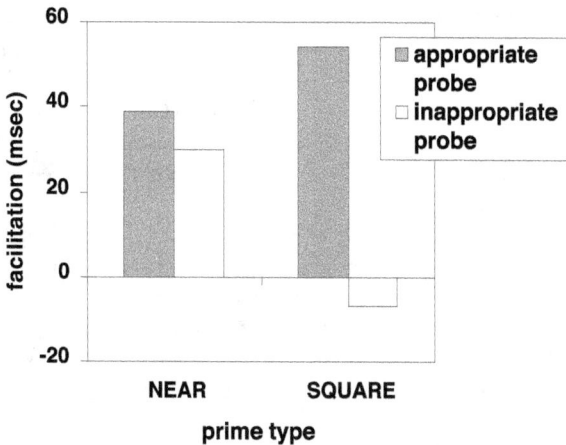

Figure 6

Average facilitation times (in milliseconds, relative to the control condition) for appropriate and inappropriate probes following NEAR and SQUARE primes (e.g., from left to right in the figure, cheer–shout, cheer–sit, chair–sit, chair–shout).

A further observation from our results supports this view that NEAR forms are homophonous but SQUARE forms are not. This relates to the difference in facilitation levels after NEAR and SQUARE. Work by Rodd and her colleagues (Rodd, Gaskell, & Marslen-Wilson, 2002) has shown that homophones are responded to more slowly than unambiguous words in a lexical decision task, reflecting competition between two different words with the same form. Analysis of lexical decision responses to the NEAR and SQUARE words in our experiment confirms that the former are responded to more slowly (894 vs. 868 msec, $t = 2.94$, df: 15, $p < .02$). A knock-on effect of this disadvantage for ambiguous words would be that their associates are less strongly primed than words associated with unambiguous words. The data shown in Figure 6 appear to support this position, with lower levels of facilitation for either word following NEAR primes than for the SQUARE word following the SQUARE prime. Note though that compared to the control condition there is still facilitation of probe words related to both meanings, so that any disadvantage is relative to priming by unambiguous words, rather than a claim that uncertainty about the lexical identity of NEAR words results in inhibition of lexical representations.

Discussion

What type of model of variation and word recognition best accounts for this set of results from young NZE participants? Recall that the production data show a high degree of overlap of NEAR and SQUARE pronunciations, particularly for our Wellington participants. Recall also that the results of the identification task show that despite this overlap in production, speakers can hear the difference between NEAR and SQUARE. Although this overall result appears to indicate something of a disjuncture between production and perception, we noted that identification scores are nevertheless better for the participants who distinguish the forms more in their own production, and that when there is sufficient variation in extent of production to allow a correlation (i.e., among the Christchurch speakers) then there is a positive relationship between production and perception.

Recall further that our speaker group (the Wellingtonians) that was least able to distinguish the vowels in production appears to have almost completely merged the diphthongs onto NEAR. Furthermore, on hearing NEAR forms in the lexical decision task this group gains access to both NEAR and SQUARE items in the lexicon. Nevertheless this group is able to correctly identify SQUARE on hearing the SQUARE form, and to access SQUARE forms (and only SQUARE forms) on hearing SQUARE in the lexical decision task.

The nature of variation for these young Wellington speakers is such that they exhibit little variation in production (i.e., they appear to have undergone a merger of approximation on NEAR); clearly they hear more variation from others in their environment (e.g., from older speakers, but even the similar aged Christchurch speakers here show more variation than the Wellingtonians), and they hear tokens from speakers who maintain a clear distinction between NEAR and SQUARE (cf. the older speakers in the studies by Gordon and Maclagan and by Holmes and Bell referred to earlier in this chapter). This experience of different patterns of distribution of diphthong forms surely contributes to the pattern of production, identification and lexical access data outlined in this chapter.

But how do they do this, and how might models of the mental lexicon and of word recognition account for this set of results? Under FUL we might imagine that the NEAR vowel is underspecified for some relevant vowel height feature and that hearing a NEAR token in the lexical decision task would therefore not lead to conflict with SQUARE on this parameter. But it is not entirely clear how this account would explain the good performance in the identification task. It is also not clear how FUL can cope with lexical diffusion of the NEAR-SQUARE merger. If the nature of the preceding consonant is influential in the initial diffusion of the change, then it is clear that a phonological inferencing account may be able to cope with diffusion (the inference being that a preceding coronal is a causal factor in a closer articulation of the first element of the SQUARE diphthong), but once the change has spread throughout the system (i.e., beyond the coronal context) it is not clear what role processes of phonological inferencing would have to play. If we abandon the single-entry assumption and posit additional lexical entries, then we might argue that the lexical representation with a NEAR vowel has NEAR in its form-based representation while SQUARE words have recognition elements with both SQUARE and NEAR vowels. This would plausibly cope with our production result (NEAR realised with the NEAR vowel; SQUARE more variable) and with the result of the priming task (NEAR tokens are ambiguous and map onto NEAR or SQUARE, while SQUARE tokens map only onto underlying SQUARE forms), but it would presumably predict that in the identification task there would be a lot of errors resulting from exposure to NEAR forms.

It seems to us that an important weakness of each of these accounts is that they fail to fully account for the participants' experiences with NEAR and SQUARE forms. Since the merger is ongoing within the community at large, it is inevitable that our participants will have encountered both merged and non-merged systems, and that this experience, particularly of the asymmetry of the merger, will influence their interpretation of the inputs that they hear. Crucially, though, part of this experience involves developing knowledge (explicit or implicit) of the kinds of speakers who do or do not have a merged system. As a consequence of their experiences, our participants have developed something of a hybrid system, where their own merged production system exists alongside a perceptual system that is sensitive to characteristics of the speaker.

We have already noted that an experience-based account such as this may be involved in the slightly higher level of errors for SQUARE tokens in the identification task — we suggested that greater exposure to NEAR forms may result in a greater likelihood that a rapid phonological preprocessor will select NEAR as a response to an item in the NEAR/SQUARE region. On the whole, though, our participants are accurate in their identification of the NEAR and SQUARE tokens, even for the less distinct productions of the Wellington speaker. It would appear that overall, the participants are able to posit a non-merged system for the speaker on top of their own merged system. The difference between the identification and lexical decision tasks is that in the former participants are able to make a cautious evaluation of the input against the posited non-merged system. In the latter, the more automatic processes of lexical access mean that the input is interpreted asymmetrically — NEAR tokens activate both NEAR and SQUARE representations, reflecting the merged system of the speaker, while SQUARE tokens give selective access to SQUARE representations.

Our further research will explore the possibility that older subjects, who feature both vowels more consistently in their productions, do not show the same asymmetry of priming in the lexical decision experiment. In addition, we wish to test whether more explicit age information about the speaker will affect the interpretation of NEAR and SQUARE forms by subjects. In other words, will subjects who are given different age information about the speaker adjust their interpretation of the same phonetic forms in a way that reflects the age-related differences in the extent of the merger? Such a finding would support a general notion that exemplar-type lexical representations for words are not only phonetically rich, but also indexed for social and demographic characteristics of the speakers who have contributed to each individual's experience of language (see Hay et al., 2006).

Endnotes

1   While read (rather than spontaneous) materials are not ideal, Gimson (1963, p. 143), referring to the original study by Fry (1947), lists the NEAR and SQUARE vowels as only the 17th and 18th most frequent out of 20 English vowels. It therefore becomes necessary to use read materials in order to elicit sufficient tokens for analysis.

2   The difference between NEAR and SQUARE in NZE, for those speakers that distinguish the vowels, largely involves the height of the first element of the diphthongs (the [i] and [e] of /iə/ and /eə/ respectively). NEAR has a higher first element, since the tongue is higher in the mouth. *High* and *low* vowels are also known as *close* and *open* respectively, reference here being made to the degree of opening between the tongue and the palate.

3   F1 and F2 give a good index of the location of the highest point of the tongue, and as such are a useful measure of the articulation of vowels. Clearly, though, the use of a single measurement point for each vowel is a gross simplification of the dynamic nature of diphthongs. Nevertheless, the height of the starting portion of the vowel is a key feature for distinguishing between the /iə/ and /eə/ diphthongs, as reflected in the transcription symbols for the vowels. The specific measurement point used here corresponds to the location of the peak F2 value in the first portion of the vowel.

4   Three sets of association norms were consulted: the Edinburgh Associative Thesaurus (URL listed in references under *Edinburgh Associative Thesaurus*, 2003), the Florida Free Association Norms (Nelson, McEvoy, & Schreiber, 1998) and the Birkbeck Association Norms (Moss & Older, 1996).

References

Bell, A. (1984). Language style as audience design. *Language in Society, 13*(2), 145–204.

Edinburgh Associative Thesaurus. (2003). Retrieved August 12, 2003, from http://www.eat.rl.ac.uk/

Fry, D. B. (1947). The frequency of occurrence of speech sounds in Southern English. *Achives Néerlandaises de Phonétique Expérimentale, XX*, 103–106.

Gaskell, M. G., & Marslen-Wilson, W. D. (1996). Phonological variation and inference in lexical access. *Journal of Experimental Psychology: Human Perception and Performance, 22*, 144–158.

Gimson, A. C. (1963). An *introduction to the pronunciation of English*. London: Edward Arnold.

Gordon, E., & Maclagan, M. (2001). Capturing a sound change: A real time study over 15 years of the NEAR/SQUARE diphthong merger in New Zealand English. *Australian Journal of Linguistics, 21*(2), 215–238.

Grosjean, F. (1985). The recognition of words after their acoustic offset: Evidence and implications. *Perception and Psychophysics, 38*, 299–310.

Hawkins, S. (2003). Contribution of fine phonetic detail to speech understanding. In M.J. Solé, D. Recasens, & J. Romero (Eds.), *Proceedings of the 15th International Congress of Phonetic Sciences, Barcelona, Spain* (pp. 293–296). Rundle Mall: Casual Productions.

Hawkins, S., & Warren, P. (1994). Phonetic influences on the intelligibility of conversational speech. *Journal of Phonetics, 22*, 493–511.

Hay, J., Warren, P., & Drager, K. (in press). Factors influencing speech perception in the context of a merger-in-progress. *Journal of Phonetics*.

Holmes, J., & Bell, A. (1992). On shear markets and sharing sheep: The merger of EAR and AIR diphthongs in New Zealand English. *Language Variation and Change, 4*, 251–273.

Johnson, K. (1997). Speech perception without speaker normalization. In J. W. Mullennix (Ed.), *Talker variability in speech processing* (pp. 145–166). New York: Academic Press.

Johnson, K. (2004). Massive reduction in conversational American English. In K. Yoneyama & K. Maekawa (Eds.), *Spontaneous speech: Data and analysis. Proceedings of the 1st Session of the 10th International Symposium* (pp. 29–54). Tokyo, Japan: The National International Institute for Japanese Language.

Johnson, K., Strand, E. A., & D'Imperio, M. (1999). Auditory-visual integration of talker gender in vowel perception. *Journal of Phonetics, 24*(4), 359–384.

Klatt, D. H. (1979). Speech perception: A model of acoustic-phonetic analysis and lexical access. *Journal of Phonetics, 7*, 279–312.

Klatt, D. H. (1989). Review of selected models of speech perception. In W. D. Marslen-Wilson (Ed.), *Lexical representation and process* (pp. 169–226). Cambridge, MA: MIT Press.

Labov, W. (1994). *Principles of linguistic change.* Oxford, UK: Blackwell.

Lahiri, A. (1999). Speech recognition with phonological features. In J. J. Ohala, Y. Hasegawa, M. Ohala, D. Granville, & A. C. Bailey (Eds.), *Proceedings of the 14th International Congress of Phonetic Sciences, San Francisco, California* (pp. 715–718). San Francisco, CA: Regents of the University of California, Berkeley.

Lahiri, A., & Marslen-Wilson, W. D. (1991). The mental representation of lexical form: A phonological approach to the recognition lexicon. *Cognition, 38,* 245–294.

Lahiri, A., & Reetz, H. (2003). Retroflexes and dentals in the FUL model. In M.J. Solé, D. Recasens, & J. Romero (Eds.), *Proceedings of the 15th International Congress of Phonetic Sciences, Barcelona, Spain* (pp. 301–304). Rundle Mall: Causal Productions.

Maclagan, M., & Gordon, E. (1996). Out of the AIR and into the EAR: Another view of the New Zealand diphthong merger. *Language Variation and Change, 8,* 125–147.

Marslen-Wilson, W. D., & Warren, P. (1994). Levels of perceptual representation and process in lexical access. *Psychological Review, 101,* 653–675.

Moss, H. E., & Older, L. (1996). *Birkbeck word association norms.* Hove, UK: Lawrence Erlbaum.

Nelson, D. L., McEvoy, C. L., & Schreiber, T. A. (1998). *The University of South Florida word association, rhyme, and word fragment norms.* Retrieved August 12, 2003, from http://www.usf.edu/FreeAssociation/

Ohala, J. J. (1992). What's cognitive, what's not, in sound change. In G. Hellermann (Ed.), *Diachrony within synchrony* (pp. 309–355). Frankfurt, Germany: Peter Verlag.

Pierrehumbert, J. (2001). Why phonological constraints are so coarse-grained. *Language and Cognitive Processes, 16,* 691–698.

Pitt, M., & Johnson, K. (2003, August). *Using pronunciation data as a starting point in modelling word recognition.* Paper presented at the 15th International Congress of Phonetic Sciences, Barcelona, Spain.

Rae, M., & Warren, P. (2002a). The asymmetrical change in progress of EAR and AIR vowels in NZE: Psycholinguistic evidence. *Wellington Working Papers in Linguistics, 14,* 33–46.

Rae, M., & Warren, P. (2002b). Goldilocks and the three beers: Sound merger and word recognition in NZE. *New Zealand English Journal, 16,* 33–41.

Rodd, J., Gaskell, M. G., & Marslen-Wilson, W. D. (2002). Making sense of semantic ambiguity: Semantic competition in lexical access. *Journal of Memory and Language, 46,* 245–266.

Strand, E. A. (1999). Uncovering the role of gender stereotypes in speech perception. *Journal of Language and Social Psychology, 18*(1), 86–99.

Strik, H., & Cucchiarini, C. (1999). Modeling pronunciation variation for ASR: A survey of the literature. *Speech Communication, 27,* 225–246.

Swinney, D. A. (1979). Lexical access during sentence comprehension: (Re) consideration of context effects. *Journal of Verbal Learning and Verbal Behaviour, 18,* 645–659.

Warren, P. (2006). Word recognition and sound merger. In J. Luchjenbroers (Ed.), *Cognitive linguistics investigations* (pp. 169–186). Amsterdam: John Benjamins.

Wells, J. C. (1982). *Accents of English.* Cambridge, UK: Cambridge University Press.

Conflicting Theories on the Developmental Progression of Phonological Awareness in Children: A Further Test of the Psychological Processing Account

William E. Tunmer and James W. Chapman

A considerable amount of research indicates that the ability to segment spoken words into subcomponents is fundamental for learning to read and spell (for reviews, see Adams, 1990; Blachman, 2000; Goswami, 2000; Goswami & Bryant, 1990; Share, 1995; Tunmer & Rohl, 1991). Making use of letter–sound relationships to identify unfamiliar printed words is the basic mechanism for acquiring sight word (i.e., word-specific) knowledge in alphabetic orthographies, including knowledge of irregularly spelled words (Ehri, 1992, 1997; Ehri & McCormick, 1998; Gough & Walsh, 1991; Share, 1995; Share & Stanovich, 1995; Tunmer & Chapman, 1998, 2006). The process of phonologically recoding a specific printed word a few times (i.e., translating the letters and letter patterns of the word into a familiar phonological form) ultimately cements the word's orthographic representation in lexical memory. Phonological recoding therefore functions as a self-teaching mechanism that enables beginning readers to acquire sight word knowledge, which in turn frees up cognitive resources for allocation to comprehension and text integration processes (Share, 1995; Share & Stanovich, 1995).

This is not to suggest that all, or even most, letter–sound relationships need to be explicitly taught. In their influential theory of reading acquisition, Gough and Hillinger (1980) pointed out that there are simply too many letter–sound relationships for children to acquire by direct instruction. As the reading attempts of beginning readers with a firm understanding of the alphabetic principle become more successful, they will begin making greater independent use of letter–sound information (possibly supplemented by sentence context cues) to identify unfamiliar words in text. These positive learning trials, in turn, facilitate the development of beginning readers' word-specific orthographic knowledge from which additional spelling–sound relationships can be induced without explicit instruction (see Thompson & Fletcher-Flinn, this volume, for a discussion of the development of *lexicalised phonological recoding*). As Juel (1991) put it, a little explicit phonics instruction may go 'a long way' in facilitating the process by which children induce untaught spelling-sound relationships (p. 783). What is crucial is that children become conceptually aware that print is encoded speech, which Gough and Hillinger (1980) refer to as *cryptanalytic intent*.

To discover mappings between spelling patterns and sound patterns, children must be able to segment spoken words into subcomponents, an ability referred to as *phonological awareness*. For beginning readers who experience ongoing difficulties in detecting phonological sequences in words, progress in learning to read will be impeded, which in turn may trigger negative Matthew (poor-get-poorer) effects in reading (Stanovich, 1986, 1996). Stanovich (1996) succinctly describes the canonical model of reading difficulties as follows: 'Impaired language segmentation skills lead to difficulties in phonological coding which in turn impede the word recognition process which underpins reading comprehension' (p. 155). Many beginning readers find it extraordinarily difficult to detect phonological sequences in spoken words even though they are clearly capable of discriminating between speech sounds, as indicated by their ability to use phonological contrasts to signal and comprehend meaning differences from an early age (e.g., 'dad' vs. 'bad'). Young children's ability to produce and extract phonological segments when speaking and listening is an automatic function of the speech system that occurs below conscious awareness. In contrast, the *metalinguistic* ability to deliberately reflect on and manipulate the subcomponents of spoken words emerges later in development and depends on aspects of general cognitive development, vocabulary development, and environmental experiences (Goswami, 2000, 2001; Tunmer & Hoover, 1992, 1993; Tunmer, Herriman, & Nesdale, 1988; Tunmer & Rohl, 1991).

The Sequence of Phonological Awareness Development

Phonological awareness comprises three levels of awareness of the phonological structure of language (Goswami, 2000). *Syllabic awareness* is the ability to detect constituent syllables in words (e.g., a word like *teacher* has two syllables). *Onset-rime awareness* is the ability to detect two units within the syllable, the *onset* and the *rime*, where the onset is the (optional) initial consonant or consonant cluster of the syllable, and the rime is the (obligatory) vowel plus any remaining consonants (e.g., the onset of the spoken word 'ship' is [ʃ] and the rime is [ɪp]). *Phoneme awareness* is the ability to detect the individual phonemic elements of spoken words (e.g., a word like 'ship' comprises three segments; [ʃ], [ɪ], and [p]).

Results from several studies indicate that the ability to segment by syllables is easier, and develops earlier in children, than the ability to segment words into phonemes (Content, Kolinsky, Morais, & Bertelson, 1986; Fox & Routh, 1975; Liberman, Shankweiler, Fischer, & Carter, 1974; Morais, Cluytens, & Alegria,

1984; Treiman & Zukowski, 1991, 1996). For example, Liberman et al. (1974) asked 4- to 6-year-old children to tap out the number of syllables or phonemes in orally presented words and found that syllables were easier to detect than phonemes at all age levels. Unlike phonemes, which are coarticulated and overlap acoustically with neighbouring phonemes within words, syllables have well-defined acoustic properties, most notably a high-acoustic-energy vocalic center. Because syllables are more clearly marked acoustically, they are easier for young children to detect, whereas phonemes are more difficult to untangle and distinguish in speech due to the parallel transmission of phonemic content (Liberman, Cooper, Shankweiler, & Studdert-Kennedy, 1967).

More recent research supports a developmental sequence in which children first become aware of syllabic units in speech, then onset and rime units, and finally phonemic units (see Treiman, 1992, for a review). Treiman and Zukowski (1991), for example, used a same–different task in which children aged 4, 5, and 6 years were asked whether two words presented to them had any sounds in common. In the beginning-sound version of the task, the shared sounds constituted initial syllables (*ham*mer, *ham*mock), onsets (*pl*ank, *pl*ea), or initial phonemes (*s*teak, *s*ponge). In the end-sound version of the task, the shared sounds constituted final syllables com*pete*, re*peat*), rimes (sp*it*, w*it*), or final phonemes (smo*ke*, ta*ke*). A criterion of six consecutive correct responses was used to indicate task mastery. In support of a developmental progression from awareness of syllables, to onsets and rimes, and finally to phonemes, Treiman and Zukowski found that for the 4- and 5-year-olds, the syllable tasks were easier than the onset and rime tasks, which in turn were easier than the phoneme tasks. For example, 90% of the 5-year-olds reached criterion on the syllable tasks, 74% reached criterion on the onset-rime tasks, and 39% reached criterion on the phoneme tasks. The 6-year-olds, who had begun to receive literacy instruction, reached the criterion on all tasks and made relatively few errors.

Similar findings have been reported by researchers employing other tasks. Using a phoneme oddity task in which children were asked to judge which spoken word out of three contained an end sound not shared by the other two, Kirtley, Bryant, MacLean, and Bradley (1989) found that 5-year-olds performed better when the common end sound was the same as the rime (*top, rail, hop,* where the correct response is *rail*) than when it was only part of the rime (*mop, lead, whip,* where the correct response is *lead*). Further evidence that the ability to segment by phonemes is preceded by the ability to segment words into onsets and rimes comes from studies in which young children were asked to delete the initial consonant of words; for example, say *stop* without the [s] sound (Morais, Cluytens, & Alegria, 1984; Perfetti, Beck, Bell, & Hughes, 1987). The results of these studies revealed that children performed better when the consonant was an onset (e.g., *f*at) rather than when it was part of an onset (e.g., *f*lat).

The Nature of the Subsyllabic Division Between Onset and Rime

The question that arises from these findings, however, is why does awareness of the onset-rime division within syllables precede awareness of phonemic units? There are two conflicting views on the nature of this developmental progression, *the linguistic structure account* (which focuses on the hypothesised internal hierarchical structure of syllables in English and closely related languages) and the *psychological processing account* (which focuses on the coarticulatory properties of speech). According to the linguistic structure account the syllable is not a string of phonemes but has an internal hierarchical organisation comprising the onset and the rime, with the rime being further subdivided into the vowel nucleus and coda, which is any following consonants (Fudge, 1987, 1989; MacKay, 1972; Selkirk, 1982; Treiman, 1989). The developmental progression of children's awareness of syllables, onsets and rimes, and phonemes is thought to reflect the hierarchical organisation of these naturally occurring linguistic units (Treiman, 1992).

Evidence in support of the onset/rime view of the structure of English syllables comes from many sources, including spontaneous and elicited speech errors, word games, and constraints on the distributions of phonemes in syllables (for reviews, see Treiman, 1989; Treiman, Fowler, Gross, Berch, & Weatherston, 1995; Treiman & Kessler, 1995). For example, in speech errors adults tend to interchange whole onsets (e.g., 'coat thrutting' for 'throat cutting') rather than parts of onsets or other parts of the syllable (MacKay, 1972). However, as Morais (1991) argued, whatever value the onset-rime distinction has as a linguistic concept, the claim that a stage of onset-rime awareness occurs developmentally between syllabic and phonemic awareness requires a more detailed explanation of *how* these linguistic units are extracted by children at different stages of development. As Morais put it, 'a linguistic notion does not have the power to explain a mental capacity' (p. 40).

Supporting an alternative view to the linguistic structure account, Morais suggested that 'future work be more inspired by the hypothesis of an influence of coarticulatory properties ... on the development of segmental abilities, rather than by the intent to merely confirm or disconfirm the onset-rime hypothesis' (p. 41). Calfee (1991) expressed a similar view, arguing that the motor theory of speech perception (the notion that phonemes are perceived according to how they are produced) proposed by Liberman and colleagues (Liberman, 1970; Liberman et al., 1967; Liberman & Mattingly, 1985) provides the basis for understanding the development of phonological awareness in children. According to Calfee, 'kindergarteners can produce and perceive speech, but they don't know how they do it ... Motor theory suggests that young children grasp the concept of "speech sounds" when they attend to articulation rather than audition, when they understand the process of making sounds rather than fine tuning their ears' (p. 84).

Building on these ideas, Tunmer and Rohl (1991) proposed a psychological processing account of the developmental progression of children's phonological

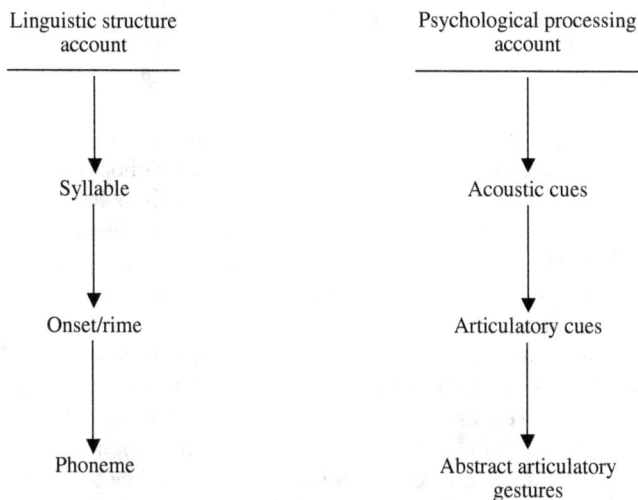

Linguistic structure account	Psychological processing account
↓	↓
Syllable	Acoustic cues
↓	↓
Onset/rime	Articulatory cues
↓	↓
Phoneme	Abstract articulatory gestures

Figure 1
Two views on the developmental progression of phonological awareness in children.

awareness. According to their model, children initially rely on acoustic cues, which enables them to detect syllables; then articulatory cues, which enables them to break syllables into onsets and rimes; and finally abstract articulatory gestures, which enables them to extract phonemes. The psychological processing account is contrasted with the linguistic structure account in Figure 1.

As noted earlier, detecting phonological units smaller than syllables is difficult for young children because there is no simple physical basis for recognising these units in speech. Syllables, however, do have a physical correlate in relative amplitude. Moreover, syllables are independently articulable. Because syllables are marked acoustically, and because children can say individual syllables to themselves, children do not need to gain access to abstract representations when segmenting multisyllabic words into syllables. Syllables are therefore easier to detect than onsets, rimes, or phonemes.

During the next stage of development children are hypothesised to undergo a gradual transition period preceding fully developed phonological awareness during which they rely heavily on monitoring articulatory cues (often subvocally) as an initial strategy for subdividing syllables into smaller units. The notion that children may segment words by initially relying on the strategy of saying to themselves sound segments that can be pronounced in isolation may explain children's initial resistance to segmenting words at points other than the onset-rime division. The obligatory vowel segment of the syllable is always the easiest phonemic segment to perceive (Brady, Shankweiler, & Mann, 1983) and pronounce in isolation and, in many instances, it is the only phonemic segment of the syllable that can be pronounced in isolation because of coarticulatory properties. When attempting to segment a syllable, children may adopt what appears to be the natural strategy of first focusing on the steady-state vowel portion of the syllable, treating the vowel and any following sounds as an unsegmented whole and likewise for any segments preceding the vowel. This would explain why children are initially more likely to produce *ap* rather than the correct response, *lap*, when asked to say a word like *clap* without the [k] sound. Consistent with the articulatory cue monitoring hypothesis is Fox and Routh's (1975) finding that when children from 3 to 7 years of age were asked to listen to two- or three-phoneme monosyllabic words and to say 'just a little bit' of the word, even children as young as 4 years were able to segment most of the words into onsets and rimes.

An advantage of the articulatory cue monitoring hypothesis is that it provides an explanation of Bradley and Bryant's (1985) finding that when 4- and 5-year-old children were asked to identify which of four words did not share a sound in common with three other words, the children performed much better when they were asked to categorise words on the basis of rime (e.g., *weed, peel, need, deed*, where the correct response is *peel*) than on the basis of the onset (e.g., *sun, sea, sack, rag*, where the correct response is *rag*). Kirtley et al. (1989) reported a similar pattern of results. The rime is often the only independently articulable segment of syllables. This would have the effect of making rimes easier to detect than onsets, which comprise single consonants or consonant clusters. Because of the coarticulatory properties of speech, there is no one-to-one correspondence between most consonantal phonemes and segments of the acoustic signal. Consequently, the beginning reading strategy of simple 'sounding out' a printed word like *bag* will result in 'buh ah guh', a nonsense word comprising three syllables (Liberman & Shankweiler, 1985). Letter sounds and letter names are only imprecise physical analogues of most phonemes in spoken words. Whether children learn to associate the sound 'buh' or the name 'bee' or both with the letter *b*, they must still be able to segment the sound or name to make the connection between the letter *b* and the abstract phoneme [b], which cannot be pronounced in isolation. This is true of all consonantal phonemes, with the exception of continuant consonants (e.g., [f], [ʃ], [s]). According to the articulatory cue monitoring hypothesis, onsets should therefore generally be more difficult to detect than rimes. Consistent with this claim, Treiman and Baron (1981) found that consonant–vowel–consonant (CVC) syllables in which both consonants were fricatives (a subgroup of continuants) were easier for children to segment than CVC syllables in which both consonants were stops (a subgroup of non-continuants). In contrast to the articulatory cue monitoring hypothesis, the onset-rime hypothesis does not appear to provide an explanation for the alliteration-rhyme performance difference.

In the final stage of the development of phonological awareness, children begin to focus more on the abstract articulatory gestures that are associated with phonemes, where a phonetic gesture is defined as the 'class of movements by one or more articulators that results in a particular, linguistically significant

Table 1

Mean Correct Scores in Initial Sound Different Task Under Four Conditions

Condition	Form of categorisation	Nature of odd word	Examples	5-year-old means
1	By single C	Different C	doll, deaf, *can*	3.67
2	By CV	Different C and V	*cap*, doll, dog	4.33
3	By CV	Different V	cap, can, *cot*	3.08
4	By CV	Different C	can, cap, *lad*	4.21

Note: Kirtley et al. (1989).

deformation, over time, of the vocal-tract configuration' (Liberman & Mattingly, 1985, p. 21). According to the motor theory of speech perception, the processes by which the sounds of speech are produced provide the invariant source of the phonetic percept. Onset-rime awareness appears to be a natural developmental precursor of the ability to fully segment words into phonemes (Tunmer & Rohl, 1991). The process of monitoring articulatory cues as an initial strategy for subdividing syllables into smaller units often results in children focusing on individual phonemic elements, as when the onset comprises a single consonant (e.g., *f*-un), or the rime comprises a single vowel (e.g., *z*-oo). Such a strategy gradually draws children's attention to the abstract representations of phonemic elements, eventually enabling them to gain conscious access to the cognitive products of the speech perception module.

Evidence in Support of the Psychological Processing Account

Support for the psychological processing account of the development of phonological awareness in children comes from a study by Kirtley et al. (1989). The aim of the study was to provide further evidence that children divide syllables into onsets and rimes before they are able to segment by phonemes. Kirtley et al. used the oddity task developed by Bradley and Bryant (1985) in which children are asked to listen to a group of words and then select the word that has a different sound from the others. In one part of the study children were asked to identify which of the three words did not share a beginning sound with two other words under four categorisation conditions: by initial consonant which was different; by initial consonant and vowel in which both the consonant and vowel were different; by initial consonant and vowel in which the vowel was different; and by initial consonant and vowel in which the consonant was different (see Table 1 for examples).

According to the linguistic structure account, there should be no difference in performance between Conditions 1 and 2, and between Conditions 1 and 4. As Kirtley et al. predicted, children 'should find it no easier to judge that words start in the same way when they start with the same consonant-vowel combination ("cat", "cap") than when they start with the same opening phoneme ("cat", "cup")' (p. 234). However, according to the psychological processing account, performance should be better under both Conditions 2 and 4 than in Condition 1.

Because of coarticulation effects, the words *doll* and *dog* (and *can* and *cap*) should feel more alike in the mouth at the beginning than do *doll* and *deaf*. Consequently, a word with a different opening sound should be easier to identify. Both the psychological processing and linguistic structure accounts predict that performance should be relatively poor under Condition 3, as the different beginning sound cuts across the onset-rime boundary (linguistic structure account) and the articulatory cues at the beginning of all three words are very similar (psychological processing account). As can be seen in Table 1, the pattern of results supports the psychological processing account.

Similar results have been obtained in studies in which children were asked to make judgments about end sounds in the oddity task. Snowling, Hulme, Smith, and Thomas (1994) found that children performed less well when asked to select the odd word out in items like *job, rob, nod* (where the correct response is *nod*) than in items like *job, rob, knock* (where the correct response is *knock*). While the linguistic structure account predicts no difference in performance between these items, the psychological processing account predicts that items like *job, rob, nod* should be more difficult because the articulatory cues for *od* and *ob* are more similar than those for *od* and *ock* ([b], [d], and [k] are all stops, but only [k] is unvoiced).

A prediction that can be derived from the psychological processing account is that vowel–consonant (VC) syllables should be easier for young children to segment than consonant–vowel (CV) syllables because initial vowels are independently articulable whereas most initial consonants are not due to the coarticulatory properties of consonants. Children should therefore be better at pronouncing in isolation (and therefore segmenting) the first phoneme of VC syllables than CV syllables. The linguistic structure account, however, predicts the opposite. CV syllables should be easier to segment than VC syllables because the division within CV syllables coincides with the onset-rime boundary, whereas the division of VC syllables occurs within an intrasyllabic unit, the rime (as noted earlier, the onset is optional).

Some preliminary evidence in support of this prediction comes from a secondary analysis (Tunmer & Rohl, 1991) of data from a longitudinal study of early literacy development carried out by Tunmer et al. (1988). As part of this study children in Year 1 were given a phoneme-counting task that included five VC syllables and five CV syllables. In support of the psychological processing account, Tunmer and Rohl found a clear advantage of VC syllables over CV syllables (81.6% vs. 65.8%). Collapsing across the 110 children, the scores of the five VC items ranged from 77% to 85% and for the five CV items, 51% to 72%. A difficulty with this study, however, is that the same consonants and vowels were not used in the VC and CV conditions of the task. The differences obtained could therefore reflect differences in the materials used in the two conditions.

Uhry and Ehri (1999) obtained similar findings in a study in which kindergarten children were asked to move small wooden blocks as they segmented VC, CV, and CVC words into phonemes. They hypothesised that VC words should be easier to segment than CV words because vowels in the initial position of words are especially salient. In contrast to consonants, vowels have higher acoustic energy, have longer duration, and can form syllables or words in isolation. Uhry and Ehri argued that the rime-cohesion hypothesis (as they described it) makes the opposite prediction because VC words constitute cohesive units on their own (i.e., rimes), whereas CV words constitute two units, an onset and a rime. In support of their vowel salience hypothesis, Uhry and Ehri found that VC words were in fact easier to segment than CV words. A shortcoming of their theoretical analysis, however, is that focusing on perceptual salience rather than coarticulatory properties does not appear to provide an explanation for the alliteration-rhyme performance difference noted earlier (Bradley & Bryant, 1985; Kirtley et al., 1989), or the pattern of results reported in the Kirtley et al. (1989) and Snowling, Hulme, Smith and Thomas (1994) studies. According to the psychological processing account, the degree of coarticulation between phonemes is greater when a consonant precedes a vowel, as in CV words, than when a vowel precedes a consonant, as in VC words. VC words should therefore be easier to segment.

There are also some methodological problems with the Uhry and Ehri study, as the authors themselves acknowledged. First, as with Tunmer and Rohl's (1991) secondary analysis, the same consonants and vowels were not used in the VC and CV conditions of the segmentation task, which leaves open the possibility of materials confounding. Second, the children were asked to segment the VC words before the CV words, which might have resulted in an unintended order effect. Third, the test items used in the study included high frequency words (e.g., *up, it, at, on*) and words containing digraphs (letter pairs which represent single phonemes, such as *sh, th, oa, oo*) or silent letters in their printed forms (e.g., *eat, say, zoo, bite*). Studies have shown that phonemic segmentation tasks including such words may provide inaccurate estimates of phonemic awareness because children who are familiar with the words are much more likely to make overshoot errors based on the word's orthographic image (Tunmer & Nesdale, 1982, 1985). That is, when orally presented with the word [it] (eat), they mentally count the letters in the orthographic image of the word and incorrectly indicate that *eat* has three sounds rather than two. Using the same strategy, they are able to indicate correctly that *up* has two 'sounds', a response that does not assess phonemic segmentation ability. The following study was therefore designed to overcome these methodological shortcomings.

A Further Test of the Psychological Processing Account

As part of a larger study, 141 children in Year 1 were given a test designed to measure phonemic segmentation ability toward the end of the school year when the mean age of the children was 5 years, 9 months. The test was a modified version of a phoneme counting task developed by Tunmer et al. (1988). The children were required to use counters to represent the sounds in orally presented pseudowords of varying length. Pseudowords were used to control for

Table 2

Predictions of the Onset-Rime and Articulatory Cue Monitoring Hypotheses

Hypothesis	Predictions	Examples
1. Onset-rime	$C_1V_1 > V_1C_1$	[kɛ], [ɛk]
	$C_1V_1C_2 = C_2V_1C_1$	[kɛb], [bɛk]
2. Articulatory cue monitoring	$V_1C_1 > C_1V_1$	[ɛk], [kɛ]
	$C_1V_1C_2 = C_2V_1C_1$	[kɛb], [bɛk]

possible contaminating effects relating to word frequency and digraphs. The task was presented in the form of a game in which the children were asked to identify the sounds in 'funny sounding names of children who live in far away lands'. One demonstration item was given, followed by four practice items with corrective feedback. The test items were then presented with no corrective feedback.

There were 24 test items: 4 single-phoneme sounds (all short vowels), 8 two-phoneme syllables (4 VC syllables and 4 CV syllables; the latter were transposed versions of the former), 8 three-phoneme syllables (4 CVC syllables that were constructed by adding a different consonant to the beginning of each of the 4 VC syllables, and 4 CVC syllables that were constructed by adding the same consonants to the ends of the 4 CV syllables), and 4 four-phoneme syllables (2 CCVC syllables and 2 CVCC syllables). The order of presentation of the different item types for the two-, three-, and four-phoneme syllables was counterbalanced within the item list, and the order of presentation of the items was counterbalanced across children. Scoring was based on the percentage of items correctly segmented in each category.

The onset-rime hypothesis predicted that the children should have performed better on the CV syllables than on the matched VC syllables, whereas the articulatory cue monitoring hypothesis predicted the opposite. Both hypotheses predicted no differences in performance when the VC and CV pairs were embedded in CVC syllables containing the same consonant added to either the beginning or the end (see Table 2).

Presented in Figure 2 are the mean percentages of correct responses for the two-phoneme syllables as a function of presentation condition and cluster type. A 2 (presentation condition: not embedded vs. embedded) × 2 (cluster type: VC vs. CV) ANOVA was performed on the data. As expected, there were significant main effects for presentation condition, $F(1, 140) = 25.2$, $p < .001$, and cluster type, $F(1, 140) = 37.7$, $p < .001$, and a significant presentation condition × cluster type interaction, $F(1, 140) = 24.6$, $p < .001$. The results provide further strong support for the articulatory cue monitoring hypothesis, as the children performed significantly better on the VC syllables than on the CV syllables.

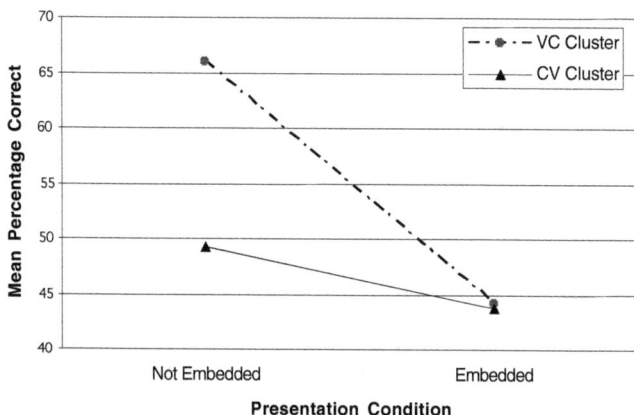

Figure 2
Mean percentages of correct responses as a function of presentation condition and cluster type.

Concluding Remarks

In this chapter we presented two views of the nature of the developmental progression of phonological awareness in children, the linguistic structure account (which focuses on the hypothesised internal hierarchical structure of syllables) and the psychological processing account (which focuses on the coarticulatory properties of speech). According to the linguistic structure account, the developmental progression of children's awareness of syllables, onsets and rimes, and phonemes reflects the hierarchical organisation of these naturally occurring linguistic units. In contrast, the psychological processing account proposes that children initially rely on acoustic cues, which enables them to detect syllables; then articulatory cues, which enables them to break syllables into onsets and rimes; and finally abstract articulatory gestures, which enables them to extract phonemes. On the basis of an examination of the theoretical arguments and empirical evidence in support of each position, and the results of a recent study we carried out, we conclude that the available research favors the psychological processing account of the developmental progression of phonological awareness in children.

Given the important role that phonological awareness plays in the development of basic literacy skills, our findings have implications for the manner in which phonological awareness skills are taught to children. In particular, the results of our analysis suggest an approach in which onset-rime units are emphasised in early reading instruction with attention placed on the monitoring of articulatory cues as an initial strategy for segmenting spoken words into smaller components.

References

Adams, M. J. (1990). *Beginning to read: Thinking and learning about print*. Cambridge, MA: MIT Press.

Blachman, B. A. (2000). Phonological awareness. In M. L. Kamil, P. B. Mosenthal, P. D. Pearson, & R. Barr (Eds.), *Handbook of reading research* (Vol. 3, pp. 483–502). Mahwah, NJ: Lawrence Erlbaum Associates.

Bradley, L., & Bryant, P. (1985). *Rhyme and reason in reading and spelling*. Ann Arbor, MI: University of Michigan Press.

Brady, S., Shankweiler, D., & Mann, V. (1983). Speech perception and memory coding in relation to reading ability. *Journal of Experimental Child Psychology, 35*, 345–367.

Calfee, R. (1991). Decoding and spelling: What to teach; when to teach it; how to teach it. *Psychological Science, 2*, 83–85.

Content, A., Kolinsky, R., Morais, J., & Bertelson, P. (1986). Phonetic segmentation in pre-readers: Effect of corrective information. *Journal of Experimental Child Psychology, 42*, 49–72.

Ehri, L. (1992). Reconceptualizing the development of sight word reading and its relationship to recoding. In P. Gough, L. Ehri, & R. Treiman (Eds.), *Reading acquisition* (pp. 107–143). Hillsdale, NJ: Lawrence Erlbaum Associates.

Ehri, L. (1997). Sight word learning in normal readers and dyslexics. In B. Blachman (Ed.), *Foundations of reading intervention and dyslexia: Implications for early intervention* (pp. 163–189). Mahwah, NJ: Lawrence Erlbaum Associates.

Ehri, L., & McCormick, S. (1998). Phases of word learning: Implications for instruction with delayed and disabled readers. *Reading and Writing Quarterly, 14*, 135–163.

Fox, B., & Routh, D. K. (1975). Analyzing spoken language into words, syllables, and phonemes: A developmental study. *Journal of Psycholinguistic Research, 4*, 331–342.

Fudge, E. (1987). Branching structure within the syllable. Journal of Linguistics, 23, 359–377.

Fudge, E. (1989). Syllable structure: A reply to Davis. *Journal of Linguistics, 25*, 219–220.

Goswami, U. (2000). Phonological and lexical processes. In M. L. Kamil, P. B. Mosenthal, P. D. Pearson, & R. Barr (Eds.), *Handbook of reading research* (Vol. 3, pp. 251–267). Mahwah, NJ: Lawrence Erlbaum Associates.

Goswami, U. (2001). Early phonological development and the acquisition of literacy. In B. S. Neuman & D. K. Dickinson (Eds.), *Handbook of early literacy research* (pp. 111–125). New York: Guilford Press.

Goswami, U., & Bryant, P. (1990). *Phonological skills and learning to read*. Hillsdale, NJ: Lawrence Erlbaum Associates.

Gough, P. B., & Hillinger, M. (1980). Learning to read: An unnatural act. *Bulletin of the Orton Society, 30*, 179–196.

Gough, P. B., & Walsh, M. (1991). Chinese, Phoenicians, and the orthographic cipher of English. In S. Brady & D. Shankweiler (Eds.), *Phonological processes in literacy* (pp. 199–209). Hillsdale, NJ: Lawrence Erlbaum Associates.

Juel, C. (1991). Beginning reading. In R. Barr, M. L. Kamil, P. B. Mosenthal, & P. D. Pearson (Eds.), *Handbook of reading research* (Vol. 2, pp. 759–788). New York: Longman.

Kirtley, C., Bryant, P., MacLean, M., & Bradley, L. (1989). Rhyme, rime, and the onset of reading. *Journal of Experimental Child Psychology, 48*, 224–245.

Liberman, A. M. (1970). The grammars of speech and language. *Cognitive Psychology, 1*, 301–323.

Liberman, A. M., Cooper, F. S., Shankweiler, D., & Studdert-Kennedy, M. (1967). Perception of the speech code. *Psychological Review, 74*, 431–461.

Liberman, A. M., & Mattingly, I. G. (1985). The motor theory of speech perception revised. *Cognition, 21*, 1–36.

Liberman, I. Y., & Shankweiler, D. (1985). Phonology and the problem of learning to read and write. *Remedial and Special Education, 6,* 8–17.

Liberman, I. Y., Shankweiler, D., Fischer, F. W., & Carter, B. (1974). Explicit syllable and phoneme segmentation in the young child. *Journal of Experimental Child Psychology, 18,* 201–212.

MacKay, D. G. (1972). The structure of words and syllables: Evidence from errors in speech. *Cognitive Psychology, 3,* 210–227.

Morais, J. (1991). Phonological awareness: A bridge between language and literacy. In D. J. Sawyer & B. J. Fox (Eds.), *Phonological awareness in reading* (pp. 31–71). New York: Springer-Verlag.

Morais, J., Cluytens, M., & Alegria, J. (1984). Segmentation abilities of dyslexics and normal readers. *Perceptual and Motor Skills, 58,* 221–222.

Perfetti, C., Beck, I., Bell, L., & Hughes, C. (1987). Phonemic knowledge and learning to read are reciprocal: A longitudinal study of first grade children. *Merrill-Palmer Quarterly, 33,* 283–319.

Selkirk, E. O. (1982). The syllable. In H. Van der Hulst & N. Smith (Eds.), *The structure of phonological representations (part II)* (pp. 337–383). Dordrecht, the Netherlands: Foris.

Share, D. L. (1995). Phonological recoding and self-teaching: Sine qua non of reading acquisition. *Cognition, 55,* 151–218.

Share, D. L., & Stanovich, K. E. (1995). Cognitive processes in early reading development: Accommodating individual differences into a model of acquisition. *Issues in Education, 1,* 1–57.

Snowling, M. J., Hulme, C., Smith, A., & Thomas, J. (1994). The effects of phonemic similarity and list length on children's sound categorization performance. *Journal of Experimental Child Psychology, 58,* 160–180.

Stanovich, K. E. (1986). Matthew effects in reading: Some consequences of individual differences in the acquisition of literacy. *Reading Research Quarterly, 21,* 340–406.

Stanovich, K. E. (1996). Toward a more inclusive definition of dyslexia. *Dyslexia, 2,* 154–166.

Thompson, G. B., & Fletcher-Flinn, C. M. (2006). Lexicalised implicit learning in reading acquisition: The knowledge sources theory. In C. M. Fletcher-Flinn & G. M. Haberman (Eds.), *Cognition and language: Perspectives from New Zealand* (pp. 141–156). Brisbane, Australia: Australian Academic Press.

Treiman, R. (1989). The internal structure of the syllable. In G. Carlson & M. Tanenhaus (Eds.), *Linguistic structure and language processing* (pp. 27–52). Dordrecht, the Netherlands: Reidel.

Treiman, R. (1992). The role of intrasyllabic units in learning to read and spell. In P. B. Gough, L. Ehri, & R. Treiman (Eds.), *Reading acquisition* (pp. 65–106). Hillsdale, NJ: Lawrence Erlbaum Associates.

Treiman, R., & Baron, J. (1981). Segmental analysis ability: Development and relation to reading ability. In G. E. MacKinnon & T. G. Waller (Eds.), *Reading research: Advances in theory and practice* (Vol. 3, pp. 159–198). New York: Academic Press.

Treiman, R., Fowler, C., Gross, J., Berch, D., & Weatherston, S. (1995). Syllable structure or word structure? Evidence for onset and rime units with disyllabic and trisyllabic stimuli. *Journal of Memory and Language, 34,* 132–155.

Treiman, R., & Kessler, B. (1995). In defense of an onset-rime syllable structure for English. *Language and Speech, 38,* 127–142.

Treiman, R., & Zukowski, A. (1991). Levels of phonological awareness. In S. A. Brady & D. P. Shankweiler (Eds.), *Phonological processes in literacy: A tribute to Isabelle Y. Liberman* (pp. 67–83). Hillsdale, NJ: Lawrence Erlbaum Associates.

Treiman, R., & Zukowski, A. (1996). Children's sensitivity to syllables, onsets, rimes, and phonemes. *Journal of Experimental Child Psychology, 61,* 193–215.

Tunmer, W. E., & Chapman, J. W. (1998). Language prediction skill, phonological recoding ability, and beginning reading. In C. Hulme & R. M. Joshi (Eds.), *Reading and spelling: Development and disorders* (pp. 33–67). Mahwah, NJ: Lawrence Erlbaum Associates.

Tunmer, W. E., & Chapman, J. W. (2006). Metalinguistic abilities, phonological recoding skill, and the use of sentence context in beginning reading development: A longitudinal study. In R. M. Joshi & P. G. Aaron (Eds.), *Handbook of orthography and literacy* (pp. 617–635). Mahwah, NJ: Lawrence Erlbaum Associates.

Tunmer, W. E., Herriman, M. L., & Nesdale, A. R. (1988). Metalinguistic abilities and beginning reading. *Reading Research Quarterly, 23*, 134–158.

Tunmer, W. E., & Hoover, W. (1992). Cognitive and linguistic factors in learning to read. In P. Gough, L. Ehri, & R. Treiman (Eds.), *Reading acquisition* (pp. 175–214). Hillsdale, NJ: Lawrence Erlbaum Associates.

Tunmer, W. E., & Hoover, W. (1993). Components of variance models of language-related factors in reading disability: A conceptual overview. In M. Joshi & C. K. Leong (Eds.), *Reading disabilities: Diagnosis and component processes* (pp. 135–173). Dordrecht, the Netherlands: Kluwer Academic Publishers.

Tunmer, W. E., & Nesdale, A. R. (1982). The effects of digraphs and pseudowords on phonemic segmentation in young children. *Applied Psycholinguistics, 3*, 299–311.

Tunmer, W. E., & Nesdale, A. R. (1985). Phonemic segmentation skill and beginning reading. *Journal of Educational Psychology, 77*, 417–427.

Tunmer, W. E., & Rohl, M. (1991). Phonological awareness and reading acquisition. In D. J. Sawyer & B. J. Fox (Eds.), *Phonological awareness in reading* (pp. 1–30). New York: Springer-Verlag.

Uhry, J. K., & Ehri, L. C. (1999). Ease of segmenting two- and three-phoneme words in kindergarten: Rime cohesion or vowel salience? *Journal of Educational Psychology, 91*, 594–603.

Lexicalised Implicit Learning in Reading Acquisition: The Knowledge Sources Theory

G. Brian Thompson and Claire M. Fletcher-Flinn

The knowledge sources theory of word reading acquisition, having been developed and tested by the authors, is a predominantly New Zealand creation. Nevertheless, it has appeared in international literature over the past 10 years and has received increasing attention in literature reviews in cognitive science (e.g., Jackson & Coltheart, 2001; Ramus, 2004), and applications to understanding the learning of non-alphabetic orthographies, such as Chinese (Wang, Liu, & Perfetti, 2004) and the Hiragana syllabary of Japanese (current project of Fletcher-Flinn, Thompson and Abe).

This chapter provides an up-to-date description of the theory, along with brief citations of evidence, with a focus on beginning readers. By way of introduction and background the chapter examines other influential theories of word reading acquisition.

Theories of Word Reading Acquisition

Learning to read comprises two main skills: the skill of identifying printed words, and the skill of comprehending text. However, comprehension cannot proceed without the reader identifying most of the words of the text. Over the past 20 years a great deal of time and effort has been devoted to understanding how children learn to identify print words. Theories of acquisition of word reading have appeared, some more fashionable at times than others, depending on the psychological and educational *Zeitgeist* (e.g., the general influence of Piaget; connectionist modelling). Developmental stage theories (e.g., Chall, 1983; Marsh, Friedman, Welch, & Desberg, 1981) have given way to 'developmental phase' theories (e.g., Ehri, 1991, 1994, 1999; Frith, 1985). More recently there is a self-teaching learning theory (Share, 1995), an analogy account (Goswami, 1993), and most recently, 'connectionist' (computational associationist) models have been applied to reading acquisition (Hutzler, Ziegler, Perry, Wimmer, & Zorzi, 2004; Zorzi, Houghton, & Butterworth, 1998). We will briefly review a selection of these theories which have had continuous influence.

Ehri's (1999) developmental phase theory has had continuous influence, especially among education researchers in the United States (US). The theory has four successive 'phases' of development that are related to the type of information that children use to identify words. ('Phases' are similar to stages that overlap in the developmental sequence.) In the *pre-alphabetic* (also called 'logographic') phase, children use partial and arbitrary visual cues, or global visual features, to identify the meanings of words. The processing of print words is similar to any visual object or non-language symbol. Children do not need to know anything about sounds of letters. During the next phase, *partial-alphabetic* reading, children attend to letters and letter order, and recognise that letters imply sounds within spoken words. Readers form partial connections between words and their pronunciations and use these connections to generate a pronunciation for an unfamiliar print word. Ehri stresses the joint role of phonemic awareness and explicit letter–sound knowledge in forming these partial connections.

The third phase is called *full-alphabetic* reading and, as the name implies, all letters in words are linked to their pronunciations. That is, children have a full complement of grapmeme–phoneme correspondences available for use. Graphemes are letters, or letter combinations, for example, *th*, that correspond to phonemes. Ehri also states that in this phase children have a substantial 'sight word' vocabulary of frequently occurring words which can be recalled from memory. The fourth and final phase of development is called the *consolidated alphabetic* phase because subword units larger than individual graphemes can be used (e.g., rimes, syllables, affixes, and stems). As fluency and the sight word vocabulary continues to develop, lexical processes become influential. This fourth phase is said to commence at 7 to 8 years of age for children of average progress.

Although phonological recoding is important in Ehri's theory, Share's account (Share, 1995; Jorm & Share, 1983; Share & Jorm, 1987) specifies it as a self-teaching mechanism that allows the learner to acquire orthographic representations of print words. Each new encounter with a word, for which phonological recoding is successful, provides opportunities for the reader to acquire word-specific and more general orthographic representations. There are two co-requisites for this phonological recoding, phoneme awareness and explicit knowledge of letter–sound relations. As the reader progresses toward maturity of reading skill there is a developmental change as phonological recoding becomes 'lexicalised', the letter–sound relationships are induced by the reader from his/her accumulated reading vocabulary.

Although Byrne (1996, 1998; Byrne, Fielding-Barnsley, & Ashley, 1996) does not propose a comprehensive theory, he has explored an important theoretical issue by conducting experimental studies on the acquisition of the 'alphabetic principle' (that letters relate to sounds within words). The results showed that pre-reading 4-year-old children expect writing to map onto meaning, not onto language sounds; and that children lack awareness that letters represent sound at the level of the phoneme. Byrne (1998, p. 50) concedes that learning to induce rule-governed relationships without awareness is well documented in the psychological literature, and that it is a basis of connectionist accounts of reading. However, he questioned whether children at the pre-reading level could induce the alphabetic principle when taught to read a few words, given their apparent expectation that writing has no mapping to language sounds. Most of Byrne's experiments were based on teaching 4-year-old pre-reading children two words, for example, *fat* and *bat*, then presenting them with a forced-choice transfer task in which they had to decide if the new printed word *fun* was read as 'fun' or 'bun'. Although the children were not successful at this task, which represented induction at the phonemic level, they were successful when the induction involved mapping at the syllable level. In a further experiment, Byrne increased the set of words to be learnt to four, to provide more contexts for the two letter–phoneme exemplars examined. This did not change the conclusion. However, he did not increase the number of exemplars of the alphabetic principle beyond these two. Nonetheless, Byrne concluded that learning to read words does not lead *automatically* to acquisition of the alphabetic principle, but does not deny it is possible that children can acquire the principle by induction from words they have learnt to read (1998, p. 62).

All theorists reviewed above ascribe a necessary role to phoneme units in the process of phonological recoding. Rime, a larger phonological unit, has been implicated by others as important, but there is debate about exactly what its role is, and whether print body units (corresponding to the phonological rime, or rhyming part, e.g., *-ot* in *pot*) are particularly salient to young children beginning to read. Goswami and Bryant (1990) and Goswami (1993) have proposed a special link between rhyming skills and the use of orthographic analogies in early reading, by maintaining that onset-rime units are used to map letters onto pronunciations prior to the reader's acquisition of grapheme–phoneme correspondences. Ehri (1999), in contrast, maintains that reading by onset-rime analogies is not an early developing skill, occurring much later during the consolidated-alphabetic phase.

It is noted that in all the theories reviewed there is a specific role for explicit awareness of some aspect of the learning process, for example, taught letter–sound correspondences, phonemic awareness, or analogy formation. None have a specific role for implicit non-conscious learning. In this respect, they are not consistent with other cognitive theories (e.g., Karmiloff-Smith, 1992; Sun, Merrill, & Peterson, 2001) that have an important role for implicit learning and knowledge in skill acquisition.

It is also noted that the theories of Ehri and Share imply that effective teaching of beginning reading requires instruction in explicit letter–sound relations. Most of the research on these theories has been with children who have received such instruction. Research on the learning of children without this teaching is also important, if theoretical and methodological circularity is to be avoided (Thompson & Johnston, 1993). Moreover, the very existence of such children making effective progress in reading is contrary to the implications of the two theories. Unlike most countries, in New Zealand for the past 35 years schools have been without instruction in explicit phonics. Although during the past 10 years there has been a decline here in the uniformity of this situation across schools, New Zealand has provided the authors, and colleagues, with an opportunity to study the learning of reading under such a teaching condition.

The Knowledge Sources Theory

The theoretical account of the learning of any cognitive skill requires consideration of (a) the various sources of knowledge used by the reader's brain, and (b) the procedures the learner's brain has for using that knowledge. These features are represented in Figure 1 for part of the knowledge sources theory of learning word identification in reading. The figure shows the learning processes after the child has made an initial exploration to determine the relevant sources of information for learning. For normal 5- or 6-year-old children receiving appropriate teaching guidance this will take just a few weeks. (Byrne's, 1998, studies of the acquisition of the 'alphabetic principle' by 4-year-old pre-readers are relevant to this critical but brief period of learning.) The theory represents the subsequent learning processes of the beginning reader, as well as the learning of the more advanced reader. It represents learning processes over time periods of months and years, not just processes for a response to a word stimulus at a point in time. Hence Figure 1, which describes part of the theory, does not show input from stimulus words and corresponding response output. Such is subsumed in the learning which is represented.

Orthographic Lexicon

One source of stored knowledge is the reader's orthographic lexicon (labelled 5 in Figure 1). This is the reader's 'reading vocabulary'. It is a letter-based memory of print words the reader has experienced. For each word of the orthographic lexicon there are normally connections with the corresponding word of the phonological lexicon (labelled 6 in Figure 1; stored representations of the sound of each word), and with representations of the semantic characteristics of the word, that is, word meanings (not shown in Figure 1). Along with these connections, the orthographic lexicon enables the reader to identify the sound and/or the meaning(s) of familiar print words (and sometimes partly correct responses to unknown words). Young children, as they begin learning to read, do in fact store in memory the representations of the specific letters (and their sequence) of print words as they become familiar with them (e.g., Ehri & Saltmarsh, 1995; Martinet, Valdois, & Fayol, 2004; Reitsma, 1983a, 1983b). They acquire an orthographic lexicon. For young children, this will be of smaller size than their phonological lexicon (as shown in Figure 1).

The account given here proposes that the components of the orthographic representation of a word in the orthographic lexicon are acquired with a pattern

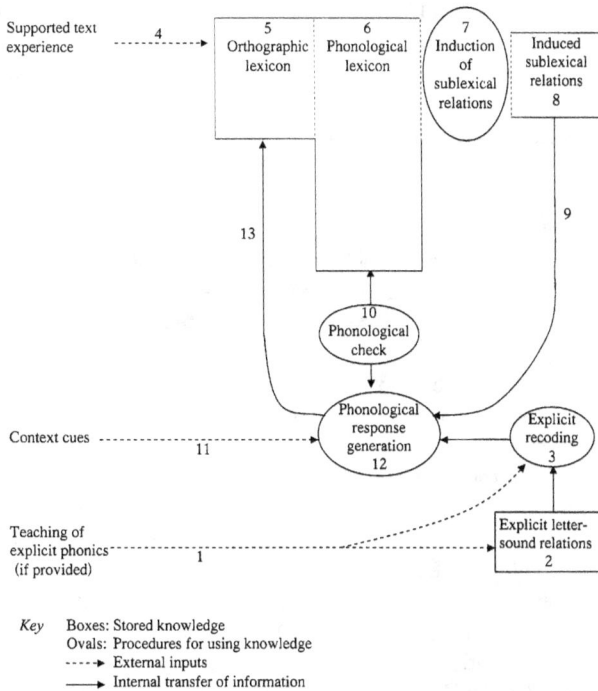

Figure 1
Some aspects of the learning of word identification in reading according to the knowledge sources theory.

of priority in the temporal sequence of learning. During the initial weeks of reading instruction, the child is at first ignorant of positional and order constraints on any letters stored to represent a print word. Cassidy (1992) has conducted a series of computational simulations, using a corpus of initial level school reading texts as input, to explore models of the kind of elementary orthographic word representation the child acquires before any reliable sublexical orthographic–phonological relations can be formed. The left and right word-boundary positions were important early reference points for representation of a partial ordering of the orthographic components in these initial elementary orthographic word representations, consistent with the extensive data on substitution errors reported by Stuart and Coltheart (1988).

In the theory there are two sources of information for acquiring and expanding the reader's orthographic lexicon. There is the 'supported text' experience of parent or teacher (4 in Figure 1). This support can cover a range of actions: the parent or teacher providing a response to the print word as they read a text to the child while the child is looking at the text; the teacher providing corrections for the child's attempt at an oral reading of the print word. The other information source for the reader to expand the orthographic lexicon is the output (13) of the reader's procedures (12) for generating a phonological response to a print word not yet established in the reader's orthographic lexicon. This generating procedure can enable acquisition of 'reading vocabulary' (here specified as the orthographic lexicon) when neither teacher nor parent is present to provide a response or correction for a print word.

Response Generation

The learning reader has the goal not only to acquire reading vocabulary knowledge but to maximise that which is veridical among knowledge acquired. Provision of correct word responses by external agents, such as teacher or parent, should achieve this better than the generation procedure which would be more prone to errors of veridicality. But the learner's goal of maximising veridical knowledge is constrained by another goal, that of being able to function without assistance from an external agent. It is this goal which requires learners to acquire procedures for generation of responses to words not yet familiar enough to be established in their reading vocabularies.

According to the theory there are potentially four information sources for the response generation procedures (12, in Figure 1) of the beginning reader. These are (a) teaching of explicit letter–sound relations, (b) the context of the word, (c) the phonological lexicon, and (d) induced sublexical relations. If it is provided, there is teaching of explicit letter–sound relations for letters of the alphabet, and some letter combinations may also be taught. Such teaching of 'explicit phonics' (1, in Figure 1) provides for the children a sound label, or 'phonic sound' for letters, for example, 'tuh' for the letter *t*, 'a' (as in 'apple') for the letter *a*. These responses are learnt as items of declarative knowledge (2, in Figure 1) that are not dependent on any pattern of letter–sound relations that children may induce from their current word reading vocabulary. Children are also taught to use the letter–sound knowledge (2) in procedures of 'explicit phonological recoding' (3); that is, translation of letters of unfamiliar words into phoneme segments which the children consciously attempt to assemble into word or word-like pronunciations. The sequence 1, 2, 3, represents the teaching and learning of 'explicit phonological recoding'. As children's reading levels advance, this recoding changes from being mainly overt to being internalised and at least in part non-conscious. In the knowledge sources theory explicit phonological recoding is optional for learning of word reading. Children can learn to read effectively without it, as had most 15-year-olds in the New Zealand sample of a recent international comparison (Ministry of Education, 2001). In neither the theories of Ehri nor Share would this be possible.

The second information source (11) for generation of a response is activated by the context of the print word. This context may be linguistic, the syntactic and semantic information already processed from the text. It may also be information from the illustrations, and from prior knowledge about the content of the text. A set of plausible candidate responses to the print word can be derived from the other information sources. Those which are inconsistent with the contextual information are registered as unlikely response candidates.

The third information source for response generation is the phonological lexicon, accessed via a 'phonological check' (10). If the phonological information being generated (from other sources) is found to be a sufficiently close match to a stored phonological word, then that word becomes a component of the output (13) of the generation procedures.

The fourth information source (8) for generation of a response comprises knowledge stored from the induction of sublexical relations between orthographic components and phonological components common to print words experienced by the learner. An example is given in Figure 2 for a segment of the reading vocabulary of a beginning reader. For illustrative purposes this is but six of all the words from the child's print experience. They provide exemplars for numerous sublexical orthographic–phonological relations that the child's brain induces. The figure illustrates just two, the relation between letter s and the phoneme 's', and between letter t and the phoneme 't'. The brain is an organ that (among other functions) finds patterns among information it receives and stores. The child has awareness of the items of the orthographic and phonological lexicons. The formation of induced sublexical relations (ISRs) involves relationships between the components of these items. This multiplicity of relationships would be overwhelming to readers if they were to attempt to gain explicit awareness of them during learning. The formation of ISRs is an implicit, nonconscious, process for both children and adults. Some of the product of this learning, the ISR knowledge, can on occasions be explicit and conscious, although most would be implicit. This aspect will be elaborated in the research evidence below.

The acquired ISRs are used to generate responses to unfamiliar print words by a process that may be described as *lexicalised phonological recoding*, which in Figure 1 is represented by 8, 9, 10, 12. This form of phonological recoding can commonly be implicit for beginning readers, which is unlike explicit phonological recoding.

Induction of Sublexical Relations

The induction of sublexical relations is a cumulative process that is continuously updated as words are added to the child's orthographic lexicon (5 in Figure 1). To form sublexical relations, it is supposed that the child's implicit procedure (7) can access the identity of components of the orthographic word as small as the letter, and of phonological segments as small as the phoneme, and align their temporal order with the stored position of orthographic components within the word. The identity of the phoneme segment is abstracted by the systems of the child's brain from the phonological forms of several words in which it is a common component. The identity of both initial and final position phonemes can be learnt in a few sessions from several exemplars via classification and matching tasks by many children as young as 4 years (Byrne & Fielding-Barnsley,

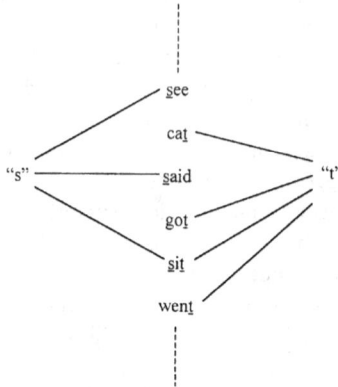

Figure 2
Illustration of induction of sublexical relations from a segment of a beginning reader's orthographic and phonological lexicons.

1990, 1991). During the early months of the child's reading instruction, access to phoneme segments and their identity will not be complete at the phoneme level, particularly for positions other than initial and final.

The implicit procedure for forming an ISR is illustrated in Figure 3 in a simplified form for just two words of a child's reading vocabulary. Having some familiarity with the print word *cat*, a relation will be formed between the orthographic component *c-* and the item of the phonological lexicon, 'cat'. The letter *c* is represented in the positional context of the left-hand boundary of the orthographic representation of the word. There will also be a relation between 'cat' and the orthographic component *-t*, where the letter *t* is represented in the positional context of the right-hand boundary of the orthographic representation of the word. (The relation between *-a-* and 'cat' may be formed later in acquisition.) Similarly, having some familiarity with the print word *got*, a relation will be formed between *g-* and 'got' and between *-t* and 'got'; and also for other lexical contexts, for example, *sit*, *went*, as in Figure 2. The orthographic component *-t* then has relations with several items of the reader's phonological lexicon, 'cat', 'got', 'sit', 'went'. One phonological component '-t' is common to those items. The child's brain can induce that the orthographic component *-t* relates to '-t', thus forming an ISR.

If the child is then presented with a previously unlearned print word which includes the orthographic component *-t*, this stored ISR (from 8 in Figure 1) can be used by the child when attempting to generate a response to that word. This ISR will be frequently used implicitly, without pronunciation of segmented components of the word, that is, without 'sounding out'. Similar ISRs will be formed among all relevant and sufficiently well established representations of other orthographic and phonological components in the various positional contexts,

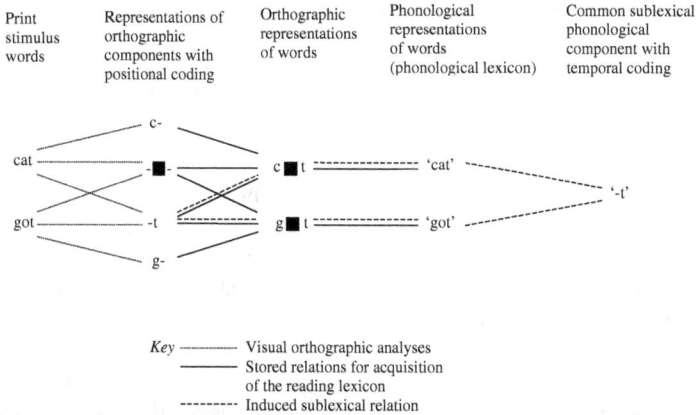

| Print stimulus words | Representations of orthographic components with positional coding | Orthographic representations of words | Phonological representations of words (phonological lexicon) | Common sublexical phonological component with temporal coding |

Figure 3

Example of a beginning reader's procedure for forming an induced sublexical relation between an orthographic component, -t, and a sublexical phonological component '-t'.

for example, initial *s* as in Figure 2, for all print words the child has experienced. For illustration, only one ISR in the final position has been described in the example in Figure 3.

Recursive Accommodation to the Orthography and Reading Vocabulary

The ISRs that are induced will depend on what the orthography can yield in the reading vocabulary the child is learning. English orthography is only partially consistent in letter–sound relationships. The systems of the child's brain learns that most words of English have at least some letters that exhibit a consistent letter–sound relationship. For example, at a very early reading level the child's brain will identify the letter sequence *th* of the word *the* as belonging to the pattern of letter–sound relationship in the words *there*, *they*, *this*, all of which are in the child's orthographic lexicon. However, the letter *e* of *the* will be identified as having an inconsistent letter–sound relationship, as the child experiences the letter *e* in the word *he*.

Orthographic units which show no consistency of phonological relationships in the child's current reading vocabulary are not ignored. To do so would often interfere with the subsequent learning of ISRs as the child's reading vocabulary expands. For example, subsequently the child will learn to read the words *me*, *she*, *we*, *be*, as well as *he* (order based on decreasing word frequencies in initial reading books; *Children's printed word database*, 2002). At this point of learning, the phonological relations to final *e* letters that fully represent the vowel of such words, comprising a single open syllable, are consistent for all but the word *the*. At the same time, the child will be experiencing the letter *e* in words such as *went*, *help*, *then*, *yes*, *bed*, *red*, *get*, and, if taught explicit letter–sound relationships (phonic sounds), the child will learn the same 'short sound' as a response for the letter *e*. If this latter letter–sound relationship were identified by the child as the standard and the others which did not match it were ignored, then there would be no learning of ISRs for *e* in *he*, *me*, *she*, *we*, *be*, and no (implicit) learning of the influence of position of the letter within the word and of the influence of syllable structure.

The child's set of ISRs derives from the total current reading vocabulary of the child. The ISRs, therefore, change to match the letter–sound relations of the expanding reading vocabulary. ISRs are thus attuned to each child's current reading vocabulary in a way not possible with a prescribed set of explicitly taught letter–sound relations. ISRs thus provide a *lexicalised* form of phonological recoding (of letters to sound).

Lexicalised phonological recoding is based on knowledge of letter–sound relationships obtained implicitly from the reading vocabulary acquired by the child. This type of phonological recoding, in turn, assists the child in responding to many unfamiliar words, thus expanding the child's reading vocabulary, which in turn provides a basis for more advanced knowledge of ISRs, and so on. In Figure 1 this repeated sequence is 4, 5, 6, 7, 8, 9, 12, 13. This recursive process can get started as the child learns to identify just a few print words by his orthographic lexicon. In contrast, explicit phonological recoding (and its subsequent internalisation) does not have this recursive characteristic, as it can only facilitate, and is not facilitated by, gains in reading vocabulary. In Figure 1, this non-recursive sequence is 1, 2, 3, 12, 13.

In contrast to many other theories of reading acquisition, the knowledge sources theory has no need for developmental phases, or stages, at successive levels of reading attainment. Although there will be an initial 'exploration' to determine the relevant sources of information for learning, thereafter the child's brain uses both the letter-based memory of words (orthographic lexicon) and lexicalised phonological recoding. If it is taught, the child also uses explicit phonological recoding. These sources of knowledge do not belong to successive phases or reading levels, as in the theories of Ehri and Share. However, for any particular word that a child experiences in print form, there will be a progression from use of phonological recoding to an increasingly dominant use of letter-based memory of the word as it becomes familiar in print form.

Research Evidence

What is the empirical evidence against which this theory has been tested? There is published evidence from two sets of studies of normal 5- and 6-year-old readers that indicated such children did use ISRs (Thompson, Cottrell, & Fletcher-Flinn, 1996; Thompson, Fletcher-Flinn, & Cottrell, 1999). In the first set of studies the children were given reading experience of words with a particular positional letter–phoneme relationship (*b* in final position) that had not previously been encountered. The resulting gain in reading vocabulary spontaneously transferred to the acquisition of the new letter–phoneme relationship. Beginning readers do induce letter–sound patterns from their limited experience of print words. The use of analogies did not account for the obtained results. In the second set of studies, on 5-year-olds, the results provided the same conclusion, from an examination of the sounds given as responses to letters by children who had not been taught explicit letter sounds.

A recent US study (Fletcher-Flinn, Shankweiler, & Frost, 2004) on normal 6-year-olds who had been taught explicit phonics but had not yet received instruction on the *th* digraph showed that a large proportion of them had apparently induced a correct pronunciation for the digraph. Induction of untaught sound correspondences for the letter *y* in final position has also been reported for the same age level, for both 2-syllable and single-syllable words (Thompson & Fletcher-Flinn, 1993, pp. 48–51). An independent research group in the United Kingdom (Stuart, Masterson, Dixon, & Quinlan, 1999) has reported that 6-year-olds can induce from their experience of reading words the correct pronunciations of vowel digraphs, for example, *ee*, *ea*, that have not been taught. Another independent research group in Europe (Martinet, Valdois, & Fayol, 2004) has published evidence from the spelling performance of phonics-taught beginners. This evidence indicates that beginners who use explicit letter–sound relationships are also using both an orthographic lexicon and induction of sublexical relations, as predicted by the knowledge sources theory.

ISRs will not only be sensitive to position within the word but also to the context of other graphemes, and corresponding phonological components, within the word. For example, among 6-year-olds the ISR for the grapheme *y* in final position of two-syllable words such as *baby*, *happy*, was distinguished not only by position from the ISR for *y* in *yes*, *you*, but also contextually from the ISR for occurrences in single open syllable words such as *by*, or *my* (Thompson & Fletcher-Flinn, 1993).

Lexicalised phonological recoding, being at least in part an implicit process, can function at relatively high speed. Explicit phonological recoding is slower, being more dependent on slower serial processing. A cross-national study of beginning readers has contributed evidence consistent with this claim (Connelly, Johnston, & Thompson, 1999, 2001). Also, the theory has been applied to the consideration of reading disability. It has provided interpretations and explanations for a variety of research results on reading disabilities. These have been presented elsewhere (Thompson, McKay, & Fletcher-Flinn, 2004).

Lexicalised Phonological Recoding Is Not an Analogy Process

Case study evidence shows that exceptionally advanced reading can develop with lexicalised phonological recoding, and without advanced explicit letter–sound recoding (Fletcher-Flinn & Thompson, 2000). Further evidence (Fletcher-Flinn & Thompson, 2004) confirms that normal readers, too, can acquire advanced lexicalised phonological recoding, despite having underdeveloped explicit letter–sound skills. In both reports, evidence was presented which showed that the child's exceptionally advanced reading did not depend on the use of analogies.

In theories of reading in which use of analogy is a principal mechanism (e.g., Goswami, 1993) the reader attempting an unfamiliar word, for example, *hump*, identifies an analogue word in his reading vocabulary by determining the one word that has the best match of a grapheme sequence and is the most accessible in memory at the time, for example, *jump*. This contrasts with the present theory in which many ISRs are for single graphemes, not just sequences. In general, ISRs possess higher productivity for learning than analogues. An ISR for a single grapheme is usually a component in a much larger number of words of the child's reading vocabulary than any analogue. Moreover, ISRs have been formed by the child's brain taking into account all words in the child's reading vocabulary that provide exemplars of the orthographic–phonological relationship, not just one word from the vocabulary that is identified to provide an analogue. In addition, the former is an implicit learning procedure while the analogy procedure can (at least in part) be explicit to the reader.

Relationships Between Explicit and Lexicalised Letter–Sound Knowledge

In the knowledge sources theory, the formation of ISR knowledge is an implicit process, but some of the product of this knowledge can on occasions be explicit. It has been shown (Thompson, Fletcher-Flinn, & Cottrell, 1999) that in 5-year-olds knowledge of ISRs provides the basis for a small set of simple letter–sound responses which have not been taught (and are those which cannot be inferred by the child from knowledge of letter names). These are instances of explicit, but untaught, letter–sound knowledge which derives from ISRs. However, explicit phonological recoding (3, in Figure 1) does not automatically result from such knowledge of letter sounds. (The relationships between explicit and lexicalised letter–sound knowledge are not depicted in Figure 1.)

If the child were taught letter–sound knowledge and how to use it for explicit phonological recoding, can this teaching influence the nature of the child's learning of ISRs? A result in a recent study (Fletcher-Flinn, Shankweiler, & Frost, 2004) suggests it can. Children in their first year of schooling who had received phonics instruction were asked to read non-words comprising just two graphemes, and their performance was compared with results from children without phonics instruction. The children without phonics showed better performance for *th* in non-words with *th* in initial position (e.g., *thu*) than in final position (e.g., *uth*), as would be expected if this phonological recoding were lexicalised. In the vocabulary of first-year reading books there are fewer words with *th* in the final position relative to the much greater number with *th* in initial position. Results for other consonant graphemes showed the effect to be largely specific to such positional distributions of the grapheme in the vocabulary. The children with phonics instruction, although equal in overall accuracy on these non-words, showed no effect of position of *th*. As the *th* letter–sound relationship had not yet been taught to these children, they had apparently induced this relationship from their print lexical experience. But, also in their experience was phonics teaching of a number of other explicit letter–sound relationships. The authors concluded that 'phonics instruction results in the storage of letter–sound associations from which is formed a general implicit principle that sounds for letters are the same irrespective of position. This principle then has a direct impact on the formation of induced sublexical relations at this early level'.

There is evidence from a large number of studies (reviewed by Ehri, Nunes, Stahl, & Willows, 2001) that increasing the teaching of explicit letter–sound relations and explicit phonological recoding for beginning readers will increase their accuracy of word reading (though unfortunately information on speed of reading is lacking). From the evidence of these studies it cannot be inferred that lexicalised phonological recoding is not of fundamental importance for beginning reading. These studies have not considered it, nor the relationships between it and explicit phonological recoding.

Some Implications of the Theory for Educational Practice

The knowledge sources theory has implications for decisions on educational practices for teaching children to read. The position of the theory has been set out within a wide-ranging examination of commonly debated issues on the teaching of reading (Thompson, 2002). Here we can provide only brief mention of three issues in the teaching of beginning readers. First, there is the question of the extent to which there ought to be teaching of explicit phonics. According to the theory this would be an optional supplementary source of information, if it does not interfere too much with the child's learning of lexicalised phonological recoding. The potential for such interference is a matter which will be enlightened by further research on the relationships between explicit and lexicalised letter–sound knowledge. Both the theories of Ehri (1999) and Share (1995), in contrast, imply that teaching of explicit phonics is required for satisfactory progress in beginning reading.

Second, there is the question of whether for beginners there should be concentration on teaching of explicit letter–sound relations before teaching for the development of reading vocabulary. In the knowledge sources theory, once the child has responded to initial teacher guidance on the relevant sources of information for learning, knowledge of ISRs is learnt implicitly from the reading vocabulary acquired by the child. In a recursive process, knowledge of ISRs is used in lexicalised phonological recoding which in turn assists the expansion of the child's reading vocabulary (orthographic lexicon) which in turn provides the basis for learning more advanced knowledge of ISRs, and so on. In view of this recursive process and the fact that the orthographic lexicon, which is a letter-based memory of words, is used by the child from near the beginning of reading acquisition, the teacher ought to be strongly supporting the child's learning of it at all reading levels. The child's implicitly acquired letter–sound knowledge is attuned to the child's current reading vocabulary.

Third, there is the question of whether beginning readers ought to be taught to use analogies for phonological recoding, a teaching practice implied by Goswami's (1993) theory. In common with Ehri's theory, but for some different reasons, the use of analogies by beginning readers is not implied by the knowledge sources theory.

Author Note

Cited print letters/words are in italic; cited spoken/heard sounds/words are in quotation marks.

References

Byrne, B. (1996). The learnability of the alphabetic principle: Children's initial hypotheses about how print represents spoken language. *Applied Psycholinguistics, 17*, 41–426.

Byrne, B. (1998). *The foundation of literacy: The child's acquisition of the alphabetic principle*. Hove, UK: Psychology Press.

Byrne, B., & Fielding-Barnsley, R. (1990). Acquiring the alphabetic principle: A case for teaching recognition of phoneme identity. *Journal of Educational Psychology, 82*, 805–812.

Byrne, B., & Fielding-Barnsley, R. (1991). Evaluation of a program to teach phonemic awareness to young children. *Journal of Educational Psychology, 83*, 451–455.

Byrne, B., Fielding-Barnsley, R., & Ashley, L. (1996). What does the child bring to the task of learning to read? A summary of the New England Reading Acquisition Projects. *Australian Journal of Psychology, 48*, 119–123.

Cassidy, S. (1992). *A computer model of reading development*. Unpublished doctoral dissertation, Victoria University of Wellington, New Zealand.

Chall, J. S. (1983). Learning to read, reading to learn: An interview with J. S. Chall. *Curriculum Review, 22*, 11–15.

Children's printed word database. (2002). Department of Psychology, University of Essex, UK. Available: http://www.essex.ac.uk/psychology/cpwd

Connelly, V., Johnston, R. S., & Thompson, G. B. (1999). The influence of instructional approaches on reading procedures. In G. B. Thompson & T. Nicholson (Eds.), *Learning to read: Beyond phonics and whole language* (pp. 103–123). New York: Teachers College Press.

Connelly, V., Johnston, R. S., & Thompson, G. B. (2001). The effects of phonics instruction on the reading comprehension of beginning readers. *Reading and Writing: An Interdisciplinary Journal, 14*, 423–457.

Ehri, L. C. (1991). Development of the ability to read words. In R. Barr, M.L. Kamil, P. Mosenthal, & P. D. Pearson (Eds.), *Handbook of reading research* (Vol. 2, pp. 385–419). New York: Longman.

Ehri, L. C. (1994). Development of the ability to read words: Update. In R. B. Ruddell, M. R. Ruddell, and H. Singer (Eds.), *Theoretical models and processes of reading* (4th ed., pp. 323–358). Newark, DE: International Reading Association.

Ehri, L. C. (1999). Phases of development in learning to read words. In J. Oakhill & R. Beard (Eds.), *Reading development and the teaching of reading* (pp. 79–108). Oxford, England: Blackwell.

Ehri, L. C., Nunes, S. R., Stahl, S. A., & Willows, D. M. (2001). Systematic phonics instruction helps students learn to read: Evidence from the National Reading Panel's meta-analysis. *Review of Educational Research, 71*, 393–447.

Ehri, L. C., & Saltmarsh, J. (1995). Beginning readers outperform older disabled readers in learning to read words by sight. *Reading and Writing: An Interdisciplinary Journal, 7*, 295–326.

Fletcher-Flinn, C. M., Shankweiler, D., & Frost. S. (2004). Coordination of reading and spelling in early literacy development: An examination of the discrepancy hypothesis. *Reading and Writing: An Interdisciplinary Journal, 17*, 617–644.

Fletcher-Flinn, C. M., & Thompson, G. B. (2000). Learning to read with underdeveloped phonemic awareness but lexicalized phonological recoding: A case study of a three-year-old. *Cognition, 74*, 177–208.

Fletcher-Flinn, C. M., & Thompson, G. B. (2004). A mechanism of implicit lexicalized phonological recoding used concurrently with underdeveloped explicit letter-sound skills in both precocious and normal reading development. *Cognition*, 90, 303–335.

Frith, U. (1985). Beneath the surface of developmental dyslexia. In K. E. Patterson, J. C. Marshall, & M. Coltheart (Eds.), *Surface dyslexia: Neuropsychological and cognitive studies of phonological reading* (pp. 301–330). London: Lawrence Erlbaum.

Goswami, U. (1993). Toward an interactive analogy model of reading development: Decoding vowel graphemes in beginning reading. *Journal of Experimental Child Psychology*, 56, 443–475.

Goswami, U., & Bryant, P. (1990). *Phonological skills and learning to read*. Hove, UK: Lawrence Erlbaum.

Hutzler, F., Ziegler, J. C., Perry, C., Wimmer, H., & Zorzi, M. (2004). Do current connectionist learning models account for reading development in different languages? *Cognition*, 91, 273–296.

Jackson, N. E., & Coltheart, M. (2001). *Routes to reading success and failure: Toward an integrated cognitive psychology of atypical reading*. New York: Psychology Press.

Jorm, A. F., & Share, D. L. (1983). Phonological recoding and reading acquisition. *Applied Psycholinguistics*, 4, 103–147.

Karmiloff-Smith, A. (1992). *Beyond modularity: A developmental perspective on cognitive science*. Cambridge, MA: MIT Press.

Marsh, G., Friedman, M., Welch, V., & Desberg, P. (1981). A cognitive-developmental theory of reading acquisition. In T. G. Waller & G. E. McKinnon (Eds.), *Reading research: Advances in theory and practice* (Vol. 3, pp. 199–221). New York: Academic Press.

Martinet, C., Valdois, S., & Fayol, M. (2004). Lexical orthographic knowledge develops from the beginning of literary acquisition. *Cognition*, 91, B11–B22.

Ministry of Education. (2001). *Assessing knowledge and skills for life: First results from the Programme for International Student Assessment (PISA 2000), New Zealand summary report*. Wellington, New Zealand: Ministry of Education.

Ramus, F. (2004). The neural basis of reading acquisition. In M. S. Gazzaniga (Ed.), *The cognitive neurosciences* (3rd ed., pp. 815–824). Cambridge, MA: MIT Press.

Reitsma, P. (1983a). Word-specific knowledge in beginning reading. *Journal of Research in Reading*, 6, 41–55.

Reitsma, P. (1983b). Printed word learning in beginning readers. *Journal of Experimental Child Psychology*, 36, 321–339.

Share, D. L. (1995). Phonological recoding and self-teaching: Sine qua non of reading acquisition. *Cognition*, 55, 115–149.

Share, D. L., & Jorm, A. F. (1987). Segmental analysis: Co-requisite to reading, vital for self-teaching, requiring phonological memory. *European Bulletin of Cognitive Psychology*, 7, 509–513.

Stuart, M., & Coltheart, M. (1988). Does reading develop in a sequence of stages? *Cognition*, 30, 139–181.

Stuart, M., Masterson, J., Dixon, M., & Quinlan, P. (1999). Interacting processes in the development of printed word recognition. In T. Nunes (Ed.), *Learning to read: An integrated view from research and practice* (pp. 105–120). Dordrecht, the Netherlands: Kluwer.

Sun, R., Merrill, E., & Peterson, T. (2001). From implicit skills to explicit knowledge: A bottom-up model of skill learning. *Cognitive Science*, 25, 203–244.

Thompson, G. B. (2002). Teaching and the phonics debate: What can we learn? *New Zealand Annual Review of Education*, 11, 161–178.

Thompson, G. B., Cottrell, D. S., & Fletcher-Flinn, C. M. (1996). Sublexical orthographic-phonological relations early in the acquisition of reading: The knowledge sources account. *Journal of Experimental Child Psychology*, 62, 190–222.

Thompson, G. B., & Fletcher-Flinn, C. M. (1993). A theory of knowledge sources and procedures for reading acquisition. In G. B. Thompson, W. E. Tunmer, & T. Nicholson (Eds.), *Reading acquisition processes* (pp. 20–73). Clevedon, UK: Multilingual Matters.

Thompson, G. B., Fletcher-Flinn, C. M., & Cottrell, D. S. (1999). Learning correspondences between letters and phonemes without explicit instruction. *Applied Psycholinguistics, 20,* 21–50.

Thompson, G. B., & Johnston, R. S. (1993). The effects of type of instruction on processes of reading acquisition. In G. B. Thompson, W. E. Tunmer, & T. Nicholson (Eds.), *Reading acquisition processes* (pp. 74–90). Clevedon, UK: Multilingual Matters.

Thompson, G. B., McKay, M. F., & Fletcher-Flinn, C. M. (2004). New theory for understanding reading and reading disability. *Australian Journal of Learning Disabilities, 9*(2), 3–7.

Wang, M., Liu, Y., & Perfetti, C. A. (2004). The implicit and explicit learning of orthographic structure and function of a new writing system. *Scientific Studies of Reading, 8,* 357–379.

Zorzi, M., Houghton, G., & Butterworth, B. (1998). The development of spelling-sound relationships in a model of phonological reading. *Language and Cognitive Processes, 13,* 337–371.

Part 3

Cognition in Development

Internal Constraints on Representational Flexibility: Reformulating the Research Evidence From Children's Drawings

Jason Low

There are several reasons for the psychological study of children's drawings. One popular reason is to explore the acquisition of relevant graphic skills (e.g., foreshortening, pattern organisation, visuo-spatial realism; e.g., Freeman, 1980; Goodnow & Levine, 1973, Low & Hollis, 2003; van Sommers, 1984). Researchers following this line of inquiry often seek to chart the slow developmental progression toward adult-like pictorial competence. However, following Karmiloff-Smith (1990), this chapter will demonstrate that another important reason for studying children's drawings is that we can use it as a source of evidence with respect to understanding the more general process of representational change, that is, the way in which knowledge in the mind becomes transformed into knowledge to the mind.

To forecast, the chapter will be structured as follows. First, to set the scene, I will introduce the theoretical model driving Karmiloff-Smith's early research (i.e., the representational redescription model). Second, I will briefly describe the seminal evidence from Karmiloff-Smith for the process of representational redescription as observed in the micro-domain of children's drawings and contrast it with findings from other laboratories. Next, I shall pause to assess some of the theoretical issues raised by the conflicting findings on children's drawings and internal representational change. Following this, I shall attempt to integrate the conflicting findings with the original Karmiloff-Smith (1990) study by weaving in research evidence from my own laboratory. Finally, I shall conclude the chapter by highlighting theoretical issues that need resolution where Karmiloff-Smith's model of cognitive development is concerned.

Representational Redescription Model

In 1992, Karmiloff-Smith formally presented an influential account of cognitive developmental change known as the representational redescription model (hereafter also referred to as RRM). According to Karmiloff-Smith, one way in which new knowledge may be acquired is through the internal process of representational redescription (RR), where information already present in the mind is repeatedly redescribed into different representational formats. The process of RR involves three specific recurrent phases. First, in the Implicit phase, the child's main source of information is external in locus or data driven. The Implicit phase does not involve any representational change per se, but rather involves collecting and practising new representations from outside sources and storing them independently (formally termed as adjunctions). Representations in this phase are in the form of procedures for responding to the environment, and are sequentially specified. The representations are also bracketed, and consequently, they remain unconnected with other pieces of knowledge. Consistent successful performance (behavioural mastery) within a certain task means that phase one is coming to an end.

With the advent of representational change, the second phase, Explicit-1, comes into play. Phase 2 signifies the child's new focus on the internal knowledge within his or her mind. Here, stable representations within a particular domain of knowledge start undergoing redescription to allow it to be related with others within or between domains. While existing information becomes the main focal point of introspection, the first rounds of redescription can lead to temporary inflexibility in a child's task performance. At this phase, feedback will be ignored and errors made will not be rectified.

Eventually, by the third Explicit 2/3 phase, there is a combining of the internally held representations with external data. Simply put, the child reconciles external data with existing information in the mind. By this phase of redescription, representations are now accessible verbally and consciously.

Clearly, an insightful aspect of RRM is that behavioural mastery is not the end point of development but a prerequisite for further representational change (Karmiloff-Smith, 1994). However, it is important to note that RRM is not a stage model and hence these phases are not age related, rather these phases occur repeatedly within different micro-domains throughout development.

Evidence From Children's Drawings: Karmiloff-Smith (1990)

To demonstrate the general process-oriented framework of RRM, Karmiloff-Smith (1990) attempted to investigate in the drawing micro-domain whether, even at the first level of representational redescription, the initial representation continues to be governed by procedural inflexibilities held over from the Implicit behavioural mastery phase — specifically, a sequentially fixed list. The issues of constraints on internal representational change and flexibility of knowledge were addressed by asking children between the ages of 5 and 11 years to draw a man, and then a man who did not exist. In keeping with RRM, Karmiloff-Smith (1990) selected children from the ages of 5 upwards because behavioural mastery is a prerequisite for the first level of representational redescription to take place. Indeed, she observed that a significant majority of the children were able to draw pictures of normal men, and executed these sequential procedures rapidly. These observations fit with existing research documenting that by 5 years of age children are likely to show a serial or sequential order in their graphic productions of the human figure. For example, Bassett (1977) reported that a majority of the 5-year-olds in her study, when asked to draw a man, started with the head, then drew the trunk in the middle of their sequence, and ended their serial ordering with the legs.

The pretend people drawings revealed significant developmental differences between the age groups. Younger children tended to delete elements (e.g., missing leg), make modifications to shape of elements (e.g., one leg in a shape of a triangle) or to the whole figure (e.g., a star-shaped person). Older children tended to make insertions (e.g., extra torsos), position-orientation changes (e.g., head switched with leg), or cross-category changes (e.g., half man, half animal). Furthermore, there were differences in the way the age groups deleted elements. Karmiloff-Smith (1990) observed that the younger age group finished their drawings after they have made a deletion, while the older age group regularly continued their drawings after deleting an item. A second experiment with 5-year-olds revealed that young children failed to draw 'a man with two heads' even when instructed to do so — children ended up drawing two men each with one head. This reduplication error shows that the absence of certain types of creative modifications in the younger children's drawing repertoire was not due to a simple lack of imagination.

Karmiloff-Smith (1990) concluded that the different graphic behaviours produced by children in the different age groups clearly showed the different levels of RR that the children achieved. Having accomplished behavioural mastery, the younger children were viewed to have gone through the first round of RR. However, even at this level, their knowledge remains bound by a sequential constraint. Here children are able to make certain kinds of modifications that do not interrupt significantly the sequential procedure (e.g., shape of element changes) but still find it difficult to make modifications that involve insertions of substantial subroutines in the middle of the drawing procedure (e.g., position-orientation changes). Furthermore, at this level of RR, children's knowledge has not become available as data structure to other parts of the cognitive system. Hence, young children made few modifications that involved combining concepts about personhood with concepts about animalhood. It is only with additional rounds of RR that the sequential constraint is relaxed, and knowledge becomes available across domains.

Research Post-Karmiloff-Smith (1990): The Emperor is Naked

While Karmiloff-Smith interpreted her findings to support the presence of an endogenous cognitive constraint upon representational change (i.e., a sequential constraint), Zhi, Thomas, and Robinson (1997) decided to test whether the constraint is instead exogenous and task related. Testing 3-year-old children, the researchers showed one group a picture of a woman with two heads, while the other group was not shown an example. Participants were then asked to draw a person with two heads. The effect of the illustration was significant, indicating that a pictorial example is a precondition for success among very young children. Further challenging Karmiloff-Smith's (1990) findings, Zhi et al. observed that of the 11 children who successfully drew a man with two heads in the illustration example condition, 10 inserted the second head immediately after drawing the first head. Overall, then, Zhi et al.'s findings reveal that even 3-year-olds can successfully interrupt their drawing sequence to produce a picture of a man with two heads. This constitutes more representational flexibility in young children than allowed by RRM. Additionally, it may be that the young children misunderstood the original instructions as presented by Karmiloff-Smith (1990), and hence it is communicating task requirements through external examples, rather than redescriptions of internal constraints, that lead to flexibility.

Aside from the benefits of visual examples, other researchers have documented that directed verbal prompts can also promote representational flexibility among young children. Using Karmiloff-Smith's (1990) pretend-person drawing paradigm, Spensley and Taylor (1999) requested 4- to 6-year-old children to draw highly specific 'strange-looking' men (e.g., a man with some part of his body the wrong shape). The results revealed that only 1 out of 15 children had any problems with these specific drawing requests. Moreover, the majority of the participants made the imaginative alterations in the middle of their drawing procedures.

Why do young children show more representational flexibility when they are cued with visual examples or directed instructions beforehand? Berti and Freeman (1997) explain that when the child is asked to draw a novel instantiation of a human being, the first aim is to make the picture recognisable as a man. The problem that arises is that, in trying to accomplish the first goal, the child may fall short of the second (i.e., the picture should also contain fictional features). The end result is that the picture looks like a normal man. Children need assistance to monitor what is emerging on paper to ensure that both pictorial aspects are recognisable: it is a man and a man that does not exist. Berti and Freeman suggest that dual recognition can be accomplished when visual or verbal cues help young children plan and pick out distinctive shapes from different categories that will trigger the two recognitions.

Overall, in the case of children's imaginative drawings, researchers have argued that since young children can draw novel innovations to the human form after being asked to come up with a particular category (e.g., verbally requested to draw a man with arms and legs displaced) or shown a visual example (e.g., a woman with two heads), RRM has underestimated the age at which representational flexibility can be observed.

Evaluation of Research Post-Karmiloff-Smith (1990): The Emperor Isn't Naked

In response to the uptake of her 1990 findings, Karmiloff-Smith (1999) explains that critics of her 1990 drawing study appear to be arguing that there is no change in representational format during development, and all that changes with age is that greater amounts of information can be brought to bear in working memory. Furthermore, simply showing that young children can reproduce high-level innovations to the human form as a result of task manipulations confuses the external drawing product with the internal cognitive processes underlying behaviour. Certainly, there are multiple sources of information in the environment about imaginative or hypothetical instantiations (e.g., television, books, comics) that children come to learn through complex social interactions (e.g., Low & Durkin, 1998; Mitchell & Riggs, 2000; White & Low, 2002). However, RRM stresses the point that we need to distinguish between the content and sources of children's knowledge as exhibited (drawn) on paper and the processes by which children integrate that knowledge into their minds. The extant research evidence suggesting that the task context determines how young children perform on Karmiloff-Smith's (1990) drawing paradigm (e.g., Berti & Freeman, 1997; Spensley & Taylor, 1999; Zhi et al., 1997) does not fully explain how knowledge in the mind might become transformed into knowledge to the mind.

It is often overlooked that even in the original 1990 report on children's drawings, Karmiloff-Smith argued that when young children are successful at drawing or copying, for instance, a two-headed man after being shown a visual example, they are not using the flexibility of a redescribed man-drawing procedure that can be pursued rapidly. Instead, under these exogenously provoked circumstances, young children are creating de novo a new implicit procedure (an adjunction). This needs to be contrasted with the explicit representational format that sustains behaviour among older children whereby they can spontaneously insert subroutines into their rapid drawing procedure. In other words, in studies where children can reproduce or copy a two-headed person when shown a similar visual aid, RRM views such evidence as indicating that children have only added a new procedure that will still have to undergo redescription before becoming data structure available to other parts of the system.

It is only when researchers show that with the passage of time, young children continue to induce (and sustain) more advanced representations after displaying behavioural success with external input, can we say that the adjunctions have undergone RR to allow more flexible instantiations. Of course, if these arguments are to retain their relevance toward RRM theorising, it is important to chart whether knowledge structures continue to change even after behavioural success, and whether RR must occur before external input becomes generalised and available for wider use. I turn now to highlight research from my laboratory that aims towards these goals.

Evidence From Children's Drawings: New Clothes for the Emperor

For the distinction between representational redescription and representational adjunction to become a powerful one, we need to search for particular kinds of experimental evidence. First, we need to show that young children can exhibit behavioural success in their drawings of a pretend man when shown visual examples. This would suggest that external input could assist children's solving of the task. However, while such results would confirm criticisms of Karmiloff-Smith's (1990) study that early representational flexibility in children's drawings of novel forms has been underestimated, such data alone would confuse the external drawing product with the internal cognitive processes that drive behaviour. Hence, the second type of evidence we would need to search for, to further consolidate the distinction between representational adjunctions and redescriptions, is whether recently activated knowledge in the mind (i.e., the visual examples) might become transformed into knowledge to the mind. According to Karmiloff-Smith (1990), under such exogenously provoked circumstances, children are creating de novo a new procedure, an adjunction. In contrast, research from criticisms of her drawing evidence would suggest that young children are using the flexibility of a redescribed man-drawing procedure that can be pursued rapidly, representations that are identical to those of older children. To determine whether the successful external drawing product generated after the visual feedback is generated from redescriptions or adjunctions, we need to observe whether there is subsequent representational change.

Within the research from my laboratory, the predictions of RRM provide the motivation to investigate whether external assistance in the form of visual examples is only temporarily helpful, and further internal change must still occur before young children reliably call upon advanced representations, and that even when behavioural change can be induced immediately after the introduction of the visual examples, the transfer of training effect is weak, if any. Together with Steve Hollis and Ron Atkins, I have been testing RRM predictions by charting representational changes after children receive external input consisting of examples of improbable looking human beings. Since some of these studies are still ongoing, I shall primarily provide illustrative data to highlight theoretical arguments.

Hollis and Low (2005) sought to investigate how children's representations in the Karmiloff-Smith (1990) drawing task might change over time (approximately 5 months), and whether redescription of external knowledge (via visual examples) must still take place before it is generalised and available for wider use. The first time point of the study involved a replication of Karmiloff-Smith's (1990) findings, asking younger (5- to 7-year-olds) and older children (8- to 9-year-olds) to draw a person and a pretend looking person. Representational level scores were allocated depending upon the type of modification made and where in the

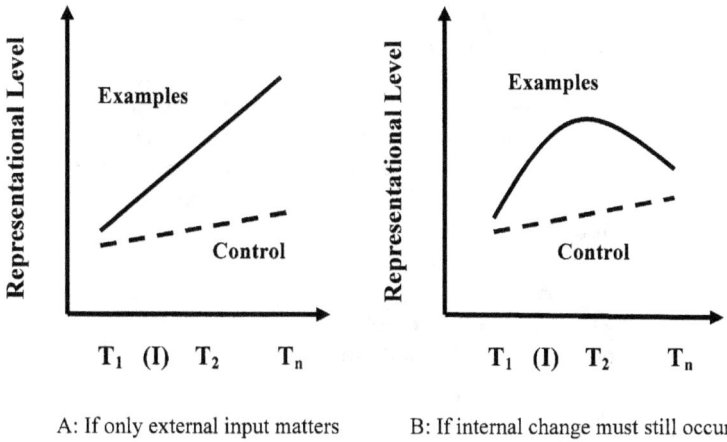

A: If only external input matters   B: If internal change must still occur

Figure 1

Potential changes in level of representational flexibility over time depending upon one of two possibilities: (A) external input drives development and hence young children's task performance reliably improves from example cuing, or (B) external input needs to be internally redescribed before advanced representations can be sustained and hence young children's improved task performance from example cuing is temporary.

Note: Key: T_1 = baseline; (I) = intervention — example cuing or control; T_2 = one week intervention; T_n = several weeks after intervention.

drawing sequence the modification was executed. One week later, an intervention phase took place. Participants in the experimental examples-provided group were shown instances of pretend-looking people (e.g., a man with a triangle-shaped leg, a man with 4 arms, a man with a deleted right leg) and told why they were considered as such. Participants in the control groups were either asked to draw impossible-looking people again but without being shown examples (the draw-again condition) or asked to build a tower of blocks (the distracter condition). This was followed by three further drawing sessions, which took place 1 week, 5 weeks and 17 weeks after the intervention. In these three post-intervention time points, children were again asked to draw new and different pretend-looking people, and the experimenter noted the type of change made and where in the drawing sequence the modifications were executed. With this design, Hollis and Low sought to separate changes in children's drawing output due to RR, from changes due to general information processing limitations (see Figure 1).

Looking at Figure 1, there are two possibilities in terms of how representational flexibility could potentially unfold for children in the example-shown group as compared to children in the control groups as per Hollis and Low's (2005) study. If the ability to introduce innovations with subroutines in the middle of the drawing procedure is independent of the distinction between representational adjunctions and redescriptions, young children who are argued to be unable to complete Karmiloff-Smith's (1990) drawing task because of information processing task demands (e.g., inability to monitor what constitutes a recognisably pretend man, lack of imagination) should perform better in the examples group across all post-intervention time points compared to their counterparts in the control groups where no external input was provided (see illustration A in Figure 1). In contrast, to the extent that advanced and generalised representations only occur after there has been sufficient developmental time for redescription of external input to take place (Karmiloff-Smith, 1990, 1992), children in the examples group should only outperform their same-age counterparts in the control groups for a brief period of time after the intervention (see illustration B in Figure 1). Extending from RRM predictions, as time passes, young children in the examples group should regress to a lower representational level that is closer to their post-intervention performance, and also similar to their same age counterparts' performance in the control groups.

Hollis and Low (2005) expected that their 5-month longitudinal study would not be sufficient to wipe out approximately 5 years of reiterated rounds of RR as suggested by the developmental differences found by Karmiloff-Smith (1990) between 5- and 11-year-olds. At the Time 1 baseline session, it was found that compared to older children (8- to 9-year-olds), younger children (5- to 7-year-olds) demonstrated significantly more conceptual and procedural rigidity. Young children often attempted shape of element changes or deletions, and made these modifications at the end of the drawing sequence. A week after having seen examples of pretend-looking people, the measures of young children's representational flexibility were higher in comparison with their baseline measures. There was also no significant difference between the representational scores of younger and older children 1 week after the examples viewing. In this manner, the results confirm extant research showing that young children's attempts at representational flexibility benefit from external supports (e.g., Spensley & Taylor, 1999; Zhi et al., 1997). However, important to confirming RRM expectations, Hollis and Low found that the utility of external input (i.e., the examples) on children's drawing behaviour was only a temporary one. Over time (by Time 4, 17 weeks after the examples viewing), the young children in the examples group regressed close to their baseline representational level scores, and their scores were also similar to their same age counterparts' performance in the control groups (graphically, their findings looked like illustration B in Figure 1). Older children, in contrast, continued to sustain high representational flexibility in their drawings across the time points. Finally, since redescription of external knowledge (via visual examples) must still take place before it is generalised and available for wider use, Hollis and Low also documented convergent findings of poor transfer of learning effects exhibited by young children in the examples group when completing the analogous task of drawing pretend houses.

Why did the younger children in the examples group only show flexible drawing behaviour for a short period of time? As expected by RRM, younger children in the examples group may have abstracted and learned specifically defined rules from the cued example set (e.g., draw a triangle for the leg, delete the right leg and so on) and stored it in working memory as a representational adjunction that is unconnected with other existing representations in order to gain rapid success in their generation of types of modifications for the drawing task. The upshot of this representational adjunction is that the learned skills may be prone to memory decay over time, and are difficult to transfer to new situations. The Hollis and Low (2005) study through its longitudinal nature, then, makes important contribution to knowledge in the area of representational flexibility by showing how externally provoked behavioural change may be a product of representational adjunctions that themselves still need to undergo RR.

However, the participants in Hollis and Low's (2005) example group viewed illustrations across the Karmiloff-Smith (1990) identified categories of drawing modifications (an element change, a deletion, an insertion, and a position-orientation change). Having children view illustrations each with different features did not permit a thorough analysis of whether children copied the features exactly specified in the illustrations (e.g., if children saw a leg drawn in a shape of a triangle, they also drew a leg in the shape of a triangle) or whether they drew different features (e.g., a leg in the shape of a square or a head in the shape of a triangle). Cognitive psychologists have reported that prior experiences can bias the production of new category exemplars. For example, Smith, Ward, and Schumacher (1993) reported that adults who had first seen examples of space creatures (creatures with four legs, tail and antenna) were more likely than matched controls to produce drawings that contained features of the examples (i.e., four legs, tail and antenna). In addition, Smith and Blankenship (1991) have suggested that such conformity effects can potentially reduce over time when the examples are no longer salient in memory and have been sufficiently incorporated into participants' existing concepts. In the language of RRM, it is through the occurrence of RR when the examples become transformed into data structure accessible for wider creative uses that adults no longer simply replicate example features for their own imaginative drawings. In terms of a better design to look at RRM distinctions between adjunctions and redescriptions, one could, for example, show young children a group of examples depicting only deletion changes. Following RRM expectations, we would expect children at Time 1 to produce only deletion changes. Important to the theoretical consolidation of RRM with respect to drawing modifications would be to demonstrate that at Time 1 the deletion examples did not trigger children to draw other high-level changes (e.g., position-orientation or cross-category changes), at Time 2 children reverted back to drawing low-level changes (e.g., element changes), and only further along in developmental time (Time N) did children induce high-level graphic changes not depicted in the original examples.

Here I shall just focus on Atkins and Low's (in preparation) findings regarding micro-genetic changes in children's (6- and 9-year-olds) drawing strategies in response to *cross-category* example cuing. Performances among control group participants revealed that 9-year-olds were more likely to make cross-category

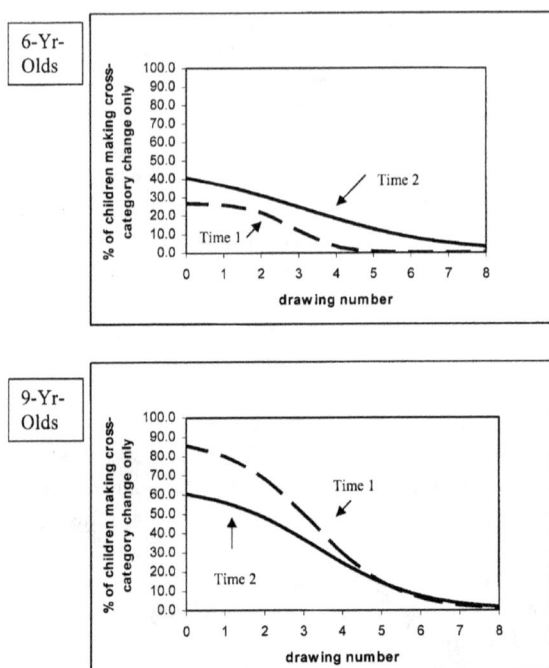

Figure 2
Generation and maintenance of cross-category changes in 6- and 9-year-old children's drawings after cross-category example cues.

changes than 6-year-olds, replicating Karmiloff-Smith's (1990) macro-developmental findings. For the experimental groups, after introducing a set of cross-category examples (people with fish parts) and explaining why they constituted instances of pretend people, the researcher invited the children to again draw as many new and different pretend-looking people of their own design as they could. The main question to be addressed was how representational flexibility was provoked immediately after receiving the external input (Time 1) and also 1 week later (Time 2). Six-year-olds in the examples condition generated more cross-category changes than their control counterparts at Time 1, and continued to draw even more cross-category changes at Time 2. The effect of the examples was greater for younger than older children. In this way, the examples seemed to benefit younger children's uptake of cross-category modifications more than older children (see Figure 2). These results are consistent with studies by Berti and Freeman (1997), Spensley and Taylor (1999) and Zhi et al. (1997) indicating that young children may be more reliant upon external drawing cues where representational flexibility is concerned.

But the most important question Atkins and Low (in preparation) sought to answer was whether the cross-category examples also provoked and inspired

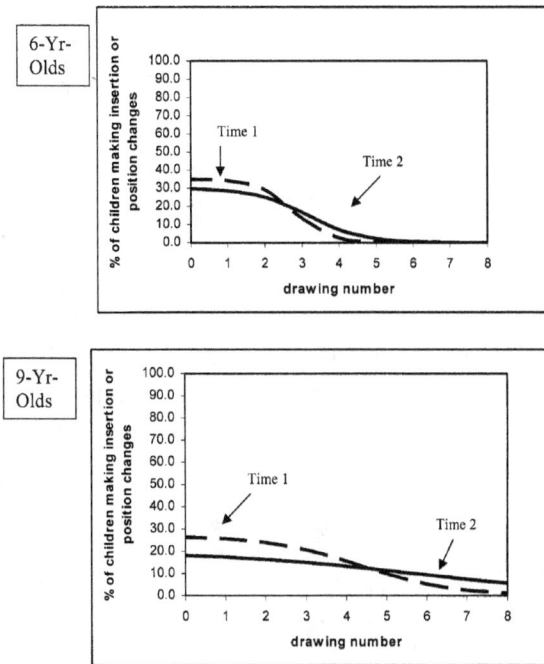

Figure 3

Generation and maintenance of insertion or position-orientation changes in 6- and 9-year-old children's drawings after cross-category example cues.

participants to spontaneously generate other high-level solutions (i.e., position-orientation changes and insertions) not shown in the examples. Again, if the ability to introduce high-level graphic changes is independent of the distinction between representational adjuncts and redescriptions, young children who are argued to be unable to complete the drawing task because of information processing task demands should be able to generate and sustain position-orientation and insertion changes over a lengthy drawing span as well as their older counterparts. In contrast, to the extent that advanced representations only occur after there has been sufficient developmental time for RR to take place (Karmiloff-Smith, 1992), young children, in comparison to older children, should only be able to induce other high-level solutions for a small number of drawings in the drawing span. The results supported RRM predictions. Atkins and Low observed that while the cross-category examples did provoke young children to generate other different kinds of high-level modifications, these rapidly declined in the drawing cycle (sustained only until drawing number 4; see Figure 3). Older children, in comparison, were able to spontaneously generate and sustain the other different kinds of high-level changes across a greater number of drawings in the cycle (even until drawing number 6).

Overall, evidence from the Hollis and Low (2005) and the Atkins and Low (in preparation) experiments reveal that Karmiloff-Smith (1990) is correct in urging researchers to recognise that it is important not to confuse external output with the internal representations that sustain them. Even when young children can demonstrate representational flexibility as a result of external input, the representations governing the behaviour are still in the form of newly created and isolated procedures. Internal system dynamics still needs to impose redescription upon those procedures before young children can go beyond mimicking the external input, and spontaneously gain wider creative insights in their problem solving.

Thoughts Towards Fine Tuning RRM: Gilding the Emperor's New Clothes

There are other ways in which RRM could be theoretically fine tuned with further investigations into children's drawings as a source of evidence for internal constraints upon representational change. As Karmiloff-Smith (1994) has already pointed out, the precise nature of behavioural mastery needs to be explicated. Since redescription is trigged by stable states giving rise to successful performance, future research needs to provide some index of what it means for a child to achieve behavioural mastery. The operationalisation of behavioural mastery in the drawing micro-domain is important because researchers have pondered whether redescription may instead occur when stable states have *not* given rise to successful performance (Goldin-Meadow & Alibali, 1994) or whether behavioural mastery is a consequence of the first round of RR when children become explicitly aware of the products of rules (Vinter & Perruchet, 1994). Goldin-Meadow and Alibali's suggestion follows the Piagetian tradition, whereby it is certainly the case that failure (or disequilibrium) can promote representational change. However, RRM views that there can be other triggers of developmental change as well, in particular success driven states. Vinter and Perruchet's comment makes sense given the research extensions of Karmiloff-Smith's (1990) study revealing that 3- to 6 year-olds show improved performance as a result of task parameter manipulations, suggesting that their behaviour may be governed by a direct awareness of the products of drawing rules rather than an implicit encoding of the rules themselves. However, as I have argued, data from my laboratory show that even when young children exhibit elevated levels of representational flexibility after receiving external directions, their improved performance is only temporary and, over time, representational flexibility returns to levels close to baseline. Moreover, young children, unlike their older counterparts, seem to fixate upon the attributes of the external input and do not derive their own unique and creative representations. These findings suggest that external input is stored as representational adjunctions and not as explicit manipulable redescriptions. In the drawing micro-domain, early changes in young children's knowledge base appear to be largely due to the acquisition and practice of procedural representations for responding to the environment.

Nevertheless, it is important for researchers to try to be clear regarding what exactly it is about behavioural mastery that triggers representational change. Drawing researchers have noted that graphic skills continue to develop and refine even when children are able to draw a recognisable human figure. These developments include manipulations of the body axis and integration of diverse shapes to form a visually realistic contour (e.g., Lange-Kuttner, Kerzmann, & Heckhausen, 2002). Another important developmental index might be the consistency of the sequence in which the common elements of canonical forms are drawn. RRM theorising in the drawing micro-domain could be refined if it could specify whether it is the progression from simple additive combination of shapes to visually realistic contour with internal differentiation of parts, or whether it is the long-term stability of the drawing procedure, that are the important recognisable points of behavioural success that is followed by RR during micro-development. It is not unreasonable to postulate that it is when drawing procedures have characteristic features and statistical regularity that afford pattern matching or generalisation, speedy retrieval, category learning, and concept organisation into larger networks, that the first round of the endogenous metaprocess of RR is activated to form higher level representations that permit the discovery of creative drawing solutions.

Related to the issue of behavioural mastery and representational change, Hollis and Low (2005) and Atkins and Low (in preparation) have observed that all of their participants, regardless of whether they generated low- or high-level modifications, were able to provide verbal explanations that corresponded with their drawings. For example, a 6-year-old who drew an element change provided the corresponding explanation that it was a pretend person 'because his legs are different sizes'. Another 6-year-old who drew insertions stated that the drawing was appropriate 'because he has two bodies and four arms'. Consequently, in our research we have not been able to find distinguishing characteristics of representational flexibility in terms of verbal and non-verbal distinctions as outlined by RRM. These findings are parallel to those observed by Pine and Messer (1999) who looked at representational flexibility through Karmiloff-Smith and Inhelder's (1974) block balancing task. Pine and Messer found that children of different representational levels did not differ significantly in terms of their verbal ability. Nevertheless, RRM still speaks of knowledge acquisition in terms of producing explicit representational formats that take accessibility to verbal report into account.

Does the observation, then, that young children are able to verbally explain the content of their pretend people drawings suggest that they are operating via explicit representations? I do not believe that this is the case. It is not unreasonable to argue that even when young children are able to verbally state the content of their drawings, they are still drawing from level implicit representations. For example, factual statements such as 'Because he's missing a leg' can still be argued to be implicit in its application because it does not represent the content of the child's beliefs. In contrast, in statements such as 'I know that human beings have two legs so my drawing shows an impossible person because he's got five legs and it's also difficult to stand with five legs', both explicit representation of attitude is demonstrated with explicit representation of what the drawing contains and how it works. Gauging children's agentic or propositional attitudes in the Karmiloff-Smith (1990) drawing paradigm while controlling for general verbal ability might help verify the precise characteristics of representational formats in the implicit/explicit continuum as suggested by RRM.

If the full engagement of flexible drawing behaviour becomes available though the redescription of existing implicit procedures into abstract and manipulable formats, as RRM hypothesises, why are people more generally inclined to engage in lower-level strategies when it comes to imaginative drawings? Several researchers have noted that adults are often less imaginative in their attempts at drawing unusual instantiations of existing concepts than children are (e.g., Davis, 1997; Ward, 1994). Individual differences in our deployment of flexible drawing representations suggest that there is more to the process by which representational flexibility unfolds than the principle of redescription alone. For instance, in order to spontaneously generate a novel drawing solution, we also need to reflect on concepts such as: desires and intention (e.g., I wish to draw a funny looking person), beliefs (e.g., I know that human beings have bilateral symmetry, but I do not see any reason why creatures on other planets must also be bilaterally symmetrical), and acting on the basis of our representations of reality and not on the basis of reality itself (e.g., I am just pretending that my friend has turned into an alien and I am going to draw his arm where is leg is). These concepts fall under the umbrella of theory of mind (ToM), the understanding that beliefs and desires may determine behaviour and that people may act on their beliefs even if they are not consistent with reality (Wimmer & Perner, 1983). It is not just sufficient for our minds to be able to develop more flexible representations of knowledge through redescription, we need also to be aware of what we know and how we have used the knowledge in the past, and what flexible strategies remain possible (see also Freeman, 1994). While RR may work to re-represent the procedural inflexibilities in children's drawing routines into flexible formats, children may only be able to seize upon those transformed knowledge structures when their theory of mind is sufficiently mature.

Are there other cognitive underpinnings to representational flexibility apart from the acquisition of a theory of mind? In terms of the theory of art that potentially infuses children's understanding of how drawings and pictures operate, Freeman (1991) has indicated that children need to not only grasp what the referent is in the outside world and how clearly the picture affords the recognition, but also how the picture works in the manner in which it 'projectively maps onto the referent in space' (p. 69). An example of a statement showing how the latter is grounded in an understanding of drawings as being artefacts of intentional artistic practice might be, for example: 'the black mass where the head would otherwise be drawn is meant to portray the frailty of the human condition'. In other words, children's developing intuitive understandings of how drawings work as artefacts with aesthetic, symbolic, and intentional properties that connect the artist, the beholder, and the world, may also contribute to the development, use, and recognition of flexible drawing strategies.

So far I have canvassed how representational flexibility in young children's drawing behaviour may be underpinned by developments in the progressive redescription of a sequential constraint, and in children's theory of mind and theory of art. It is even possible that young children's intuitive biological understandings about human form and functioning may place limitations on what they are willing to draw in Karmiloff-Smith's (1990) creative generation task. Given that children reliably turn to domain-specific causal explanations that they use only for biological phenomena (Gelman & Wellman, 1991), young children could perseverate upon normative attributes of human beings (bilateral symmetry, making a few deletions while retaining standard appendages and senses) in their pretend-people drawings because they believe that these are important for life maintenance, even those of imaginary looking people. If RR permits representations in the drawing micro-domain to cut across representations pertaining to biological and psychological phenomena, then larger theoretical questions about cognitive development may be raised. Do the redescriptions that occur in the notational domain involve a radical restructuring of knowledge (akin to a theory change) that has fundamentally different meanings for children in the latter phases of RR than children in the earlier phases of RR? Or do the redescriptions that occur in the notational domain simply result in gaining more consciously accessed classifications that are looser and better hierarchically organised? While RRM has no definitive answers to issues of whether cognitive development involves children gaining better access to better structured representations, or children introspecting and constructing completely new and radical ideas, these topics are ripe for further theoretical and research exploration.

Conclusion

A deep-seated research issue for cognitive developmentalists is the nature of the different types of internal constraints upon representational change, and how external manipulations affect representational flexibility. In this chapter I have focused on sequential procedures as a curtailing constraint on drawing flexibility. I have also argued that while external manipulations can improve young children's representational flexibility, such behaviour should not be equated with behaviours among older children that are sustained by redescribed representations. Young children's flexibility in the Karmiloff-Smith (1990) drawing paradigm seen after external provocation tends to be short lived. As a result, there is data to support the RRM expectation that momentary flexibility seen among young children that is triggered by external cues is driven by representational adjunctions. These adjunctions need to go through the cycle of redescription before they will become a part of a child's drawing repertoire and larger knowledge network. Finally, RRM may be theoretically refined through determining the structural characteristics of behavioural mastery that trigger redescription, and how data structures concerning propositional attitudes may be necessary operators for seizing and deploying flexible problem solving in the drawing micro-domain. In conclusion, the discussion of research findings presented here illustrates that children's drawings continue to be an exciting and challenging source of evidence for understanding the general processes of internal representational change. At least one message from RRM rings loud and clear: If we want to get ahead, we need to start redescribing and reformulating what we already know.

References

Atkins, R., & Low, J. (in preparation). *Effects of examples on children's imaginative drawings: Micro-genetic analyses of representational redescription.*

Bassett, E. M. (1977). Production strategies in the child's drawing of the human figure: Towards an argument for a model of syncretic perception. In G. Butterworth (Ed.), *The child's representation of the world* (pp. 49–59). New York: Plenum Press.

Berti, A. E., & Freeman, N. H. (1997). Representational change in resources for pictorial innovation: A three-component analysis. *Cognitive Development, 12,* 405–426.

Davis, J. H. (1997). The what and the whether of the U: Cultural implications of understanding development in graphic symbolization. *Human Development, 40,* 145–154.

Freeman, N. H. (1980). *Strategies of representation in young children: Analysis of spatial skills and drawing processes.* London: Academic Press.

Freeman, N. H. (1991). The theory of art that underpins children's naïve realism. *Visual Arts Research, 17,* 56–75.

Freeman, N. H. (1994). Redescription of intentionality. *Behavioral and Brain Sciences, 17,* 717–718.

Gelman, S. A., & Wellman, H. M. (1991). Insides and essences: Early understandings of the non-obvious. *Cognition, 38,* 213–244.

Goldin-Meadow, S., & Alibali, M. W. (1994). Do you have to be right to redescribe? *Behavioral and Brain Sciences, 17,* 718–719.

Goodnow, J., & Levine, R. A. (1973). The 'grammar of action': Sequence and syntax in children's copying behavior. *Cognitive Psychology, 4,* 82–98.

Hollis, S., & Low, J. (2005). Karmiloff-Smith's RRM distinction between adjunctions and redescriptions: It's about time (and children's drawings). *British Journal of Developmental Psychology, 23,* 623–644.

Karmiloff-Smith, A. (1990). Constraints on representational change: Evidence from children's drawings. *Cognition, 34,* 57–83.

Karmiloff-Smith, A. (1992). *Beyond modularity: A developmental perspective on cognitive science.* Cambridge, MA: MIT Press.

Karmiloff-Smith, A. (1994). Précis of beyond modularity: A developmental perspective on cognitive science. *Behavioral and Brain Sciences, 17,* 693–745.

Karmiloff-Smith, A. (1999). Taking development seriously. *Human Development, 42,* 325–327.

Karmiloff-Smith, A., & Inhelder, B. (1974). If you want to get ahead, get a theory. *Cognition, 3,* 195–212.

Lange-Kuttner, C., Kerzmann, A., & Heckhausen, J. (2002). The emergence of visually realistic contour in the drawing of the human figure. *British Journal of Developmental Psychology, 20,* 439–463.

Low, J., & Durkin, K. (1998). Children's understanding of structure and causal relations in television narratives: What develops? *Cognitive Development, 13,* 203–227.

Low, J., & Hollis, S. (2003). The eyes have it: Development of generative thinking. *International Journal of Behavioral Development, 27*, 97–108.

Mitchell, P., & Riggs, K. J. (2000). *Children's reasoning and the mind.* Hove, UK: Psychology Press.

Pine, K., & Messer, D. (1999). What children do and what children know: Looking beyond success using Karmiloff-Smith's RR framework. *New Ideas in Psychology, 17*, 17–30.

Smith, S. M., & Blankenship, S. E. (1991). Incubation and persistence of fixation in problem solving. American Journal of Psychology, 104, 61–87.

Smith, S. M., Ward, T. B., & Schumacher, J. S. (1993). Constraining effects of examples in a creative generation task. *Memory & Cognition, 21*, 837–845.

Spensley, F., & Taylor, J. (1999). The development of cognitive flexibility: Evidence from children's drawings. *Human Development, 42*, 300–324.

van Sommers, P. (1984). *Drawing and cognition.* Cambridge: Cambridge University Press.

Vinter, A., & Perruchet, P. (1994). Is there an implicit level of representation? *Behavioral and Brain Sciences, 17*, 730–731.

Ward, T. B. (1994). Structured imagination: The role of category structure in exemplar generation. *Cognitive Psychology, 27*, 1–40.

White, S., & Low, J. (2002). When mothers turn a visual story into a verbal one for their children: Previewing helps with the telling, conversing, and remembering. *International Journal of Behavioral Development, 26*, 360–370.

Wimmer, H., & Perner, J. (1983). Beliefs about beliefs: Representation and constraining function of wrong beliefs in young children's understanding of deception. *Cognition, 13*, 103–128.

Zhi, Z., Thomas, G. V., & Robinson, E. J. (1997). Constraints on representational change: Drawing a man with two heads. *British Journal of Developmental Psychology, 15*, 275–290.

The Emergence of Autobiographical Memory: Cognitive, Social, and Emotional Factors

Elaine Reese, Rhiannon Newcombe, and Amy Bird

At its heart, autobiographical memory is a cognitive process. Personal memories depend upon basic cognitive functions for their existence. An event must first be attended to and encoded for it to be stored and later retrieved as personally relevant. Yet autobiographical memories are much more than a basic cognitive process.

Autobiographical memories are also inherently about emotions (Pillemer, 1998). Why do we remember one personal experience with greater vividness than another? Why do we choose to discuss one personal experience with our friends and family, but we remain mute about other personal experiences? We argue that one defining feature of an autobiographical memory, as opposed to simply an episodic memory, is its personal meaning. Along with many other theorists (e.g., Brewer, 1986; Fivush, 2001; Nelson, 1996; Nelson & Fivush, 2004), we are demarcating autobiographical memories as a particular kind of episodic memory. We have many personal experiences every day that count as episodic memories, but only some of these memories will last, and even fewer will become autobiographical. For instance, what I eat for lunch today will almost certainly not become an autobiographical memory, and will fade quickly even as an episodic memory, unless something of great significance occurs at that lunch. My sandwich may take on greater personal significance if I experience food poisoning that necessitates a trip to hospital later in the day.

What event characteristics have the power to promote a simply episodic memory to autobiographical status? Certainly the distinctiveness and uniqueness of the event play a large role. My first ride in an ambulance, the first time I have my stomach pumped — these characteristics would work to enhance the memorability of the event. But it is emotion that endows an event with personal significance. In this case the emotion is negative, and strongly so. Yet even highly emotional experiences vary in terms of personal significance. Although dramatically negative at the time, my episode of food poisoning would not have any lasting personal significance, although it might serve to change my behaviour in the future to avoid lunch products with salad dressing. This event would only take on lasting significance if, as a result of my experience, I decided to make a career change to become an emergency medical technician, or if while I was in hospital I lost my child to a bike accident. Thus, an event can be distinctive, emotional, and meaningful at the time, without earning a lasting place in the life story. The most conservative definition of an autobiographical memory is one that is in a form that can be and is discussed with others, and that has a lasting place in the life story (Linde, 1993; McAdams, 2003; Nelson, 1996).

The problem with this definition, especially when studying this issue from a developmental perspective, is that it is nearly impossible to know which events might ultimately take on lasting significance for the life story. The lunch example illustrates that even a seemingly mundane event can take on lasting significance, sometimes even much later than its original occurrence. Therefore, our approach to studying autobiographical memory prospectively is to include all memories that are potentially autobiographical. A child's memory of winning a colouring competition at age 3 is probably only going to take its place in the life story if the child becomes an artist. Otherwise, the event will be contained to childhood as a positive but not especially memorable event that resulted in a gift certificate for new toys.

We take the view that an equally important determinant to an event becoming autobiographical is not only its immediate and long-term emotional valence, but also the frequency and quality with which an event is discussed in childhood and beyond. We know that parents who discuss events in a rich manner have children who go on to discuss past events in more detail, both with their parents (e.g., Fivush & Fromhoff, 1988; Reese, Haden, & Fivush, 1993) and with others (Haden, Haine, & Fivush, 1997; Hudson, 1993). Recent experimental evidence bolsters this argument. Peterson, Jesso, and McCabe (1999) trained one group of mothers to talk in a more elaborative way with their 3-year-olds about past events through using open-ended questions containing new information and by praising children's responses. By the time the children were 5 years old, those whose mothers had been trained in the elaborative and evaluative style told richer, more complex stories of personal experience to a researcher than did children whose mothers were not trained. With New Zealand mothers, Reese and Newcombe (2005) trained one group of mothers to reminisce more elaboratively with their 1^1/2 year old children. By the time the children were 3^1/2 years old, they discussed memories more comprehensively and more accurately with researchers compared to children of mothers in a control group. These effects of an elaborative style appear to be event-specific as well as general. Boland, Haden, and Ornstein (2003) trained one group of mothers to be more elaborative during children's initial experience of a novel event. The children of trained mothers remembered more details of the event, but not necessarily more core features at a 2-week delay, than did children of untrained mothers. McGuigan and Salmon (2004) compared an adult's elaborative interviewing style before, during, or after a novel event for children's memory. They found that although 5-year-olds' memory reports benefited from an elaborative style both during and after the event, 3-year-olds benefited most from an elaborative style after the event had occurred. The mechanism for these effects is probably occurring both at the encoding phase, during which elaborative adults are describing events for children in more detail, and at the consolidation, storage, and retrieval phases, during which elaborative adults are highlighting children's correct memories as well as amplifying aspects of the past and giving children richer cues by which to retrieve personal memories.

Our current focus is on the way that parents socialise the emotional and evaluative content of children's past event narratives for these potentially autobiographical memories. From the research cited above, we know that parents who talk in more elaborative ways have children with richer memories of those experiences. Do these same children also retain more emotional information about these past events? If so, how does this emotional aspect of memory affect their sense of self? Nelson (1993) and Singer and Salovey (1993) proposed that autobiographical memories are critical determinants of the self-concept. Of course, these theorists, along with others, acknowledge the impact of self-concept and self esteem in biasing personal memories (cf. Christensen, Wood, & Barrett, 2003). We wanted to know how children's understanding of the emotional, evaluative component of memory arises out of the emotional bond between parent and child, and what would be the consequences for the self-concept of children who were exposed to more emotional and evaluative memory narratives. In this sense, we are moving away from the strictly memorial aspects of autobiographical memory into social and emotional spheres. But if we are to take seriously the role of self and emotion in the cognitive skill of autobiographical memory, we must consider the emotional origins and consequences of talking about the past.

A Longitudinal Study of Autobiographical Memory

We are examining these social and emotional factors in an ongoing study of autobiographical memory. We began the study with $1^1/2$-year-old children and their primary caregiver mothers. We studied the children's autobiographical memory development through to $5^1/2$ years. In the process, we also collected information on the children's language skills, attachment security, temperament, and their developing self-awareness and self-concept. Throughout the study, we measured the mothers' naturally occurring style of discussing unique past events with their children.

Our first goal in the study was to explore the emotional basis for the socialisation of autobiographical memory. Bowlby (1969/1984) defined a child's secure attachment to parent as the ability for the child to use the parent in times of stress. Bowlby theorised that by the age of around 3 years, children relied upon an internal working model or representation of their everyday interactions with the caregiver to inform their behaviour. One way that children develop a secure internal working model of self and others, Bowlby (1988) reasoned, is through frank and open discussions about the meaning of everyday and emotional events. Representations of individual past events consolidate into a general model of the caregiver as reliable or unreliable in times of stress, and of the self as worthy or unworthy of care and affection. We predicted that children who were more securely attached to their mothers would take on the mothers' reminiscing style to a greater extent than children who were insecurely attached to their mothers. Our reasoning was that children in an emotionally secure environment would be more trusting and open to their mothers' emotional interpretation of events. Second, we were interested in the social and emotional consequences of autobiographical memory for children's self-concept. Children have largely internalised their mothers' reminiscing style by the time they are 5 years old (Haden et al., 1997; Reese et al., 1993). We wanted to know if children who had internalised a more emotional and evaluative approach to autobiographical memory would have a stronger sense of who they are, or a more coherent self-concept, by the time they were 5^1/2 years old. If autobiographical memories serve to inform or even comprise our identities, then children with a more evaluative style of discussing the past should also have a stronger sense of self. In other words, these are children who have developed an evaluative perspective for events and who should be able to use the past to inform their sense of who they are at present (Fivush, 2001; Nelson & Fivush, 2004).

Method

We began the study with 58 New Zealand children and their primary caregiver mothers when the children were 19 months old. Further measurement points occurred when children were 25, 32, 40, 51, and 65 months of age. At the 51-month measurement point, we retained 56 dyads, and by 65 months, 50 families (25 girls and 25 boys) participated in the study. Most families reported European ancestry, but in one family, the primary caregiver was Asian, and in five families, one or both parents were of Maori ancestry. Relevant measures follow:

Language Skill

Children's language was assessed at the early measurement points (19–32 months) with the MacArthur Communicative Development Inventory: Words and Sentences (Fenson et al., 1993), adapted for New Zealand vocabulary (NZ CDI:WS; Reese & Read, 2000). Mothers completed an inventory of children's current expressive vocabulary. At the later measurement points (32–65 months), children's language was assessed with the Peabody Picture Vocabulary Test-III (PPVT-III; Dunn & Dunn, 1997) and the Expressive Vocabulary Test (EVT; Williams, 1997). Mothers' verbal abilities were also measured with the PPVT-III. Standard scores were used for analyses.

Attachment Security

Children's attachment security was assessed at the beginning of the study using Water's (1987) Attachment Q-set. In this task, mothers are given a list of 90 attachment-related behaviours and are asked 1 week later to sort the behaviours into a continuum from most characteristic to least characteristic of their child. Their sorts are compared to a criterion sort of an ideally secure child (for scoring details, see Newcombe & Reese, 2004; Posada et al., 1995).

Self-Concept

The coherence or integration of children's self-concept was assessed at the final measurement point with the Children's Self-View Questionnaire (CSVQ; Eder, 1990). In this task, children endorse their view on 35 items describing 9 different dimensions of self, from achievement (e.g., 'I like to do hard puzzles' vs. 'I like to do easy puzzles') to harm avoidance (e.g., 'I like to go down a slide headfirst' vs. 'I don't like to go down a slide headfirst'). For the coherence score, children's choices are assessed within each dimension for consistency and then averaged across dimensions (see Bird & Reese, 2006, for scoring details). This measure of self-concept is content-free and only addresses the internal consistency of the child's responses.

Past Event Narratives

At each measurement point, mothers and children discussed several unique past events together. Prior to the conversation, which was videotaped and audiotaped, the researcher helped mothers select events that were novel and spanned no more than one day. Most of the events mothers selected were positive or neutral in overall theme (88%). Examples of events discussed ranged from going to a wedding to having an operation. These conversations were transcribed and coded for their narrative content (see Newcombe & Reese, 2004) and their emotional and evaluative content (see Bird & Reese, 2006). The specific utterances of interest here are mothers' and children's use of orientations to time, person, and place ('We were in Wanaka at Christmastime when we saw Nana and Papa') versus their evaluations of people and of the event. The evaluative category was subdivided into emotion references ('You were happy'; positive vs. negative), person and event evaluatives ('The dress was yucky'; positive vs. negative), and compulsion terms (e.g., 'I had to get a haircut') at the later measurement points (51–65 months). At the early measurement points, children did not provide enough evaluative terms for us to subdivide the overall category of evaluations.

Socioemotional Origins of Evaluative Past Event Narratives

Our main question centered on the role of children's attachment security in the origins of an evaluative perspective in children's past event narratives. Would securely attached children show a different path of socialisation than insecurely attached children? We predicted that these socialisation differences would be primarily for the emotional and evaluative aspects of past event talk, and not for the more objective aspects of such talk. As such, we compared the socialisation patterns for securely and insecurely attached children for their use of evaluations and orientations in the narratives (see Newcombe & Reese, 2004, for coding details). Words or phrases coded as evaluations always involve an emotional

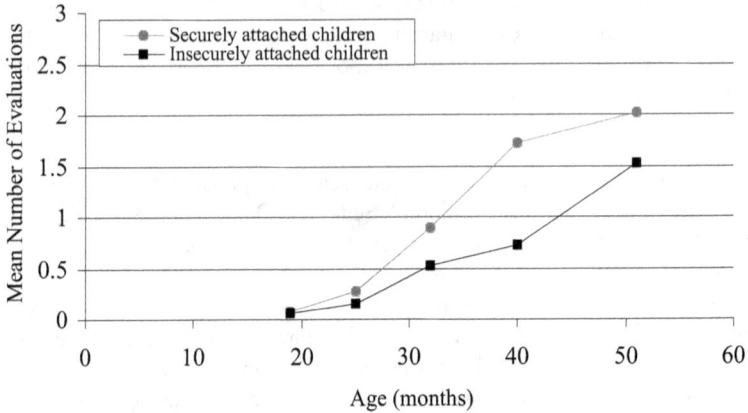

Figure 1
Children's use of evaluations in mother–child past-event narratives as a function of attachment security.

component, either about a person or about the event (e.g., the slide was *fun*). In contrast, words or phrases coded as orientations are more factual in their content because they involve mentioning the time, place, or people from an event without any explicit linguistic reference to emotion (e.g., We were with *Nana and Papa* in *Wanaka* at *Christmastime*). Orientations and evaluations are both critical components for a coherent narrative about a past event (Labov & Waletzky, 1967/1997). Both are also complex narrative devices with a more protracted development than children's mention of actions and objects (Fivush, Haden, & Adams, 1995). Thus, they provide a good comparison because although they are both more advanced narrative techniques, only evaluations involve an explicit emotional component. For this initial question, we only utilised the first five measurement points of the study as children were still developing their evaluative styles up to this point. We divided the sample into groups with securely attached (*n* = 38) and insecurely attached children (*n* = 18), in accord with past theory and research (e.g., Posada et al., 1995; van IJzendoorn & Sagi, 1999).

Our analyses first addressed mothers' and children's use of orientations and evaluations over time as a function of children's attachment security with a 5 (age) × 2 (attachment status) mixed MANOVA on children's evaluations and orientations. Although children used more evaluations and orientations as they got older, $F(4, 220) = 49.71$, $p < .01$, only evaluations, and not orientations, differed as a function of children's attachment security, in line with our predictions. Mothers' and children's growing use of orientations was similar in dyads with securely attached and insecurely attached children. Children's and mothers' use of evaluations differed, however, depending upon the child's attachment security. Securely attached children used more evaluations overall

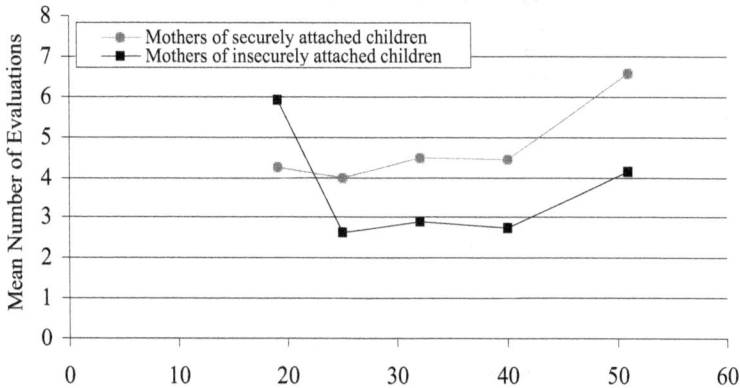

Figure 2
Mothers' use of evaluations in mother–child past-event narratives as a function of children's attachment security.

than insecurely attached children, $F(1, 54) = 4.54$, $p < .05$ (see Figure 1). Mothers' use of evaluations over time interacted with children's attachment security, $F(1, 54) = 5.33$, $p < .05$ (see Figure 2). Mothers of securely attached children steadily increased their use of evaluations as children got older and used more evaluations themselves, $F(1, 37) = 5.18$, $p < .05$. Mothers of insecurely attached children used a great many evaluations at the first measurement point, but then decreased their use of evaluations dramatically at the next measurement point, with a slow increase thereafter. We argue that the mothers of securely attached children are doing a better job of matching their use of evaluations with their children's growth in evaluations over time.

A series of cross-lagged correlations between mothers' and children's use of evaluations over time, separately for dyads with securely attached and insecurely attached children, was consonant with this interpretation. Mothers and securely attached children matched each others' use of evaluatives in the same conversations (see the correlations along diagonals in Table 1). Moreover, there were long-term relations between mothers' earlier use of evaluations and securely attached children's later use of evaluations, as well as between securely attached children's earlier use of evaluations and mothers' later use of evaluations. In stark contrast, there was not a single significant positive correlation between mothers' and insecurely attached children's use of evaluatives, either within the same conversation or across time (see Table 2). In fact, the only significant long-term correlation for dyads with insecurely attached children was negative. Fisher z tests confirmed the different pattern of correlations for dyads with securely attached and insecurely attached children, regardless of the different sample sizes (i.e., 25% of the pairs of correlations were significantly different from each other). Thus, only the conversations with securely attached children were

Table 1
Correlations Between Mothers' and Children's Evaluations Within Dyads
With Securely Attached Children

Children

Mothers	EVAL19	EVAL25	EVAL32	EVAL40	EVAL51
EVAL19	.31	.23	.25	.10	.03
EVAL25	.30	.36*[b]	.10	−.04	.29
EVAL32	.21	.47**	.35*[a]	.17	.34*
EVAL40	.16	.03	.13	.31	.53**
EVAL51	.00	.18	.22	.34*	.71**

Note: *$p < .05$; **$p < .01$.
[a] Correlation no longer significant or marginally significant ($p < .10$) once children's earlier language ability was partialled out.
[b] Correlation no longer significant or marginally significant ($p < .10$) once mothers' language ability was partialled out.

increasingly evaluative and collaborative over time as each partner adapted to the other's evaluative style. The effects were bidirectional, but mothers appeared to play a significant role in children's later use of evaluations. In hierarchical regression analyses that controlled for children's language and earlier evaluative skill, mothers' 40-month evaluative usage uniquely predicted their own later evaluations at 51 months ($\beta = .61$, $p < .01$) and, more importantly, their securely attached children's later use of evaluations at 51 months ($\beta = .37$, $p < .05$). Children's earlier evaluations at 40 months did not uniquely predict their own later evaluations ($\beta = .10$, ns) or their mothers' later evaluations at 51 months ($\beta = .00$, ns). At least prior to age 4, children's use of evaluatives appears to be driven by mothers' use of evaluatives.

Consequences of an Evaluative Perspective Toward the Past

In the earlier measurement points of the study, we discovered that securely and insecurely attached children were being socialised differently in their development of an evaluative perspective toward past events, although in more factual

Table 2
Correlations Between Mothers' and Children's Evaluations Within Dyads
With Insecurely Attached Children[a]

Children

Mothers	EVAL19	EVAL25	EVAL32	EVAL40	EVAL51
EVAL19	.11	.15	.12	−.05	−.30
EVAL25	.14	.09	−.17	−.53*	.33
EVAL32	.02	−.12	.06	.09	−.29
EVAL40	.30	−.14	.02	.18	−.03
EVAL51	.26	.27	.10	−.10	−.09

Note: *$p < .05$; **$p < .01$.
[a] Maternal and child language partialled out.

respects (e.g., orientations), children with differing attachment statuses were being socialised similarly. This finding is important, theoretically and practically, because it restricts the impact of the socioemotional basis of autobiographical memory to emotional outcomes. The next step was to look at the implications of having an evaluative perspective toward the past for children's self-concept. Given that by 51 months, children had developed at least some semblance of an evaluative perspective, regardless of whether they achieved this with or without the help of their mothers, how would this evaluative perspective relate to their sense of self? By the time children were 51 and 65 months old, we were able to separate out mothers' and children's references to positive and negative emotional states, almost all of which referred to the child's emotional states and not the mother's or others' emotional states (e.g., 'I was *sad*'; 'You *liked* that part'; see Bird & Reese, 2006, for additional coding details). In only one other study to date has a link been identified between mother–child emotional talk about the past and children's self-concept. Welch-Ross, Fasig, and Farrar (1999) found a concurrent correlation between dyadic references to emotion in past-event talk and the coherence of children's self-concept. Dyads that made more emotion references had children with more coherent self-concepts. They were not able to differentiate between positive and negative states, between mothers' and children's emotion references, or to look at these effects with self-concept over time in their study.

There was a consistent pattern of correlations between the negative emotion references and children's self-coherence across time and partner. At each measurement point, regardless of conversational partner, references to children's negative emotional states were negatively correlated with children's self-concept coherence (rs ranged from $-.28$, $p < .05$, to $-.46$, $p < .01$). The same pattern and strength of these correlations with self-concept was evident regardless of children's attachment security. In other words, dyads that dwelled on negative emotional states in these conversations about mostly positive past events had children who later had a less coherent self-concept. Through regression analyses contrasting mothers' and children's negative emotion references, we did not obtain a strong mother-to-child direction in this effect on children's self-concept coherence. In fact, only children's concurrent use of negative emotion references was uniquely predictive of their self-concept coherence ($\beta = -.47$, $p < .01$). We were able to uncover, however, a unique long-term relation between dyads' use of negative emotion terms at 51 months and children's later self-concept coherence, even after dyadic 65-month use of negative emotions had been entered into the regression ($\beta = -.29$, $p < .05$). By 51 months, in line with the first set of analyses, children already have or do not have a propensity to discuss past events in an evaluative way. For securely attached children, this evaluative propensity may have been socialised in part by the parent. Regardless of its origins, however, the propensity toward discussing negative emotional states in the context of a positive past event is negatively linked with an integrated self-concept. We explored this relation qualitatively by examining the number of past-event discussions that contained an explanation of mentioned emotions or a resolution to the emotional state. For example, a mother might explain a child's feeling of anger toward a friend by explaining that sometimes we get angry even with those we care about. Or, a mother might attempt to resolve a child's fear of the dark by suggesting a practical solution, such as installing a nightlight in the child's room. As we suspected, very few of the conversations about negative emotions involved an explanation of the emotion (18%) or a resolution (28%). Instead, these dyads are bringing up negative emotions in the context of a positive event and are not exploring those negative emotions in depth. In further work, we are exploring the links between evaluative talk in primarily negative events and children's self-concept (Reese, Bird, & Tripp, in press).

Conclusions

What do these results mean for the development of autobiographical memory and self-concept? One implication is that the way parents are talking about the past, and in particular the evaluative perspective they set up for children in interpreting the past, is important for children's interpretation of the past. Mothers of securely attached children are setting the evaluative stage for their children in a way that is more sensitive to their children's capacities, by steadily increasing their use of evaluatives as their children are using more of these utterances in their own narratives.

By 51 months, all children were using evaluatives in their conversations, but as we saw in the first set of analyses, some children were doing this without as much help from their mothers. It turns out that the degree to which dyads are able to discuss and resolve negative emotions in everyday past events is consistently linked to the coherence of children's self-concepts. Children who discussed their own negative emotions with mothers in the context of a positive event, and who did not receive support for the resolution of these negative emotions, had less organised self-concepts by age 5^{1}/2. These children were not as consistent in the way they viewed their likes, dislikes, and abilities.

These findings are consonant with Bowlby's predictions about the importance of parent–child conversation in children's internal working models about self, others, and relationships. Bowlby (1988) hypothesised that in a secure attachment relationship, children are able to discuss and explore emotions openly with parents. These emotional and evaluative conversations ultimately lead to a representation of the parent as someone who can be trusted, and a representation of the self as someone worthy of affection. We extend this argument to propose that children who are able to discuss emotions in greater depth with their parents are also gaining a more organised sense of who they are: 'I am a person who likes to take some risks' (e.g., 'I had fun on the roller coaster') but 'I am not as interested in school achievement' (e.g., 'I got really frustrated the time I tried to do a hard puzzle'). Recall that in the past-event conversations between insecurely attached children and their parents, mothers were not matching their use of evaluatives with their children's use of evaluatives, even in the same conversation. These insecurely attached children were indeed using evaluatives in conversation and growing in their use of evaluatives at a similar rate to the securely attached children, but they were not gaining an evaluative perspective from their parents. It is not enough to assign emotion to an experience; emotions (perhaps especially negative emotions) must be interpreted and resolved for an event to make sense, especially for very young children (Bretherton & Munholland, 1999).

What, then, is the mechanism by which an evaluative perspective is critical in our developing autobiography? The securely and insecurely attached children in our study may have similar basic memory abilities for the facts of an event, as illustrated by their comparable use of orientations. They are likely to differ, however, in their ultimate ability to draw meaning from an event and to place it in the context of the larger life story. Insecurely attached children may not be as good at drawing upon the meaning of an event to inform their behaviour in the future, and they may not be as good at connecting events with similar emotional themes for use in understanding themselves. We speculate that it is possible that these children will grow into adults who have fewer, later, and less elaborate autobiographical memories across the lifespan. They may also be less able to use the events of their lives as a means of self-reflection. Research using the Adult Attachment Interview, a narrative measure of adults' ability to resolve early childhood attachment experiences, reveals individual differences in the coherence with which adults relate their childhood memories (Main, Kaplan, & Cassidy, 1985). We are currently exploring the link between mothers' secure and insecure orientations toward their own early experiences and their ability to talk openly and deeply with their children about emotional past events. As we continue to study their children over time, we will be able to examine the emotional themes of their memories from early childhood, and the growth of their life stories.

Acknowledgments

This research was conducted with the help of the Marsden Fund of the Royal Society of New Zealand. We thank the Language and Memory team for their help with all phases of this project. We are grateful for the long-standing participation of the families in this project.

References

Bird, A., & Reese, E. (2006). Emotional reminiscing and the development of an autobiographical self. *Developmental Psychology, 42*, 613–626.

Boland, A. M., Haden, C. A., & Ornstein, P. A. (2003). Boosting children's memory by training mothers in the use of an elaborative conversational style as an event unfolds. *Journal of Cognition and Development, 4*, 39–65.

Bowlby, J. (1984). *Attachment and loss: Attachment Vol. 1* (2nd ed.). New York: Basic Books. (Original work published 1969)

Bowlby, J. (1988). *A secure base: Clinical applications of attachment theory.* London: Routledge.

Bretherton, I., & Munholland, K. A. (1999). Internal working models in attachment relationships: A construct revisited. In J. Cassidy, & P. R. Shaver (Eds.), *Handbook of attachment: Theory, research and clinical applications* (pp. 89–111). New York: Guilford.

Brewer, W. F. (1986). What is autobiographical memory? In D. C. Rubin (Ed.), *Autobiographical memory*. Cambridge, England: Cambridge University Press.

Christensen, T. C., Wood, J. V., & Barrett, L. F. (2003). Remembering everyday experience through the prism of self-esteem. *Personality and Social Psychology Bulletin, 29*, 51–62.

Dunn, L. M., & Dunn, L. M. (1997). *Peabody Picture Vocabulary Test* (3rd ed.). Circle Pines, MN: American Guidance Service.

Eder, R. (1990). Uncovering young children's psychological selves: Individual and developmental differences. *Child Development, 61*, 849–863.

Fenson, L., Dale, P. S., Reznick, J. S., Thal, D., Bates, E., Hartung, J. P., et al. (1993). *The MacArthur Communicative Development Inventory: Words and Sentences*. San Diego, CA: Singular.

Fivush, R. (2001). Owning experience: Developing subjective perspective in autobiographical narratives. In C. Moore & K. Lemmon (Eds.), *The self in time: Developmental perspectives*. Mahwah, NJ: Erlbaum.

Fivush, R., & Fromhoff, F. A. (1988). Style and structure in mother–child conversations about the past. *Discourse Processes, 11*, 337–355.

Fivush, R., Haden, C., & Adam, S. (1995). Structure and coherence of preschoolers' personal narratives over time: Implications for childhood amnesia. *Journal of Experimental Child Psychology, 60*, 32–56.

Haden, C. A., Haine, R. A., & Fivush, R. (1997). Developing narrative structure in parent–child reminiscing across the preschool years. *Developmental Psychology, 22*, 295–307.

Hudson, J. A. (1993). Reminiscing with mothers and others: Autobiographical memory in young two-year-olds. *Journal of Narrative and Life History, 3*, 1–32.

Labov, W., & Waletzky, J. (1997). Narrative analysis: Oral versions of personal experience. *Journal of Narrative and Life History, 7*, 3–38. (Reprinted from *Essays on the verbal and visual arts*, pp. 12–44, by J. Helm, Ed., 1967, Seattle, WA: University of Washington Press)

Linde, C. (1993). *Life stories: The creation of coherence*. New York: Oxford University Press.

Main, M., Kaplan, N., & Cassidy, J. (1985). Security in infancy, childhood and adulthood: A move to the level of representation. In I. Bretherton & E. Waters (Eds.), Growing points of attachment theory and research. *Monographs of the Society for Research in Child Development, 50*, 66–104.

McAdams, D. P. (2003). Identity and the life story. In R. Fivush & C. A. Haden (Eds.), *Autobiographical memory and the construction of a narrative self: Developmental and cultural perspectives* (pp. 187–207). Mahwah, NJ: Lawrence Erlbaum Associates.

McGuigan, F., & Salmon, K. (2004). The time to talk: The influence of the timing of adult–child talk on children's event memory. *Child Development, 75*, 669–686.

Nelson, K. (1993). Developing self-knowledge from autobiographical memory. In T. K. Srull & R. S. Wyer (Eds.), *The mental representation of trait and autobiographical knowledge about the self* (pp. 111–121). Hillsdale, NJ: Lawrence Erlbaum Associates.

Nelson, K. (1996). *Language in cognitive development: The emergence of the mediated mind*. Cambridge, UK: Cambridge University Press.

Nelson, K., & Fivush, R. (2004). The emergence of autobiographical memory: A social cultural developmental theory. *Psychological Review, 111*, 486–511.

Newcombe, A., & Reese, E. (2004). Evaluations and orientations in mother-child narratives as a function of attachment security: A longitudinal investigation. *International Journal of Behavioral Development, 28*, 230–245.

Peterson, C., Jesso, B., & McCabe, A. (1999). Encouraging narratives in preschoolers: An intervention study. *Journal of Child Language, 26*, 49–67.

Pillemer, D. (1998). *Momentous events, vivid memories*. Cambridge, MA: Harvard University Press.

Posada, G., Gao, Y., Wu, F., Posada, R., Tascon, M., Schoelmerich, A., et al. (1995). The secure-base phenomenon across cultures: Children's behavior, mothers' preferences, and experts' concepts. *Monographs of the Society for Research in Child Development, 60* (2–3, Serial No. 244), 27–48.

Reese, E., Bird, A., & Tripp, G. (in press). Children's self-esteem and moral self: Links to parent–child conversations about emotion. *Social Development*.

Reese, E., Haden, C., & Fivush, R. (1993). Mother–child conversations about the past: Relationships of style and memory over time. *Cognitive Development, 8*, 403–430.

Reese, E., & Newcombe, R. (2005). *Mothers' elaborative talk about the past enhances children's language and memory*. Manuscript under review.

Reese, E., & Read, S. (2000). Predictive validity of the New Zealand MacArthur Communicative Development Inventory: Words and sentences. *Journal of Child Language, 27*, 255–266.

Singer, J. A., & Salovey, P. (1993). *The remembered self: Emotion and memory in personality*. New York: US Free Press.

van IJzendoorn, M. H., & Sagi, A. (1999). Cross-cultural patterns of attachment: Universal and contextual dimensions. In J. Cassidy & P. R. Shaver (Eds.), *Handbook of attachment: Theory, research and clinical applications* (pp. 713–734). New York: Guilford Press.

Waters, E. (1987). *Attachment Behavior Q-Set* (Version 3.0). Unpublished instrument, State University of New York at Stony Brook, Department of Psychology.

Welch-Ross, M. K., Fasig, G., & Farrar, M. J. (1999). Predictors of preschoolers' self-knowledge: Reference to emotion and mental states in mother–child conversation about past events. *Cognitive Development, 14*, 401–422.

Williams, K. T. (1997). *Expressive Vocabulary Test*. Circle Pines, MN: American Guidance Service.

The Ontogeny of Serial-Order Representation

Michael Colombo, Michelle Gulya, and Carolyn Rovee-Collier

The importance of serially ordered information for human cognition cannot be overstated. Indeed one could argue that all human behaviours consist of a sequence of smaller behaviours. Citing examples such as a rat running a maze, an architect designing a house, and a human uttering a sentence, Lashley (1951) noted long ago that most activities involve memory for temporal (serial) information. Lashley (1951) also asserted that understanding how memory for serial-order information affects behaviour is crucial for understanding the activity and connectivity of the brain. A similar sentiment was echoed by Murdock (1974), who listed serial-order information as one of the three main types of information important for human memory. Murdock (1974) also argued that the basic questions to consider is how serial-order information is encoded, stored, and retrieved. Despite the significance of serial-order learning for human behaviour, very little is known about its ontogeny. The present series of studies addressed this issue.

Serial-Order Representation in Adults

The procedure that we adopted in our studies was originally developed by Terrace (1986, Straub & Terrace, 1981) for use with pigeons. D'Amato and Colombo (1988) adapted the serial-order task for use with monkeys, and more recently, we have used this task extensively with human participants to chart the ontogeny of serial-order representation. The procedure is quite simple, and because it forms the basis for the series of studies that will be described in this chapter, it is worth going over in some detail. The participants are shown five simultaneously displayed stimuli presented at the four corners and midpoint of a touchscreen monitor (see Figure 1A). For ease of exposition, these stimuli will be referred to as A, B, C, D, and E. A correct trial was defined as pressing all five stimuli in a specific order (A→B→C→D→E), which resulted in the display of the word 'CORRECT' on the monitor. Although on each trial the five stimuli

A. Basic 5-Item Task

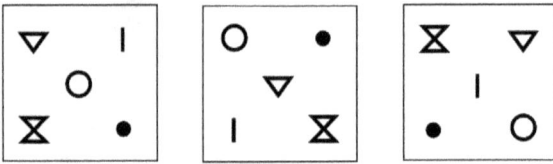

B. Pairwise Test

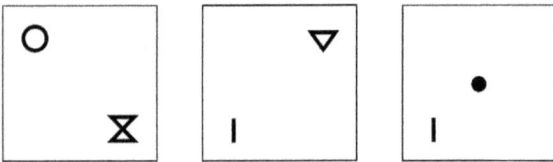

C. Triplet Test

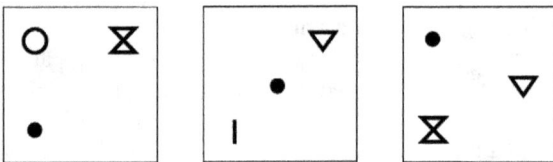

Figure 1

A. The Basic 5-Item Serial-Order Task. On each trial the same five stimuli are displayed in different spatial locations, and the participant must learn to press the stimuli in the same order, for example, circle→vertical line→dot→triangle→hourglass. B. The Pairwise Test. For the pairwise test, two of the five stimuli are presented. Adult participants will respond to the two stimuli in the order in which they appear in the original sequence. C. The Triplet Test. For the triplet test, three of the five stimuli are presented. Again, adult participants will respond to the three stimuli in the order in which they appear in the original sequence.

appeared in different locations, the order in which they needed to be pressed (A→B→C→D→E) remained the same. Any deviation from the assigned order was considered an error, immediately resulted in all the stimuli being turned off, and was followed by the display of the word 'INCORRECT' on the monitor. There are two types of errors that can be made, a forward error consisting of skipping over an item that should have been pressed (e.g., A→B→D or A→B→C→E), or a backward error consisting of responding to an item that has already been pressed (e.g., A→B→A or A→B→C→D→B). Repeat responses to the most recent item pressed was not considered an error and was allowed (e.g., A→B→B→B→C→D→D→E).

It would be quite difficult to learn the serial-order task with all five stimuli displayed from the onset, so initially the participants are trained to execute the serial-order task with only one stimulus (A), then two stimuli (A→B), three stimuli (A→B→C), four stimuli (A→B→C→D), and finally all five stimuli (A→B→C→D→E) until they achieve a reasonable level of performance. Not surprisingly, adult humans can be taught to perform the serial-order task to a high level of competence. The critical question, however, is: *What have they learned?* To assess the nature of the representation that is learned in the serial-order task, once criterial performance has been achieved on the 5-item task, a pairwise test and a triplet test are conducted. The pairwise test (see Figure 1B) consists of presenting the participants with all possible pairs of stimuli that can be generated from the five items, 10 in all (AB, AC, AD, AE, BC, BD, BE, CD, CE, and DE). The triplet test is similar, and consists of all possible triplets of stimuli that can be generated from the five items, again 10 in all (ABC, ABD, ABE, ACD, ACE, ADE, BCD, BCE, BDE, CDE). Note that the way the pairs are written (e.g., AB) does not imply any particular spatial organisation of the stimuli. Pair AB merely indicates that the two stimuli A and B are presented to the participant in no particular spatial organisation; A may be on the left and B on the right, or B may be on the left and A on the right.

When given the pairwise and triplet tests, adult human participants responded to the items in the test pair or test triplet in the order in which they appear in the original sequence. The data from a study we conducted with human adult participants (Colombo & Frost, 2001) are shown in Figure 2. Performance on all test pairs and all test triplets was significantly above chance (50% for the pairwise test and 8.3% for the triplet test) and most often close to 100% correct. In other words, the participants responded to the stimuli in the test pair or test triplet in the order in which they occurred in the original 5-item task. Given pair BD, for example, the participants first responded to stimulus B and then responded to stimulus D. Given triplet BDE, the participants first responded to B, then D, and finally E.

The high levels of performance on the ten pairwise and ten triplet combinations indicated that in the course of learning to respond to the five stimuli in the order A→B→C→D→E, the participants formed a linear representation of the stimuli, and used that representation to guide their behaviour. By 'guide their behaviour' we mean that when a pair or triplet was displayed, the participants accessed the list at item A and then progressed through the list in a serial fashion, comparing the current item in the linear representation with the items being displayed. If this was the case, then an interesting prediction can be made regarding the latency to respond to the first item in the pairwise and triplet test. Take the case where pair BD is presented. The participant says 'A' (i.e., accesses the representation of A) and then looks for stimulus A on the display, fails to find it so then moves on and says 'B' and looks for stimulus B on the display. The participant sees stimulus B and makes a response to it. Now imagine that pair CD is presented. If the participant again engages the same mechanism and compares the current

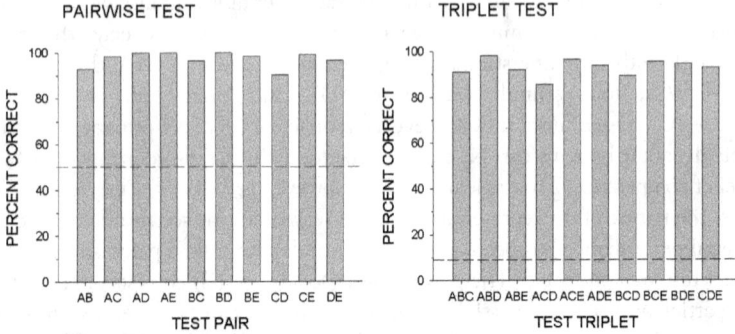

Figure 2

Performance of adult participants on the pairwise and triplet tests.

Note: The dashed line represents chance levels of performance.

Adapted from 'Representation of serial order in humans: A comparison to the findings with monkeys (*Cebus apella*)', by M. Colombo and N. Frost, 2001, *Psychonomic Bulletin & Review, 8*, p. 265. Copyright 2001 by Psychonomic Society Inc. Adapted with permission.

accessed item with the displayed items, then the latency to respond to stimulus C in pair CD should be longer than the latency to respond to stimulus B in pair BD. This is because in the case of pair CD, the participant has to access two items (A and B) before finding a match. Likewise, the latency to respond to stimulus A in pair AD should be faster than either the latency to respond to stimulus B in BD or C in CD. This is exactly what we found.

Figure 3 shows that there was a strong linear relationship between the latency to respond to the first item and the position of that item in the series. We termed this effect the *first-item effect*, and we believe it provides a window into the structure of the representation that the participants construct when learning to solve the five-item task. In effect, it shows that in the course of learning the five-item task, a linked representation of the five items is formed, and that the participants do indeed then use this linear representation to guide their choices on the pairwise and triplet tests.

Taken together, the high levels of performance on the pairwise test, as well as the presence of a first-item effect, suggested that in the course of learning to respond to the five items in a specific order, the adult participants in our study formed a linear representation of the sequence and used that representation to guide their behaviour. Equipped with these basic findings our first question was: *Are there differences in the structure of the serial-order representation across development?*

Experiment 1: Ontogeny of Serial-Order Representation — Representation of a List

Human adults seem to form a linear representation of the five-item list, and use that representation to guide their behaviour when components of the list are absent, such as during the pairwise test and triplet test. Not all animals, however,

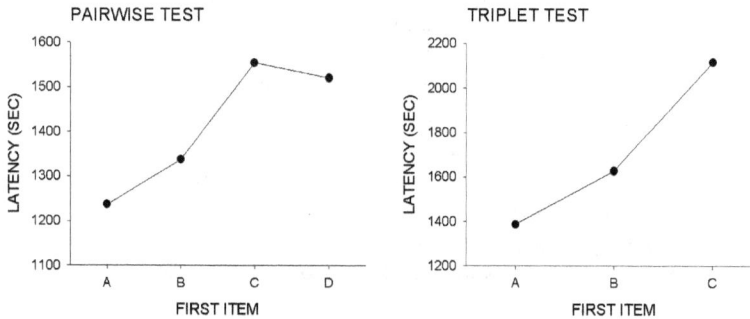

Figure 3
The first-item effect generated during the pairwise test (left) and the triplet test (right).

Note: It is not possible to generate a first-item latency for stimulus D on the triplet test because no test triplet begins with stimulus D.
Adapted from 'Representation of serial order in humans: A comparison to the findings with monkeys (*Cebus apella*)',
by M. Colombo and N. Frost, 2001, *Psychonomic Bulletin & Review, 8*, p. 266. Copyright 2001 by Psychonomic Society Inc.
Adapted with permission.

form such a linear representation. For example, birds also learn to perform the basic serial-order task with five stimuli (Terrace, 1993), and other than some small differences in the speed of learning the task, they can achieve levels of performance that are not too different from that of human adults. Unlike the human adults, however, birds perform quite differently on the pairwise test. Although birds perform quite well on pairs that contain either stimulus A or E (AB, AC, AD, AE, BE, CE, and DE), they perform at chance levels on the three pairs that do not contain these stimuli (BC, BD, and CD). Likewise, the birds do not show a first-item effect. Together, these findings indicate that although birds can learn to perform the five-item serial-order task, they do not develop a linear representation of the list. Thus when confronted with only components of the list, they seem to rely on an inventory of simple discriminative rules such as 'always peck A first' and 'always peck E last' (Terrace, 1993). The point we are trying to make is that learning the basic five-item task is no guarantee that a linear representation of the items will be formed. Our question then is: At *what point in development do children form a linear representation of a list?*

Despite the recognised importance of serial-order information for human behaviour, few studies have explored the ontogeny of list representation. In one of the earliest studies, Stromer and Mackay (1993) showed that a 9-year-old child trained on two different five-item series performed at 100% correct on pairwise tests that were based on each series. Similarly, Terrace and McGonigle (1994) looked at the acquisition of three different five-item series by 5- and 7-year-old children. One series was based on stimuli of different colours, whereas the other two were based on stimuli of different sizes, one series (monotonic) with the response sequence ordered according to the size of the stimuli, and the other one (nonmonotonic) with the response sequence mapped randomly onto the size of the stimuli. Both the 5- and 7-year-olds learned the colour sequence and the monotonic size sequence more easily than the nonmonotonic size sequence. Finally, Holcomb, Stromer, and Mackay (1997) trained 4- and 5-year-olds on a six-item variant of the serial-order task in which the children were trained to respond in a specific way to each of the six pairs of stimuli (AB, BC, CD, DE, and EF). Once trained on these pairs, the children were able to respond correctly to all other pairs that could be generated from the six stimuli as well as to reproduce the entire six-item sequence when all six stimuli were presented simultaneously.

The above studies show that young children are able to reproduce an ordered list containing as many as six items and of responding to subsets of those items in the correct order. Unfortunately, because the age groups used in these studies were so restricted, it is hard to construct a developmental picture of serial-order representation. Furthermore, none of the studies looked at the interesting latency differences, such as the first-item effect, that can provide a window into the structure of the representations. In our first study (Gulya & Colombo, 2004) our goal was to chart the development of serial-order representation using 3-, 4-, 7-, and 10-year-old children and adults. We tested 3- and 4-year-olds in order to gain an understanding of very young children's capacity to learn and recall a list of arbitrary items, 7- and 10-year-olds because previous research had shown that these were ages where rehearsal strategies and increased verbal abilities facilitate memory for list performance, and adults because presumably list representation is most fully developed in adulthood. Based on previous studies we expected the 7- and 10-year-olds to perform well on the pairwise test and show a first-item effect, in other words, provide evidence that they formed a linear representation of the five-item series. But how would the very young children fare?

The procedure that we used was similar to that used by Colombo and Frost (2001) with adult participants. So that differences in verbal competence would not differentially affect the results at different ages, a non-verbal task with stimuli appropriate for even the youngest children was used. A touch-sensitive screen with a viewing area of 28.6 cm by 21.6 cm displayed the stimuli. The stimuli used for the serial-order task consisted of brightly coloured 3.3 cm × 3.1 cm pictures of five Sesame Street® characters — Big Bird, Scooter, Cookie Monster, Kermit, and Bert. Throughout the rest of this chapter, the five stimuli will be denoted as A, B, C, D, and E.

When the participant touched the display, the sound 'ta-da' was heard (this sound combination is commonly heard when turning on or shutting down an IBM-compatible computer with Windows), and simultaneously an animated visual display of Elmo jumping up and down in an 11.7 cm × 8 cm black rectangle was shown for 2 s. All correct trials were followed by this audio and visual presentation (the reinforcer). After an incorrect response, the screen darkened for 1 s. No instructions about the task were given during either training or testing. During the warm-up session, all age groups were merely encouraged to touch the visual display. During training and testing, all participants were told to try and make Elmo jump. The phrases 'Can you make Elmo dance?' and 'Good job!'

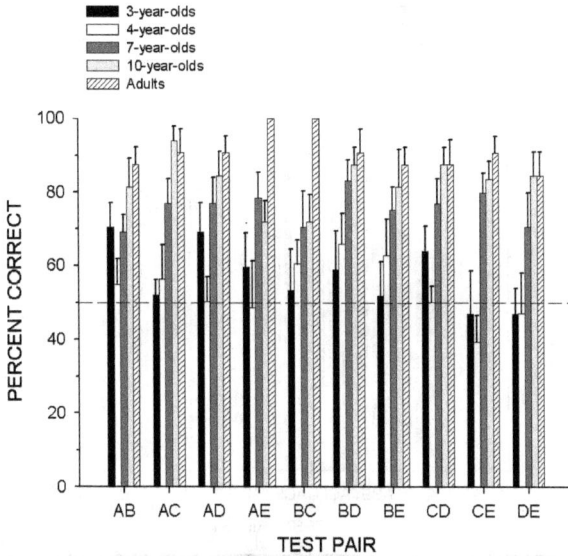

Figure 4

Performance of 3-, 4-, 7-, and 10-year-olds and adults on the pairwise test.

Note: The dashed line represents chance levels of performance.

were often repeated with the 3- and 4-year-olds. It was not uncommon for the younger children to clap for themselves when they were correct. When this occurred, the experimenter and the caregiver joined in this behaviour. All children selected a small prize upon completion of training and testing. Further details about the procedure can be found in Gulya and Colombo (2004). All reported outcomes were based on a Greenhouse-Geisser-corrected repeated-measures analysis of variance evaluated at $p < .05$. Tukey's honestly significant differences (HSD), evaluate at $p < .05$, were used for post hoc tests.

Not surprisingly, there was an inverse relationship between age and the number of trials required to learn the five-item serial-order task (3-year-olds: 79.9 trials; 4-year-olds: 64.7 trials; 7-year-olds: 39.5 trials; 10-year-olds: 34.9 trials; adults: 34.5 trials). Post hoc tests revealed two non-overlapping age groups, one consisting of the 3-, 4-, and 7-year-olds, and the second consisting of the adult participants. The 10-year-olds overlapped with both of these age groups. Although there were differences in the number of trials needed to learn the five-item serial-order task, it is important to keep in mind that all age groups learned the five-item task to the same level of proficiency.

Performance across the 10 test pairs is shown in Figure 4. As the age of the participants increased, there was a gradual increase in performance. The 3- and 4-year-olds performed at or close to chance (50%) on almost all of the test pairs, the exceptions being performance on pairs AB, AD, and CD by the 3-year-olds

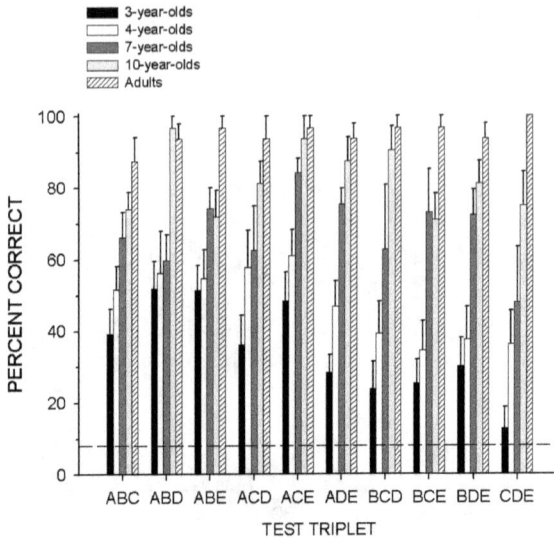

Figure 5

Performance of 3-, 4-, 7-, and 10-year-olds and adults on the triplet test.

Note: The dashed line represents chance levels of performance.

(the 4-year-olds performed at chance on all test pairs). In contrast, the 7- and 10-year-olds' and adults' performance was significantly above chance on all of the test pairs.

Performance across the 10 test triplets is shown in Figure 5. A similar pattern was evident on the triplet test as on the pairwise test. With the exception of performance on test triplet CDE by the 3-year-olds, all age groups performed above chance on all of the test triplets. Although the 3- and 4-year-olds performed significantly above chance on the test triplets, their performance was inferior to that of the older children and the adults.

The high levels of performance exhibited by the 7- and 10-year-olds and adults on the test pairs and test triplets suggest that in the course of learning to perform the five-item task, these participants had formed a linear representation of the series and used that representation to guide their behaviour. If the participants had formed a linear representation of the five stimuli, then the latency to respond to the first item of a test pair or test triplet should increase as a function of the position of that item in the series. Figure 6 shows the latency to respond to the first item on the pairwise and triplet test for each of the age groups. In line with their performance data, there was no first-item effect present on the pairwise test for either the 3- or 4-year-olds, whereas a clear first-item effect was demonstrated by the 7- and 10-year-olds, as well as by the adult participants. The same pattern was evident on the triplet test: the 3- and 4-year-olds failed to

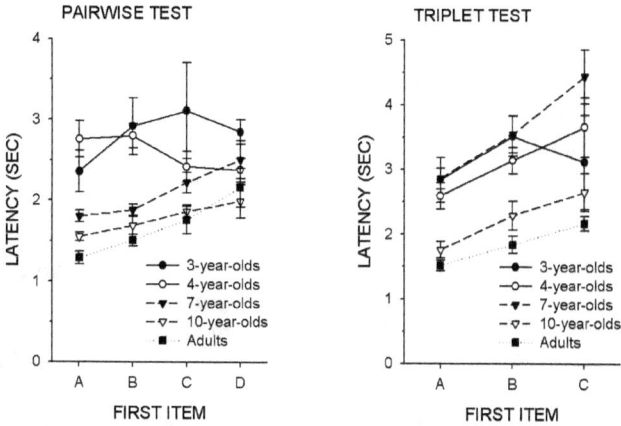

Figure 6

The first-item effect on the pairwise test (left) and triplet test (right) for the 3-, 4-, 7-, and 10-year-olds and adults.

show a first item effect (note, however, that the effect fell just short of significance for the 4-year-olds), whereas the 7- and 10-year-olds and adult participants did show the effect.

Our data suggest that in the course of learning to respond to the five items, the
older children and the adult participants formed a linear representation of the series.
Such a representation likely has two properties. The first property is an internal representation of each of the stimuli used on the five-item task, symbolised as a, b, c, d,
and e. The second property is the organisation of these representations as an asso-
ciative chain, symbolised as $a \rightarrow b \rightarrow c \rightarrow d \rightarrow e$. The associative chain representation is
not a full-fledged visual representation of the entire sequence but only a series of
directions to guide the participant from one stimulus to the next. When the subject
retrieves the associative chain, he or she is merely retrieving the instruction, *given
the current stimulus, the next stimulus to press is x*. These two properties, the representation of each stimulus and the associative chain, are sufficient to account for all of
the data just described. According to this view, when a test pair or triplet is displayed, the 7-, 10-year-olds and the adult participants begin by accessing the associative chain at a and progress in a linear fashion through the chain until a recalled
item matches a displayed item. The high levels of performance on the pairwise and
triplet tests, along with a clear first-item effect, suggest that the 7- and 10-year-olds
and adults had both well-formed representations of each item and a well-formed
associative representation of the list. In contrast, the poor performance of the 3-
year-olds and the 4-year-olds, together with no evidence of a first-item effect,
suggests that the younger children had either failed to form a representation of each
item and/or formed, at best, a very crude associative representation of the list. We
take up this point again in the Discussion section.

Experiment 2: Ontogeny of Serial-Order Representation
— Knowledge of Ordinal Position

One limitation of the associative chain account is that it does not impart to the participant any knowledge of the ordinal position of the items in the series. In other words, when presented with pair BD, the participant responds to stimulus B because the representational component a elicits the representational component b (i.e., $a{\rightarrow}b$), and not because the participant knows that stimulus B comes before stimulus D. When we speak of the participant knowing that B comes before D, we mean that they possess a spatial representation of the list, that is, a representation of the list showing at the same time all of the stimuli and their relationship to one another. With such a representation, the subject can look at the list and see that B comes before D without having to progress in a linear fashion throughout the associative chain.

Surprisingly, very few studies have examined the ability of adults (Ebenholtz, 1963; Lovelace & Snodgrass, 1971; Murdock, 1968) or children (Cohen, Quinton, & Winder, 1983; Fivush & Slackman, 1986) to extract ordinal information. More importantly, none has examined the ontogeny of this ability. In the next study, therefore, we examined the ontogeny of knowledge of ordinal position. We consider the spatial representation to be a higher-order representation that develops at a later time than the associative representation. With this in mind, we predicted that the 3- and 4-year-olds, who provided limited evidence for an associative representation, should not be able to extract ordinal information from a list. But how would the 7- and 10-year-olds fare on this task?

Our procedure was based on studies that we had conducted with monkeys (D'Amato & Colombo, 1989) and that Terrace and colleagues had conducted with pigeons (Terrace, Chen, & Newman, 1995). The participants once again were 3-, 4-, 7- and 10-year-old children and adults. Separate groups of participants of each age were trained on either a three-item (ABC), four-item (ABCD), or five-item (ABCDE) serial-order task. Once they achieved a certain level of proficiency on these baseline series, they were given a wild card test in which half the trials in a session consisted of the baseline series, and the other half consisted of wild card series, randomly mixed. Participants were required to complete the entire sequence, responding to the wild card stimulus in place of the missing Sesame Street® character stimulus. In other words, for those participants who were trained on the ABC series, once they reached criterion, they were given a test on which the ABC configuration was presented on half the trials, and the wild card configurations were presented on the other half of the trials.

For the ABC wild card configurations, any two of the original three stimuli were presented in the same ordinal position, but a novel third 'wild card' (W) stimulus was substituted for the remaining original stimulus. Thus there were three wild card configurations (WBC, AWC, ABW). For the ABCD series and ABCDE series, there were either four (WBCD, AWCD, ABWD, ABCW) or five (WBCDE, AWCDE, ABWDE, ABCWE, ABCDW) wild card configurations. The wild card stimuli consisted of either a white diamond on a black background or a black plus sign on a white background (both were 3.3 cm × 3.1 cm). Their presentation was counterbalanced within groups.

Generating chance levels of performance on the wild card tests following ABC, ABCD, and ABCDE training is not a simple matter. Take, for example, the case of wild card testing after training on the ABCDE sequence. The probability of responding by chance alone to all five items on a wild card trial is .0008. This calculation, however, does not take into account the fact that the participant was able to perform the baseline ABCDE task at a high level. A more realistic level of chance is based on the assumptions that participants positioned the wild card stimulus by chance alone, but that when they guessed the position of the wild card correctly, they then completed the entire sequence without further errors. On this basis, chance level of performance on the ABC, ABCD, and ABCDE wild card trials is 33.3%, 25%, and 20%, respectively.

The performance on the baseline and wild card trials for the ABC, ABCD, and ABCDE series is shown in Figure 7. The pattern is quite consistent across the three series and reveals that the 3- and 4-year-olds performed at chance on almost all of the wild card trials except trial ABCDW by the 3-year-olds. In contrast, the 7- and 10-year-olds, and the adult participants performed significantly above chance on all of the wild card trials. These data indicate a clear developmental difference in the ability to solve the wild card trials and suggest that the 3- and 4-year-old children did not have knowledge of the ordinal position of the items in the series, whereas the 7- and 10-year-olds and adults did. This conclusion, however, must remain tentative, given that the 3-year-old children were also unable to solve the baseline series when it was embedded in the wild card trials, suggesting that a failure to understand the requirements of the task, rather than an inability to extract ordinal knowledge, may have been the basis for their poor performance. Likewise, the 4-year-old children, although performing above chance on the baseline series, still performed well below the level of the older children and adults on the baseline series; thus, they too may have suffered from a failure to understand the requirements of the task.

We argued earlier that an associative chain mechanism was sufficient to account for the performance and latency effects observed on the pairwise and triplet test. It is harder, although not impossible, to account for the wild card data with just the associative chain mechanism because no associations have been established between any of the training items and the wild card stimulus. How does the participant know to respond to W after responding to items A and B in the wild card trial ABWDE? Surely the participant learned a remote association between B and D in original training which ought to override any tendency to respond to W after B, which is a completely unestablished association. Instead, the older children and adults suppressed their tendency to choose D after B and chose W instead. We believe they were able to do this because they can extract ordinal information, and at the same time, appreciate that the task requires responding to the W stimulus in place of the missing original stimulus.

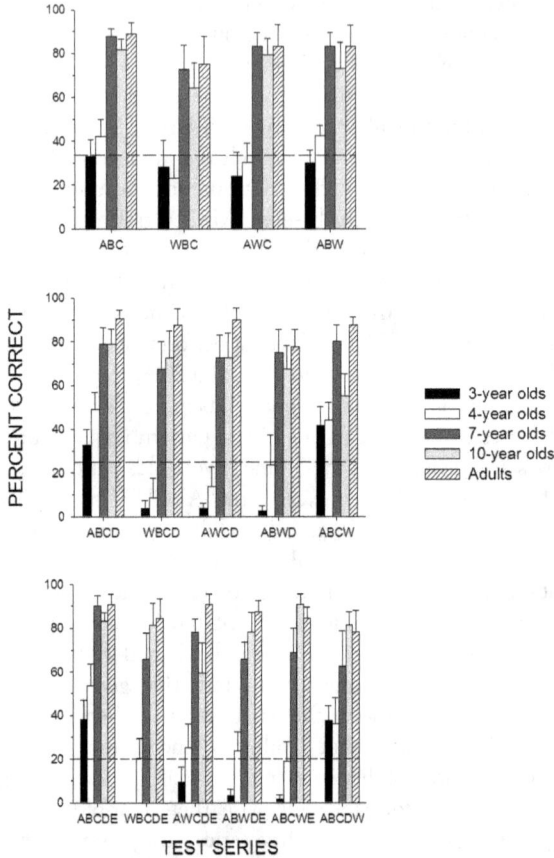

Figure 7

Performance of the 3-, 4-, 7-, and 10-year-olds and adults on the wild card trials after training on the ABC (top), ABCD (middle) or ABCDE (bottom) series.

Note: The dashed line represents chance levels of performance.

Discussion

Our findings show that children of different ages extract different levels of information when learning to solve the five-item serial-order task. Our data suggest that in the course of learning to solve the five-item task, children 7 years of age and older form a linear representation of the items and access that representation to guide their behaviour. The 3- and 4-year-olds could respond correctly to the five items during training, and their performance on the triplet test suggests that they possess some rudimentary linear representation of the five items. That they possess, *at best*, a rudimentary representation of the series is underscored by the fact that they performed poorly on the pairwise test, failed

A. Associative Chain: All links of full strength

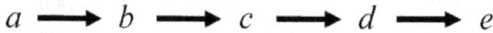

$$a \longrightarrow b \longrightarrow c \longrightarrow d \longrightarrow e$$

B. Associative Chain: Fewer Links

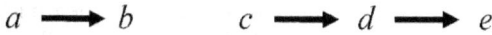

$$a \longrightarrow b \qquad c \longrightarrow d \longrightarrow e$$

C. Associative Chain: Weaker Links

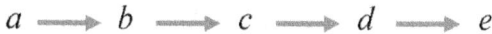

$$a \longrightarrow b \longrightarrow c \longrightarrow d \longrightarrow e$$

Figure 8

Different types of associative chain representations. A. An associative chain representation with all links formed and of full strength. B. An associative chain representation in which the links are of full strength but not all have been formed. In this case, the link between stimuli B and C is missing. C. An associative chain representation in which all the links are formed, but the links are weak, signified by the arrows drawn in gray.

to show a first-item effect on both the pairwise and triplet tests, and were unable to place the wild card stimulus in the proper position.

It is unclear at present in what way the representation of the 3- and 4-year-olds differs from that of the older children and adults. As we argued earlier, high levels of performance on the pairwise and triplet tests, and evidence of a first-item effect can all be accommodated by the formation of an associative chain that consists of two properties. The first property is that each of these items is part of a well-organised internal representation, symbolised as a, b, c, d, and e. The second property is that these items are organised in an associative chain symbolised as $a \rightarrow b \rightarrow c \rightarrow d \rightarrow e$. If we assume these two properties, then one possibility why the younger children did not perform as well as the older children is that they have not developed well-organised internal representations of each of the items. This seems unlikely, however, for even children as young as 2 months of age can form representations of highly complex objects (Hayne, Greco, Early, Griesler, & Rovee-Collier, 1986).

An alternative possibility is that the associative chain of the 3- and 4-year-olds was not as robust as that of the older children. In this regard, there are two further possibilities, illustrated in Figure 8. First, the 3- and 4-year-olds might have formed fewer links than the older children. Second, the 3- and 4-year-olds might have formed as many links as the older children but the links were weaker. Given that the younger children did perform above chance on the triplet test, our operating hypothesis at present is that they formed the associative chain, but its links were weaker.

Although we are still in the early phases of research in this area, the data from the wild card experiment suggest that children 7 years of age are also able to extract ordinal information from a list. We have argued elsewhere (Gulya & Colombo, 2004) that the ability to proceed in a linear fashion through a list is evidence of an associative representation, whereas the ability to extract ordinal information is indicative of a spatial representation. Quite possibly there is a hierarchy of list representation with an associative representation being the foundation for a spatial representation. If this is true, then there might be a point in developmental when these representations are experimentally dissociable.

The ability to learn and remember serially ordered information is not a late ontogenetic development; rather, the brain mechanisms that mediate it are functional in some rudimentary form by the third postnatal month (Gulya, Rovee-Collier, Galluccio, & Wilk, 1998). The appearance and elaboration of this capacity are critical to the subsequent development of language and several important concepts that are based on sequential understanding, including time and number.

A longstanding debate among cognitive psychologists pertains to the emergence and structure of conceptual representations, specifically, whether conceptual development entails a fundamental reorganisation of the way concepts are represented in later childhood (Bruner, Olver, & Greenfield, 1966; Carey, 1985; Inhelder & Piaget, 1964; Piaget, 1962; Vygotsky, 1934, 1978) or whether conceptual development is a continuous process. Those who subscribe to the first position hold that young minds differ fundamentally from older ones, and so the concepts of younger and older children must differ fundamentally as well. Thus, for example, the concepts of younger children have been characterised as concrete (Piaget, 1962) and perceptual (Bruner et al., 1966), whereas the concepts of older children have been characterised as abstract and conceptual, respectively.

Advocates of the other position have focused on the development of a few basic concepts that are ubiquitous across cultures and are used to a greater or lesser degree beginning early in infancy (Keil, 1989; Mandler, 1998, 2004; Spelke, Breinlinger, Macomber, & Jacobson, 1992). Mandler (2004), for example, argued that traces of the hierarchical organisation of conceptual representations that is characteristic of adults can be seen in the concept learning of young infants. She concluded, 'most of what has been documented … in the literature consists of enrichment and differentiation rather than fundamental reorganisation' (p. 216).

Our data are consistent with the latter position. Even in early infancy, list learning ability changes gradually. For example, 3-month-olds can learn and remember the serial order of items in a three-item list (Gulya et al., 1998), and 6-month-olds can learn and remember the items but not their order if the list contains five items (Gulya, Sweeney, & Rovee-Collier, 1999). Here, Experiment 1 documents the continued continuity of the representation of serially ordered information through adulthood. We interpret the apparent developmental discontinuity between 4 and 7 years of age on the ordinal knowledge task in Experiment 2, not as a fundament change in conceptual representation, but as evidence that the representation of serial order is simply the *precursor* of the representation of ordinal knowledge.

Acknowledgments

This research was supported by a Royal Society of New Zealand Marsden Foundation Grant UOO040 to Michael Colombo and an NIMH Grant No. MH32307 to Carolyn Rovee-Collier.

References

Bruner, J., S., Olver, R. R., & Greenfield, P. M. (1966). *Studies in cognitive growth*. New York: John Wiley & Sons.

Carey, S. (1985). *Conceptual change in childhood*. Cambridge, MA: MIT Press.

Cohen, R. L., Quinton, C., & Winder, S. (1983). Critical processes in serial short-term memory: A developmental study. *Intelligence, 9*, 171–188.

Colombo, M., & Frost, N. (2001). Representation of serial order in humans: A comparison to the findings with monkeys (*Cebus apella*). *Psychonomic Bulletin & Review, 8*, 262–269.

D'Amato, M. R., & Colombo, M. (1988). Representation of serial order in monkeys (*Cebus apella*). *Journal of Experimental Psychology: Animal Behavior Processes, 14*, 131–139.

D'Amato, M. R., & Colombo, M. (1989). Serial learning with wild card items by monkeys (*Cebus apella*): Implications for knowledge of ordinal position. *Journal of Comparative Psychology, 103*, 252–161.

Ebenholtz, S. M. (1963). Serial learning: Position learning and sequential associations. *Journal of Experimental Psychology, 66*, 353–362.

Fivush, R., & Slackman, E. A. (1986). The acquisition and development of scripts. In K. Nelson (Ed.), *Event knowledge: Structure and function in development* (pp. 71–96). Hillsdale: Erlbaum.

Gulya, M., & Colombo, M. (2004). The development of serial-order behaviour: Representation of a list. *Journal of Comparative Psychology, 118*, 71–81.

Gulya, M., Rovee-Collier, C., Galluccio, L., & Wilk, A. (1998). Memory processing of a serial list by young infants. *Psychological Science, 9*, 303–307.

Gulya, M., Sweeney, B., & Rovee-Collier, C. (1999). Infants' memory processing of a serial list: List length effects. *Journal of Experimental Child Psychology, 73*, 72–91.

Hayne, H., Greco, C., Earley, L.A, Griesler, P.C., & Rovee-Collier, C. (1986). Ontogeny of early event memory: II. Encoding and retrieval by 2- and 3-month-olds. *Infant Behavior and Development, 9*, 461–472.

Holcomb, W. L., Stromer, R., & Mackay, H. A. (1997). Transitivity and emergent sequence performances in young children. *Journal of Experimental Child Psychology, 65*, 96–124.

Inhelder, B., & Piaget, J. (1964). *The early growth of logic in the child*. New York: Norton.

Keil, F. C. (1989). *Concepts, kinds, and cognitive development*. Cambridge, MA: MIT Press.

Lashley, K. S. (1951). The problem of serial order in behavior. In L. A. Jeffress (Ed.), *Cerebral mechanisms in behavior: The Hixon Symposium* (pp. 112–146). New York: Wiley.

Lovelace, E. A., & Snodgrass, R. D. (1971). Decision times for alphabetic order of letter pairs. *Journal of Experimental Psychology, 88*, 258–264.

Mandler, J. M. (1998). Representation. In W. Damon (Ed.), *Handbook of child psychology: Cognition, perception, & language* (Vol. 2, pp. 255–307). New York: Wiley.

Mandler, J. M. (2004). *The foundations of mind: Origins of conceptual thought*. New York: Oxford University Press.

Murdock, B. B. (1968). Serial order effects in short-term memory. *Journal of Experimental Psychology Monograph Supplement, 76,* (No. 4, Pt. 2).

Murdock, B. B. (1974). *Human memory: Theory and data*. Potomac, MD: Erlbaum.

Piaget, J. (1962). *Play, dreams, and imitation in childhood* (C. Gattegno & F. M. Hodgson, Trans.). New York: Norton.

Spelke, E. S., Breinlinger, K., Macomber, J., & Jacobson, K. (1992). Origins of knowledge. *Psychological Review, 99,* 605–632.

Straub, R. O., & Terrace, H. S. (1981). Generalization of serial learning in the pigeon. *Animal Learning & Behavior, 9,* 454–468.

Stromer, R., & Mackay, H. A. (1993). Human sequential behavior: Relations among stimuli, class formation, and derived sequences. *The Psychological Record, 43,* 107–131.

Terrace, H. S. (1986). A nonverbal organism's knowledge of ordinal position in a serial learning task. *Journal of Experimental Psychology: Animal Behavior Processes, 12,* 203–214.

Terrace, H. S. (1993). The phylogeny and ontogeny of serial memory: List learning by pigeons and monkeys. *Psychological Science, 4,* 162–169.

Terrace, H. S., Chen, S., & Newman, A. B. (1995). Serial learning with a wild card by pigeons (*Columba livia*): Effect of list length. *Journal of Comparative Psychology, 109,* 162–172.

Terrace, H. S., & McGonigle, B. (1994). Memory and representations of serial order by children, monkeys, and pigeons. *Current Directions in Psychological Science, 3,* 180–185.

Vygotsky, L. S. (1934). *Thought and language*. New York: John Wiley & Sons.

Vygotsky, L. S. (1978). *Mind in society: The development of higher mental processes*. Cambridge, MA: Harvard University Press. (Original works published in 1930, 1933, and 1935).

Assessing Selective Attention in ADHD, Highly Creative, and Normal Young Children via Stroop Negative Priming Effects

Verena E. Pritchard, Dione Healey, and Ewald Neumann

Selective attention is conventionally taken to indicate the selection of one set of sensory inputs over others. The selection of relevant over irrelevant stimuli is fundamental for efficient interaction with the visual world. Such interaction relies on selection mechanisms that allow for the direction of action to behaviourally relevant items. Attention is influenced by both stimulus-driven (bottom-up) and goal-directed (top-down) processes. According to one view of selective attention, along with the enhancement of selected targeted information, there is a screening-out or gating of unwanted, competing non-target stimuli (e.g., Cohen, Dunbar, & McClelland, 1990; Desimone & Duncan, 1995). An alternative view regarding such non-targets holds that they are not simply screened out, but implicitly registered and subjected to active inhibition (see Tipper, 2001, for a review). The current study looks for evidence of active inhibition in groups of children with potential differences relating to attentional processing.

Negative Priming and the Stroop Colour-Word Task

The active inhibition view can be traced to the seminal work of Dalrymple-Alford and Budayr (1966) using Stroop stimuli. Stroop tasks typify a class of interference effects whereby the introduction of task-irrelevant stimulus characteristics slows reaction time. In Stroop interference tasks the naming of hues is slowed by the presence of a word that consists of a task-irrelevant colour name that differs from the ink colour of the task-relevant target stimulus. For example, it takes longer to say 'red' to a red-coloured word when the word is incongruent (e.g., *green*), than if it consists of a neutral stimulus comprising random letters (e.g., *iiiii*).

While examining the effect of Stroop stimuli sequencing on interference, Dalrymple-Alford and Budayr (1966) discovered an increased delay and greater error rate for items appearing in the hue that had been the ignored word of the previous Stroop stimulus. More specifically, response time was slower for a related condition in which the colour specified by the colour-word in the preceding trial matched the hue of the subsequent target than for an unrelated condition in which the target hue was unrelated to the colour specified by the colour-word in the preceding trial. This phenomenon is now called negative priming (Tipper, 1985) and refers to the finding that when a distracting, non-target stimulus is ignored, a subsequent response to that stimulus (or a conceptually similar stimulus) is typically slowed or less accurate, or both. Although negative priming (NP) tasks have been used extensively to understand the nature of inhibitory mechanisms underlying visual selective attention in adults, they have been under-utilised in the assessment of these abilities in children. A primary goal of the present chapter was to redress the neglect of this tool for investigating potential inhibitory capacities in different populations of children. We thus employed a Stroop negative priming task modeled on the early work of Dalrymple-Alford and Budayr to measure attentional processing in three distinct populations of children: 30 diagnosed with attention-deficit/hyperactivity disorder (ADHD); 30 designated highly creative; and 30 matched controls.

The Active Inhibition Explanation of Negative Priming

In initial interpretations, the response cost associated with an ignored item was attributed to the active suppression or inhibition of the ignored item's representation or to suppression of the access from that item to action (Tipper & Cranston, 1985). This account of the NP phenomenon stems from activation–suppression models of attention emphasising the operation of a dual mechanism during selection (e.g., Neill & Westberry, 1987; Neumann & DeSchepper, 1991; Tipper, 1985). According to these models selection is postcategorical; initial analysis of both attended and unattended stimuli takes place in parallel prior to selection. For a response to be directed towards the target, an excitatory mechanism functions to enhance or maintain the internal representation of the target, while an inhibitory mechanism acts to suppress the competing distractor representation. From this perspective, inhibition functions to enhance response to the target on a trial containing a specified target and distractor by reducing potential interference from the distractor.

Inhibition-based theories of NP suggest that the NP effect may reflect inhibition elicited as part of the selection process. Impaired or delayed response to the target on the subsequent trial of an ignored repetition (IR) pair (whereby a distractor becomes the subsequent target) in a NP task is attributed to inhibitory processes associated with the distractor on the prior trial (Houghton & Tipper, 1994; Neumann & DeSchepper, 1992; Strayer & Grison, 1999). Such NP effects are reliably demonstrated by young adults in a variety of NP tasks employing a wide range of stimuli such as pictures, letters, words, novel shapes, structurally possible and impossible three-dimensional shapes, and numbers (Driver & Tipper,

1989; Neumann, 1999; Tipper, 1985; Tipper & Cranston, 1985; Treisman & DeSchepper, 1996). The observation of NP across such a wide range of stimuli suggests that the associated inhibitory mechanism may be a general property of the selection process in situations with intensively clashing target and concurrent non-target information. It should be noted, however, that a competing explanation for NP, known as episodic retrieval theory, denies any role for an inhibitory selective attention mechanism (Neill, 1997; Neill & Mathis, 1998; Neill & Valdes, 1992). Because findings from most recent studies suggest an inhibition-based explanation remains the most influential account of NP (Buchner & Steffans, 2001; Conway, 1999; Fuentes, Humphreys, Agis, Carmona, & Catena, 1998; Hughes & Jones, 2003; Khurana, 2000; Kramer & Strayer, 2001; Lavie & Fox, 2000; Neumann, McCloskey, & Felio, 1999; Strayer & Grison, 1999; Wong, 2000), episodic retrieval theory will not be dealt with further. For a more detailed discussion, however, see Pritchard and Neumann (2004).

Negative Priming and Attentional Deficits

Negative priming procedures are currently deemed the best available index for investigating inhibitory processes in visual selective attention. Research examining NP effects in atypical adult populations has found that generalised cognitive failures (Tipper & Baylis, 1987), certain brain pathologies such as schizophrenia (Beech, Powell, McWilliam, & Claridge, 1989; Laplante, Everett, & Thomas, 1992), aging (Hasher, Stoltzfus, Zacks, & Rypma, 1991; McDowd & Oseas-Kreger, 1991; Tipper, 1991), and Alzheimer's syndrome (Sullivan, Faust, & Balota, 1995) are associated with a reduced or reversed NP effect. This suggests that the efficiency of the distractor inhibition mechanism has direct ramifications for attentional processing. Absent or reversed NP effects, for instance, might imply a dysfunctional inhibitory processing mechanism, which may in turn account for variability in cognitive performance.

Recent research investigating NP effects in varying age ranges of typical children has shown that conceptual (i.e., identity or semantic) NP effects occur in children as young as 5 years old (Pritchard & Neumann, 2004). These findings contradict earlier work that suggested deficiencies in the inhibitory mechanism of children (Tipper, Bourque, Anderson, & Brehaut, 1989). The present study used a Stroop negative priming task to investigate and compare potential differences in inhibitory processing in three distinct populations of children (ADHD versus Highly Creative versus Control) between the ages of 10 and 12 years. Our primary objectives were (a) to assess whether conceptual NP is a replicable phenomenon in children, (b) to investigate inhibitory processing in children with recognised deficits in attentional processing in an attempt to resolve discrepancies in the existing literature in this area, and (c) to investigate the contribution of cognitive inhibition to the information processing style of highly creative children. In the sections that follow, we provide a brief overview of existing NP studies concerned with inhibitory function in children with ADHD and creative individuals.

Negative Priming Effects in Children With ADHD

ADHD has become one of the most common developmental disorders of child-hood affecting 3% to 6% of children from varied cultures and geographical regions (Hart, Leahy, Loeber, Applegate, & Frick, 1995). The core behavioural symptoms of ADHD are inattention, impulsivity, and hyperactivity (American Psychiatric Association, 2000). A deficit in behavioural inhibition (impulsiveness) is the most distinguishing characteristic. This involves a failure to inhibit or delay a behavioural response and is associated with a significant disruption in the ability to control and regulate response and behaviour (Barkley, 1998; Tannock, 1998).

Many studies point to a dysfunction in inhibitory control as the cause for the major deficits in children with attention deficit disorder (Barkley, 1997; Quay, 1988; Schachar & Logan 1990). Inhibitory control is classified as the ability of an individual to delay a response, to interrupt an initiated response, to withhold a planned response, and to protect an ongoing activity from interference (Rubia, Oosterlann, Sergeant, Brandeis, & Leeuwen, 1998). Deficits in behavioural inhi-bition and inhibitory control in ADHD may relate to a dysfunction associated with the neurotransmission of dopamine (a neurotransmitter implicated in the brain's braking or inhibiting system) in the prefrontal cortex (Hynd et al., 1993).

The prefrontal cortex is assumed to modulate executive functions involved in complex goal-directed behaviour and play a paramount role in the mediation of various types of inhibitory function. Barkley (1994) assigns a central role to inhibitory control in executive function, arguing that impairments in inhibitory function in ADHD children may cause deficits typically shown by these children across a range of executive tasks designed to tap or assess prefrontal function (Barkley, Grodzinsky, & DuPaul, 1992; Pennington & Ozonoff, 1996; Ross, Hommer, Breiger, Varley, & Radant, 1994). Effective performance on executive function tasks often demands the ability to screen out, or in some way eliminate or reduce, intrusion from task-irrelevant information via inhibition and attentional control (Roberts & Pennington, 1996). A good example of this is the Stroop colour-naming task where the salient feature is the prepotent–alternative response dynamic. The prepotent tendency is to read the word while the alternative (correct) response is to identify the colour of the ink. Children with ADHD typically demon-strate heightened Stroop interference in comparison to typical children (see Harnishfeger & Bjorklund, 1994, for a review). Researchers using the NP paradigm to investigate central or cognitive inhibitory mechanisms in children with ADHD have proposed that poor behavioural inhibition and inhibitory control, along with increased susceptibility to interference in these individuals, may show up as a reduced NP effect in comparison to NP effects in typical children.

Results from the few studies that have investigated NP effects in children with ADHD are contradictory. Marriott (1998) used a letter-matching NP task to assess possible deficits in underlying attention mechanisms in hyperactive and ADHD children aged 10 to 12 years. Stimuli in this task consisted of a five-letter array (e.g., TVTVT). The first, third, and fifth letters are always classified as distractors and always identical to each other, while the second and fourth letters always function as targets, and may differ from one another. On half of the trials, target letters do not match (e.g., FTFXF), while on the remaining trials the target letters are the same (e.g., FTFTF). The task requires participants to judge whether the target letters are 'same' or 'different'. Two conditions are compared; unrelated (distractor and target letters are novel for consecutive trials) and IR (one or both target letters appear as distractors on the immediately preceding trial). Negative priming scores are calculated by taking the difference in reaction time or error rate between the two conditions. Marriott (1998) found, that in comparison to age-matched peers, hyperactive and ADHD children demonstrated a significantly reduced NP effect on such a task. Diminished NP effects have also been reported for 11- and 12-year-old children with Tourette syndrome with comorbid ADHD on a letter NP task similar to that used by Marriott, in comparison to age-matched children with Tourette syndrome but without ADHD comorbidity and typical children (Ozonoff, Strayer, McMahon, & Filloux, 1998). According to Ozonoff et al., these findings suggested that the presence of ADHD in individuals with Tourette syndrome impairs performance on select variables indicative of a specific inhibitory deficit.

In contrast, a study by Gaultney, Kipp, Weinstein, and McNeill (1999) employing a Stroop NP task found significant NP effects for both ADHD and typical children matched in age (9 to 12 years) and IQ. Participants in their study were all required to complete two identical versions of the Stroop NP task. Because Gaultney et al. were also interested in assessing the effects of stimulant medication on NP effects, children with ADHD were required to complete double administrations of the Stroop NP tasks: one session while medicated and one session while unmedicated. These sessions were counterbalanced. Typical children in their study were only required to complete one session. Gaultney and colleagues predicted that because ADHD is associated with deficits in behavioural inhibition and inhibitory control, a deficit in cognitive inhibition may also be implicated. Thus, children with ADHD may present with a diminished NP effect. An additional prediction made by these authors was that NP effects for ADHD participants would increase when these individuals were medicated. Neither hypothesis was supported. Negative priming effects were invariant across the two versions and both sessions of the Stroop NP task for the ADHD participants. More importantly, while children with ADHD demonstrated a significant increase in response latency on both unrelated and IR priming conditions on the second version of the two Stroop NP tasks relative to typical children in the first session, the critical NP effect was significant and invariant across the two groups on both the first and second versions of the task.

Contradictions in the literature concerning the relationship between ADHD and NP effects do not allow for any clear-cut conclusions to be drawn regarding the ability of these children to inhibit distracting information. Rather they beg the question — are the inhibitory mechanisms underlying visual selective attention dysfunctional in children diagnosed with ADHD?

Negative Priming Effects in Creative Individuals

There has been some speculation that enhanced creativity may be associated with reduced cognitive inhibition (Green & Williams, 1999; Stavridou & Furnham, 1996). By definition, creativity is demonstrated by some sort of novel outcome, whether it be a solution to a problem, a completed communicable idea, or something tangible like a work of art or an invention (Akande, 1997; Bogen & Bogen, 1999; DuBrin, 1994; Parkhurst, 1999; Pearlman, 1983; Piirto, 1998). One prominent thought process involved in creativity is divergent thinking; the production of a large number of original and unexpected ideas to form solutions for a given problem.

Stavridou and Furnham (1996) proposed that divergent thinking may relate to a weakness in cognitive inhibition. This conjecture was loosely based on research concerning reduced NP effects in individuals diagnosed with schizophrenia. Stavridou and Furnham argued that a deficit in inhibitory selective attention mechanisms may make individuals with schizophrenia unable to inhibit irrelevant information and prevent it from entering consciousness. Consequently, many unrelated ideas become interconnected resulting in 'widened associative connections'. This then results in more unusual associations between words and ideas compared with typical individuals. Stavridou and Furnham go on to suggest that the 'wide associative horizons' that typically characterise individuals with schizophrenia are similar to the thought processes that define creativity; that is, attention to multiple variables of a given stimulus and the subsequent production of more varied associations. In accordance with this logic, they predicted that because individuals with schizophrenia present with reduced NP effects, individuals who score highly on measures of divergent thinking may also exhibit diminished NP effects. Results from their NP Stroop task failed to support this hypothesis. Significant and similar NP effects were obtained for both high and low divergent thinking scorers. However, Stavridou and Furnham did note that, although not statistically significant, participants who scored highly on divergent thinking measures did present with a smaller NP effect in comparison to low scorers. Green and Williams (1999) suggested that Stavridou and Furnham's failure to find any significant association between NP and divergent thinking scores may relate to the small sample size that was used, or to modifications that were made to the timing of stimulus presentation within the priming procedure used in the study. Green and Williams (1999) employed a larger sample size and used a modified version of Stavridou and Furnham's (1996) Stroop NP task. Again, the prediction was that high scores in divergent thinking tasks would associate with a reduced NP effect in comparison to low scores. This was not supported. In fact, results from Green and Williams's study were characterised by an overall absence of NP effects across all participants. Green and Williams (1999) acknowledge that their failure to achieve NP effects may relate to problems with the experimental design they employed, such as the non-randomisation of priming conditions across trials. Green and Williams's Stroop NP task consisted of three experimental conditions; neutral, unrelated, and IR. The presentation order for all participants was always IR trials followed by unrelated trials followed by neutral trials. Because IR trials were never interspersed with unrelated or neutral trials, participants may have noticed the relationship between prime distractor and probe target stimuli in this condition (i.e., the distractor colour word on the prime trial names the probe trial target colour). It is well documented that when participants become aware of the NP manipulation, they can potentially use this information to predict test targets on ignored repetition probe trials (Hasher et al., 1991; Neumann & DeSchepper, 1991; Stoltzfus, Hasher, Zacks, Ulivi, & Goldstein, 1993). This may result in a decreases rather than increases in response latency on IR trials, relative to unrelated trials where prime distractor and probe target are never related (see May, Kane, & Hasher, 1995, for a review). Clearly, the evidence for compromised inhibition in creative individuals is equivocal. Research by Stavridou and Furnham (1996) points to the faint possibility of a link between reduced NP effects and divergent thinking. Attempts to follow up this study have been unsuccessful, marred by potential methodological problems (Green & Williams, 1998). There is no conclusive evidence to suggest that divergent thinking, possibly a dominant feature of the creative process, is associated with a deficit in inhibitory capacity.

In the present experiment, children ranging in age between 10 and 12 years old were tested to see if they would produce NP in the present Stroop NP task. In addition, children with ADHD were specifically tested to determine if they would show evidence for a diminished NP effect, in comparison to control children. Lastly, the performance of highly creative children was assessed in order to determine if they would produce a reduced NP effect relative to controls in light of recent speculations that creativity may be associated with weakened cognitive inhibition. Because of the variety of discrepancies in the literature, the present results should enable either verification or disconfirmation of the studies covered in our review.

Method

Participants

Ninety children aged between 10 and 12 years participated in the experiment. The children were divided into three groups: 30 (23 male, 7 female) were diagnosed with ADHD, 30 (14 male, 16 female) were identified as highly creative, and 30 (13 male, 17 female) were classified as controls with normal creativity scores and no indication of ADHD. Hereafter, these will be referred to as the ADHD, Creative, and Control groups, respectively. The mean age for the respective groups was 11 years 2 months (SD = 0.82), 11 years 5 months (SD = 0.85), and 11 years 10 months (SD = 0.89). Recruitment was conducted through advertisements in local newspapers, school notices, an ADD support group newsletter, and a Gifted Children's Society newsletter. The ADHD group was established by confirming that each child was diagnosed with ADHD by a psychiatrist or registered psychologist. Participants in the ADHD group were unmedicated on the day of testing. Participants in the ADHD group who were receiving psychostimulant (dextroamphetamine or methylphenidate) medication discontinued their treatment 24 hours before the day of testing because of the known effects of methylphenidate on cognitive functioning (e.g., Berman, Douglas, & Barr, 1999). As methylphenidate has an approximate half-life of 4.5 hours (Shader, Harmatz, Oesterheld, Parmelee, Sallee, & Greenblatt, 1999), a 24-hour elimination period should have ensured that the majority of the active ingredient had been eliminated prior to testing. The Creative group was established by confirming that each child scored in the 92nd percentile, or higher, on the Torrance Test of Creative Thinking (TTCT; Torrance, 1962). Participation was voluntary and included parental consent and child assent. All children had normal colour vision and normal or corrected to normal visual acuity. Participants were predominantly Caucasian of varying socioeconomic score (SES) backgrounds residing in Christchurch, New Zealand.

Design

The study employed a mixed design. The between-subjects variable was group (ADHD versus Creative versus Control) and the within-subjects variable was priming condition (Unrelated versus IR). Half the trials in the experiment were Unrelated (UR) trials (where neither the hue nor distractor colour word in a display were repeated in the subsequent display) and half IR trials (where the distractor word in a previous display repeated as the subsequent target hue). See Figure 1 for a sample of these conditions.

Apparatus and Stimuli

The stimuli were presented on 26 cm × 18 cm laminated cards and consisted of the words BLUE, RED, PURPLE, PINK, ORANGE, YELLOW, BROWN, GREEN, WHITE, GREY, and BLACK. These were all printed as a vertical list and displayed against a light grey background on each UR and IR card. Lettering measured 1.0 cm in height with each word spaced at 1.0 cm intervals down the list. The 11 Stroop items in each card were arranged in a single vertical column with the print of each word presented in one of the 11 corresponding colours. The first two items on each IR card were unrelated in order to reduce the saliency of this condition (see Figure 1). Test cards consisted of six IR cards and six UR cards. Four additional UR cards were used for practice trials. Each word and each ink colour appeared only once on a given card.[1] Presentation orders in the experiment were counterbalanced so that half of the participants began with a UR card and the remaining half began with an IR card. Subsequent cards were presented in regular alternation of the two conditions. A stopwatch was used to measure response latencies to complete the colour naming for each card.

Procedure

In a double-blind experiment, participants were tested individually in a quiet room. Prior to the experiment, participants completed a colour vision task requiring identification of the 11 ink colours used in the experiment. The colours

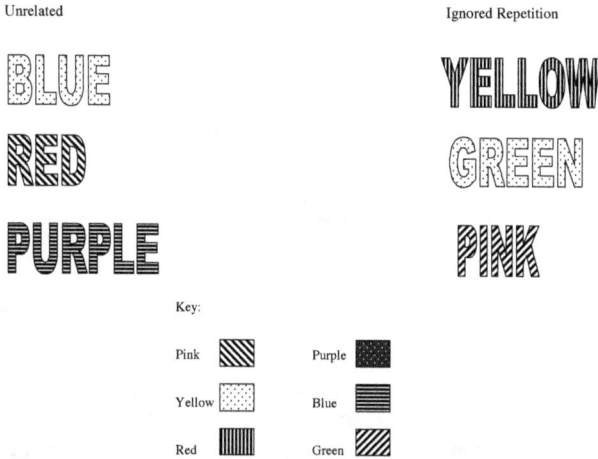

Unrelated   Ignored Repetition

BLUE   YELLOW

RED   GREEN

PURPLE   PINK

Key:

Pink   Purple

Yellow   Blue

Red   Green

Figure 1

Example of unrelated and ignored repetition trials.

Note: Children were asked to name the ink colour of the Stroop item in each column as quickly and accurately as possible from the top to the bottom of each card.

were presented in a vertical column of small squares on a 26 cm × 18 cm laminated card. This was done both as a test of colour vision and to ensure familiarity with the entire set of colour names used in the experiment. Participants were then verbally instructed to name as quickly and accurately as possible the colour of the ink that each word was printed in from the top to the bottom of the column on a card. They were asked not to stop if an error was made but to continue until the colour naming for the card was completed. Each participant encountered four UR practice cards before the commencement of test cards for the experiment. In the experiment proper, participants were given the 12 test cards (six per condition presented in alteration). For each card the experimenter said 'Ready' as a warning and on the word 'Go' a blank card covering the test card was removed and the stopwatch started. The stopwatch was stopped in synchrony with the naming of the last colour on a card. Error scores for each card were recorded and classified as either omissions or verbalisations of an incorrect colour.

Results

For each participant a mean response time per item (RT) was computed for the six cards representing the UR condition and the six cards representing the IR condition. Mean RTs and percentage of errors for the UR and IR conditions are shown for the three groups in Table 1.

A two-way mixed analysis of variance (ANOVA) was carried out on the mean RTs. The between-subjects variable was group (ADHD versus Creative versus Control) and the within-subjects variable was priming condition (UR versus IR).

Table 1

Mean Reaction Time in Milliseconds per Item and Percentage of Errors for Each Group Type as a Function of Priming Condition

	Group					
	ADHD		Highly Creative		Control	
	UR	IR	UR	IR	UR	IR
M	1436	1500	1122	1175	1089	1125
SD	423	410	315	354	286	255
ER (%)	5.9	6.9	3.2	4.1	3.5	3.7

The between-subjects variable of group was significant, $F(2, 87) = 10.57, p < .001$. In order to determine whether there were differences in the overall RTs between the groups, Newman-Keuls post hoc analyses were conducted. The results indicated that the ADHD group responded significantly more slowly than both the Creative and Control groups, ($ps < .001$), but there was no difference between the Creative and the Control groups. More critically, the within-subjects variable of priming condition (UR versus IR) was significant, $F(1, 87) = 6.74, p < .02$, and there was no hint of an interaction, $F < 1$. Participants responded slower on the IR trials than on the UR trials. The NP effect was thus similar across the three groups and was unrelated to overall processing speed. Additional support for the statistical outcome was evidenced in the percentage of participants showing NP effects in each group; 60% (ADHD), 63% (Creative), and 63 % (Control).

Similar analyses were conducted for error scores. The between-subjects variable of group (ADHD versus Creative versus Control) was significant, $F(2, 87) = 8.06, p < .001$. Newman-Keuls analyses indicated that the ADHD group made significantly more errors than the other two groups ($ps < .01$). No other error effects were significant. Because each of the three groups produced numerically more errors in the IR than the UR condition, there is no indication of speed-accuracy trade-offs that could compromise the RT analyses.

Discussion

The specific purpose of this study was to examine potential differences in NP effects between three distinct populations of children. With regard to earlier empirical discrepancies and ambiguities in studies with typical, ADHD, and highly creative children, results from our Stroop NP task revealed conceptual NP to be both significant and invariant between these groups. Children with ADHD, however, do appear to encounter significantly more Stroop interference than either creative or control children, as evidenced by their longer RTs in both UR and IR conditions. These findings make direct contributions to the existing literature on NP effects in children and may also have important implications for research concerned with ADHD. Contrary to the findings from previous studies by Marriott (1998) and Ozonoff et al. (1998) that failed to obtain significant NP effects in children with ADHD, results from our study showed that cognitive inhibitory capacity is intact in these individuals. Our results provide further empirical support for the similar findings reported by Gaultney et al. (1999). Taken together, the outcome of these later studies afford an opportunity to discuss potential sources of inhibitory processing in NP tasks, in contrast with other tasks commonly employed in testing children with ADHD. Much of the contemporary research literature on ADHD points to a widespread deficit in inhibitory function in individuals with ADHD. In accordance with this literature, researchers using the negative priming paradigm to investigate cognitive inhibition in children with ADHD have predicted, not unreasonably, that a deficit in cognitive inhibition may also underlie the symptoms of ADHD. Therefore, children with ADHD should present with a reduced NP effect. This is questionable on the basis of findings by Gaultney et al. (1999) and the current study, however. Instead, these studies seem to imply that NP may reflect a specific type of cognitive inhibition, one that may operate independently of other inhibitory processes deemed to play a pivotal role in prefrontal function.

Two typical tasks that have been used to assess inhibitory function in ADHD children are the go/no-go task and the stop-signal task. The go/no-go task taps behavioural inhibition, requiring either the execution or the inhibition of a response to a stimulus in a series of sequential trials depending on whether the stimulus has been previously specified as a 'go stimulus' or a 'no-go stimulus'. The stop signal task tends to rely on inhibitory control. Participants need to inhibit or interrupt a planned, but not yet initiated, response to the target stimulus presented on screen when a stop signal, either auditory or visual, is presented directly after the onset of the target stimulus. Hyperactive and ADHD children demonstrate impairments on both of these tasks, usually presenting with an increased rate of errors in comparison to typical children (Rubia et al., 1998; Vaidya et al., 1998). From our perspective, the type of inhibition that is implicated in the go/no-go task and the stop signal task are unlikely to relate to the distractor inhibition that may underlie NP effects. While children with ADHD demonstrate inhibitory impairment in the go/no-go and the stop signal tasks, they do not present with any evidence to suggest impairment in inhibitory processes underlying NP. There is also empirical evidence with adults to suggest that go/no-go tasks and NP tasks measure distinct types of inhibition. A study by Kramer, Humphery, Larish, Logan, and Strayer (1994), for example, found no correlation between NP effects and performance on the go/no-go task.

Although we found NP effects for ADHD children to be equivalent to those of highly creative and control children, the response latency for both UR and IR conditions of our Stroop NP task was significantly greater for ADHD children in comparison to the other two groups. Note that similar trends were found by Gaultney et al. (1999) for UR and IR priming conditions on both versions of their Stroop NP task for ADHD children relative to typical children. This difference between the groups reached statistical significance for the second version of their Stroop NP task. There is some debate as to whether the noted increase in response latency on the Stroop test for ADHD children relates to heightened susceptibility to distractor intrusion (see Harnishfeger & Bjorklund, 1994; Pennington & Ozonoff, 1996; Rucklidge & Tannock, 2002, for reviews). Given that we found intact NP effects for this group, the above conjecture loses some credibility, at least in the Stroop NP paradigm. Rucklidge and Tannock (2002) suggested that increased naming latencies for ADHD individuals may relate to an overall slowness in information processing and name retrieval rather than to interference effects associated with distractor intrusion. When comparing interference effects on the Stroop Colour and Word Naming test between adolescents with ADHD and age-matched controls, Rucklidge and Tannock found that in comparison to controls, while those with ADHD were slower to name colour words, colours, and incongruent colour-words, there were no group differences in interference scores. A more recent study by Pritchard, Neumann, and Rucklidge (in press) lends further empirical support to conjectures arising from findings in the current study and those by Rucklidge and Tannock (2002) regarding issues of Stroop interference and NP levels in ADHD individuals. Pritchard et al. (in press) used a similar technique to Rucklidge and Tannock to compare Stroop interference levels in addition to comparisons of NP effects between typical adolescents and those with ADHD. It was found that, while the ADHD group was consistently slower to name target stimuli in comparison to the typical group, there were no differences in interference or NP between the two groups. Increased response latencies in both conditions of the Stroop NP task in children with ADHD imply a possible maturational lag in some aspects of information processing. That is, the performance of 10- to 12-year-old children with ADHD on the Stroop negative priming task mirrors the performance of five to six year old children on the same task. A developmental study by Pritchard and Neumann (2004), found that while 5- and 6-year-old children produce similar magnitudes of NP to children between the ages of 8 and 12 years, overall response latencies for the younger children were significantly greater compared to those for the older children. Further research is clearly required to establish the nature of this maturational lag for children with ADHD, if indeed such a lag exists.

Our final goal was to test hypotheses concerning possible associations between creativity and cognitive inhibitory function. Recall that Stavridou and Furnham (1996) and Green and Williams (1999) suggested that compared with typical individuals, creative individuals may demonstrate a reduced NP effect. Results from our study failed to support this prediction, at least with children. Instead, our results imply that the inhibitory process implicated in the NP effect appears to be invariant across typical and creative children. Thus, the creative thought processes implicated in divergent thinking do not necessarily appear to be associated with a deficit in cognitive inhibitory capacity.

Toward Resolving Discrepancies

The specific reasons for the discrepancies between the results of the present experiment and others regarding NP effects with typical children and in children with ADHD are unclear. It is worth noting, however, that the contradictory results with atypical children emulate previous contradictions in NP studies with older adults, typical children, and Alzheimer's disease where early reports of inhibitory impairment are being supplanted by studies revealing intact and comparable NP effects in these individuals. A clear example of this trend is evident in the early developmental NP literature. While Tipper et al. (1989) failed to find significant NP effects for children between the ages of 7 and 8 years, Pritchard and Neumann (2004) found significant levels of NP in children as young as 5 years. A similar pattern exists in investigations of NP effects in older adults and patients with Alzheimer's (cf. Langley, Overmier, Knopman, & Prod'Homme, 1998; Sullivan et al., 1995; see also Gamboz, Russo, & Fox 2002). The specific reasons for discrepancies between the earlier and more recent studies in these domains remain unresolved.

Given the discrepancies that exist in the ADHD NP literature regarding the prevalence of this effect, however, it is suggested that NP effects in ADHD populations, like those in typical developmental populations, may be sensitive to variations in task design (see Pritchard & Neumann, 2004). Moreover, the typically small size of the NP effect coupled with a propensity for increased variability in ADHD individuals, or the use of too small sample sizes, might help explain the lack of NP in some of these studies. Buchner and Mayr (2004) provide a particularly cogent discussion on how these issues apply more generally to atypical populations engaged in NP tasks. What seems clear, however, is that generally impaired performance in attentional tasks is not necessarily associated with a deficit relating to the inhibition of irrelevant information during selection. Thus, impaired performance across a range of attentional tasks that require various sources of inhibition and resistance to distractor intrusion does not necessarily lead to decreased NP effects.

Cognitive Inhibition: A Rudimentary Information Processing Mechanism?

The negative priming paradigm offers a unique opportunity to investigate dedicated inhibitory mechanisms involved in the selection of relevant over irrelevant information. Findings from the current study support the contention that the inhibitory mechanism underpinning conceptual NP effects may be a basic or primitive processing resource (Neumann & DeSchepper, 1991, 1992). If so, negative priming effects may reflect a fundamental information processing mechanism inherent across a wide range of distinct populations and largely distinct from other processes implicated in reduced or enhanced cognitive performance. The failure to find any significant variability between the NP effects for three distinct populations of children supports the view that NP effects reflect the workings of a primitive and fundamental information processing mechanism which develops at an early age and is unlikely to become defective even in persons with known attentional deficits. Here the specific cognitive inhibitory mechanism implicated in NP does not appear to contribute to, or mediate, individual differences in cognitive performance. This is not to say that other specific inhibitory functions may not show declines in various populations. On a more theoretical note, if nontarget information in strong conflict with concurrent target information undergoes active inhibition, and the resulting suppression of irrelevant (or unwanted) items produces NP effects, then cognitive psychology's most influential general models of selective attention (Desimone & Duncan, 1995) and more particularly Stroop interference resolution (Cohen et al., 1990) should be questioned. Since these theories do not contain this type of inhibition-based processing in their frameworks, it is possible they are missing one of the key information processing mechanisms in the human repertoire (cf. Cohen, Dunbar, Barch, & Braver, 1997; Schooler, Neumann, Caplan, & Roberts, 1997a, 1997b).

Endnote

1   This did not hold for IR cards as the inclusion of one unrelated prime-probe couplet at the beginning of each IR card meant that one ink colour had to appear twice as a target to the exclusion of another. Consequently, whereas each control card had 11 different target colours to be named, an IR card had only 10 with one reappearing to be named for a second time so that the total number of target colours to be named was the same for both the control and IR cards. A supplementary control experiment using Stroop stimuli was conducted to determine whether any detrimental artefact could have emerged from presenting a duplicate colour only in the IR condition. Two conditions were assessed. Naming 11 unique colours once versus naming nine unique colours and one duplicate colour. The results from that experiment ruled out the possibility that including one duplicated target colour could yield a delay compared to cards with no duplicated target colours. Thus, it is unlikely that the interpretation of IR NP effects in the present experiment would be compromised by this potential artefact.

References

Akande, A. (1997). Creativity: The caregiver's secret weapon. *Early Childhood Development and Care, 143,* 89–101.

American Psychiatric Association. (2000). *Diagnostic and statistical manual of mental disorders* (4th ed.; Text rev.). Washington, DC: Author.

Barkley, R. A., Grodzinsky, G., & DuPaul, G. J. X. (1992). Frontal lobe functions in attention deficit disorder with and without hyperactivity: A review and research report. *Journal of Abnormal Child Psychology, 20,* 162–188.

Barkley, R. A. (1994). Impaired delayed responding: A unified theory of attention-deficit hyperactivity disorder. In D. K. Routh (Ed.), *Disruptive behavior disorder in childhood: Essays honouring Herbert C. Quay* (pp. 11–57). New York: Plenum Press.

Barkley, R. A. (1997). Behavioural inhibition, sustained attention, and executive function: Constructing a unifying theory of ADHD. *Psychological Bulletin, 121,* 65–94.

Barkley, R. A. (1998). *Attention-deficit hyperactivity disorder: A handbook for diagnosis and treatment* (2nd ed.). New York: Guilford Press.

Beech, A. R., Powell, T., McWilliam, J., & Claridge, G. S. (1989). Evidence of reduced 'cognitive inhibition' in schizophrenia. *British Journal of Clinical Psychology, 28,* 109–116.

Berman, T., Douglas, V. I., & Barr, R. G. (1999). Effects of methylphenidate on complex cognitive processing in attention-deficit/hyperactivity disorder. *Journal of Abnormal Child Psychology, 108*, 90–105.

Bogen, J. E., & Bogen, G. M. (1999). Split-brains: Interhemispheric exchange in creativity. In M. A. Runco & S. R. Pritzker (Eds.), *Encylopedia of creativity*. New York: Academic Press.

Buchner, A., & Steffens, M. C. (2001). Auditory negative priming in speeded reactions and temporal order judgements. *Quarterly Journal of Experimental Psychology, 14*, 27–48.

Buchner, A., & Mayr, S. (2004). Auditory negative priming in younger and older adults. *Quarterly Journal of Experimental Psychology, 57A*, 769–787.

Cohen, J. D., Dunbar, K. O., & McClelland, J. L. (1990). On the control of automatic processes: A parallel distributed processing account of the Stroop effect. *Psychological Review, 97*, 332–361.

Cohen, J. D., Dunbar, K. O., Barch, D. M., & Braver, T. S. (1997). Issues concerning relative speed of processing hypotheses, schizophrenic performance deficits, and prefrontal function: Comment on Schooler et al. (1997). *Journal of Experimental Psychology: General, 126*, 19–36.

Conway, A. R. A. (1999). The time-course of negative priming: Little evidence for episodic trace retrieval. *Memory & Cognition, 27*, 575–583.

Dalrymple-Alford, E. C., & Budayr, B. (1966). Examination of some aspects of the Stroop colour-word test. *Perceptual and Motor Skills, 23*, 1211–1214.

Desimone, R., & Duncan, J. (1995). Neural mechanisms of selective visual attention. *Annual Review of Neuroscience, 18*, 193–222.

Driver, J., & Tipper, S. P. (1989). On the nonselectivity of selective seeing: Contrasts between interference and priming in selective attention. *Journal of Experimental Psychology: Human Perception and Performance, 15*, 304–314.

DuBrin, A. J. (1994). *Applying psychology.* New York: Plenum.

Fuentes, L. J., Humphreys, G. W., Agis, I. F., Carmona, E., & Catena, A. (1998). Object-based perceptual grouping affects negative priming. *Journal of Experimental Psychology: Human Perception and Performance, 24*, 664–672.

Gamboz, N., Russo, R., & Fox, E. (2002). Age differences and the identity negative priming effect: An updated meta-analysis. *Psychology and Aging, 17*, 525–530.

Gaultney, J. F., Kipp, K., Weinstein, J., & McNeill, J. (1999). Inhibition and mental effort in attention deficit hyperactivity disorder. *Journal of Developmental and Physical Disabilities, 11*, 105–114.

Green, M. J., & Williams, L. M. (1999). Schizotypy and creativity as effects of reduced cognitive inhibition. *Personality and Individual Differences, 27*, 263–276.

Harnishfeger, K. K., & Bjorklund, D. F. (1994). A developmental perspective on individual differences in inhibition. *Learning and Individual Differences, 6*, 331–355.

Hart, E., Leahy, B. B., Loeber, R., Applegate, B., & Frick, P. J. (1995). Developmental change in attention-deficit hyperactivity disorder in boys: A four-year longitudinal study. *Journal of Abnormal Child Psychology, 23*, 729–749.

Hasher, L., Stoltzfus, E. R., Zacks, R. T., & Rypma, B. (1991). Age and inhibition. *Journal of Experimental Psychology: Learning, Memory and Cognition, 17*, 163–169.

Houghton, G., & Tipper, S. P. (1994). A model of inhibitory mechanisms in selective attention. In D. Dagenbach & T. Carr (Eds.), *Inhibitory mechanisms in attention, memory and language* (pp. 53–112). San Diego, CA: Academic Press.

Hughes, R., & Jones, D.M. (2003). A negative order-repetition priming effect: Inhibition of order in unattended order sequences? *Journal of Experimental Psychology: Human Perception and Performance, 29*, 199–218.

Hynd, G. W., Hern, K. L., Novey, E. S., Eliopulos, R. T., Marshall, R., Gonzalez, J. J., et al., K. K. (1993). Attention deficit-hyperactivity disorder and asymmetry of the caudate nucleus. *Journal of Child Neurology, 8*, 339–347.

Khurana, B. (2000). Not to be and then to be: Visual representation for ignored unfamiliar faces. *Journal of Experimental Psychology: Human Perception and Performance, 26*, 246–263.

Kramer, A. F., Humphrey, D. G., Larish, J. F., Logan, G. D., & Strayer, D. L. (1994). Aging and inhibition: Beyond a unitary view of inhibitory processing in attention. *Psychology and Aging, 9*, 491–512.

Kramer, A. F., & Strayer, D. L. (2001). Influence of stimulus repetition on negative priming. *Psychology and Aging, 16*, 580–587.

Langley, L. K., Overmier, J., B., Knopman, D. S., & Prod'Homme, M. M. (1998). Inhibition and habituation: Preserved mechanisms of attentional selection in aging and Alzheimer's disease. *Neuropsychology, 12*, 353–366.

Laplante, L., Everett, H., & Thomas, J. (1992). Inhibition through negative priming with Stroop stimuli in schizophrenia. *British Journal of Clinical Psychology, 31*, 307–326.

Lavie, N., & Fox, E. (2000). The role of perceptual load in negative priming. *Journal of Experimental Psychology: Human Perception and Performance, 26*, 1038–1052.

Marriott, M. (1998). *Selective attention, negative priming, and hyperactivity: Investigating the 'AD' in ADHD.* Unpublished doctoral dissertation, McMaster University, Canada.

McDowd, J. M., & Oseas-Kreger, D. M. (1991). Aging, inhibitory processes, and negative priming. *Journal of Gerontology: Psychological Sciences, 46B*, 340–345.

May, C. P., Kane, M. T., & Hasher, L. (1995). Determinants of negative priming. *Psychological Bulletin, 118*, 35–54.

Neill., W. T. (1997). Episodic retrieval in negative priming and repetition priming. *Journal of Experimental Psychology: Learning, Memory, and Cognition, 6*, 1291–1305.

Neill, W. T., & Mathis, K. M. (1998). Transfer-inappropriate processing: Negative priming and related phenomena. In D. L. Medlin (Ed.), *The psychology of learning and motivation: Advances in research and theory* (Vol. 38, pp. 1–44). San Diego, CA: Academic Press.

Neill, W. T., & Valdes, L. A. (1992). Persistence of negative priming: Steady state or decay. *Journal of Experimental Psychology: Learning, Memory, and Cognition, 18*, 565–576.

Neill, W. T., & Westberry, R. L. (1987). Selective attention and the suppression of cognitive noise. *Journal of Experimental Psychology: Learning, Memory, and Cognition, 13*, 327–334.

Neumann, E. (1999, October). *Ignored impossible 3D objects produce long-term negative priming: Evidence of structurally intact mental representations.* Poster presented at the 34th Annual Meeting of the Australian Psychological Society in Hobart, Tasmania.

Neumann, E., & DeSchepper, B. G. (1991). Costs and benefits of target activation and distractor inhibition in selective attention. *Journal of Experimental Psychology: Learning, Memory, and Cognition, 17*, 1136–1145.

Neumann, E., & DeSchepper, B. G. (1992). An inhibition based fan effect: Evidence for an active suppression mechanism in selective attention. *Canadian Journal of Psychology, 46*, 1–40.

Neumann, E., McCloskey, M. S., & Felio, A. C. (1999). Cross-language positive priming disappears, negative priming does not: Evidence for two sources of selective inhibition. *Memory and Cognition, 27*, 1051–1063.

Ozonoff, S., Strayer, D. L., McMahon, W. M., & Filloux, F. (1998). Inhibitory deficits in Tourette syndrome: A function of comorbidity and symptom severity. *Journal of Child Psychiatry, 39*, 1109–1118.

Parkhurst, H. B. (1999). Confusion, lack of consensus and the definition of creativity as a construct. *Journal of Creative Behaviour, 33*, 1–21.

Pearlman, C. (1983). A theoretical model for creativity. *Education, 103*, 294–305.

Pennington, B. F., & Ozonoff, S. (1996). Executive functions and developmental psychopathology. *Journal of Child Psychology and Psychiatry, 37*, 51–87.

Piirto, J. (1998). *Understanding those who create* (2nd ed.) Scottsdale, AZ: Gifted Psychology Press.

Pritchard, V. E., & Neumann, E. (2004). Negative priming effects in children engaged in nonspatial tasks: Evidence for early development of an intact inhibitory mechanism. *Developmental Psychology, 40*, 191–203.

Pritchard, V. E., Neumann, E., & Rucklidge, J. J. (in press). Interference and negative priming effects in adolescents with attention deficit hyperactivity disorder. *American Journal of Psychology.*

Quay, H. C. (1988). Attention deficit disorder and the behavioural inhibition systems: The relevance of the neuropsychological theory of Jeffrey A. Gray. In L. M. Bloomingdale & J. A. Sergeant (Eds.), *Attention deficit disorder: Criteria, cognition and intervention* (pp. 117–125). New York: Pergamon.

Roberts, R. J., & Pennington, B. F. (1996). An interactive framework for examining prefrontal cognitive processes. *Developmental Neuropsychology, 12*, 105–126.

Ross, R. G., Hommer, D., Breiger, D., Varley, C., & Radant, A. (1994). Eye movement task related to frontal lobe functioning in children with attention deficit disorder. *Journal of the American Academy of Child and Adolescent Psychiatry, 33*, 869–974.

Rucklidge, J. J., & Tannock, R. (2002). Neuropsychological profiles of adolescents with ADHD: Effects of reading difficulties and gender. *Journal of Child Psychology and Psychiatry, 43*, 988–1003.

Rubia, K., Oosterlaan, J., Sergeant, J .A., Brandeis, D., & Leeuwen, T. (1998). Inhibitory dysfunction in hyperactive boys. *Behavioural Brain Research, 94*, 25–32.

Schachar, R., & Logan, G. D. (1990). Impulsivity and inhibitory control in normal development and childhood psychopathology. *Developmental Psychology, 26*, 710–20.

Schooler, C., Neumann, E., Caplan, L. J., & Roberts, B. R. (1997a). A time course analysis of Stroop interference and facilitation: Comparing normal individuals and individuals with schizophrenia. *Journal of Experimental Psychology: General, 126*, 19–36.

Schooler, C., Neumann, E., Caplan, L. J., & Roberts, B. R. (1997b). Stroop theory, memory, and prefrontal cortical functioning: Reply to Cohen et al. (1997). *Journal of Experimental Psychology: General, 126*, 42–44.

Shader, R. I., Harmatz, J. S., Oesterheld, J. R., Parmalee, D. X., Sallee, F. R., & Greenblatt, D. J. (1999). Population pharmacokinetics of methylphenidate in children with attention-deficit/hyperactivity disorder. *Journal of Clinical Pharmacology, 39*, 775–785.

Stavridou, A., & Furnham, A. (1996). The relationship between psychoticism, trait-creativity and the attentional mechanism of cognitive inhibition. *Personality and Individual Differences, 21*, 143–153.

Stoltzfus, E. R., Hasher, L., Zacks, R. T., Ulivi, M. S., & Goldstein, D. (1993). Investigation of inhibition and interference in younger and older adults. *Journal of Gerontology, 48*, 179–188.

Strayer, C. D., & Grison, S. (1999). Negative priming is contingent on stimulus repetition. *Journal of Experimental Psychology: Human Perception and Performance, 25*, 24–38.

Sullivan, M. P., Faust, M. E., & Balota, D. A. (1995). Identity negative priming in older adults and individuals with dementia of the Alzheimer type. *Neuropsychology, 9*, 537–555.

Tannock, R. (1998). Attention deficit hyperactivity disorder: Advances in cognitive, neurobiological and genetic research. *Journal of Child Psychology and Psychiatry, 39*, 65–99.

Tipper, S. P. (1985). The negative priming effect: Inhibitory effects of ignored primes. *Quarterly Journal of Experimental Psychology, 37A*, 571–590.

Tipper, S. P. (2001). Does negative priming reflect inhibitory mechanisms? A review and integration of conflicting views. *Quarterly Journal of Experimental Psychology, 54*, 321–345.

Tipper, S. P. (1991). Less attentional selectivity as a result of declining inhibition in older adults. *Bulletin of the Psychonomic Society, 29*, 45–47.

Tipper, S. P., & Baylis. G. C. (1987). Individual differences in selective attention: The relation of priming and interference to cognitive failure. *Personality and Individual Differences, 8*, 667–675.

Tipper, S. P., Bourque, T. A., Anderson, S. H., & Brehaut, J. C. (1989). Mechanisms of attention: A developmental study. *Journal of Experimental Child Psychology, 48*, 353–378.

Tipper. S. P., & Cranston, M. (1985). Selective attention and priming: Inhibitory and facilitatory effects of ignored primes. *Quarterly Journal of Experimental Psychology, 37A*, 591–611.

Torrance, E. P. (1962). *Thinking creatively with pictures: Figural booklet A*. Bensenville, IL: Scholastic Testing Service

Treisman, A., & DeSchepper, B. G. (1996). Object tokens, attention, and visual memory. In I. Inui & J. McClelland (Eds.), *Attention and performance XVI: Information integration in perception and communication* (pp. 15–46). Cambridge, MA: MIT Press.

Vaidya, C. J., Austin, G., Kirkorian, G., Ridlehuber, H. W., Desmond, J. E., Glover, G. H., et al. (1998). Selective effects of methylphenidate in attention deficit hyperactivity disorder: A functional magnetic resonance study. *Neurobiology, 95*, 14494–14499.

Wong, K. F. E. (2000). Dissociative prime-probe contextual similarity effects on negative priming and repetition priming: A challenge to episodic retrieval as a unified account of negative priming. *Journal of Experimental psychology: Learning, Memory, and Cognition, 26*, 1411–1422.

Part 4

Theoretical Insights and Future Challenges

Elements of an Evolved Conceptual Framework

Steve Stewart-Williams, John V. Podd, and Stephen R. Hill

It is sometimes suggested that the ways in which people carve up the flow of their experience — that is, people's conceptual frameworks — are shaped largely by general mechanisms of concept formation, or by the categories made available to them by their language or culture. However, there are good reasons to suppose that certain basic conceptual distinctions have an evolutionary origin, and that the tendency to make these distinctions contributed to the persistence of the genetic material contributing to that tendency. The goal of this chapter is to sketch a speculative outline of the basic categorical framework of human experience, and to summarise relevant evidence for the universality, innateness, and evolutionary function of the elements in this framework. Among the most fundamental elements of the proposed framework are the distinction between self and not self, and the concept of *physical object*. These elements underlie people's basic perceptual representation of the world. Other suggested components include the distinction between animate and inanimate, and that between human and nonhuman. These distinctions may be tied to characteristic affective and cognitive responses that helped to solve adaptive challenges faced by our ancestors. Finally, it is argued that the capacity to frame mentalist concepts has an evolutionary origin. Taken together, these elements constitute an intuitive ontology, and form the skeletal structure of human phenomenology.

Concepts, Innateness, and Evolutionary Theory

Concepts are among the most important elements of theories of the mind. One of the major tasks facing concept theorists is to provide an account of the origin of our concepts. Discussion of this issue traces back at least as far as the empiricist–rationalist debate in the 17th and 18th centuries. Roughly speaking, the empiricists argued that all concepts derive from experience, whereas the rationalists argued that some concepts are innate. Until recently, there has been no naturalistic account of the origin of any innate mental content. As a result, naturalistically oriented thinkers have tended to shy away from anything resembling the rationalist position. As various commentators have recognised, however, Darwin's theory of evolution by natural selection radically changed the landscape in regard to the question of innate mental content (Lorenz, 1982; Plotkin, 1993). Especially important is the fact that the theory provides a naturalistic account of the origin of any innate conceptual content.

One of the key changes ushered in by an evolutionary perspective concerns the subject matter of any such content. Among the innate ideas suggested by the rationalists were such notions as the concept of God (Descartes, 1641/1986). However, in the wake of evolutionary theory, the innate conceptual divisions one would expect to find, if any, concern more mundane adaptive challenges. The context of these challenges is not the modern environment. For most of the period of our evolution, hominids lived as hunter-gatherers in the African savannah. It is only around 10,000 years since humans began inventing radically different ways of life. This is a mere blink of an eye in evolutionary terms, and it is unlikely that complex adaptations have changed a great deal in that time (Tooby & Cosmides, 1992). As such, it is the challenges associated with the hunter-gatherer lifestyle of our ancestors that are most likely to be reflected in any innate conceptual content. Among the most important adaptive challenges were obtaining suitable food, predator avoidance, reproduction, parenting, helping kin, and cooperating with non-kin (Buss, 2004).

The present analysis is based on inclusive fitness theory, or the genes' eye-view of evolution (Dawkins, 1982; Hamilton, 1964; Williams, 1966). According to this view, phenotypic features are not selected because they are advantageous to the species, to the group, or even to the individual organisms bearing those features. They are selected if they are advantageous to the genes giving rise to them, where this advantage is defined in terms of the replication rate of those genes relative to competing versions of the same genes (competing alleles). The implication of this perspective for the present topic are that if any concept or conceptual distinction is a product of evolutionary selection, each stage in the cumulative shaping of that distinction was presumably advantageous to the genes contributing to it, because it enhanced individual fitness and/or the fitness of kin.

The Distinction Between Self and Not Self

Arguably, the most fundamental distinction in people's representation of the world is that between self and not self. The self is the referent of terms such as *I* and *me*. However, though people may not be aware of this, these terms are used in different ways at different times. Sometimes the body is construed as part of the self ('that hit me'), whereas at other times it is construed as distinct from the self ('that hit my body'). In the following, we limit ourselves to the former definition, that is, the self as the whole organism. The first task, then, is to explain why a tendency to partition the world into the-organism-that-is-me vs. everything else might have an evolutionary origin. There is an obvious clue in the fact that the organism is an important unit in evolution. In humans and most sexually reproducing species, the replication success of the genes in any particular genome depends primarily on the survival and reproductive success of the organism in which that genome is found. As such, there would be a selective advantage in a tendency to distinguish self from not self, coupled with motivational dispositions that guide voluntary behaviour that typically promotes the interests of the self.

The conscious concept of self may be a product of a general selection pressure to create boundaries distinguishing the organism from the rest of the environment. As Dennett (1991) has pointed out, 'if you are setting out to preserve yourself, you don't want to squander effort trying to preserve the whole world: you draw the line. You become, in a word, *selfish*' (p. 174). Non-conscious analogues of the self–other distinction can be seen in various products of natural selection. This includes the immune system, which attacks entities it encounters that are 'categorised' as not self. (Autoimmune disorders involve mistakenly categorising aspects of self as not self.) Similarly, the self–other distinction is implicit in the fact that animals usually only eat parts of the environment other than themselves. For organisms with simple and relatively inflexible patterns of action, there is presumably no conscious understanding of this distinction. Instead, their hardwired patterns of behaviour simply lead them to act *as if* they possessed such an understanding. However, the same selection pressures that shaped these behaviours, and shaped the immune system, may also have given rise in some lineages to a conscious understanding of the self–other distinction.[1] The concept of self may therefore be one example of a wider biological phenomenon, of which the immune system and other adaptations are also examples.

Why might a conscious understanding of the self–other distinction be evolutionarily useful, and what might it achieve that the implicit understanding could not? To answer this question, it may be useful to consider the characteristics of conscious mental processing in general. Conscious awareness is most strongly associated with the execution of novel and unpractised behaviours; well-practised and habitual behaviours tend not to occupy the spotlight of consciousness. If consciousness in general is associated with novel behaviour, it seems reasonable to suppose that the biological function of a conscious understanding of the self–other distinction relates to novel behaviour. This distinction may be an evolutionarily crucial ingredient in the formulation of any new behavioural plan. Though such plans are not directly innate, the disposition to distinguish self from other may be.

But what evidence is there that this conceptual distinction is innate? An initial precondition for its innateness would be that the self–other distinction is universal across cultures. It might be argued, however, that this is not the case. According to the Buddhist teaching of 'No self' (anātman), for example, the self–other distinction is an illusion. But the denial of the reality of self provides no evidence that the concept is not universal. After all, to deny the concept, one must first possess the concept. So, the doctrine of anātman does not eliminate the possibility that the concept of self is universal. Another objection might be that the concept of the individual self is a product of individualistic western culture, and that the idea that it is universal simply betrays an ethnocentric bias. According to social psychologists, cultures vary on a continuum spanning from individualism to collectivism (Hofstede & Hofstede, 2005). In individualistic cultures, people typically put the individual above the group, but in collectivist cultures, people put a greater premium on the group. But this is another red herring. The individualism–collectivism dimension relates to the value people in different cultures officially attach to the individual versus the group (on average); it is not a question of whether or not they divide the world into individuals. Certainly, people sometimes construe themselves as components of more inclusive entities (e.g., the family, the group or nation, the biosphere), but this is not inconsistent with the notion that they possess the self–other distinction also.

Nonetheless, even if it is accepted that the concept of self is universal among human cultures, this does not necessarily mean it is innate. The universality of the distinction may reflect the fact that it is just too obvious to miss. The body is the only part of the universe that is directly controllable by the mind/brain, and is the only part of the universe from which the mind/brain receives sensory input concerning contact with other objects, temperature, and so on. This may make the boundaries of the self so obvious that no innate contribution is required beyond the basic design of the sensory-motor apparatus and an ability to form concepts. As plausible as this argument might sound, there is evidence to suggest that the tendency to distinguish self from not self is something over and above an awareness of sensory input from the periphery. Certain brain lesions can result in the sense that parts of an individual's body are no longer parts of that individual, despite the fact that the individual is still fully aware of these parts. According to Melzack (1992):

> Patients who have suffered a lesion of the parietal lobe in one hemisphere have been known to push one of their own legs out of a hospital bed because they were convinced it belonged to a stranger. Such behavior shows that the damaged area normally imparts a signal that says, 'This is my body; it is a part of my self'. (p. 93)

That the awareness of self in humans can be selectively impaired suggests that distinguishing between self and not self is something that the brain has specifically evolved to do. That is, there is reason to believe that the concept of self has an evolutionary origin.

The Object Concept

Another plausible element of the evolved conceptual framework of *Homo sapiens* is the concept of *object*. Like the self–other distinction, this concept is fundamental to people's experience of the world. The application of the object concept involves grouping some sensations into wholes, while excluding others. However, it also goes beyond simply putting borders around portions of the sensory landscape. It incorporates the assumption that identified wholes persist through time, and continue to exist even when beyond the range of the senses (what Piaget called *object permanence*). Spelke (1990) explicated some of the other assumptions that people make about objects. Her suggestions have a *prima facie* plausibility, and include (a) continuity: objects occupy connected paths in space and time; (b) solidity: two objects cannot occupy the same portion of space simultaneously or pass through one another intact; and (c) no action-at-a-distance: objects only affect one another if they collide or otherwise make contact with one another.

Various commentators have suggested that the object concept has an evolutionary origin (Jackendoff, 1987; Leslie, 1994). As Campbell and Paller (1989) remarked, 'The perceptual reification of independent objects ... will have been naturally selected for the usefulness available when stable discreteness, manipulability, and reoccurrence are typical' (p. 239). There are several ways that an understanding of objects could contribute to adaptive behaviour. First, an understanding of the solidity of objects allows us to weave our way efficiently around impenetrable portions of the environment, such as trees, rocks, and other people. Second, the ability to predict the future motion of objects allows us to take anticipatory action, such as moving to avoid a collision with a rapidly approaching object. Third, an understanding of objects allows us to manipulate the environment to satisfy evolved needs and motivations, for example, guiding certain objects into our mouths for nutritional purposes. Finally, the understanding that objects persist beyond the range of the senses underpins various adaptive activities (Stewart-Williams, 2003). For example, a predator without this understanding would stop pursuing its prey the instant it slipped from view.

There are various reasons to accept that the object concept has an evolutionary origin. First, Leibniz claimed that language is the window to the mind and, as such, universal aspects of language may reveal universal aspects of the human mind. All languages have words for objects (Dixon, 1977). In fact, across cultures, objects are among the most common concepts that words label (Brown, 1991). Beyond this, Spelke (1991) has suggested that continuity and solidity are assumptions found in all humans. An understanding of object permanence has also been experimentally demonstrated in other species, including dogs and nonhuman apes (Wynne, 2001). The presence of the object concept in other animals militates against the idea that this concept is just an artefact of certain human languages, and is acquired when people acquire such a language. It seems more likely that it is the other way around: The object concept provides basic perceptual units that serve as a necessary foundation for the acquisition of language.

Suggestive empirical evidence for the innate origin of the object concept comes from research in developmental cognitive psychology that shows that infants' understanding of objects is remarkably similar to that of adults. For example, ingenious experiments by researchers such as Baillargeon and Spelke have demonstrated that infants as young as $3^{1}/2$ months represent the continued existence and continued motion of objects hidden from view (Baillargeon, 1999; Carey & Spelke, 1994). Spelke (1990) has also shown that infants expect objects to be cohesive and solid. The fact that some basic components of the object concept emerge as young as 3 or 4 months is not conclusive proof of innateness. Nonetheless, it does make it considerably less plausible that the concept is acquired solely from experience. At the very least, the evidence is consistent with the view that the object concept has an evolutionary origin.

Animal and Non-Animal

There is reason, then, to believe that human beings have been 'designed' by natural selection to construe the external world in terms of objects in space (one of which is them). Among these objects, certain important distinctions are drawn, and some of these are plausible candidates for evolved tendencies of cognition. One area in which such distinctions might be found is the biological domain. Various possibilities could be suggested here, including the tendency to distinguish between biological and non-biological entities; to divide the former group into plants and animals; and to divide plants and animals into species. In this section, we focus on the distinction that we consider most plausibly traced to evolutionary selection: that between animal and non-animal, or between animate and inanimate entities. There are grounds for believing that humans are specialised for the rapid detection of animals, including one another, from among the objects in their environment, and to attend preferentially to these parts of the environment. These are discussed more fully in the next section. The basic idea, though, is that animate agents generally have greater evolutionary relevance (e.g., are more useful or more dangerous) than are inanimate objects.

Many aspects of the basic object concept apply to animals and non-animals. For example, members of both categories are solid, and move on connected tracks through space and time. There are also differences, though, one of the most important being that, whereas inanimate objects only move when external forces act on them, animals exhibit unpredictable, self-generated motion. There is widespread agreement that such motion is one of the key criteria by which animals are distinguished from non-animals (Heider & Simmel, 1944; Leslie, 1994; Premack, 1990). In addition, like many other animals, humans may be specialised to identify and attend to patterns that have a vertical axis of symmetry (Dennett, 1991). This pattern is biologically important because it tends to indicate, first, that another animal is present, and second, that it may be facing you and observing you. The abstract concept of animate being, rather than being directly innate, may emerge from simple innate pattern detectors such as these, in conjunction with general mechanisms of concept formation.

If the animate concept can be traced to innate aspects of the human mind, it should be found in all human cultures. Consistent with this prediction, there is evidence that the concept is a semantic universal (Wierzbicka, 1992). But is it really the same concept across cultures? The American linguist Benjamin Whorf (1956) suggested that, although the Hopi Indians of Arizona distinguish between animate and inanimate, they place items such as clouds and stones in the animate category. This may seem to undermine the notion that they possess the same conception of animacy as is common in the West. However, Whorf's conclusion is highly suspect. It stemmed from an analysis of the grammatical structure of the Hopi language, but the same method would lead to conclusions such as that French people believe that tables are female and all cats are male (Yule, 1996). In any case, there is no claim that any evolved conceptual division will always be uniformly deployed. As long as familiar, local animals are universally classed as animate, it is no threat to an evolutionary account that the concept is sometimes also extended somewhat beyond this. Indeed, there are grounds to expect that, when in doubt, people will tend to err on the side of assuming that stimuli are animate rather than inanimate. For obvious reasons, it is less costly in fitness terms to mistake a vine for a snake than it is to mistake a snake for a vine. Therefore, the prevalence of animistic and anthropomorphic thinking in belief systems is no threat to an evolutionary account of the animate–inanimate distinction. Indeed, it makes good sense from an evolutionary psychological perspective.

Human and Non-Human

Just as the concept of object can be divided into animals and non-animals, the concept of animal can be divided into humans and non-humans. The human–non-human distinction is deep seated, and implicit in various psychological tendencies. For example, people fear negative evaluation almost exclusively by members of their own species. To illustrate: People may feel self-conscious when observed by a crowd of people, but they are unlikely to feel self-conscious in the presence of, say, a flock of seagulls. Some evidence suggests that there is an innate contribution to the human–non-human distinction, and to people's typical responses to entities assigned to each category. The concept of human is a semantic universal (Wierzbicka, 1992), and from a very young age, infants can distinguish members of their own species from others (Morton & Johnson, 1991). There are also good reasons to think that natural selection would favour this capacity. People's species-typical relationships with other humans differ markedly from those they have with members of other species, in ways that have clear evolutionary relevance. Some non-humans are potential predators and prey. In contrast, some humans are potential mates, others are kin, and others still are friends, allies, leaders, and subordinates. Some are also rivals for mates and status. If these different relationships have an evolutionary origin, they presumably rest on an innate tendency to distinguish humans from other animals, and on innate patterns of response to entities categorised as one or the other.

The capacity to distinguish members of one's own species (conspecifics) from others is widespread in the animal kingdom. This ability can be related to a number of adaptive tasks, including mating, feeding, and predator avoidance. From an evolutionary perspective, sexual behaviour is most usefully confined to members of one's own species. The fact that there is occasional cross-species sexual interaction does not invalidate this claim; the vast majority of sexual acts throughout the animal kingdom are within-species. The ability to distinguish conspecifics from others also relates to the adaptive challenge of feeding, and is particularly relevant to species that eat meat. Eating members of one's own species carries a greater risk than eating members of other species, due to the danger of picking up species-specific parasites. Ruse and Wilson (1986) hypothesised that repugnance towards cannibalism is likely to be a species-typical adaptation. Again, cannibalism in humans is not unheard of, but it is relatively rare. For reasons such as these, it is plausible that selection would equip people with a tendency to distinguish conspecifics from non-conspecifics.

Mind

So far, the focus has been on concrete entities, such as objects, animals, and conspecifics. These concepts may be found in many other species. One set of concepts that may be largely unique to humans is mentalist concepts. As the ability to mentally represent the environment evolves in a lineage, a new entity arrives in that environment: representations themselves. These are then available for organisms to track. Most species appear not to have taken this 'option'. However, one of the distinguishing features of Homo sapiens is the ability to represent representations, an ability known as 'theory of mind' (ToM). Various theorists have suggested that the human brain is specialised for thinking about minds (Baron-Cohen, 1995; Frith, 1989; Leslie, 1994; Premack & Woodruff, 1978). According to this view, the belief–desire model of mind and behaviour is not a cultural product. Instead, people are innately disposed to construe others as possessing conscious mental states, such as beliefs, desires, and intentions, and to explain voluntary behaviour in terms of constructs such as these.

The presence of ToM may only become apparent when one encounters someone in whom it is absent. A number of researchers have suggested that ToM is absent or poorly developed in people with autism (Baron-Cohen, 1995; Frith, 1989; Leslie, 1992). An important component of ToM is the understanding that other people's beliefs can differ from one's own, and that beliefs can be false. In most people, the understanding of false beliefs develops by about 4 or 5 years of age (Leslie, 1994). However, autistic children continue to find it difficult or impossible to understand that others can have false beliefs. It is thought that such problems might contribute to autistic symptoms such as deficits in social interaction and communication. Baron-Cohen (1995) coined the term mindblindness to describe this aspect of autism. Autistic people are not completely mindblind; they may be better described as mind-myopic (Badcock, 2000). In contrast, most animals are probably mindblind, although some of our close relatives, such as chimpanzees, may instead be mind-myopic (Premack & Woodruff, 1978; Whiten, 2001).[2]

A number of suggestions have been made concerning the evolutionary function of ToM. One view is that the capacity to represent the motivations, intentions, and beliefs of others allows people to predict others' behaviour (Baron-Cohen, 1995; Leslie, 1994). Understanding that others have belief states and intentions also seems to be part-and-parcel of the capacity to comprehend and successfully use language. Another social skill that characterises human beings is purposeful deception (Byrne & Whiten, 1988; Humphrey, 1988). Deception involves shaping false beliefs in others, and purposeful deception presupposes an understanding that beliefs may be false. Employed in the service of evolved motivations, the ability to deceive would enjoy a selective advantage. It would also create selection pressure for ToM itself; after all, not only does the ability to understand beliefs and intentions make deception possible, but it can also help to defend against deception. Finally, in addition to understanding conspecifics, ToM may have helped our ancestors to understand and predict the behaviour of other animals, including predators and prey (Mithen, 1996).

What evidence and arguments are there that the ability to frame mentalist concepts has an innate basis? First, it might be possible to invoke a 'poverty-of-the-stimulus' argument to show that such concepts are probably not derived solely from personal experience. In principle, people could interpret behaviour (their own included) in infinitely many ways. However, no-one spontaneously interprets behaviour in, say, the non-mentalist terms of the early behaviourists. It is sometimes commented that, when 'off duty', even radical behaviourists do not explain behaviour in such terms (Dennett, 1991). Across cultures, people (including off-duty behaviourists) appear to explain behaviour in terms of desires, beliefs, and intentions. Wierzbicka (1992) noted that in all languages there are words for such mentalist terms as think, know, feel, and want (although see Astington, 1993). Similarly, Brown (1991) reported that people in all cultures 'have a concept of the person in the psychological sense ... They understand the concept of intention. They know that people have a private inner life ... can feel pain and other emotions' (p. 135). He also noted that, across cultures, people use language to deceive, a talent that implies an understanding that other people may possess false beliefs. Furthermore, there is research suggesting that the timing of ToM's development in children is similar across cultures. For example, an understanding of false beliefs develops at around four or five years not only in western children but in Pygmy children as well (Avis & Harris, 1991). This is consistent with the view that ToM is the product of an evolved developmental timetable, and is a universal aspect of normal human development. So, the situation appears to be this: The belief-desire model is only one possible interpretation of the evidence, but in every culture, people seem to arrive at this interpretation. This argues that ToM has an evolutionary origin.

However, perhaps we are being too hasty in rejecting the possibility that ToM could be wrested from experience. People do not directly observe mental states in others, but perhaps it could be argued that they observe them in themselves and extend them to others by analogy. This suggestion might initially sound plausible — but only if one maintains a narrow focus on just one species: our own. Adopting a cross-species perspective, it becomes apparent that, for the vast majority of species, four or five years of experience of their own mental states does not lead to the acquisition of ToM. Therefore, something must distinguish humans from most other animals in this respect. It might be responded that human brains are not necessarily specialised for this task. The ability to identify mental states within ourselves and extend them to others might just be an offshoot of a greater general intelligence found in humans. But this proposal does not square well with evidence that autistic children have a relatively selective loss of abilities (Baron-Cohen, 1995). That the ability to represent representations is impaired in people with autism, while some cognitive abilities remain largely intact, argues that ToM is not simply an offshoot of a general intelligence, or language ability, or anything else, but is instead a specific competency with identifiable seats in the brain.

Summary

William James (1978) once suggested that the categories of common sense were a discovery of our distant ancestors, presumably passed on via cultural transmission. We have argued that some of these categories were instead 'discoveries' of natural selection, and that their presence in our distant ancestors helps to explain the fact that these individuals *were* our ancestors. There are an infinite number of ways to divide up and categorise experience. If experience itself provided the only guidance people had in this task, one would not expect the inter-individual and cross-cultural commonalities found in people's conceptual frameworks. It would also be a notable coincidence that these frameworks make such sense in evolutionary terms. Taken together, the evidence and arguments suggest that the conceptual framework underlying people's experience of the world is not derived solely from experience. Instead, some elements appear to have their origin in the evolutionary history of the species.

Endnotes

1   It is reported that mystics and people using hallucinogenic drugs sometimes have the experience that there is no distinction between themselves and external objects. In evolutionary terms, this perception is functionally equivalent to an immune disorder. Both involve the failure of a mechanism involved in distinguishing self from not self.

2   These terms are relative, of course. Humans would be considered mind-myopic by an intelligent being with a more formidable intuitive psychology than our own.

Acknowledgments

This article was supported by a Bright Future Top-Achiever Doctoral Scholarship, administered to the first author by the Foundation for Research, Science, and Technology (FRST), New Zealand. Thanks go to James Battye for valuable input and challenges.

References

Astington, J. W. (1993). *The child's discovery of mind*. Cambridge, MA: Harvard University Press.

Avis, J., & Harris, P. L. (1991). Belief-desire reasoning among Baka children: Evidence for a universal conception of mind. *Child Development, 62*, 460–467.

Badcock, C. (2000). *Evolutionary psychology: A critical introduction*. Cambridge, UK: Polity Press.

Baillargeon, R. (1999). The object concept revisited: New directions in the investigation of infant's physical knowledge. In E. Margolis & S. Laurence (Eds.), *Concepts: Core readings* (pp. 571–612). Cambridge, MA: MIT Press.

Baron-Cohen, S. (1995). *Mindblindness: An essay on autism and theory of mind*. Cambridge, MA: MIT Press.

Brown, D. E. (1991). *Human universals*. New York: McGraw-Hill.

Buss, D. M. (2004). *Evolutionary psychology: The new science of the mind* (2nd ed.). Needham Heights, MA: Allyn & Bacon.

Byrne, R. W., & Whiten, A. (Eds.). (1988). *Machiavellian intelligence: Social expertise and the evolution of intellect in monkeys, apes, and humans*. Oxford: Clarendon Press.

Campbell, D. T., & Paller, B. T. (1989). Extending evolutionary epistemology to 'justifying' scientific beliefs (a sociological rapprochement with a fallibilist perceptual foundationalism?). In K. Hahlweg & C. A. Hooker (Eds.), *Issues in evolutionary epistemology* (pp. 231–257). Albany, NY: State University of New York Press.

Carey, S., & Spelke, E. (1994). Domain-specific knowledge and conceptual change. In L. A. Hirschfeld & S. A. Gelman (Eds.), *Mapping the mind: Domain specificity in cognition and culture* (pp. 169–200). New York: Cambridge University Press.

Dawkins, R. (1982). *The extended phenotype: The long reach of the gene* (Rev. ed.). Oxford: Oxford University Press.

Dennett, D. C. (1991). *Consciousness explained*. New York: Little, Brown.

Descartes, R. (1986). *Meditations on first philosophy* (J. Cottingham, Trans.). Cambridge: Cambridge University Press. (Original work published 1641)

Dixon, R. M. W. (1977). Where have all the adjectives gone? *Studies in Language, 1*, 19–80.

Frith, U. (1989). *Autism: Explaining the enigma*. Oxford: Blackwell.

Hamilton, W. D. (1964). The genetical evolution of social behaviour: I & II. *Journal of Theoretical Biology, 7*, 1–52.

Heider, R., & Simmel, M. (1944). An experimental study of apparent behavior. *American Journal of Psychology, 57*, 243–259.

Hofstede, G., & Hofstede, G. J. (2005). *Cultures and organizations: Software of the mind* (2nd ed.). New York: McGraw Hill.

Humphrey, N. K. (1988). The social function of intellect. In R. W. Byrne & A. Whiten (Eds.), *Machiavellian intelligence: Social expertise and the evolution of intellect in monkeys, apes, and humans* (pp. 13–26). Oxford: Clarendon Press.

Jackendoff, R. S. (1987). *Consciousness and the computational mind*. Cambridge, MA: MIT Press.

James, W. (1978). *Pragmatism: A new name for some old ways of thinking. The meaning of truth: A sequel to pragmatism*. Cambridge, MA: Harvard University Press.

Leslie, A. M. (1992). Pretense, autism, and the theory-of-mind module. *Current Directions in Psychological Science, 1*, 18–21.

Leslie, A. M. (1994). ToMM, ToBy, and Agency: Core architecture and domain specificity. In L. A. Hirschfeld & S. A. Gelman (Eds.), *Mapping the mind: Domain specificity in cognition and culture* (pp. 119–148). New York: Cambridge University Press.

Lorenz, K. (1982). Kant's doctrine of the a priori in the light of contemporary biology. In H. C. Plotkin (Ed.), *Learning, development, and culture: Essays in evolutionary epistemology* (pp. 121–143). Chichester, UK: Wiley.

Melzack, R. (1992, April). Phantom limbs. *Scientific American, 271*, 90–96.

Mithen, S. J. (1996). *The prehistory of the mind: The cognitive origins of art, religion, and science*. London: Thames & Hudson.

Morton, J., & Johnson, M. H. (1991). CONSPEC and CONLERN: A two-process theory of infant face recognition. *Psychological Review, 98*, 164–181.

Plotkin, H. C. (1993). *Darwin machines and the nature of knowledge*. Cambridge, MA: Harvard University Press.

Premack, D. (1990). The infant's theory of self-propelled objects. *Cognition, 36*, 1–16.

Premack, D., & Woodruff, G. (1978). Does the chimpanzee have a theory of mind? *Behavioral and Brain Sciences, 1*, 515–526.

Ruse, M., & Wilson, E. O. (1986). Moral philosophy as applied science. *Philosophy, 61*, 173–192.

Spelke, E. S. (1990). Principles of object perception. *Cognitive Science, 14*, 29–56.

Stewart-Williams, S. (2003). Darwin and Descartes' demon: On the possible evolutionary origin of belief in an external world. *Evolution and Cognition, 9*, 123–130.

Tooby, J., & Cosmides, L. (1992). The psychological foundations of culture. In J. H. Barkow, L. Cosmides, & J. Tooby (Eds.), *The adapted mind: Evolutionary psychology and the generation of culture* (pp. 19–136). New York: Oxford University Press.

Whiten, A. (2001). Theory of mind in non-verbal apes: Conceptual issues and the critical experiments. In D. M. Walsh (Ed.), *Naturalism, evolution, and mind* (pp. 199–223). Cambridge: Cambridge University Press.

Whorf, B. L. (1956). *Language, thought, and reality: Selected writings of Benjamin Lee Whorf*. Cambridge, MA: MIT Press.

Wierzbicka, A. (1992). *Semantics, culture, and cognition*. Oxford: Oxford University Press.

Williams, G. C. (1966). *Adaptation and natural selection: A critique of some current evolutionary thought*. Princeton, NJ: Princeton University Press.

Wynne, C. D. L. (2001). *Animal cognition: The mental lives of animals*. Basingstoke, UK: Palgrave.

Yule, G. (1996). *The study of language* (2nd ed.). Cambridge: Cambridge University Press.

Chapter

16

The Chinese Room
and Thinking Machines

Peter Jackson

The debate on thinking machines, originating with Alan Turing (Turing, 1950; Leiber, 2006), has been going on for around 6 decades. In 1980 John Searle (1980a) published a seminal paper consisting of a thought experiment which has become known as the Chinese Room Experiment (CRE) from which he derived a syllogism, his Chinese Room Argument (CRA). In the 25 years since Searle's original paper, the debate has progressed through many twists and turns of argument, counterargument and rebuttal. Over the course of the quarter of a century the original CRE has evolved in subtlety, and ideas have arisen and fallen by the wayside. However, across this span of 25 years, Searle's CRE with its defining syllogism has remained essentially unchanged. After a brief review of Alan Turing's work, this chapter reviews the unfolding of this remarkable debate over its past 25-year history. A chronological sequence allows the reader to note the progression of ideas as they lead to the current state of play in the debate. The main purpose of the chapter is to show that Searle's CRE, with its CRA, is valid and has yet to be successfully refuted. That is, the weak artificial intelligence (AI) hypothesis (computers cannot think) remains the valid view and awaits undermining by the strong AI view (computers can think). A secondary purpose is to demonstrate that this longstanding debate may have run its course, leaving little of further novelty or value to be added.

A useful point of departure for examining the debate is Alan Turing's proposal for a logical computing machine (LCM), later to become known as a Universal Turing Machine. This machine was, in essence, the precursor of the modern stored-program computer. It was based on the notion of a tape containing coded instructions. In this way, the same basic hardware could perform a range of tasks for which there was an existing algorithm and a feasible solution. The origins of Turing's LCM concept lay in the work that he (contemporaneously, with Alonzo Church: Church, 1936) did on replacing informal effective methods with a formally exact predicate calculus (Turing, 1936; Leiber, 2006).

In his paper in *Mind* (Turing, 1950), Turing's proposed a *Gedankenexperiment* that he called an imitation game. In this game, initially, a judge had to decide of two hidden respondents, which was the male and which the female. Part way through this game, Turing replaced one human with a logical computing machine, where the judge's task changes to that of deciding which is the human and which the machine. Where the judge was unable to differentiate between human and machine, the machine was deemed to have passed what has gone down in AI history as the 'Turing Test'. In his Mind paper, Turing was convinced that by the 21st century, machines would be able to think. His conviction gave rise to what Searle (1980a) defined as the strong AI hypothesis. Tragically, unable to live with the judgments of his era in regard to homosexuality, Turing took his life on June 7, 1954 (Leiber, 2006).

Searle and the Chinese Room

The Turing Test (and more recent versions of it — see below), coupled with the strong AI hypothesis provided the basis for the ongoing debate within AI and the philosophy of mind on whether machines can, or ever will think. From the 1950s the focus was on the technology underpinning AI, and remarkable advances were made in terms of hardware and software. In this technological phase, the philosophical debate took a back seat. However, in the late 1960s and early 1970s, the technological platforms for AI had reached a stage where some (cf. Minsky & Papert, 1969) claimed that AI machines either could already think, or soon would: the 'strong AI view'. Such claims caught the attention of Searle (1980a) who proposed his Gedankenexperiment (i.e., the CRE) to refute the strong AI hypothesis, taking the stance that, while AI machines can and do emulate human thinking, they do not in fact think. This came to be known as the 'weak AI hypothesis'. From the thought experiment, Searle derived the CRA which has acquired the status of one of the most widely debated arguments in the philosophy of mind (Harnad, 1991). It takes the form of a syllogism:

- Computers operate on syntax.
- Thought is semantical.
- Syntax does not produce semantics.
- Therefore, computers do not think.

The original CRE consisted of a non-Chinese-speaking person (Searle himself) sitting in a room with a long list of rules for translating strings of Chinese characters into new strings of Chinese characters. When a string of characters is slipped under the door, the person consults the rules and slips back an appropriate response under the door. If the incoming strings actually represented questions (as in a Turing Test), then a particularly cleverly contrived and exhaustive set of rules could conceivably allow the person in the room to produce outgoing strings that furnished answers to the questions. From the point of view of a person outside, the room would seem to contain an intelligent Chinese-speaking person who is responding to the questions. But the person in the room has no understanding of the content of these questions (he/she has no understanding of the Chinese language) — and is merely acting out a set of rules, translating one set of random symbols into another. It could, just as well, be an AI machine in the room, and not a person.

The strong AI position argues that an appropriately programmed computer has a mind, in the sense that computers, given the right programs, can be said to understand and have other cognitive states. This is also known as the computationalist argument. Thus, strong AI argues that the programs are themselves the cause of mind in the machine (Searle, 1980a). Searle's CRE aims to show that, although the 'Room' appears to have an understanding of the Chinese Language and is evidencing thought processes, no such thing is actually happening. The 'Room' is not thinking, nor does it possess intelligence. It is simply following a set of instructions in just the way that a stored program machine is doing.

Searle is willing to consider that an AI machine might pass the Turing Test, but considers that it will not think or possess intentionality, two attributes he considers central.[1]

Objections and Rebuttals

Various objections were put forward to rebut Searle's stand during the drafting of his article (Searle, 1980a) while he discussed his thought experiment with a number of AI workers. In his article he responds to each objection. Searle categorised these as:

- **Systems:** In this objection, it is suggested that the non-Chinese speaker is only a part of the system, where the whole system does understand the strings of Chinese characters. That is, it is false to claim that the entire system does not think and understand simply because one component (the human in this case) does not. This objection is linked to a related objection known as the Virtual Mind objection. In this linked objection, it is argued that the 'mind' that understands is not identical to the human in the system. That is, this objection is distinguishing between mind and the system hardware that hosts it.

- **Robot:** This objection arises from the view that the person in the Chinese Room is prevented from understanding by a lack of sensori-motor connection with the reality that the Chinese characters represent. The idea here is to put the Chinese Room into a robot that has sensori-motor capabilities, which impart perception and locomotion, hence engagement with reality.

- **Brain simulator:** The argument in this objection is that the 'program' implemented by the person in the Room simulates the actual sequence of neuron firings at the synapses of the Chinese speaker who receives the outputs from the Room. Thus, at the synaptic level of neuronal firing, there is no difference between the 'program' in the Chinese Room, and the program in the Chinese reader's brain. This being so, then the 'Room' has just as much understanding as the Chinese reader.

- **Combination:** In this objection, it is supposed that the Chinese Room is lodged in a robot, which is running a brain simulation program. In this, it is argued that now we would have to ascribe intentionality to the entire system, in that the whole behaves indistinguishably from a human.

- **Other minds:** This objection arises out of the consideration that we know that others have minds (and so think) by inferring this from their behaviour. Thus, if one can legitimately attribute cognition to humans based on their behaviour, then one is required to do the same in the case of the Chinese Room.

- **Many mansions:** This objection suggests other means than programming in order to confer intentionality and cognition on the Chinese Room. The implication is that these other means are non-computational.

Searle responded to each of the objections in turn. The rebuttals can be summarised as follows:

- **Systems rebuttal:** Searle responds by imagining himself to internalise all the elements of the system, by memorising the instructions, and so on. However, he still understands nothing of the Chinese language and neither does the system.

- **Robot rebuttal:** Searle replies that the addition of such perceptual and motor capacities adds nothing in the way of understanding. He imagines himself in the room inside the robot, computationally acting as the robot's homunculus. He argues that by instantiating the program he has no intentional states of the relevant type (to the Chinese language).

- **Brain simulator rebuttal:** Searle replies, that even getting close to the operation of the brain is still not sufficient to produce understanding. He envisages a system of valves and water pipes that simulate the neuronal structure of the Chinese reader, such that instead of manipulating pieces of paper, the person in the Room operates the valves, where each water connection corresponds to a synapse in the Chinese Reader's brain. Searle argues that the person still has no understanding of the Chinese Language, and nor have the valves and pipes. The key word for Searle seems to be 'simulator', in that this is all the system does: simulate intentionality and thought. This harks back to the debate about Turing's Test, which, in this author's view, is a behavioural test only.

- **Combination rebuttal:** Searle replies — in effect — three times nil is still nil. He does concede that it is tempting to attribute intentionality to the robot-combination if we do not know how it works. However, Searle argues, once we can account for the behaviour of the combination, then we cannot attribute intentionality to it. That is, we now know what is occurring inside the Room and so must concede that there is no intentionality, nor thinking nor understanding, despite appearances.

- **Other minds rebuttal:** Searle dismisses this as an epistemological worry beside his metaphysical point. 'The problem in this discussion,' he says, 'is not about how I know that other people have cognitive states. But rather what it is that I am attributing to them when I attribute cognitive states' and 'it couldn't be just computational processes and their outputs because the computational processes and their outputs can exist without the cognitive state' (Searle, 1980a, pp. 421–422).

- **Many mansions rebuttal:** Searle replies that this 'trivialises the project of strong AI by redefining it as whatever artificially produces and explains cognition' (Searle, 1980a, p. 422). In conclusion, Searle advances his own thought that the brain must produce intentionality by some non-computational means which are 'as likely to be as causally dependent on ... specific biochemistry ... as lactation, photosynthesis, or any other biological phenomenon' (p. 424).

Searle's original paper (Searle, 1980a) explains that he has not offered a proof that computers are not conscious. Rather, the proof is to show that computational operations by themselves, that is, formal symbol manipulations by themselves are not sufficient to guarantee the presence of consciousness. Symbol manipulations are defined in abstract syntactical terms, and syntax by itself has no mental content, conscious or otherwise. Furthermore, the abstract symbols have no powers to cause consciousness because they have no causal powers at all. All the causal powers are in the physical system as a medium. A particular medium in which a program is implemented, a brain for example, might independently have causal powers to cause consciousness. However, the operation of the program has to be defined totally independently of the medium since the definition of the program is purely formal and thus allows implementation in any medium whatever.

In a companion article (Searle, 1980b), Searle expands on his CRA, the objections to it, and the rebuttals. He elucidates the distinction between intrinsic intentionality and observer-relative ascriptions of intentionality, defining the former as the kind of intentionality that we humans have and the latter as the ways we have of talking about machines or similar entities that lack intrinsic intentionality. Searle argues that we cannot attribute intrinsic intentionality to machines (e.g., carburetors and thermostats) because machines do not possess beliefs, whereas humans do. He also argues that the fact that he cannot explain how the brain works to possess intrinsic intentionality is not grounds for dismissing his view. No one can yet explain it, but this does not alter the fact that people possess intrinsic intentionality. While not subscribing to some 'numinous Cartesian glow' (Rorty, 1980),[2] Searle argues that mental states are not dispositions in the sense that temperature responsiveness is a material disposition of a thermostat. He says that mental states cannot be explained in terms of dispositions as they are 'made' of qualia and partake of ontological subjectivity.

Searle explored these arguments further still in the book *Mind, Brains and Science* (Searle, 1984). In chapter 2, 'Can Machines Think?', he argues that his Chinese Room is a refutation of the strong AI view that 'mind is to brain what program is to computer'. In his book, Searle states his axiomatic premises in this way:

1. Brains cause minds.
2. Minds have mental contents; specifically, they have semantic content.
3. Syntax is not sufficient for semantics.[3]

4. Computer programs are entirely defined by their formal, or syntactical, structure.

5. Therefore, computer programs are not minds nor can they give rise to minds.

As follows from these premises and their conclusion:

- No computer program by itself is sufficient to give a system a mind.

Programs, in short, are not minds; they are not by themselves sufficient for having minds.

- The way that the brain functions to cause minds cannot be solely by virtue of running a computer program.
- Anything else that caused minds would have to have causal powers at least equivalent to those of the brain.
- For any artifact that we might build which had mental states equivalent to human mental states, the implementation of a computer program would not by itself be sufficient. Rather, the artifact would have to have powers equivalent to the powers of the human brain.

Responding to counter-arguments, Searle has actively continued the debate (Searle, 1984, 1990, 1991, 1997). The following sections summarise key proposals of some contributors since Searle's 1980 paper.

The Strong AI Position

Dennett (1988, 1990, 1995), a firm believer in strong AI, was an early opponent of Searle's weak AI view. Dennett was convinced that not only could AI machines think, they were already doing so. He often cited IBM's Deep Blue computer that took part in the series of chess games with the grand master Kasparov in the 1990s. Dennett argued that a suitably programmed AI machine would have a mind, and therefore could think. For Dennett, the flaw in Searle's CRA syllogism lays in the fact that programs contain both syntactical and semantical content.

Hauser (1997) rejects Searle's CRA and describes it as an *ignoratio elenchi* (a logical fallacy that argues beside the point, reaching a conclusion that is irrelevant to the proof that was attempted). He regards the CRA as sophistry (a plausible but fallacious argument). He also accuses Searle of an *ad hominem* (personal rather than logical) appeal. Finally, he regards the CRA as logically and scientifically a dud, having mainly historical interest, which survives only as a sociological phenomenon. However, part of the strength of Hauser's arguments is that he chooses to see AI as synonymous with thinking. This is similar to Turing's original ideas in that Turing didn't distinguish between intelligence and thought. This seems fallacious, in that intelligent behaviour doesn't imply thought or thinking. After all, many mammals display intelligent behaviour in acting in a problem-solving and adaptive way. The debate engaged in by Searle is about thinking machines, not machines that exhibit intelligent behaviour. Most would agree that modern AI systems behave in an intelligent fashion. The Turing test is a test of intelligent behaviour (or at least the simulation of such behaviour). But, the key thing is that intelligent behaviour is not synonymous with thinking.

Hauser categorises the various arguments within the debate as follows:

- Possible AI (PAI): the claim that computers will one day think.

- Actual AI (AAI): the claim that computers already do think.

- Essential AI (EAI): this is computationalism in which program is identified with mind, where the claim is that anything that computes entails thinking. It is what Searle calls strong AI.

The first two above are, collectively, AI proper. Hauser distinguishes the above three claims from epistemological or methodological claims that programs explain human cognition (calling these latter claims 'cognitivism').

With regard to Searle's syllogism, Hauser chose (for purposes of further analysis) to rephrase the argument. Searle's original formulation is contrasted by italics:

1. Programs are formal (syntactical). *Computers operate on syntax.*

2. Minds have mental contents (semantical). *Thought is semantical.*

3. Syntax by itself is neither constitutive nor sufficient for minds. *Syntax does not produce semantics.*

4. Therefore, programs are neither constitutive of, nor sufficient for, minds. *Therefore, computers do not think.*

Although, on the face of it, Hauser's version seems to amount to what Searle gave us, there are differences. Axiom 1 is pretty much as Searle intended. In the case of Axiom 2, there is a departure, in that Searle was talking specifically of thought and not mental content. Some mental content is not normally associated with semantics (for example, imagery or the flow of rhythm in a musician's mind). Axiom 3 is quite a radical departure in that Hauser is bringing in minds (Searle did not, at this point). The conclusion, thus, departs from Searle's; it does not refer to thinking.

For this author, Hauser's reconstituted syllogism lacks the clarity of Searle's, and may fall into a circularity trap depending on what Hauser meant by mental content. Aside from those issues, Hauser argues that his rephrased syllogism's point is to show that you cannot get the mental content from syntax alone. He claims that it is not at all obvious that existing AI systems do not have causal powers equivalent to brains. It begs the question against AAI to assume computers lack these powers. He views the argument as little better than claiming: 'Human brains cause mental states'; 'No digital computers are human brains', therefore, 'No digital computers cause mental states'. He explores the notion of equivalence, looking at what it means for something to have the causal equivalence to a human brain. Does it mean having the equivalent brainpower? Is it equivalent to behave 'as if', or does it require true possession of equivalent mental powers?

In this context, the issue of hierarchical levels of 'mental powers' arises. Searle has argued that many species display intentional actions, yet lack intentionality.

According to Hauser, we don't know what features of human brains determine their mental capacities. Searle has suggested that intentionality (hence mental powers) is dependent on biochemistry. But, this, in itself, doesn't disconfirm AI proper. For Hauser, Searle seems to be arguing that it is a certain kind of chemistry (X) that leads to intentionality. Thus, any nonhuman system lacking X lacks intentionality.

Hauser regards Searle's arguments as sophistry, in that Searle classes what Hauser has dubbed essential AI ('Turing Machine functionalism' as Searle had called it) as strong AI while, in the same breath, contrasting strong AI to the thesis that computers merely simulate the mental abilities that they seem to manifest (called weak AI by Searle). This author finds it hard to see the sophistry of Searle's argument. Essential AI (computationalism by Hauser's term) is clearly what Searle is talking about in his definition of Strong AI (that computers can think). There is no falsity then in claiming that this is in contradistinction to what Searle is calling weak AI (computers do not think). Besides, Hauser believes that, in part, AI's detractors are motivated by a fear of thinking machines (as raised in one of the objections to Turing's ideas). Turing held that those who regarded thinking machines as too dreadful were likely to be intellectuals, since they value the power of thinking and regard Man (sic) as superior. Among such intelligentsia, Hauser argues, are those who say that computers can think but don't.

Hauser gives what he terms a bare-bones version of Searle's syllogism[4] as follows:

1. If instantiating a right program R is a sufficient condition for understanding Chinese, then anything that instantiates R understands Chinese.
2. While in the Chinese Room, Searle himself instantiates R but fails to understand Chinese.
3. Instantiating a right program is *not* a sufficient condition for understanding Chinese.

Hauser relies on arguments about the inability of a human to process the card shuffling fast enough to pass the Turing Test, to dispute the conclusion (3) above. However, the CRA does not entail a speed of response criterion, only that, to someone outside the room, there appears to be someone in the room who understands Chinese. Searle does not appear to have mentioned a speed criterion. Hauser also argues that by internalising the rules (cf. premise 2 above), Searle would become cognisant of the meanings of the symbols. He further argues that one would understand unconsciously. In this, Hauser distinguishes between seeming to oneself to not understand and to really not understanding. He accuses Searle of a Cartesian identification of thought with private experience, with its corollary of private access, saying that privileging the first person fatally biases the CRA. However, there is no circular argument entailed in the CRE, which attempts to demonstrate that third-person competence is not sufficient for content attribution and that the first-person perspective is always relevant to such attributions. In raising the conscious-unconscious distinction above, Hauser himself is invoking a form of Cartesianism. Searle seems to have argued adequately that one cannot ignore the first-person subjectivity issue when considering intentionality and cognitive processes, as these relate to thought in any structure, organic or otherwise.

Hardware Dependence or Independence?

Reber (1997) accepts that Searle's CRA is correct in its essentials, but claims it does not go far enough, believing that the CRA runs afoul of the problem of emergentism.[5] Unfortunately, Reber does not clarify exactly which way the CRA runs afoul. The CRA itself does not rely on any emergent properties. There is no claim of understanding of Chinese arising from simple rules. Quite the reverse; the whole point of the CRA is to show that no such understanding arises nor is needed, even though it appears that the 'Chinese Room' does so understand.

Reber says that an interesting feature of AI is that the program is what counts, not the device on which it runs. This has been termed the 'hardware independence assumption'. No-one has ever argued that the computer used to run existing AI programs is, itself, an intelligent entity. Both strong and weak AI share the hardware independence assumption. However, strong AI claims that a properly programmed machine will exhibit subjectivity, be conscious and have mental states. That is, strong AI goes far beyond claims that an appropriately programmed machine can simulate various forms of complex behaviour, claiming that such an entity really does have a mind. Weak AI has had success in constructing useful models of human cognitive functioning, whereas strong AI has had no such success. One reason that Reber puts forward is that some people seem insecure at the thought that our precious mental capacity could be merely the carrying out of a program. Another reason comes from those who feel that the concepts of strong AI are fundamentally wrong: deeply flawed. Reber argues that this belief is the basis of Searle's approach in his CRA, which he regards as the strongest assault on strong AI.

Reber discusses the revised CRA, in which the room and all of its operations are instantiated in a human operator that Reber calls Maxine. He points out that Maxine is simply following a set of syntactic computational guidelines, satisfying the linguistic constraints of the Chinese language. In this sense, Maxine qualifies as an AI device and would pass the original Turing Test (TT) and perhaps even TTT.[6] However, she lacks understanding and true intelligence. She is likewise bereft of qualia, mental content, and semantic content. In essence, she lacks consciousness. Reber claims that the CRA is against the root assumption of hardware independence, showing that, instead, the system is extremely hardware-dependent. In fact, mind is hardware-dependent, being the property of certain classes of organic matter organised in a certain way. Reber argues that Searle (and any other opponent of the strong AI claim) has not taken this line of reasoning far enough: has not taken it to its logical conclusion. Searle, Reber claims, began to approach that view at the end of his 1980 article, where he said that strong AI told us little about machines since it was only about programs. True mental states, argues

Searle, are products of biological machines, not of mere programs. These properties of organic systems are not explicable simply by providing a formal instantiation of the processes that underlie them. They are inherent, intrinsic features of organic systems such as brains. While these systems may follow a set of instructions that can be instantiated as formal programs, they are not equivalent to the organic systems, and the carrying out of these programs is not equivalent to the carrying out of the biological functions of organic systems.

Advocates of the strong AI position are convinced that mind emerges from programs; that is, 'run the right program and mentation will appear' (here, Reber appears to be equating 'mentation' with 'mind' — this is not strictly valid in that strong AI refers to mind). Searle argues that this position is fundamentally flawed, that consciousness and other mental experiences are intimately tied not to a program but to a particular device that just happens to have consciousness as one of its emergent properties, and the brain is one such device. Reber points out that, in a sense, this raises more questions than it answers; especially, it prompts the question 'how does consciousness emerge from brains'? The seductive thing about strong AI is that, if correct, the problem of mind becomes much easier to solve. Reber states that we don't have a clue as to how mind can emerge from a brain. However, he believes that we have been asking the wrong question. The error has been to focus on the human brain and wonder how mind is produced in it. Reber proposes that phenomenal experience is an inherent property of all living organic forms. It does not emerge only when the structure gets as complex as a human brain. It is there all along. Philosophers have worried mainly about human consciousness. Reber argues that we no more have to worry about how consciousness emerges from a brain than we have to worry about how gravity emerges from mass.

What Reber pinpoints as the major problem with current theories of the origins of consciousness is that they are 'hoist by the petard of emergentism'; they 'require a miracle'. He argues that his proposal of some kind of inherent arch-consciousness in all living organisms sidesteps the emergentist problem, and avoids going down the dualist path that Chalmers (1996) feels we must travel. However, Reber admits that his proposal, although avoiding having to explain how complex biological structures give rise to consciousness, still needs to wrestle with the issue of how organic systems of varying complexity permit the evolution of systems of varying richness. He feels that the solution to this problem will not come easily.

Syntax, Semantics and Physics

Teng (2000) is generally in support of Searle's CRA and analyses it within a cognitive model based on schemas and metaphors with the notion of conceptual blending. Teng focuses on Searle's assertion that syntax is not intrinsic to physics, and argues that the assertion is a modified version of the original CRA. Strong AI claims that implementing the right program is sufficient for having a mind. That is, cognition is computation, which is a purely syntactical set of operations.

As seen earlier, in the refuting of this claim, Searle's CRA has three steps:
1. Programs are entirely syntactical.
2. Minds have a semantics.
3. Syntax is not the same as, nor by itself sufficient for, semantics.

Therefore, programs are not minds (Searle, 1990, 1997).

Teng argues that the CRE amounts to a blending of a number of cross-domain mappings. The generic space is the physical system capable of manipulating the symbols on the basis of their syntactical features, according to defined procedures. The source space is the person who understands English, but not Chinese. The target space is the computer for manipulating the Chinese characters. This is based on the computer-as-person metaphor, where Teng concludes that this metaphor does not understand Chinese solely on the basis of implementing the right program. Teng then looks at the 'syntax-is-not-physics' argument of Searle, using the cognitive modelling as above in relation to the CRE. However, Teng may be misapplying this argument, because, in the context of his 'syntax-is-not-physics' assertion, Searle was not invoking the CRA or CRE specifically (cf. Searle, 1990). He was dealing purely with digital machines in relation to their physical construction. Nonetheless, Teng correctly states that a computer operates on physical patterns without 'knowing' that these physical patterns are symbols of some language. These patterns are merely physical patterns, which suggests (as Searle argues) that syntax is not intrinsic to physics. This being the case, computation, algorithms and programs are not intrinsic to physical systems. They are notions assigned relative to observers and users.

Teng (2000) also deals with the debate between Chalmers (1994) and Searle, in which Chalmers argues that the CRE 'fails to respect' the role of implementation. According to Chalmers, implementation requires that the system have the right causal power built into it. The CRA does not rule out the possibility that semantics can arise from implementing the right program. Searle argues back that programs are purely syntactic and observer-relative. The issue for Searle is that of physical systems that are capable of having a mind. Brain processes bring about mental states, and since programs are observer-relative, there is no such thing as programs involved in the operations of brains that give rise to the basic features of minds. For Searle, the first-person point of view is essential to understanding a language. As the CRE lacks such a viewpoint, it cannot judge for itself whether or not it understands Chinese. It does not matter whether a brain or other physical system carries out the implementation, as long as the right causal dynamic is secured, in that cognitive systems have the right mental properties by virtue of their causal organisation.

Issues of Essentialism and Determinacy

Wakefield (2003) reminds us that Searle's CRA aims at refuting computationalism, hence strong AI. He believes that many will consider CRA to be refuted. As presented by Searle, CRA is a question-begging (where the evidence given for a proposition contains the proposition itself) appeal to intuition, in that it relies on faulty intuitions. Wakefield discusses the systems objection and Searle's rebuttal, in which the person in the Chinese Room instantiates the room; that is, the operator in the room *is* the system. The challenge then, for strong AI, is to demonstrate that the operator understands Chinese, because the operator instantiates the same program as a native Chinese speaker. Wakefield points out that Searle argues that instantiating the right program cannot be what confers understanding, because the operator has no such understanding despite instantiating the right program.

In his original article (1980a), in response to the 'Systems' reply, Searle instantiated the room within the operator, so that the operator internalises all the elements of the CRE. She memorises the rules in the ledger and the database of Chinese symbols, and does all of the calculations in her head. There isn't anything to the system that she does not encompass. Searle says that we can even get rid of the room and suppose that the person works outdoors. However, she still understands nothing of Chinese; thus, neither does the system. Wakefield points out that, in a republication of his original article (Searle, 1991), Searle amended the scenario, so that the process admits input sequences of sounds rather than written symbols. Rather than getting an input sequence of Chinese characters, the operator listens directly to the speaker and utters the Chinese responses herself. With practice, the operator can become flawless in her responses, so that there is no noticeable difference between her responses and those of a fluent Chinese speaker.

Wakefield argues that Block's (1998) objection to Searle's revised rebuttal stands or falls on Block's ability to draw a relevant distinction between the program's and the operator's meaning within a computationalist account of meaning. However, Searle's argument is subtler than Block allows. The program in the CRE exists as thoughts in the mind of the operator. Thus, for computationalism, the operator and program must possess the same content. As the operator understands only in a syntactic fashion (without meaning), the program cannot understand Chinese. If implemented syntax constitutes semantic content, then, because the operator does not understand Chinese, neither does the program. Wakefield asserts that Block is trying to imply a multiple personality condition, distinguishing between operator and program states. However, there is nothing in the CRE that might cause a difference in syntactic steps between program and operator. If computationalism is correct, there is no way for the program to understand Chinese unless the operator possesses the same understanding. Wakefield cites Fodor (1991), who accepts that the CRE 'does not understand' Chinese. However, Fodor argues that the program would understand Chinese without the intervention of the operator, because introducing the operator has rendered the implemented system non-equivalent to the original program of the Chinese speaker. Searle assumes that introducing the operator preserves Turing-machine equivalence. Fodor is challenging this assumption, in that transitions between program steps are not direct and involve further mediation (conscious, deliberate actions); that is, these mediating steps are part of the program. Hence, the program is not equivalent to programs lacking such mediating steps. Fodor argues thus because he claims that a transition from one state to the next is not directly and proximally caused by the prior state.

In Wakefield's view, Searle held that introducing causal relations did not affect the CRE because, whatever caused the inputs, the processing of symbols could still proceed without any understanding of the semantic content of the symbols. Searle also argued that the introduction of conscious implementation of the program by the operator did not cause the system to become a non-Turing machine. The operator is still following the program steps. In fact, conscious implementation ensures that one step is directly caused by another (Fodor's requirement). As Wakefield points out, in any case, the crucial issue is whether the operator understands the arriving sentences and not the causal relation to the emitter of these sentences. Also, because the modified CRE internalises the entire program within the operator, she is directly receiving input, is internally implementing all program steps involved in understanding the input, and is directly responding herself. Thus, the new CRE eliminates any causal chain deviance.

Wakefield turns to Hauser's (1997) argument about unconscious understanding, in which Hauser claims that, although he accepts that the operator does not consciously understand Chinese, she does unconsciously understand Chinese and has unconscious Chinese semantic content. As Wakefield reports, Searle, in relation to the unconsciousness argument, says that a person cannot have an 'unconscious understanding' unless, at least in principle, the content could become conscious (Searle, 1991). In case of the CRE, any first-person report of unconscious content becoming conscious would reveal only syntactic descriptions and not semantic content. In any case, there is no need to postulate an unconscious understanding in order to explain the system. Wakefield argues that the critical question for strong AI and the CRE is whether the operator really understands Chinese. There is a distinction between being 'unaware' of content one actually possesses unconsciously and plain ignorance, in which one does not possess the content at all, either consciously or unconsciously. Wakefield says that the CRE yields the intuition that the operator does not understand Chinese, either consciously or unconsciously. The CRA uses this result to argue that computationalism cannot be true.

Wakefield introduces an essentialist objection to the CRA, which argues that the common pretheoretical intuition that the Chinese Room operator does not understand Chinese is not an appropriate reason for concluding that she does not in fact understand Chinese. Wakefield argues that computationalism is best considered as a theoretical claim about the essence of meaning. An essential description (e.g., 'whales are mammals') contrasts with an intuitive description ('whales are fish'). Computationalism holds that the essence of standard cases of human intentional content is the running of certain formal programs. Thus, if anything shares this essence it also has intentional content. For Wakefield, the CRE presents a non-standard human instance that possesses that essence but violates our pre-theoretical intuitions regarding the possession of intentional content. The computationalists claim that the CRE essentially shares the human essence of intentionality and thought, even though it is non-standard. But this demands that computationalists successfully explain intentional content in typical human thought in computationalist terms.

Wakefield holds that the CRA poses a threat to strong AI, if reframed as an indeterminacy argument. Strong AI holds that the operator's intentional states are determined simply by the program she follows. It is difficult to counter this without question-begging (that is, there is no genuine intentionality in virtue of formal programming alone). However, Wakefield offers an indeterminacy test. If the Chinese-understanding program leaves claimed intentional contents indeterminate in a way that genuine intentional contents are not indeterminate, then we can say with confidence that the program does not constitute intentional content. Basically, this shows that computationalism is unable to account for how anyone can ever understand Chinese, even in standard cases of human thought that intuitively are clear instances of genuine Chinese understanding. The issue is that there is a distinction between manipulating the syntactical elements of a language and actually understanding that language at a semantic level.

Wakefield cites Quine (1960), who claimed that semantical and intentional content remain indeterminate (that is, open to multiple, incompatible interpretations consistent with possible evidence) if the relevant evidence is limited to syntax. Wakefield adds that the computationalist claim that to think a certain semantic or intentional content is just to be in a certain syntactic state is mutually incompatible with the claim that all the operator's thoughts and actions relate only to the program's syntactic structures and transitions (as in the CRE). The indeterminacy lies, then, in the fact that, consistent with all the syntactic and programming evidence that strong AI claims to exhaust the evidence relevant to fixing content, a person who appears fluent in a language may be meaningfully using the language or may be merely implementing the states that are identified syntactically. Thus, there may not be any meaning to her utterances.

For each brain state with a syntactic structure S that would be interpreted by strong AI as a thought with content T, the person could have T or could have the thought 'syntactic structure S'. For example, someone might make the utterance: 'Please pass the salt' and intend the meaning of that request, or they may be following some program requesting to utter the sounds: 'Please pass the salt'. There is no evidence in the program itself that could distinguish which of these two interpretations is correct. The indeterminacy argument might go as follows:

- There are determinate meanings that distinguish between thoughts and intentions, and thoughts about syntactic shape. Thoughts dealing with syntactic shape are different from those that possess semantic content as expressed by those shapes.
- All syntactic facts underrepresent (hence leave indeterminate) the content of thoughts and intentions-in-action. The syntactic structure S is ambiguous

between the meaning M of S and the meaning the program specifies to be the syntactic structure of S.

• Thus, the thoughts and intention-in-action cannot be constituted by syntactic facts.

This argument provides the support needed for Searle's third premise. In the CRE, every sentence in Chinese (with its usual semantic content) is translated into a sentence about the syntax of the original sentence. In this context, the challenge for computationalism is: 'What makes it the case that people who in fact understand Chinese do have genuine semantic understanding and that they are not, like the operator in the CRE, merely manipulating syntax where meanings are unknown to them?' Any claims that the operator does understand Chinese demand that the claimant distinguish between that and ordinary understanding of Chinese, or at least explain why they are different. However, the indeterminacy approach concludes that computationalism cannot do this; computationalism does not adequately account for meaning.

The Current 'State of Play'

It may be worthwhile to summarise views of key authors who have entered this debate in recent years. A brief mention of three views will be made. Copeland (2002) provides a detailed overview of Searle's CRA, pointing out what he regards as its three antecedents. First, the 'Mill argument' (Bolton, 1998), a thought experiment of Gottfried Leibniz, in which he asks that we consider a machine that behaves in a way such that we can infer that it thinks. Second, Turing's paper in *Mind* (Turing, 1950), as discussed earlier in this chapter. Third, the functionalist's argument of the multiple realisability of mind, in which one argument (subsequently called the 'Chinese Nation argument') goes that if each person in the entire Chinese Nation acted as a specific neuron and was instructed to behave in a certain way, consciousness would arise.

Copeland concludes that Leibniz and Searle had similar intuitions about the systems they consider in their respective thought experiments, Leibniz' Mill and the Chinese Room. In both cases they consider a complex system composed of relatively simple operations, and note that it is impossible to see how understanding or consciousness could result. Copeland argues that these simple arguments do the service of highlighting serious problems we are facing in understanding 'meaning' and 'minds', and holds that the many issues raised by the Chinese Room argument will not be settled until there is a consensus about the nature of meaning, its relation to syntax, and about the nature of consciousness.

Harnad (2001) argues that the formulation of the CRA by Searle has misled us for these past decades in that it implies that non-computational bases of AI also fail to think. This author is not aware of Searle writing that computers will never think. However he was clear that the stored-program, von Neumann type of computer (a Turing LCM) could not think. Perhaps, in hindsight, the original axiom 'computers operate on syntax' could have been more precise in qualifying the term 'computer'. Obviously, an AI machine using a non-von Neumann platform, such as artificial neural networks, may have no dependence on either syntax or programs. As much as Harnad might deplore the deficiencies in the phrasing of the CRA, its focus was the computationalist argument that the right program led to thinking. This clarifies that a program, with its syntax, was what the CRA addressed, and the force of its logic remains as strong as ever.

Rapaport (2002) has introduced the notion of 'syntactic semantics' into the CRE/CRA debate, a notion he had researched for years (cf. Rapaport, 1988). He argues that a semantic domain can be considered as a new syntactic domain, thus requiring a further semantic domain to understand it. This makes it seem that the terms 'semantic' and 'syntactic' are context-dependent, hence mutable (a view that relativises the generally accepted definition of these terms, for example, in theoretical linguistics and computer science). One can confute the CRA by playing on this mutability. But this appears to circumvent the fact that, for Searle, and most others in the debate, it is semantics that has a special relationship to thinking, hence the claims of the CRA.

Recent contributions to this debate just reviewed convince this author that after a protracted investigation, there is little left for the opponents of Searle's CRA to attack. This is not to say that nothing truly novel will come to light. However, it is hard to see what form that might take in view of the range of arguments already considered.

As pointed out at the beginning of this chapter, the AI dispute began nearly 5 decades ago, and the Chinese Room debate, a more recent aspect of it (as provoked in 1980 by Searle) has been going for a quarter of a century. The plot has evolved during this time with the twists and turns of argument and counterargument. The CRE itself has evolved from a simple room with Searle sitting in it with a book of rules, where someone pushes slips of paper under the door, to a person standing freely out in the open, who can respond orally to verbal inputs, where the programming has been entirely internalised, and yet still does not understand Chinese. During a 25-year period the essence of the CRA survived many attacks. The earliest of the objections addressed within Searle's original seminal paper (Searle, 1980a) seem, in retrospect, somewhat naïve in the light of the increasing sophistication of later arguments. There has been a shift in subtlety and sophistication both on the part of the strong AI believers, and in the rebuttals; Searle has continued to defend his view successfully.

Despite the 'red herrings' of robots, homunculi, many mansions, syntax versus semantics, and syntax-free physics, the issue of intentionality has emerged as dominant. Searle continues to assert that thinking entails intentionality, and that intentionality arises only in biological systems. This does not rule out thinking AI machines based on some biological platform, but it does rule out the computationalists' argument that thinking in AI machines is hardware-independent. Reber's point is well made that consciousness, hence thought, appears to be an innate property of biological systems (Reber, 1997); in humans, it reaches sufficient organisational complexity to permit thought. If the proponents of strong AI wish to defend computationalism, they will need to demonstrate beyond further argument that intentionality (hence a mind) can arise out of running a program on some von Neumann-type machine. The intentionality targeted here is that defined by Searle as intrinsic, as opposed to the rather loose way of referring to machines having intentions. In this author's view, the gauntlet thrown down by Searle over a quarter of century ago is still there.

Endnotes

1   The original Turing Test (TT) evolved more recently (cf. Harnad, 1991) into a Total Turing Test (TTT) for indistinguishability of response including sensorimotor measures. A further refinement was suggested by Harnad which tested right down to the neuronal and molecular levels (TTTT).

2   Rorty questions Searle's claim that human mental phenomena are dependent on physico-chemical properties of the brain, arguing that this claim is a device for insuring that the 'secret' powers of the brain are pushed further and further out of sight every time a new brain model looks as though it might explain mental content.

3   Note that in this context, the term 'syntax' is used in a narrower sense, referring to the structure of statements in a computer program (as in computer science). It does not cover all variants of syntax investigated in theoretical linguistics.

4   Searle probably never produced such a syllogism. The 'bare-bones' version of Hauser's is a derivation from the CRA; it alters the syllogism to deal with the computationalist's argument that thought in a computer depends on instantiating the right program. Searle does not claim to instantiate the right program in the computationalist's sense. He fails to understand Chinese, and the 'right' program would understand Chinese.

5   Emergentism can be defined as a focus on the process of complex *pattern* formation from simpler *rules*; that which emerges is not predictable from the lower level rules (see the papers in Forrest, 1991). In the field of AI, proponents of strong AI imply that mind emerges from instantiating the right program, even though they may not use emergentist terminology.

6   As said earlier, the original Turing Test (TT) evolved into TTT and TTTT. See Endnote 1, and Harnad (1991).

References

Block, N. (1998). The philosophy of psychology: Classical computationalism. In A. C. Grayling (Ed.), *Philosophy 2: Further through the subject* (pp. 5–47). New York: Oxford University Press.

Bolton, M. B. (1998). Locke, Leibniz, and the logic of mechanism. *Journal of the History of Philosophy, 36*, 189–213.

Chalmers, D. (1994). On implementing a computation. *Minds and Machines, 4*, 391–402.

Chalmers, D. (1996). *The conscious mind: In search of a fundamental theory.* Oxford: Oxford University Press.

Church, A. (1936). An unsolvable problem in elementary number theory. *American Journal of Mathematics, 58*, 345–363.

Copeland, J. (2002). The Chinese Room from a logical point of view. In J. Preston & M. Bishop (Eds.), *Views into the Chinese Room: New essays on Searle and artificial intelligence* (pp. 109–122). New York: Oxford University Press.

Dennett, D. (1988). When philosophers encounter AI. *Daedalus, Proceedings of the American Academy of Arts and Sciences, 117* (Winter), 283–295.

Dennett, D. (1990). *The age of intelligent machines: Can machines think?* Retrieved December 10, 2004, from http://www.kurzweilai.net/articles/art0099.html

Dennett, D. (1995). 'The unimagined preposterousness of zombies': Commentary on T. Moody, O. Flanagan and T. Polger. *Journal of Consciousness Studies, 2*, 322–326.

Fodor, J. (1991). Afterthoughts: Yin and Yang in the Chinese Room. In D. M. Rosenthal (Ed.), *The nature of mind* (pp. 524–525). New York: Oxford University Press.

Forrest, S. (Ed.). (1991). *Emergent computation: Self-organizing, collective, and cooperative phenomena in natural and computing networks*. Cambridge, MA: MIT Press.

Harnad, S. (1991). Other bodies, other minds: A machine incarnation of an old philosophical problem. *Minds and Machines, 1*, 5–25.

Harnad, S. (2001). What's wrong and right about Searle's Chinese Room Argument? In M. Bishop & J. Preston (Eds.), *Essays on Searle's Chinese Room argument*. Oxford: Oxford University Press.

Hauser, L. (1997). Searle's Chinese box: Debunking the Chinese Room argument. *Minds and Machines, 7*, 199–226.

Leiber, J. (2006). Turing's Golden: How well Turing's work stands today. *Philosophical Psychology, 19*, 13–46.

Minsky, M., & Papert, S. (1969). *Perceptrons*. Cambridge, MA: MIT Press.

Quine, W. van O. (1960). *Word and object*. Cambridge, MA: MIT Press.

Rapaport, W. J. (1988). Syntactic semantics: Foundations of computational natural-language understanding. In J. H. Fetzer (Ed.), *Aspects of artificial intelligence* (pp. 81–131). Dordrecht, the Netherlands: Kluwer Academic Publishers.

Rapaport, W. J. (2002). Holism, conceptual-role semantics, and syntactic semantics. *Minds and Machines, 12*, 3–59.

Reber, A. S. (1997). Caterpillars and consciousness. *Philosophical Psychology, 10*, 437–350.

Rorty, R. (1980). Searle and the special powers of the brain. *Behavioral and Brain Sciences, 3*, 445–446.

Searle, J. R. (1980a). Minds, brains, and programs. *Behavioral and Brain Sciences, 3*, 417–424.

Searle, J. R. (1980b). Intrinsic intentionality. *Behavioral and Brain Sciences, 3*, 450–456.

Searle, J. R. (1984). *Minds, brains, and science*. Cambridge, MA: Harvard University Press.

Searle, J. R. (1990). Is the brain's mind a computer program? *Scientific American, 262*(1), 26–31.

Searle, J. R. (1980). Minds, brains, and programs. *Behavioral and Brain Sciences, 3*, 417–457. Later version (1991) In D. M. Rosenthal (Ed.), *The nature of mind* (pp. 509–519). New York: Oxford University Press.

Searle, J. R. (1997). *The mystery of consciousness*. (Including exchanges with Daniel C. Dennett and David J. Chalmers.) New York: New York Review of Books.

Teng, N. (2000). A cognitive analysis of the Chinese Room Argument. *Philosophical Psychology, 13*, 313–324.

Turing, A. M. (1936). On computable numbers, with an application to the Entscheidungsproblem. *Proceedings of the London Mathematical Society*, Series 2, 42, 230–265.

Turing, A. M. (1950). Computing machinery and intelligence. *Mind, LIX*, 433–460.

Wakefield, J. C. (2003). The Chinese Room argument reconsidered: Essentialism, indeterminacy and strong AI. *Minds and Machines, 13*, 285–319.

Are Humans Mobot Minded? Some Implications of Embodied Cognitive Science for Cognitive Psychology[1]

Stephen R. Hill

A mobot is a mobile robot. In the past decade or so a group of breakaway researchers have built new kinds of mobots that incorporate non-traditional control architectures and make heavy use of bodily and environmental resources in the production of adaptive behaviour (Pfeifer, Iida, & Bongard, 2005). *Situated robotics*, as this new perspective is often known (Mataric, 2003), forms a central plank of a new approach to studying cognition called *embodied cognitive science* (ECS; Anderson, 2003; Clark, 1997; Keijzer, 2001; Pfeifer & Scheier, 1999; Sporns, 2003; Wilson, 2002). The primary unit of analysis for much ECS research is the *behavioural system*, which consists of dynamically coupled neural, bodily, and environmental components (Chiel & Beer, 1997; Keijzer, 2001; see also Wilson, 2002, for criticism of this idea). ECS theorists are particularly concerned with the phenomenon of *behavioural emergence* (Hendriks-Jansen, 1996), the idea that behaviour is not entirely controlled by an 'in-the-head' control system but rather arises 'from the ongoing interaction between [an agent's] brain, its body, and its environment' (Beer, 2003, p. 210).

One key question raised by this novel approach is whether natural cognisers (people and other animals) might be better understood as mobot-like *embodied* and *situated* systems rather than the reflective, world-modelling systems beloved of classical cognitive science. Both embodiment (the possession of a physical body made up of components with their own dynamics and transduction features) and situatedness (the fact that agents rely on and make use of properties of their environments in the production of behaviour) provide strong constraints on the structure of the internal architecture ('minds') of situated robots. Embodiment constraints can be further decomposed into *integration constraints* and *morphological constraints*. The former arise from the demand that a complex agent's 'brain' must combine multiple behaviour-producing subsystems into a coherent whole. The latter are a consequence of agents possessing non-neural body structures. The constraining effects of situatedness can also be examined in two ways. Many discussions of situatedness focus on *environmental constraints* — ways in which an agent's environment is used to simplify the computational demands of, and thereby the structure of the internal mechanisms that underpin, various tasks. An equally important aspect of situatedness is the concept of *interaction space*. This term refers to the ways in which important stimuli are temporally filtered so that cognitive abilities can robustly develop.

This chapter explores the idea that the design of the human mental architecture, like those of situated robots, is a product of integration, morphological, environmental, and interaction space constraints. Although much situated robotics research has focused on the generation of rather basic behaviours, rather than the kinds of complex cognitive abilities central to cognitive psychology, I want to suggest that we have much to learn from the synthetic methodology used in ECS.

Background: Mobile Robots and Cognitive Architecture

Artificial intelligence (AI) researchers have had a longstanding interest in creating robots that are self-sufficient and autonomous. However, by these standards, the early days of mobile robotics (the late 1960s and early 1970s) were not a resounding success (see Brooks, 1999). AI has attempted to circumvent the problems that gave rise to these failings in two ways: by either (a) focusing on simulating or building disembodied, function-specific systems known as expert systems, or (b) by simplifying the environments in which the classically-designed robots 'live'. In both cases, traditional assumptions about the structure and dynamics of internal processing systems remain largely unchanged.

In the mid-1980s the roboticist Rodney Brooks began to wonder whether the problem of building robust, self-sufficient robots could be due to traditional assumptions about the nature of internal mechanisms and processes. He set out to create cheap robots that could survive unaided in real environments filled with things like chairs, desks, doors, Coke cans, and graduates. On the face of it this was an incredibly ambitious undertaking considering the difficulties earlier robots had simply trying to cope with recognising and fetching a few geometrical shapes in uncluttered and simplified environments. It was amazing then that Brooks came up with a design that achieved many of his original objectives. The result was Allen, a simple wanderer of the MIT labs. 'He' was the first in a long line of increasingly sophisticated real-world MIT mobots (see Breazeal & Scassellati, 2002; Brooks, 1999).

The important point, for the purpose of this chapter, is that the innards of Brooks' robots bear almost no resemblance to the designs favoured by classical cognitive scientists (see also Harvey et al., 2005; Pfeifer et al., 2005; Pfeifer & Scheier, 1999). The reasons for this derive largely from the fact that Brooks' machines are both *embodied* and *situated* entities. Put simply, the task of building complete, physically-realised robots, which can 'survive' in real environments, has constrained the design of the robots' computational control structures.

Layered Control Architectures and Integration Constraints

A basic assumption that classical AI shares with traditional cognitive psychology is the view that cognitive architectures are best understood as sequential information-processing systems made up of complex data structures that constitute models, plans, and goals (Palmer & Kimchi, 1986). The standard information-processing architecture involves a cascade of processing that usually includes sensing, modeling, planning, and acting stages. In this sequence, information from the environment is gradually filtered by a variety of algorithms and augmented with stored knowledge until motor commands for producing appropriate behaviours are computed. This sense-model-plan-act (SMPA) scheme also lies at the heart of much thinking in cognitive psychology. Its presence is obvious, for instance, in the sequence of detection, recognition, and response selection phases psychologists have used to understand the duration of mental processes since the time of Donders and Helmholtz.

Many of the researchers within the field of situated robotics have eschewed the SMPA schema and instead have built robots utilising *layered control architectures* (LCAs). Robots built using LCAs are, on the whole, better at 'surviving' in real-world environments than are traditional machines. The best known LCA is Brooks' *subsumption architecture* (for other architectures that adopt this principle of *parallel, loosely coupled processes* see Pfeifer & Scheier, 1999). LCAs typically omit the modelling and planning phases of processing (what Brooks refers to as the 'cognition box') and link sensing directly with action. Brooks argues that building a sufficiently useful model of the world is the most computationally expensive, and most problematic, part of the traditional AI scheme. He suggests that a system that can deal with changes in the environment in real-time will not necessarily require an internal model. As Brooks and his colleagues are fond of saying, such a system instead 'uses the world as its own model'.

Excising the 'cognition box' is one strategy for building more robust and adaptive robots. Another strategy is to do away with the need to build a system with a centralised control system. In traditional models of cognition, such as that offered by Marr's (1982) theory of vision, it is the job of the agent's mind/brain to construct detailed and centralised representations of the world which can be utilised in the execution of many possible actions. These representations are typically *detailed* (encoding information about many aspects of a stimulus) and *decoupled* (accessible by many response planning systems) (Clark, 1997, chap. 8; Sterelny, 2003). Brooks has argued that centralised control systems are unnecessary and unrealistic. Instead he favours a decentralised system decomposed into behaviour-producing layers. In this kind of system each layer receives minimal sensory input — just enough necessary for triggering a specific behavioural response (e.g., backing away from looming objects). Layers

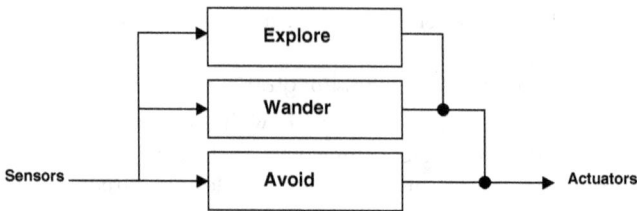

Figure 1
Schematic of the subsumption architecture of the mobile robot Allen (based on Brooks, 1999).

then compete with each other for control of the robot's actions via a network of low bandwidth connections (see Figure 1 for a simple example).

Subsumption architecture robots are built in an incremental fashion, somewhat reminiscent of the way nervous systems have evolved (see Prescott, Redgrave, & Gurney, 1999). Robot design begins by building a basic layer that utilises a narrow range of sensory information to produce a simple, reflex-like response (such as avoiding nearby objects). Once the basic layer has been perfected and debugged an additional layer is built atop the first which adds to the complexity of the robot's behaviour. It operates in parallel with the first layer and receives its own, specially tailored, sensory information, and produces its own specific motor responses (such as wandering in randomly selected directions). The second layer has access to the activity of the lower layer, and can either inhibit output from the lower layer or, less frequently, replace the lower layer's output with its own 'data'. The lower layer, however, cannot affect anything happening in the higher layer. Additional layers are added on top of lower layers following the same incremental strategy until the robot's behaviour reaches a sufficient level of complexity.

An important implication of this design is that one cannot necessarily model the structure and dynamics of a higher layer mechanism without knowing the structure and dynamics of lower systems and how the higher layer interacts with them. In fact, one is likely to 'over engineer' a higher layer unless the constraints provided by lower layers are taken into account. LCA-controlled mobots do not store or construct models of their environments in order to plan how to act. Rather, their behaviour emerges from the coupling of the mobots' simple reflex subsystems and the unique structure of the local environment. The seemingly complex and goal-oriented behaviour of these machines is not explicitly pre-specified (encoded, programmed, or discoverable) in the mobot's innards. To an observer it may *appear* that a situated robot is operating on a unified conceptual model of a complex world, when, in fact, its internal machinery does not share or bring together information from its different sensor channels.

Layered Control Architectures in Natural Cognisers

Brooks (1999) and others have suggested that the LCA strategy was partly inspired by phylogenetic and neurobiological considerations, but that the primary reason for building mobots with layered control systems was because LCAs provide a better mechanism for producing robust adaptive behaviour. It is perhaps surprising, then, that some neurobiological researchers have begun to suggest that important aspects of vertebrate nervous systems can be usefully understood as LCAs (e.g., Quartz, 2002). Prescott et al. (1999) suggest that the idea that the nervous system of vertebrates is composed of semi-independent, behaviour-producing layers was foreshadowed in the writings of the nineteenth century neurologist John Hughlings Jackson (1884/1958). They describe research that suggests that dissociations consistent with the LCA profile have been shown to exist in a number of species (rats, cats, and fish). Ethologists have also claimed that this kind of machinery underpins much animal behaviour (e.g., Baerends, 1976; see also Hendriks-Jansen, 1996). They argue that many animals do not possess unified models of their environments or centralised goal-based planning systems. Instead behaviours are produced in response to sign stimuli — once one behaviour is executed the animal becomes sensitised to another class of stimuli that 'call' other behaviours. These chains of activity are organised in such a fashion as to produce large-scale patterns of adaptive behaviour. These ideas are echoed in Milner and Goodale's (1995) discussion of the anatomy and function of frogs' visuomotor systems:

> The fact that the frog possesses this parallel set of independent visuomotor pathways does not fit well with the common view of a visual system dedicated to the construction of a unified representation of the external world. Although the outputs of the different visuomotor systems need to be coordinated, it would clearly be absurd to suppose that the different actions controlled by these networks are guided by a single visual representation of the world residing somewhere in the animal's brain. There is clearly no single representation or comparator to which all the animal's actions are referred (p. 11).

Prescott et al. (1999) have explicitly argued that the neural circuits that underpin rat defensive behaviour exhibit LCA-like features. These features include:

- *Distributed control:* Different layers make distinct contributions to the overall production of defensive behaviour.
- *Behavioural decomposition:* Evidence suggests that distinct behaviour subsystems are underpinned by separate (dissociable) neural circuits. For instance, there exist separate circuits for 'controlling' backing-off defensive behaviour and forward-locomotion defensive behaviour.
- *Increasing levels of competence:* Higher layers in the rat defence system seems to mediate more complex responses to increasingly distant (temporally and spatially) threats.
- *Communication between layers by subsumption mechanisms:* Higher layers modulate the activity of lower layers by way of simple processes such as inhibition and substitution.

- *Limited sensor fusion and lack of centralised models:* At least some layers of the rat defence system use distinct 'sensor processing channels'. Furthermore, there is evidence that information from individual sensor channels is rarely fused to generate more complex centralised models of the local environment.

The LCA perspective may cast light on a number of theoretical models within cognitive neuroscience including the distinction between 'what/where' visuo-motor systems in humans and other mammals (e.g., Milner & Goodale, 1995) and Damasio and Damasio's (1994) convergence zone theory of the neural substrate of memory. In summary, there exists evidence that vertebrate brains can be usefully thought of as layered control systems.

Morphological Constraints

Situated robotics researchers have also discovered that the structure and dynamics of a robot's body, including the placement and operation of its sensors and actuators, strongly constrains the design of the robot's internal control system. The roboticist Tim Smithers (1995) argues that '[i]f a particular robot is not well fitted morphologically to its tasks and environment, no amount of clever programming will ever overcome its deficiencies' (p. 142). Smithers has found that there are times when a robot can be best 'reprogrammed' by altering its body shape rather than changing its internal program structure. Similarly, Pfeifer and Scheier (1999) suggest that computation can be 'traded' for morphology, and that good body designs can reduce computational complexity by an order of magnitude or more.

A hopping robot built by Raibert provides a nice example of the importance of morphology in behaviour production. This one-legged robot moves by bouncing on a single compressible leg. The robot's control structure controls the direction in which the leg points when it hits the ground. The movement commands are used to balance the robot so it does not fall over, and tip the whole machine so that it moves in a certain direction. However, the control system does not provide instructions for all of the movements exhibited by the robot. The robot's body provides bouncing and tipping over 'for free'. The control system modulates this intrinsic dynamic. Global behaviour, then, is an outcome of the coupling of the dynamics of the control system and the dynamics of the robot's body. Raibert and Hodgins (1993) summarise these ideas when they write:

> We believe that *the mechanical system has a mind of its own,* governed by the physical structure and the laws of physics. Rather than issuing commands, the nervous system can only make 'suggestions' which are reconciled with the physics of the system and the task. (p. 350, italics added)

A similar claim has been made by the psychologist Esther Thelen and her colleagues (Thelen & Smith, 1994; Smith & Gasser, 2005) in their research with infants. Up until about 2 months of age infants exhibit a spontaneous stepping reflex when they are held upright. At around 2 months this pattern disappears.

It returns between 8 and 10 months when the child is beginning to support itself on two legs. Traditionally it was thought that the disappearance of this reflex was due to maturational changes in the neural motor control system of the infant. However, in several ingenious experiments Thelen showed that these changes were caused by morphological changes in the infant. By the age of 2 months the weight of an infant's leg has reached the point where it simply defeats the natural spring-like action of the muscles. Thus, the neuromuscular system cannot generate the stepping pattern. Thelen demonstrated this by effectively reducing the weight of the infant's legs (by immersing the infant's legs in water or putting them on a treadmill). This finding implies that much of neural and bodily machinery needed for stepping is intact in 'non-stepping' infants. Thelen argues that many other changes in human behaviour can be accounted for in a similar way as the outcome of the coupling of multiple neural and non-neural body systems. Non-neural systems have also been implicated as important constraints in active vision (e.g., Findlay & Gilchrist, 2003) and auditory perception (Chiel & Beer, 1997).

Environmental Constraints

The actual dynamics of body structures depend to a large degree on the environment in which they are 'used'. For instance, in microgravity Raibert and Hodgins' robot would obviously not be able hop in a terrestrial fashion. Similarly, the behaviour of Thelen's infants changes when they are placed in different environments. Many situated roboticists have argued that a robot's body and internal control system cannot be designed unless one knows about the layout of its 'species-typical' environment. The philosopher Andy Clark (1997; see also Rowlands, 1999) expands on the cognitive consequences of this idea by suggesting that '[i]n general, evolved creatures will neither store nor process information in costly ways when they can use the structure of the environment and their operations on it as a convenient stand-in for the information-processing operations concerned' (p. 46).

One can see this principle at work in the design of Polly, a mobot designed to show tourists around the MIT AI labs (see Pfeifer & Scheier, 1999). This ecological niche possessed a number of recurring features which simplified the design requirements for Polly's internal control structure. For instance, Polly needed to be able gauge the distance of various objects that lay in front of 'her'. This is a very complex problem. However, because Polly's niche consisted only of flat floors, distant objects always appeared higher on her camera sensors than closer objects. Thus, distance was a simple function of an object's Y coordinate. Polly's internal architecture was designed to exploit the unique physics of her local environment.

ECS researchers argue that the cognitive architectures of humans and other animals are also constrained by the structure and dynamics of their species-typical environments. Humans, of course, have colonised every habitat on the planet and have even begun to move beyond it. We seem to be amazingly adaptable in a wide range of environments. Despite this high level of adaptability, there are many ways in which our basic abilities work best in specific environments that include features found in our environment of evolutionary adaptedness such as illumination from above (for perceiving shapes using shading; Kleffner & Ramachandran, 1992) and natural light (for colour perception; Shepard, 1994). Both of these examples demonstrate constraints on basic perceptual abilities, but our cognitive abilities may also be designed to exploit features of our species-typical environments.

A simple example will help to illustrate this point. The visual memory literature suggests that people can remember a moderate number of features of a visuospatial layout. One might think, based on previous laboratory research, that we would make the most of this ability and fill, or nearly fill, our working memory when engaging in visuospatial tasks. However, in a number of experiments Ballard and colleagues (Ballard, Hayhoe, & Pelz, 1995; see also Ballard, Hayhoe, Pook, & Rajesh, 1997) showed that participants avoided memory-intensive activity whenever they could. The task in their experiments involved replicating a modelled pattern of coloured blocks. Ballard et al. showed that much of the time their participants often did not 'store' any more than one feature of the model (i.e., the colour or position of a single block) at a time. Indeed, it became apparent that people had no recollection of a previously 'stored' feature once a new one was 'encoded'. Simply put, people stored one feature at a time and promptly emptied their visual memory as soon as that feature had served its purpose within the larger task. Ballard et al. suggest that these results imply that we do not build complex internal models of our surroundings when we can use the environment as a kind of surrogate memory store (see also Gray & Fu, 2004).

Thus, there is reason to believe that humans, like mobots, exploit the structure of the environment when engaging in cognitive activity. The nature of the local environment provides important constraints on the structure and dynamics of the cogniser's internal cognitive mechanisms.

The Role of Interaction Spaces in the Development of Cognitive Mechanisms

Cognitive psychology often proceeds by attempting to model the cognitive abilities of *adult* humans. Although this is an admirable goal it ignores the important contribution that historical (evolutionary and developmental) analyses provide. ECS research supports the idea that a good understanding of developmental change can help to constrain our speculations about the nature of neurocognitive mechanisms that underpin various *mature* cognitive abilities. If we know something about the mechanisms and behaviour of earlier forms we can make better guesses about the structure and dynamics of internal cognitive mechanisms.

Verschure, Voegtlin, and Douglas (2003) have recently shown that early forms of a robot control system modulate the later forms by constraining the effective environment, or *interaction space* (Keijzer, 2001), to which the learning system is exposed. They constructed a simple, three-layered robot forager whose task was to learn to approach food targets and avoid obstacles. Verschure and colleagues found that performance was improved with the activation of a higher contextual layer, which enabled the robot to 'remember' extended temporal patterns of the associations between locations, obstacles, and targets. Upon investigation they found that this contextual layer influenced a lower adaptive learning layer, not by providing *internal* signals that improved the learning processes in the adaptive layer, but via an external feedback loop. That is, the contextual layer modulated the robot's activity by ensuring that the adaptive learning subsystem was provided with 'friendly' sensor input that enhanced the robot's ability to learn. Put simply, the contextual layer ensured that the robot's sensors were in the right place at the right time to make the most of the robot's limited learning capacity.

Does anything like this happen in animals? Verschure et al. (2003) think so: 'We expect that behavioural feedback would affect perceptual systems and those structures that readout from these systems, both during early development and beyond' (p. 623). They describe research that shows that the development of sensory areas (the auditory cortex, 'place' fields in the CA1 region of the hippocampus) might be influenced by behavioural feedback. In a more psychological vein several researchers have also suggested that language learning may be dependent on the structuring of interaction space by earlier forms (e.g., Deacon, 1997; Newport, 1990).

Elman (1993) has attempted to model these aspects of language acquisition using connectionist simulations. He found that in order to successfully train his networks to deal with complex sentential structures, it was necessary to constrain the stimulus array of sentence exemplars. In particular he found that two constraining strategies were helpful: *phasing training* and *phasing memory*. The former involved gradually increasing the difficulty of the training sentences, while the latter involved endowing the infant network with a small 'immediate memory' and letting it gradually grow in capacity over time. Both of these strategies can be understood to have real-world counterparts: the transition from infant-directed speech to more adult speech, and the maturation of memory (Deacon, 1997).

The net effect of both strategies was to provide the infant network with a gradually expanding world of stimulation that enabled it to avoid getting stuck in local minima solutions from which recovery was impossible. What is illustrated here is the importance of the role of temporal constraints on the structure and dynamics of internal behaviour producing systems. Earlier forms (e.g., limited memory, poor visual acuity, restricted focal length) partially structure the kind of interaction space, to which an agent, is exposed enabling the development of later forms of behaviour that would not be possible had the earlier forms been more precocious (see also Smith & Gasser, 2005; Turkewitz & Kenny, 1985).

In sum this is another example of the, by now familiar, story that without a proper appreciation of the various factors that may constrain the structure and function of underlying neurocognitive mechanisms our attempts at cognitive modeling will miss the mark. So, to the list of layered control structure, morphological, and environmental factors we can add the constraining effects of developmental change.

Conclusions and Questions

I began by asking whether humans may be, in some important sense, mobot-minded — that is, whether the insights from the engineering of the internal control structures of situated robots could cast any light on the ways in which the cognitive architectures of humans, and other animals, are structured. Since embodied cognitive science's novel robotic designs have often been more effective in creating lifelike behaviour than those machines designed using classical architectures it might be the case that the useful engineering constraints that have been unearthed in situated robotics research might also be applicable to natural cognisers like us. I have tried to make a case for considering the possibility that our traditional cognitive models are inadequately constrained, and may therefore provide an unrealistic picture of the mechanisms that underpin cognition. I have attempted to show that, in at least some cases, there is evidence that the constraints explicitly acknowledged within the embodied approach are operative in humans and thus that they are potentially important for theory development in cognitive psychology.

There are, of course, many unresolved questions that may prove damaging to my case. Paramount among these is the question of whether we can scale up the lessons of situated robotics to the level of advanced cognitive abilities (Edelman, 2003). Modern adult humans are amazingly flexible cognitive creatures. We are not purely reactive, situation-driven beings. Indeed we seem to be able respond in an almost infinite number of ways to environmental 'stimuli'. Thus, one might wonder whether the ECS framework has anything useful to offer a distinctly *human* cognitive psychology. It is relatively simple to come up with examples where each of the previously identified themes of ECS do not hold: regions of mammalian nervous systems do not exhibit layered architectures (Prescott et al., 1999); there are times when radical changes to a person's morphology do not result in significant changes in behaviour; often people find it easy to 'cognise' in a variety of environments; and sometimes early developmental forms seem to play no role in the structuring of the learning environment. These kinds of examples could be taken as evidence against the importance of ECS claims. There are many good reasons why we should not be too quick to make this theoretical leap (see, for example, Hill, 2000) but I will focus on just one: the fact that human beings are a species of animal that has evolved to cope with specific hostile environments (Sterelny, 2003) strongly suggests that our mental architecture is not fundamentally designed to enable off-line, rational pondering but rather to produce adaptive behaviour in response to (mainly local) environmental events. The flexibility we *do* possess is more than likely built on top of, and out of, previous structures that evolved as adaptations to earlier environments. Modern abilities may have arisen from *terminal additions* to the mechanisms of earlier, more restricted, abilities. For instance, Hermer-Vazquez, Moffet, and Munkholm (2001) suggest that the development of human spatial ability (from a simpler system that uses information about the macroscopic shape of the environment to a more flexible system that also utilises non-spatial information) may reflect the coming on-line of new layers of complexity. Similarly, it is possible that the increasing dominance of tertiary cortical areas in our species involves the subsumption of 'lower' cortical and subcortical systems by new control layers (Deacon, 1997). Curtis and D'Esposito (2003), echoing the claims of Hughlings Jackson (1884/1958), have recently suggested that the human prefrontal cortex, the sine qua non of pure mentality, should be understood as complex integrator of sensory and motor processes that lies 'at the apex of the motor hierarchy' (p. 421). Put simply, these examples suggest that human cognition may consist of an off-line mind built out of situated and embodied components.

If these claims about modern human cognition are anywhere near the mark, then the ideas broached in this chapter should have important implications for the ways in which we understand human cognition. We must face the possibility that the machinery that enables our flexibility rests upon, and depends upon, a reactive and situated neurocognitive bedrock.

Endnote

1   This chapter is derived from a longer manuscript (Hill, 2005) available from the author on request.

References

Anderson, M. L. (2003). Embodied cognition: A field guide. *Artificial Intelligence, 149*, 91–130.

Baerends, G. P. (1976). The functional organization of behaviour. *Animal Behaviour, 24*, 726–738.

Ballard, D. H., Hayhoe, M. M., & Pelz, J. B. (1995). Memory representations in natural tasks. *Journal of Cognitive Neuroscience, 7*, 66–80.

Ballard, D. H., Hayhoe, M. M., Pook, P. K., & Rajesh, P. N. R. (1997). Deictic codes for embodiment in cognition. *Behavioral and Brain Sciences, 20*, 723–767.

Beer, R. D. (2003). The dynamics of active categorical perception in an evolved model agent. *Adaptive Behavior, 11*, 209–243.

Breazeal, C., & Scassellati, B. (2002). Robots that imitate humans. *Trends in Cognitive Sciences, 6*, 481–487

Brooks, R. A. (1999). *Cambrian intelligence: The early history of the new AI*. Cambridge, MA: MIT Press.

Chiel, H. J., & Beer, R. D. (1997). The brain has a body: Adaptive behavior emerges from the interactions of nervous system, body and environment. *Trends in Neurosciences, 20*, 553–557.

Clark, A. (1997). *Being there: Putting brain, body, and world together again*. Cambridge, MA: MIT Press.

Curtis, C. E., & D'Esposito, M. (2003). Persistent activity in the prefrontal cortex during working memory. *Trends in Cognitive Sciences, 7*, 415–423.

Damasio, A. R., & Damasio, H. C. (1994). Cortical systems for retrieval of concrete knowledge: The convergence zone framework. In C. Koch & J. L. Davis (Eds.), *Large-scale neuronal theories of the brain* (pp. 61–74). Cambridge, MA: MIT Press.

Deacon, T. W. (1997). *The symbolic species: The co-evolution of language and the brain*. New York: W. W. Norton.

Edelman, S. (2003). But will it scale up? Not without representations. *Adaptive Behavior, 11*, 273–275.

Elman, J. L. (1993). Learning and development in neural networks: The importance of starting small. *Cognition, 48*, 71–99.

Findlay, J. M., & Gilchrist, I. D. (2003) *Active vision: The psychology of looking and seeing.* Oxford, England: Oxford University Press.

Gray, W. D., & Fu, W-T. (2004). Soft constraints in interactive behaviour: The case for ignoring perfect knowledge in-the-world for imperfect knowledge in-the-head. *Cognitive Science, 28*, 359–382.

Harvey, I., Di Paolo, E., Tuci, E, Wood, R., & Quinn, M. (2005). Evolutionary robotics: A new scientific tool for studying cognition. *Artificial Life, 11*, 79–98.

Hendriks-Jansen, H. (1996). *Catching ourselves in the act: Situated activity, interactive emergence, evolution, and human thought.* Cambridge, MA: MIT Press.

Hermer-Vazquez, L., Moffet, A., & Munkholm, P. (2001). Language, space, and the development of cognitive flexibility in humans: The case of two spatial memory tasks. *Cognition, 79*, 263–299.

Hill, S. R. (2000). *Where is cognition? Towards an embodied, situated, and distributed interactionist theory of cognitive activity.* Unpublished PhD dissertation, University of Canterbury, New Zealand.

Hill, S. R. (2005). *Situated robotic systems as models of human cognitive architecture.* Unpublished manuscript.

Jackson, J. H. (1958). Evolution and dissolution of the nervous system. In J. Taylor (Ed.), *Selected writings of John Hughlings Jackson* (Vol. 2, pp. 45–75). London: Staples Press. (Original work published 1884)

Keijzer, F. A. (2001). *Representation and behavior.* Cambridge, MA: MIT Press.

Kleffner, D. A., & Ramachandran, V. S. (1992). On the perception of shape from shading. *Perception and Psychophysics, 52*, 18–36.

Marr, D. (1982). *Vision: A computational investigation into the human representation and processing of visual information.* New York: W. H. Freeman.

Mataric, M. J. (2003). Situated robotics. In Nadel, L. (Ed.), *Encyclopedia of cognitive science.* (Vol. 4, pp. 25–30). London: Nature Publishing Group.

Milner, A. D., & Goodale, M. A. (1995). *The visual brain in action.* Oxford: Oxford University Press.

Newport, E. L. (1990). Maturational constraints on language learning. *Cognitive Science, 14*, 11–28.

Palmer, S. E., & Kimchi, R. (1986). The information processing approach to cognition. In T. J. Knapp & L. C. Robertson (Eds.), *Approaches to cognition: Contrasts and controversies* (pp. 37–77). Hillsdale, NJ: Lawrence Erlbaum.

Pfeifer, R., & Scheier, C. (1999). *Understanding intelligence.* Cambridge, MA: MIT Press.

Pfeifer, R., Iida, F., & Bongard, J. (2005). New robotics: Design principles for intelligent systems. *Artificial Life, 11*, 99–120.

Prescott, T. J., Redgrave, P., & Gurney, K. (1999). Layered control architectures in robots and vertebrates. *Adaptive Behavior, 7*, 99–127.

Quartz, S. R. (2002). Toward a developmental evolutionary psychology: Genes, development, and the evolution of the human cognitive architecture. In S. J. Scher & F. Rauscher (Eds.), *Evolutionary psychology: Alternative approaches* (pp. 185–210). Boston: Kluwer.

Raibert, M. H., & Hodgins, J. K. (1993). Legged robots. In R. D. Beer, R. E. Ritzmann, & T. McKenna (Eds.), *Biological neural networks in invertebrate neuroethology and robotics* (pp. 319–354). San Diego, CA: Academic Press.

Rowlands, M. (1999). *The body in mind: Understanding cognitive processes.* Cambridge, England: Cambridge University Press.

Shepard, R. N. (1994). Perceptual–cognitive universals as reflections of the world. *Psychonomic Bulletin & Review, 1*, 2–28.

Smith, L. B., & Gasser, M. (2005). The development of embodied cognition: Six lessons from babies. *Artificial Life, 11,* 13–20.

Smithers, T. (1995). Are autonomous agents information processing systems? In L. Steels & R. A. Brooks (Eds.), *The artificial life route to artificial intelligence: Building situated embodied agents* (pp. 123–162). Hillsdale, NJ: Erlbaum.

Sporns, O. (2003). Embodied cognition. In M. A. Arbib (Ed.), *The handbook of brain theory and neural networks* (2nd ed., pp. 395–398). Cambridge, MA: MIT Press.

Sterelny, K. (2003). *Thought in a hostile world: The evolution of human cognition.* Malden, MA: Blackwell.

Thelen, E., & Smith, L. B. (1994). *A dynamic systems approach to the development of cognition and action.* Cambridge, MA: MIT Press.

Turkewitz, G., & Kenny, P. A. (1985). The role of developmental limitations of sensory input on sensory/perceptual organization. *Developmental and Behavioral Pediatrics, 6,* 302–306.

Verschure, P. F. M. J., Voegtlin, T., & Douglas, R. J. (2003). Environmentally mediated synergy between perception and behaviour in mobile robots. *Nature, 425,* 620–624.

Wilson, M. (2002). Six views of embodied cognition. *Psychonomic Bulletin & Review, 9,* 625–636.

About the Contributors and Editors

Gjurgjica Badzakova-Trajkov

Badzakova-Trajkov is studying the neural representation of language in bilinguals for her Ph.D at the University of Auckland.

Kylie J. Barnett

Dr Barnett was awarded her Ph.D at the University of Auckland in 2005. She is now a post-doctoral fellow at Trinity College Dublin, investigating the neural basis of synaesthesia.

Amy Bird

Dr Bird received her Ph.D and Dip.P.Clin.Psych from the psychology department at the University of Otago. Her doctoral research examined the relationships among self-concept development in 5- and 6-year-old children, parent–child talk about past emotional events, and early attachment security and child temperament. She is now a clinical psychologist in Auckland. Currently she works in the area of child and adolescent community mental health serving young people with a range of presentations including depression, anxiety, and behavioural difficulties.

Heather Buttle

Dr Buttle is Lecturer in Cognitive Psychology at Massey University's Albany Campus. Her Ph.D, completed at the University of Wales, Bangor, investigated effects of high familiarity on visual processing, including attentional studies of faces, places, and products. Since then her research has investigated other aspects of visual attention, such as repetition blindness and the emotional processing of faces, and consumer issues, such as recognition of brand information (e.g., names, objects, and logos). Dr Buttle has recently been developing interests in cognitive measures of mindfulness and attentional biases in addictive behaviours. Her articles appear in journals such as *Perception & Psychophysics* and *Applied Cognitive Psychology*.

James Chapman

Dr Chapman is Professor of Educational Psychology and Pro Vice-Chancellor of the College of Education at Massey University. He has published in a range of international journals in the areas of academic self-perceptions and reading disabilities, and in 1999 was co-winner of the Dina Feitelson Award for Excellence in Research. He is President of the International Academy for Research in Learning Disabilities and has served on the editorial boards of the *Journal of Educational Psychology* and the *Journal of Learning and Disabilities*.

Zhe Chen

Dr Chen is a senior lecturer in psychology at the University of Canterbury, New Zealand. Her research explores various aspects of human visual cognition, with an emphasis on visual perception, attention, distractor inhibition, and duration estimation. Her current research has focused on the processing of irrelevant information as a result of attention, the effect of working memory and attentional focus on perception, and the mechanisms that underlie object-based distribution of attention.

Michael Colombo

Dr Colombo is an associate professor of psychology at the University of Otago in Dunedin. He received his Ph.D in behavioural neuroscience from Rutgers University and then received an NIH postdoctoral fellowship to conduct research on the neural basis of visual information processing in primates at Princeton University. He conducts both neuroscience research, exploring the role of the hippocampus in learning and memory, and developmental work looking at how serial-order information is represented in the brain. He is co-author of the book *The Developmental of Implicit and Explicit Memory*, which received a Division 7 nomination for the 'Best Book in Developmental Psychology' from the American Psychological Association in 2002.

Michael Corballis

Professor Corballis received undergraduate and masters degrees from the Universities of New Zealand and Auckland, before completing his Ph.D in psychology from McGill University in Montreal, Canada, in 1965. He was a lecturer in psychology at the University of Auckland from 1966 to 1968, when he returned to McGill as assistant, associate, and then full professor of psychology. In 1978 he came back to a chair of psychology at the University of Auckland. He has worked on mirror-image discrimination, cerebral asymmetry of function, mental imagery, and language. In 1998 he received an honorary LLD from the University of Waterloo, Canada, and in 2002 was created Officer of the New Zealand Order of Merit for contributions to psychological science.

Scott L. Fairhall

Dr Fairhall was awarded his Ph.D at the University of Auckland in 2006. He is currently a postdoctoral fellow at the University of Zürich, Switzerland, investigating the neural correlates of consciousness.

Claire M. Fletcher-Flinn

Dr Fletcher-Flinn received her Ph.D from LaTrobe University, Melbourne, Australia. In 1988 she moved to take up a postdoctoral fellowship in education, and subsequently, a lectureship in psychology at Victoria University of Wellington, New Zealand. Now at the University of Auckland, she teaches developmental psychology and maintains a range of research interests in literacy learning and reading disability.

Michelle Gulya

Dr Gulya received her Ph.D in 1999 from the Biopsychology and Behavioral Neuroscience Program in psychology at Rutgers University (the State University of New Jersey, United States). In 1994, she received the Marilyn L. Shaw Award for Excellence in Research, and a Walter Russell Academic Scholarship. She published extensively on serial learning and memory by human infants. Currently, she is a Behavior Specialist Consultant in Pittsburgh, Pennsylvania.

Gus M. Haberman

Dr. Haberman's original research area is cognition and communication. He spent his apprenticeship in psycholinguistics as an assistant in the cross-cultural network of Charles E. Osgood's CCPL. His doctoral dissertation examined how readers processed two-clause sentences with complement-governing predicates. He has spent more than 13 years in Aotearoa/ New Zealand teaching cognition and language, as well as applied psychology. Among other books he is editor of *Looking Back and Moving Forward: Fifty Years of New Zealand Psychology*.

Jen Hay

Dr Hay received a Ph.D from Northwestern University in 2000, and is now a senior lecturer in the Department of Linguistics at the University of Canterbury, New Zealand. She works on the Origins of New Zealand English Project (ONZE), and has research interests in sociophonetics, laboratory phonology and morphology. She is the author of *Causes and Consequences of Word Structure* (Routledge), co-author of *New Zealand English: Its Origins and Evolution* (Cambridge University Press), and co-editor of *Probabilistic Linguistics* (MIT Press).

Dione Healey

Dione Healey recently graduated with her Ph.D, entitled 'Attention deficit/ hyperactivity disorder and creativity: An investigation into their relationship' from the University of Canterbury. She is currently working as a postdoctoral fellow at Queens College of the City University of New York, where she is continuing her research into the cognitive and psycho-social functioning of children with ADHD.

Stephen R. Hill

Dr Hill is a lecturer in cognitive and experimental psychology at Massey University, Palmerston North, New Zealand. His Ph.D (University of Canterbury, 2001) critically evaluated the emerging embodied approach to cognitive science. His other research interests include philosophy of mind, attention, adaptive person construal, and evolutionary psychology.

Peter Jackson

Dr Jackson is a principal lecturer in psychology at the Open Polytechnic of New Zealand. He was awarded his Ph.D at Massey University. He has played an active role on the Social Sciences Committee of the Royal Society of New Zealand. Dr Jackson's research interests cluster around human consciousness, with a recent focus on its relationship with quantum physical states, also with artificial intelligence machines.

Lucy Johnston

Dr Johnston is Associate Professor of Social Psychology, specialising in social cognition, at the University of Canterbury where she has been since 1994. She received her BA (Honours) in Experimental Psychology from the University of Oxford, and her Ph.D in 1991 from the University of Bristol. In 2004 she had a visiting professorship at University of Connecticut. Her ongoing research focuses on implicit non-verbal behavior in social interaction, such as facial expressions of emotion,behavioural mimicry and synchronization, and stereotyping and discrimination.

Todd C. Jones

Dr Jones completed his BA in psychology (1990) and MA in experimental psychology (1991) from Southern Methodist University. He earned his Ph.D in cognitive psychology from Rice University (1995). He fell in love and followed his fiancée (now wife), Pamela, to New York City where he taught at Barnard College and conducted research as a postdoctoral fellow at New York University. He sneaked away to the University of Kansas for a brief stint as a visiting research scientist but returned to teach at New York University. The big shift to Wellington, New Zealand occurred in 1999, where he has remained happily. He is currently Senior Lecturer in Cognitive Psychology at Victoria University of Wellington. His general research interest is in automatic and controlled cognitive processes, with more specific interests in implicit and explicit memory, recognition memory (including false recognition), age-related memory processes, subjective memory experiences, and the neuro-anatomical underpinnings of memory.

Ian J. Kirk

Dr Kirk is a member of the psychology department and the Research Centre for Cognitive Neuroscience at the University of Auckland. He uses EEG and fMRI to investigate the neural substrates of mnemonic, attentional, and linguistic processes.

Anthony Lambert

Dr Lambert studied psychology as an undergraduate at the University of Sheffield, and as a postgraduate at the University of Leicester. After completing his Ph.D he carried out postdoctoral research at the University of Durham, working with Professors Bob Hockey and John Findlay. He has published research on laterality and language, the split-brain, human computer interaction, implicit learning, eye movements, ageing, and attention. He is currently a senior lecturer in psychology at the University of Auckland, and Director of the Research Centre for Cognitive Neuroscience.

Andrew J. Lock

Dr Lock is Professor of Psychology at Massey University. He has authored and edited a number of books on the transition from pre-linguistic to symbolic communication in infancy. His most recent book is the *Handbook of Human Symbolic Evolution* (Blackwell, 1999), co-edited with Charles R. Peters.

Jason Low

Dr. Low received his Ph.D in psychology from the University of Western Australia, Perth, in 1998. From 1998 to 1999, he was a research scholar at the University of Florida. In 1999 he was appointed Lecturer in Psychology at Victoria University of Wellington, where he is currently Senior Lecturer in Developmental Psychology. Dr. Low's research interest concerns the representational nature of children's minds. He is currently investigating the development of flexible knowledge structures by studying the cognitive domains that underpin children's imaginative thinking, and how they characterise imagination in pervasive developmental disorders (autism). He also has interests in how children process events and stories presented in audio-visual media that have creative temporal sequences.

Lynden Miles

Dr Miles is a postdoctoral fellow in the Social Perception Laboratory at the University of Canterbury, Christchurch. His research interests are centred around the application of ecological psychology to social phenomena, with a focus on perception. Lynden's recent work concerns the detection of the affective states of others and deficits in this ability within various clinical populations.

Clare Morton

Clare Morton completed her B.Sc(Hons) at the University of Auckland, and is currently studying in Melbourne.

Ewald Neumann

Dr Neumann is currently a senior lecturer in the cognitive psychology area at the University of Canterbury, specialising in (visual) selective attention research. He earned his Ph.D at the University of California, Santa Barbara. Prior to coming to New Zealand, he held research positions at the National Institute of Mental Health in Bethesda, Maryland, where he completed postdoctoral training and received a senior scientific staff fellowship. He has also taught at University of California, Santa Barbara and held faculty positions at New College (the honours college of the University of South Florida) and Middlebury College in Vermont.

Rhiannon Newcombe

Dr Newcombe completed a Ph.D and a postgraduate diploma in clinical psychology at Otago University, Dunedin, New Zealand. She investigated children's narrative development across the preschool years. In particular, she was interested in whether children's attachment security was associated with their narrative ability. She presently works as the Project Coordinator for the Environmental Risk (E-risk) Longitudinal Twin Study, investigating how genetic and environmental factors shape children's development. The longitudinal study follows a cohort of twins in England and Wales. Dr. Newcombe is based at the Social, Genetic and Developmental Psychiatry Centre, at the Institute of Psychiatry, Kings College, London, United Kingdom.

John V. Podd

Dr Podd obtained his Ph.D in psychoacoustics from Victoria University of Wellington, New Zealand, in 1983. Since that time he has been a faculty member in the School of Psychology at Massey University, now as Associate Professor. He is a member of both the American Psychological Society and the Bioelectromagnetics Society. He has many research interests, including the effects of electromagnetic radiation on biological systems, and human nutrition and brain function. Currently, his major focus is on cognitive changes that accompany aging, especially in the 'oldest old' (85+ years of age). He has also investigated the changes that take place in memory functioning in Parkinson's disease, a neuro-degenerative disorder. Aided and abetted by Dr. Stewart-Williams, he has developed a strong interest in evolutionary psychology.

Verena E. Pritchard

Verena Pritchard, M.Sc(Hons), is currently studying towards a doctorate in psychology at the University of Canterbury. A recipient of the university's doctoral scholarship, her research is in developmental cognitive psychology focusing on the role of automatic and controlled processes in attention and memory. Her research has concentrated on understanding the nature of inhibitory mechanisms underlying visual attention in various typical and atypical developmental populations, with a recent publication in the journal *Developmental Psychology*.

Elaine Reese

Professor Reese is a senior lecturer in psychology at the University of Otago and an associate research professor in psychology at Clark University in Worcester, Massachusetts. She completed her Ph.D in developmental psychology at Emory University in 1993. Her main research interest is in the way that adult–child interaction affects the development of autobiographical memory and literacy. She has an ongoing longitudinal study of autobiographical memory development with over 150 families in Dunedin, New Zealand, as well as an ongoing longitudinal study of literacy development in children from low-income families in the United States.

Carolyn Rovee-Collier

Professor Rovee-Collier is Professor of Psychology in the Department of Psychology at Rutgers University (the State University of New Jersey, United States). She is an international authority on infant memory, having published 195 scientific articles on the topic. She has received numerous awards including an NIMH (National Institute of Mental Health) Merit Award, two NIMH Research Scientist Awards, the Distinguished Scientific Contribution Award from the Society for Research in Child Development, as well as the Howard Crosby Warren Medal from the Society of Experimental Psychologists. For 18 years she served as editor of the journal *Infant Behavior and Development*; she co-edited the series Advances in Infancy Research. She served as President of the International Society for Developmental Psychobiology, the International Society for Infant Studies, and the Eastern Psychological Association.

Murray Simmonds

Dr Simmonds is a senior lecturer in psychology at the University of Canterbury. He was appointed in 1971 after completing a Ph.D on the role of verbal factors in psychophysical similarity judgements. His interests include face perception and facial attractiveness. He is currently working on a textbook of experimental aesthetics entitled *The Perception of Beauty: Modularity, Ratios and Aesthetics*.

Steve Stewart-Williams

Originally from Wellington, New Zealand, Dr. Stewart-Williams spent several years pursuing a career as a musician before going into psychology. He completed a Ph.D in psychology and philosophy at Massey University, and is now a research fellow at McMaster University in Canada. His current research takes an evolutionary perspective on kinship, and investigates how people attempt to influence the mating behaviour of their relatives. He has also done work on the perception of aggression; the mechanisms underlying the placebo effect; and the philosophical implications of evolutionary theory and evolutionary psychology.

G. Brian Thompson

Currently an academic in the School of Education Studies, Victoria University of Wellington, New Zealand, Dr. Thompson worked as a psychologist in the New Zealand school system for 7 years before taking up a position as Senior Teaching Fellow in the Faculty of Education at Monash University, Melbourne, Australia. He received his Ph.D from Monash University. Since 1978 he has been a senior lecturer, and from 2001, a senior research associate, at Victoria University of Wellington.

William E. Tunmer

Professor Tunmer is Distinguished Professor of Educational Psychology in the College of Education at Massey University. He has published several articles on language and literacy development, reading difficulties, and intervention strategies, and has served on the editorial boards of the *Journal of Learning Disabilities*, *Reading Research Quarterly*, *Reading and Writing*, and *Language and Education*. In 1999 he was co-winner of the International Reading Association's Dina Feitelson Award for Excellence in Research.

Paul Warren

Dr Warren is Associate Professor in the School of Linguistics and Applied Language Studies at Victoria University of Wellington, New Zealand. His primary research interests are in psycholinguistics, in particular, spoken word recognition and the use of intonation in sentence processing. Since moving to New Zealand in 1994, he has combined these interests with a growing fascination in the development of New Zealand English. He is the editor of the book *Prosody and Parsing* (Psychology Press) and is on the editorial board of the journal *Language and Speech*.